The Urban Fringe of Indian Cities

The Urban Fringe of Indian Cities

Professor Jaymala Diddee Felicitation Volume

Edited by

Jutta K. Dikshit

RAWAT PUBLICATIONS

Jaipur • New Delhi • Bangalore • Guwahati • Kolkata

ISBN 978-81-316-0403-8

Published by
Prem Rawat for **Rawat Publications**
Satyam Apts, Sector 3, Jawahar Nagar, Jaipur 302 004 (India)
Phone: 0141 265 1748/7006 Fax: 0141 265 1748
E-mail: info@rawatbooks.com
Website: www.rawatbooks.com

New Delhi Office
4858/24, Ansari Road, Daryaganj, New Delhi 110 002
Phone: 011 2326 3290

Also at *Bangalore, Guwahati* and *Kolkata*

Typeset by Rawat Computers, Jaipur
Printed at Chaman Enterprises, New Delhi

Contents

List of Figures

List of Tables

Chapter 15

Chapter 16

Chapter 17

Chapter 18

Chapter 20

Chapter 21

Preface

The three-day seminar on *Managing the Urban Fringe of Indian Cities* organised to felicitate Professor Jaymala Diddee on the eve of her retirement was intended to bring the scholars of different disciplines together to get their views on the problems of the urban fringe and their possible solutions. The book is a Festschrift dedicated to Professor Jaymala Diddee.

The volume is organised into four parts, besides *The City and the Urban Fringe: An Introductory Note* by Professor K.R. Dikshit, given in the beginning of the book. The first part of the book under the title *'Views on the Urban Fringe'* is a collection of mainly short papers representing different approaches by scholars of different disciplines to the problems of the fringe. This part also includes the inaugural address by late Professor V.G. Bhide, a former Vice-Chancellor of the University of Pune, and the keynote address of Professor Vinod Tewari, Director of the Institute of Urbanism. The second part looks at *'Fringe Development in France and Germany'*, both highly urbanised countries. Future urbanisation in India may follow different trends and strategies but it may be important to look at the benchmarks of development abroad. The third part includes a discussion of the *'Urban Fringe of Different Indian Cities'*, notably Kolkata, Chandigarh, Jaipur, Delhi, Mumbai and several others. The fourth part named *'Bombay Suburbs in Retrospect'* gives a detailed account of the suburbs of the city as they appeared in 1960.

Late Prof. V.G. Bhide, former Vice-Chancellor of the University of Pune, a renowned physicist and an educationalist, true to his reputation, delivered a very well-prepared inaugural address. The address begins with a brief overview of the history of urban growth in India, and the role towns played in ancient times in the economy as well as the cultural development of the country, and emphasised the interdependence of the ancient Indian towns and villages. It then explained the changed role of towns in colonial India. This, Bhide considered, brought about the urban-rural divide and the heterogeneity within the economic base and living conditions of the population of the city. The neglect of the rapidly expanding towns in independent India underestimated the wealth-promoting role of cities and lacked foresight for urban planning and development. Bhide then gives a very lucid overview of planned and unplanned urban growth, especially in the fringe areas and its social and human implications.

In his keynote address on *'Managing the Urban Fringe of Indian Cities'*, after presenting a vivid picture of the unparalleled challenges of rapidly growing towns and their negative impact on the rural–urban fringe, Vinod Tewari pleads for their appropriate planning and management including the preservation of prime agricultural lands. Giving the example of the urban fringe of Delhi, he explains the gap between the well-intended Regional Plan of 2001 for the National Capital Region and its implementation and hopes that some of the shortcomings will be avoided in the Regional Plan of 2021.

D.N. Dhanagare in his paper *'On Encounter between Urban Fringe and Neoliberal Capitalism'* views the happenings in the fringe from the point of view of political economy. He starts by distinguishing between the classical form of capitalism, which included some social concern and welfare measures, and the present-day reigning neoliberal capitalism – the latter being concerned with profit alone. As financing and profit making constitute the core of this new economy, it is the urban fringe, especially of metropolitan towns, that offers an ideal playing field for its stakeholders: financiers, builders, speculators etc. As a result, planning is poor, and so is the infrastructure, while rules are often changed to suit some interest groups. Dhanagare tries to question some of the assumptions of inevitable urban growth and unmanageable development and proposes an alternative model of development that concentrates more on the hinterland rather than on the city itself. In his model he emphasises the fringe as living space for different human groups and different social realities. Hanuman Singh Yadav too in *'Expansion of Urban Capital and Marginalisation of Fringe: An Antipode of Urban Development'* considers the fringe-city relationship under the dialectical model of political economy. Citing the example of the rapidly growing town of Bhopal, he finds that the fringe is the scene of land speculation, the accumulation of capital in fewer and fewer hands and weak governance. He, thus, considers urban growth which lacks a mechanism to improve the living conditions of the poor, counterproductive to development. Though it cannot be denied that a large group of people, being uneducated, may not know to utilise the sale proceeds of land judiciously, and in due course, find themselves in a situation worse off than before, yet it is also observed that an equally important group has made well-thought-out use of new opportunities and improved their living conditions and income levels. One may also question the assumption that urban processes in a quasi-capitalist economy are neutral to space, time and scale. The dialectical model as such is worth examining in relation to the fringe. The case study by Chinmoyee Mallik and Sucharita Sen entitled *'Land Dispossession and Changes in Rural Livelihoods: Case of Periurban Delhi'* adds to the above two contributions by analysing the change in livelihood of villagers after their land was acquired for urban expansion. They could show that the most negatively affected people were the landless agricultural workers as they lost their source of income without any compensation and being least educated found it difficult to get a job, increasing the degree of unemployment. In the absence of adequate employment opportunities, the overall shift in the occupational structure seems low; however, some landowners invested their compensation money in income generating assets.

The approach of the planners and architects to the urban fringe problems differs from those of social scientists, in so far as they focus on urban land policy, plan outlays and relevant acts. The paper of G.R. Diwan '*Planning and Managing the Urban Fringe of Indian Cities: Issues and Options*' with special reference to Pune critically examines how the legal aspects of urban land policy, especially the Urban Land Ceiling Act of 1976, had a negative effect on urban planning that resulted in a spontaneous, rapid and largely unplanned development in the fringe. He advocates the preparation of regional town planning schemes which take into account the potential of the fringe. In '*The Concept of Urban Fringe and the Basis for Delineation*' Sandeep Parkhi discusses methods to define and delineate the periurban area and explains the urban development of Pune. Taking Pune as an example and based on four determinants, he classifies 16 out of 36 villages as fringe villages. Such an objective approach in delineating fringe villages is of major importance in the future planning of urban areas. Christopher C. Benninger in '*Conundrums, Visions and Devices of Urban Form*' reacquaints the reader with the different directions town planning has taken in the last two hundred years mainly in the United States and Europe. Though conceived as an ideal solution by the then leading architects, with respect to the suburbs, they were not always satisfactory, and inadequate services, segregation of people according to their income, loss of valuable agricultural land, low housing density spread over large areas of urban land defied solution. Against these shortcomings, Benninger advocates a "Charter of Intelligent Urbanism" based on ten principles some of them being regional integration, efficiency, balanced movement. It is in the nature of architects to continue to look for ideal solutions. Rajeev Kathpalia in '*Engaging the Peripheries: In Search of India's Future Cities*' focuses on the process of urbanisation in India and its impact on the fringe development. However, his major concern relates to cities as dynamic multicultural and multilayered systems and to the challenges the new social realities pose to architects and planners. Kiran and A. Kalamdani in their short paper list some problems faced in the fringe area of Pune and offer some original solutions.

Pankaja Kulabkar has also chosen Pune to examine the role of politics in urban planning. She analyses one special aspect of town planning in Pune, namely, the reservation of the hills. This plan was sanctioned in 1987 by the State Government. However, a number of attempts were made by different stakeholders to modify the proposal or to resist its modification. An important part of her study is the detailed analytical framework consisting of the plan formulation, the strategy of implementation and lastly the implementation itself. Kulabkar applies this methodology to the special case of the reservation of hills in Pune and summarises her findings in a detailed table. The urban fringe is an area, as mentioned in other places, where often a wide gap exists between planning and implementation and it may be useful while examining developments to consider the above methodology. We may add that even in 2011 the future of the hills is not decided, the options swinging between Biodiversity Park and low density housing, each having its own set of advocates.

The second section of the volume is devoted to '*Fringe Development in Germany and France*'. Both countries have a very high degree of urbanisation spread deep into the hinterland with new modes of living, social reorganisation and adjustment, new administrative divisions and a new legal framework. India may follow a different route in its policy of urbanisation because of its large and ever-increasing population, and unending stream of rural–urban migrations. However, certain trends in fringe development in India resemble those in abroad and a comparison may be useful. Gerhard Bahrenberg in *'Recent Developments of Urban Fringes in Modern Society: An Evolutionary Perspective'* looks at the history of urbanisation in Germany. During the last thirty years, the population in the suburban hinterland steadily increased while the population in the city core decreased. This process initiated by the automobile revolution and expanding road network led to some complex and far-reaching changes in the city–fringe relationship with respect to the occupational and settlement structure. With new employment opportunities in the fringe – Bahrenberg prefers the term *cityland* – and the emergence of sub-centres and new cores, the functional linkages between the city and the fringe become less pronounced. Modern suburban society spread out in the rural surroundings has adopted a new way of life while remaining socially connected by road and telecommunication network. Though the opinions about the fringe development may be divided, especially regarding the loss of agricultural land, it seems to be an irreversible process, to which the political-administrative system had to adapt. Similarly, Jean Steinberg in *'Urban Fringes in France'* talks about periurbanisation in France, which expresses itself differently in the landscape not as the densely populated suburbs of the pre-Second World War era but as patchy settlements interspersed into the agricultural or natural landscape. Steinberg explains periurbanisation as a typical French phenomenon based on a new return to nature and supported by a number of favourable conditions like the personal transport or lower property prices in the fringe. An important aspect of the fringe is that different economic activities have also shifted into the urbanised part of the fringe, and that commuting constitutes one of the major criteria of fringe definition. Periurban areas vary in size, they are larger around million towns especially Paris. The periurban reality required the adaptation of the legal structure and administration, especially as 80 per cent of the French population is urbanised. Steinberg explains the changes from the Land Use Law of 1967 to the new laws which are related to a 'multi-municipal' structure of administration, sustainable development and an administrative framework that removes the inequalities between the income differences of rich and poor municipalities.

The third section looks at the *Urban Fringe of Different Indian Cities*. Chittaranjan Pathak in *'The Fringe Areas of Kolkata Metropolis: Nature, Problems and Prospects'* deals with Kolkata metropolis which is formed by three municipal corporations and 38 municipalities and the Panchayat Samiti areas, and represents the large fringe area. Kolkata being overpopulated, the fringe areas had to cope with the immigrants in search of jobs, but above all with the influx of refugees from erstwhile East Pakistan and later Bangladesh. The metropolis, with a ribbon-like extension along both sides of the river Hooghly, did not leave much choice to the poor people occupying the fringe in the deltaic environment. They had to live in the lowest, badly drained and mosquito-infected areas. The uncontrolled growth, the increasing population density, the lack of job opportunities, the less developed infrastructure and the encroachment on valuable agricultural land have made the planning of Kolkata Metropolitan Area extremely challenging.

K.D. Sharma, Pippa Deodhar and Bhawana Bali in *'Dynamics of the Rural Segment around a Planned City and the Need for a Broader Framework: A Case Study of Chandigarh (U.T.)'* present a comprehensive analysis of the multiple changes that the rural segment of Chandigarh Union Territory has undergone. Though, Chandigarh was carefully planned and executed, it did not take into account the need of housing for the poor, and has thus experienced unauthorised settlements in the periurban fringe, occupied by construction and other workers of the informal sector, besides displaced people. The paper carefully examines the changes in a number of villages, in respect of land use, population attributes, residential housing and the built-up areas. All these changes indicate a low income periurban development usually observed in other towns, but not expected in Chandigarh. The extended village area is exhibiting the negative aspects of fringe development like poor unauthorised housing and different commercial encroachments. The authors point out that the planning of Chandigarh has been urban-centric and little attention has been paid to the planning of the rural areas of Union Territory, and this, in spite of the rural area being earmarked for further urban development. Based on their findings they suggest a number of specific measures to be included in the second phase of the development plan of the city.

H.S. Sharma and R.N. Mishra in *'Evaluation of Master Plans and Changing Character of Fringe Areas of Jaipur Urban Complex'* are concerned with the consequences of the rapid growth of Jaipur after it became the capital of Rajasthan in 1949. Though the objectives of the First Master Plan (1971–1991) were commendable, the realisation of the plan did not come close to the objectives. Before long, the proposed green belt at the outskirt of the town was swallowed by mushrooming housing societies who paid little attention to the physical constraints of Jaipur city, especially the drainage system, and an inadequate infrastructure. Non-availability of land to development agencies held by land speculators, and legal complications further contributed to the failure of the plan. To avoid earlier mistakes the new Master Plan (1991–2011) incorporated the entire Jaipur Development Authority region. However, the authors regret that this plan lacks a regional perspective, and the proposal does not contain any zoning regulation, and the proposed low-density housing in vast areas constitutes under-utilisation of valuable urban land.

In their paper *'Integrated Approach for Characterisation of Urban Fringe Area: A Study of Bangalore City'*, Daksha C. Barai, Sudha Ravindranath and J. Krishnamurthy use both remote sensing, and household surveys of three selected inner fringe areas, thus providing an areal assessment of the changes that the different land uses in Bangalore have undergone. The statistical data provided by the application of GIS techniques emphasise, among other things, the loss of agricultural land including irrigated land – a problem mentioned by a number of authors – which nearly equals the gain in residential land use. The paper highlights differences in the development of fringe areas – much of it unplanned – with respect to the original village, the accessibility, the group of people who settle in a particular area, the perceived value given to a location and the stage of fringe development, ranging from near rural pockets to ultra-modern high rising edge cities. According to the household survey, the socio-economic conditions of the residents of the urban fringe improved considerably with the increasing urban employment opportunities.

Baleshwar Thakur gives a detailed analysis of '*The Structure and Dynamics of the Urban Fringe of Delhi*' including a discussion on environmental degradation, natural resource depletion and the policies of fringe development. The periurban fringe of Delhi spreads out in all directions wide into the hinterland which makes its delimitation difficult. Thakur sets the inner boundary of the fringe between the Delhi Urban Area and the Delhi Metropolitan Area and the outer boundary beyond the DMA. However, the boundaries are not uniform and keep changing – a fact underlined by the outward radiating corridor development. The author presents a very lively geographical picture of the different fringe areas of Delhi, taking into account differences in the micro relief, soil and drainage conditions, the history of urban expansion and the population characteristics. He, thus, provides a detailed account of the five Community Development Blocks consisting of villages and satellite towns which surround urban Delhi. Both Tewari and Thakur talk about planning of the fringe areas of Delhi, there is a certain overlap, but as their views slightly differ, both are presented here.

While Vimala Rangaswami is concerned with the '*Urban Fringe of Vadodara: Development and Transformation*', K.M. Kulkarni looks at '*The Outgrowths beyond the Municipal Limits in Gujarat*'. These two papers complement each other in so far as both are concerned with the rapid urbanisation in Gujarat fuelled by immigration, industrialisation and economic growth. Rangaswami, however, focuses on the different development plans of the Municipal Corporation and the Urban Development Authority of Vadodara, their shortcomings and their scope, and explains some of the salient features of the planning strategies. Kulkarni examines the demographic characteristics of 125 urban outgrowths in Gujarat, classifies them according to the urban agglomeration class and studies the changes between 1981 and 2001. S.R. Latkar in his study of Nashik City after looking at the urban growth of the city, identifies the urban inner and outer fringe of the city and makes suggestion for its future management.

V.S. Phadke and V.S. Rao in '*Stagnant Town in a Metropolitan Fringe: The Case of Sandor in the Shadow of Mumbai*' have tried to explain why the population of a fringe town remained stagnant, in contrast to the population of other towns of the Vasai-Virar region growing rapidly. As the accessibility, infrastructure, quality of land and water are as favourable as in the neighbouring towns, the reasons for this atypical behaviour according to them lies in the special history of this once-upon-a-time Portuguese settlement, and the existing dominant Catholic population resisting any change. Here, the role of the '*Harit Vasai Samiti*', an organisation interested in greening cities, to keep certain pockets of the Vasai-Virar region green, as mentioned in the following paper needs to be acknowledged. Gita Kewalramani, in '*Managing the Peri-urban Interface of Mumbai: A Case Study of the Vasai-Virar Region*', starts with a detailed description of the different geographical units within the region as each zone reflects different land use, different population densities and different economies, the highest densities being found in the towns along the railway line in the central lowland. Kewalramani gives a detailed account of both the problems and opportunities of the changes in land use brought about by rapid urbanisation of the region. While serious problems still exist in providing proper infrastructure, as much as in ensuring water quality, besides coastal erosion and emerging slums, new opportunities arose in the employment sector. Special consideration is given to the role of planning in the region especially since 1990 when this task was given to CIDCO. However, parts of the Development Plan could not be implemented because of non-availability of funds and lack of co-ordination between different departments. The analysis of the planning process is followed by suggestions for future improvement in the basic infrastructure of the region.

The last section of the book *'Bombay Suburbs in Retrospect'* has a chapter entitled *'The Suburbs of Bombay'* reproduced from the unpublished Ph.D. thesis of K.R. Dikshit, *'The City of Bombay: A Study in Urban Geography'*, 1961, pp. 569–648. Mumbai being one of the mega-cities of India, it was thought that a retrospective view of its suburban growth may be helpful in not only understanding the growth of this very special city, but also the process of urbanisation of towns which are at different stages of development. Some lengthy tables have been omitted. It is regretted that the blueprints of the original figures could not be improved upon much. But the well-written text and the detailed study the suburbs may compensate the reader for the shortcomings.

The editor has endeavoured to organise the papers, after having them revised by the authors, whenever possible, in a manner she thought appropriate. She is thankful to the contributors for revising their papers and lending moral support for the publication of the volume. The urban fringe is the 'happening place' in the context of the cities, and is ever changing with new problems and prospects. The editor is quite aware of the shortcomings in organising a volume which may not cover all aspects of the urban fringe. It is hoped that the articles produced here throw some light on what is currently happening in the fringe area of Indian cities, and provide some insight into challenges that need to be met, during the process of development in the fringe areas.

The editor will also like to thank Rawat Publications, not only for agreeing to publish the volume and but also bringing it out elegantly in a short time.

Jutta K. Dikshit

Prof. Jaymala Diddee addressing the audience during the inaugural function of the seminar. On the dais from left to right Prof. K.R. Dikshit, Dr P. Nag, Prof. V.G. Bhide and Prof. Vinod K. Tewari.

Professor Jaymala N. Diddee

A Profile

On 30th November 2002, Professor Jaymala N. Diddee retired as Professor and Head of the Department of Geography after twenty-five years of service at the University of Pune.

Ms Diddee (nee Kadam) was born to Maharashtrian parents on 29th November 1942, at Baroda, now known as Vadodara, in Gujarat, where she spent her childhood and had early schooling. As it turned out, her parents shifted base and moved to Pune in the fifties. Pune provided a very appropriate climate for education and growth to young Jaymala. After finishing her schooling at the secondary level, she joined the reputed Nowrosjee Wadia College from where she graduated in Science with Chemistry major. It was not a case of direct entry from the graduate to the postgraduate class in a university. Jaymala took a voluntary brake of several years during which she married, and enjoyed a family life and had two children, before deciding to go for further education. She joined the University of Pune as M. Sc. student in Geography in 1969. During her two years as a postgraduate student, she developed wider interests in the subject, especially Settlement Geography, and decided to continue as a research student. She received her Ph.D. degree from the University of Pune in 1978. The thesis titled *"Central Places in Western Maharashtra"* was completed under the guidance of Professor K.R. Dikshit.

The same year, Dr Diddee joined the University of Pune as a faculty member. She taught a wide gamut of papers including population and settlement geography, human and cultural geography, South-East Asia etc. Her research interests included studies on ethnic groups like the Dhangars and the tribes of western Maharashtra, weekly markets, medium towns, cantonments etc. These are reflected in the research papers she published and the numerous M.Phil. and Ph.D. dissertations she guided. She actively participated in the annual tours of the students to different parts of the country, ranging from Rajasthan in the west to the Kolkata and the Sunderbans in the east, Tamil Nadu and Kerala in the south and Shimla and Sikkim in the north. New Delhi was often included in the tours she conducted, as she felt the students must experience the national capital. Dr Diddee also regularly accompanied her research students for fieldwork despite difficulties of terrain and stay. She was a source of encouragement to her students, being very approachable and open to discussing their difficulties. In addition, Dr Diddee was a guest lecturer at the University of Chandigarh and the University of Bremen, Germany. She also gave lectures at various universities such as Hawai, Shillong etc.

In addition to writing a book *Central Places in Western Maharashtra*, she also edited a number of books. These included *Indian Geography, Geography of Maharashtra* and *Exploration in the Tropics*. She also edited the journal *Transactions, Institute of Geographers* for a number of years. Her love for Pune, her knowledge of the facets of the town and its history found expression in her book *Pune, the Queen of Deccan* authored jointly with another equally scholarly person Dr Samita Gupta.

During her tenure as head of the department the credit system was designed and introduced, the computer laboratory was well equipped and every faculty member was provided with a computer. She encouraged and supported the introduction of the B. Sc. Applied Course in Geographic Information Systems, now also an M. Sc. Course which has opened new career options for geography students.

Prof. Diddee is a founder member of the Institute of Indian Geographers. From its inception, she has been deeply involved in the promotion of the activities of the Institute. As its Secretary General she nurtured its growth, looked after the day-to-day affairs for more than fifteen years, supported the conveners of the conferences and encouraged young geographers at the meets.

As with many teachers, retirement for Dr Diddee has meant a change in life but not an end to academic pursuits. She continues to guide her Ph.D. students and is currently busy with a major research project, an Atlas of Maharatha Campaigns. She is also actively involved with the preservation and promotion of the heritage sites of Pune.

1

The City and the Urban Fringe

An Introductory Note

K.R. DIKSHIT

City symbolises the achievement of contemporary society. And, the structural organisation and the functional efficiency of a city have always been a measure of success in community organisation, right from the days of primitive agrarian society to the modern period of Megalopolis culture. But what has happened over the centuries, and especially after the industrial revolution, is the concentration of ever-increasing number of economic activities and people in the towns, making them multifunctional settlements. While the towns in the developed economies have almost reached a stable phase, the situation in the developing countries is drastically different, where a rapid transformation in urban structure has taken place during the last fifty years. The cities of the Third World, especially the mega-cities, have demonstrated an unprecedented growth during the closing decades of the last century and the process continues unabated. The growth of their economic base, coupled with a steady rural–urban migration stream, has rendered the administration and development of the towns extremely difficult and created in the process the problem of the FRINGE.

Though the fringe was always an entity on the periphery of the towns, it has acquired an added significance as a problem area in recent years. The spillover effects of the large towns are so apparent that the fringe can no longer be ignored. It is subjected to all kinds of unplanned growth, environmental degradation and even destruction of precious natural resources and requires serious attention, analysis of its problems and introduction of remedial measures.

The Urban Fringe

The urban fringe, also called the rural–urban fringe or simply the FRINGE, is a space segment lying between the urban complex on the one hand and the vast rural countryside, on the other. Normally, it is understood to mean, as suggested by the term, the peripheral zone of the cities and is occasionally also labelled as periurban fringe. Traditionally, the urban fringe has been complementary to the functions of the towns supplying perishables like fresh vegetables, milk, flowers, manpower and sheltering some of the nuisance causing industries like brick kilns in return to market for agricultural produce and job opportunities offered by the towns. But this was during the phase when the towns were stagnant or showed a very slow growth. Today, the physical and demographic growth of the large cities is so rapid and its spillover effects are so unrelated to the interests of the countryside that the traditional symbiotic relationship no longer exists.

The physical growth of the cities cutting into the rural landscape has changed the character of the fringe area, and produced a landscape vastly different from either the rural or the urban. Potentially a part of the town in future, the fringe experiences the spillover effects of non-agricultural functions of the towns and requires better administration, and planned development. Unfortunately and surprisingly, the fringe in most cities with the exception of a few metropolitan authorities, having regulatory power over a larger area, remains neglected. The regulation of the fringe is highly demanding yet least attended to. That is the core of the problem. The towns show no signs of being stabilised either in their population, their functional mass or in their areal spread in their peripheries, producing, in the process an amorphous zone, the fringe, an area as problematic as the main city that needs attention and careful planning.

The Fringe: An Area of Political Conflicts

The fringe represents an area of conflict of not only competing uses but also of political interests. Nothing in an urban set-up is more amenable to political and bureaucratic manoeuvres than the land. And spatial organisation of the fringe is not necessarily the result of an impartial delineation of functional areas to suit and promote the community welfare. Political decisions, seldom based on merit, and even bureaucratic bungling, often distort the arrangement from what could be optimal. The administrative overlap, involving several government departments, like State Revenue Department, State Town Planning Department, local self-body like a Municipal Corporation, and even Village Panchayats, in situations where the fringe area is not inside the corporation limit, often results in inadequate appreciation and isolated interpretation of a plethora of changing rules that remain un-enacted. The most damaging part is the residuary powers in the form of discretion given to the competent authority or the State Government. So, who should be responsible for fringe development, who will lay the ground rules and grant affirmative or restrictive permission, is uncertain?

The Urban Fringe within the Municipality/Corporation Limits

The chaos in the municipal fringe stems from the fact that many of the land uses, structures and functional locations antedate the merger of the area within the municipal limits. The expansion of the urban activities of the town, often uncontrolled, is gradual whereas the municipal expansion like a legislative statute is sudden, and overnight the area of the corporation is enlarged. The entrenched interests in the quasi-urbanised rural fringe do not quietly accept the control and regulation by the Corporation. Moreover, the haphazard growth with cart tracks, agricultural fields, brick kilns, rural community centres, existing residential houses and the tiny shops of village artisans do not quite fit in the planning scheme of the Corporation. To take a simple instance, villages are linked by age-old cart tracks, and to replace them with a modern highway requires not only widening and acquisition of land but also in some cases demolition of existing structures.

The most disputed act of the Corporation is its zoning system and reservation of land for public utilities. The owners of the land would like to benefit most from zoning system in Town Plans fixing the use of land in the existing peripheral villages for the landowners. The acquisition of land for public utility against a marginal compensation is dreaded by most, whereas its inclusion in commercial or residential zone is financially rewarding. There is no system in place, which can compensate for the loss suffered by such landowners. The result is political lobbying, delay in plans, litigation and the consequent neglect suffered by the fringe villages. Away from the downtown, the fringe has to depend on the main city-core for education, medical treatment, major shopping or even for travel. The plan proposals are modified time and again till finally a plan emerges that carries an unmistakable imprint of political interference. The story does not end here; changes in the plans are made continuously at the behest of builders and other vested interests. Urban amenities, like a hospital, a major shopping complex and educational facilities, remain a distant dream, and the area gets filled up with small manufacturing units, crowded residential clusters and slums.

The Fringe Area outside the Municipal Limits

This is a free-for-all area where low-paid workers, daily wage earners, unemployed and even those engaged in tiny industries take shelter – all within the shadow of the main village settlement. Many residential suburbs, observed inside the municipal limits and existing as an adjunct to the main village, developed to the benefit of both – the original village people as well as the commuters settled in the vicinity – the former collecting rents from the induced shantytowns and the latter finding affordable albeit very unhealthy accommodation. Apparently, the disorganised accretion to the villages outside the municipal limits may appear innocuous, but after the lapse of a few years, these villages are brought inside the municipal limits, leading to a situation where the pre-existing haphazard growth defies management and planning. Such fringes have a conglomerate of activities, where residential quarters, industries, trade, educational institutions and the like coexist juxtaposed to each other.

The Urban Fringe and the Fringe Area Problems

Criteria exist or could be established to delineate the fringe area depending on the situation. The fringe could be inside the city limit or beyond the administrative limit of the town. It will depend on whether the city is, to borrow terms from an American urbanist, 'underbound' or 'overbound'. In the former case the fringe will spill over the town's boundary while in the latter it may remain as an undeveloped or underdeveloped fringe. The problems of the fringe emerge primarily from its proximity and close link with the town and secondly from the well-recognised fact that it is considered as a part of the town in future. Many problems flow from this fact. The growth of dormitory suburbs, demand for more land for future residences, producing in the process a speculative property market and above all the fear of a planning that is more inspired than neutral – all add to the problems. The landowners are not altogether immune to this problem and they are also caught in the whirlpool of the extension of municipal limits, demarcation of zones and none too infrequent interference of politicians.

The Uniqueness of the Fringe Problems

The problems encountered in the organisation of the fringe and its assimilation in the town are vastly different from those facing the city's core or the median zone. While in the compact old core prevention of dilapidation, renewal and maintenance are the main concerns, the fringe awaiting a well-laidout spatial organisation faces the risk of a chaotic, incongruous and unregulated development. While the city cores enjoy some stability, the fringe is a flux. The growth of the fringe, or the suburbs in a large metropolis like Mumbai, is continuous, the merger of the fringe area is a statutory exercise and sudden. During this period, whatever changes take place, add to the confused mosaic of a picture that is neither planned nor regulated thoughtfully nor based on future projections. The greatest risk facing the fringe is the damage to its valuable natural resources, like land, soil, water, forests, hills, water bodies or other scenic spots. The fringe environment remains unprotected. The attitude of property sharks is too well known to be mentioned here.

Development of Infrastructure in the Fringe

The villages in the shadow of the large towns need infrastructure like transport, water supply, waste disposal, sewerage, and other services. Beyond the Corporation limit, the roads degenerate into mud tracks. The most important could be a network of arteries that could guide future development or a market that could be of use to both the town and the suburbs. With proper planning many of the higher educational institutions and medical centres, including hospitals and veterinary centres, could be located in the fringe. A swimming pool or a large playground could be planned in the fringe with proper connectivity. Besides there is also need for national parks, gardens, stadia, zoos, airports, shopping malls, nature clubs, inter-state bus terminals, and other related activities that require large areas.

The uses mentioned are only indicative and suggest that the fringe has to provide space for such uses. Often, these are likely to be considered redundant and no provisions are made for such uses. In a city like Pune with a population approximating three million, there is hardly any large open space, which an average person may think of visiting on holidays. What is seen more often in the fringe are exclusive resorts meant for the well-to-do, different from large open public places or gardens. Where are the large woodlands, green areas, lakes, or any other recreational areas? The whole countryside is sprinkled with private properties in the midst of wilderness, and even the hilltops are not spared.

Everything is decided by the legality of the case and not by the need of healthy environment. All along the crest of the Sahyadris, wherever there is agricultural land, it undergoes free trade transactions under the revenue code. The growth of elite townships and resorts and large residential colonies is definitely going to affect the available discharge of the rivers downstream and is a sure recipe for the destruction of the scenic landscape on the flanks of the Sahyadris. Already, there are reports that residential colonies build dams on small tributaries in the source region of larger rivers. What will be their impact, has to be seriously investigated. In recent history, there has been once a conflict between the farmers of the Deccan and the authorities who pioneered Bhera Ghat power project – the Mulshi dam. If a large number of elitist colonies emerge in the crest zone of the Ghats, we may see in future a far greater conflict between the elite settlements at the crest and the populous towns in the piedmont zone.

Environment of the Fringe

Nothing is as important as the quality of environment in the fringe. Today, the situation is such that most polluting and hazardous industries are either located or looking for location in the fringe. These include chemical industries and those producing toxic effluents or fumes. The most recent case is that of such industries in the periurban zone of Delhi. So is the case with Bombay suburbs. Once established, these industries cannot be easily moved out. Once outside the limits of the Corporation, today, they occupy parts of residential suburbs. Certainly, these industries could not have been established without governmental clearance at a time when environmental control was not so strict. It is important that industrial areas are allowed not in the vicinity of large towns but at distances beyond a projected expansion of the towns over the next hundred years. *Equally important is saving the natural environmental resources like soil, plants, animal life, forests and scenic landscapes, from degradation, pollution and destruction.*

The Cause for Concern

The facts and the ground realities that cause concern include recognition of the necessity for a better organised spatial structure of the fringe to be assimilated in the growing town, an appropriate placement of economic activities, a thoughtful layout of arterial network, and above all an anticipated distribution of land use that could allow the regulation of land use. Besides, the delivery of services should be made available to the fringe the same way as in the city.

The physical growth of the cities adds another dimension requiring city administration to organise, plan and administer much larger areas. The cities, specially the large ones, are not static and keep growing in the developing economy both in their population and areal spread. It is this phenomenon of unending growth in large Indian cities that has added another problem area – the fringe – that is amorphous in its structure, changing and expanding continually, and needs to be saved from chaotic growth.

Some Suggested Themes

The entire problem could be resolved into sub-themes, not all of which are mentioned here. The list given here is only suggestive.

1. Character of urban fringe illustrated with case studies.
2. Process of growth and enlargement of fringe area; the stages in development. Could there be spatial or evolutionary model? What model could apply to the Indian cities more aptly?
3. Environmental problems of degradation, degeneration and destruction of land, water, soil, plant and animal resources, water bodies, hills, forests, animal life, and scenic landscape. Problem of pollution, particularly industrial pollution.

4. The problem of existing and unregulated land use.
5. Land economics and land values in the fringe. How they vary with distance from the city core, location and potential uses?
6. Legal difficulties, individual choices, political interference in land use determination of the fringe.
7. Commuters and the fringe and the associated problem of induced slums.
8. Exclusion of the fringe from intra-urban circulation planning and the absence of arterial network.
9. Problem of polluting industries, the effluent, the noise and above all the emission of toxic fumes and gases, not infrequently next to the residential quarters.
10. Dearth of public utility services and the dependence of the fringe on the core.
11. Absence of foresight in making allowance for future development of green areas, recreational areas, sports ground and airports etc.
12. People of the fringe, growth of fringe settlements, nature of housing, occupational structure of the people. The income levels of agriculturists and the migrant population.
13. Growth potential of the fringe: the present and the optimal state.
14. Planning and managing the urban fringe of Indian cities area.

These are only a few themes; more can be added. Any study that has a bearing on the fringe is welcome. Case studies are the most valued help in our understanding. The rural–urban dichotomy is nowhere so visible as in the area just outside the municipal border represented only by a thin line on the map with perfect legal sanction, and the people on the two sides of this line, though not at cross purposes as across international borders, have different rules and share community services differently. The discussion could be area, people and development oriented with all their ramifications.

I

Views on the Urban Fringe

2

Managing the Urban Fringe of Indian Cities*

V.G. BHIDE

It is indeed a great pleasure and certainly a unique privilege to be called upon to preside over the inaugural function of a seminar on "Managing the Urban Fringe of Indian Cities" organised by the Institute of Indian Geographers and the Department of Geography of the University of Pune. I am deeply conscious that I am deputising and substituting for Dr Kolaskar, Vice-Chancellor of Pune University, who was originally supposed to preside but could not do so because of unavoidable commitment. I am equally conscious that I have no special qualifications or claims to preside but this seminar being a seminar on a subject, which affects the common man, as a sensitive citizen, I agreed to preside. Just as a substitute in a cricket match is not allowed to bowl, bat or even field in some special positions but can field at the periphery, I will also be talking to you on the fringe of the subject, namely, "Managing the Fringe of Indian Cities".

City symbolises the achievement of contemporary society and the structural organisation and the functional efficiency of a city have always been a measure of success in community living. Even in the past, with the advent of cities, it was supposed that the species have come of age and cultures have become civilisations. The stories of cities have become the stories of mankind. Jericho, Thebes, Memphis, Harappa and Mohenjodaro are examples in point. In contemporary times cities have become symbols of industrialisation and economic growth. In a sense, growth of cities or growing urbanisation has come to be recognised to be synonymous with development and economic growth.

At the beginning of the 20th century, India's population was 218 million, out of which 10 per cent lived in urban areas. At the beginning of the 21st century 350 million or 35 per cent of Indians will be town or city dwellers. That is a staggering growth, comprising of India's population of 1901 plus 130 million. Even larger population would continue to flow and merge into the urban ocean, and by 2050, India would have approximately reversed both the rural and urban percentage that was there some hundred years ago. From 350 million in 1947, the number of people living in India has more than doubled to

---

* Inaugural address delivered by the author in a seminar on "Managing the Urban Fringe of Indian Cities" organised by the Institute of Indian Geographers, Pune.

nearly 880 million in 1990 and 1,040 million in 2002. But, during the same period, the urban population grew twice as fast from 50 million in 1947 to over 200 million in 1988. The 1991 Census revealed that while the total population increased by 23 per cent, the urban population increased by 65 per cent. It is interesting to know that India entered the 20th century with an urban decennial growth rate of less than 1 per cent, and this growth rate averaged to 20 per cent in the first half of the century. The rate jumped to an average of 37 per cent in the latter half of the century to as high as 46 per cent. Approximately 37 million were added in the first fifty years to towns, whereas in the next fifty years the urban population increased to 280 million. The 20th century began with a solitary million-plus city. By 1991, we had 23, and by 2002 we have 40 million-plus cities. Some of the metropolitan cities have swollen to mega-cities as Bombay, Calcutta and Delhi. Today, we have nearly 300 towns with a population over 1,00,000. This growth rate in urbanisation matches well with the industrialisation of the country.

During the course of the last century, apart from the change in the demographic picture, there has been an economic change in the contribution of the rural and urban sectors to the Indian economy. At the turn of the 20th century, the urban contribution did not deserve even a mention. But, by 1950–51, the urban contribution had climbed to 47 per cent. Interestingly, it was close to 65 per cent in 2000. In 2050, it is expected that the rural contribution would be so low as not to deserve even a mention. In keeping with the trend in many developed countries, the towns in India would fuel Indian economy and the biggest cities would have the largest economies. It appears that the emerging picture of India would inescapably be urban.

It is indeed interesting to look at the growth of cities in India. India has a long tradition in city building and every school child may have heard of the Indus valley civilisation, which began roughly 2500 B.C. and had its antecedents in the early Harappan culture. During 1,000 years of the Indus valley civilisation, the inhabitants laid the foundation for several aspects of later Indian civilisations, and many of their cultural and religious symbols find reflection in contemporary Hinduism. As everywhere else, so in India, natural harbours had developed into port cities, wherever the hinterland was a surplus agricultural or industrial producer. Indian cities of those times were essentially an extension of the village with its hierarchically separated but economically interdependent structures.

Thus, whatever be their geographical locations, up to the 18th century, Indian cites were performing two crucial roles: first, a social role of enabling trade, commerce, employment, services and administration, and second, the cultural role of unifying myriad little traditions into a semblance of a Great Indian tradition and then disseminating it through education. It is important to realise at this point that the towns and cities of this period were essentially strengthening an Indian way of life and although they were far from perfect as habitations, they were at least Indian. There was also no sharp rural–urban divide as of today.

With the consolidation of the British rule, Indian towns and cities began singing a distant tune and marching to the beat of a distant drum. Those cities such as Bombay, Calcutta, Madras and Ahmedabad which embraced the new influence rode ahead while others were left to decay and perish. In real terms, this meant that new towns and cities developed not so much to serve the needs of the local populace but the interests of the colonialists. The heterogeneous urbanisation of British India was to inexorably change the focus of urban India and leave a troubling legacy. It is in this period that the urban-rural divide originated and grew; urban cities and rural villages differed in their social and cultural outlook and in economic status.

The heterogeneous urbanisation of British India with its perceived alien nature and manifest exploitation that led to dissenting reaction to urbanism in India's founding fathers, resulting in a disengagement from urban concern in policy making even to this day. The sharpness of reaction to urbanisation can be gauged from what Mahatma Gandhi, Father of the Nation, said, *"I regard the growth of cities as an evil thing, unfortunate for mankind and the world and certainly unfortunate for India. The British have exploited India through the cities. The latter have exploited the villages. The blood of the villages is the cement with which the edifice of the cities is built."*

However, the bitterest legacy of colonisation was to decimate the country's powers of self-generation, sap its self-confidence, and destroy its talent to find innovative solutions to India's problems.

Indian cities remained relatively small until the Second World War, only Calcutta and Bombay could be truly classified as the metropolitan centres. City management was limited to the provision of pure public services, aspects of private and civic life like trade, education, entertainment and so on. These functions were financed through grants, allocations and local taxes. Their administration, as even now, was notorious for hierarchy and compartmentalisation.

Under the colonial regime, healthy elite, comprising both the rich natives and the rulers, wielded considerable powers in various aspects of the society, commerce and government and lived in fashionable and well-provided enclaves. The rest of the urban population lived in urban villages that encircled these enclaves and were built and run in essentially rural ways with strong family ties binding the city and the villages. Things have not changed materially since then except the cities grew in numbers and generated wealth but created problems.

Urbanisation may justifiably be labelled as a quiet revolution of our time, but the challenges it has thrown up have remained largely un-addressed.

It is easy to forget that India has 5,000-year-old tradition of urbanisation, given the enduring image in the rest of the world of an emaciated farmer under the blazing sun against an impoverished rural landscape – an image that has shaped the development plans and destinies since independence. Perhaps cities were viewed as the symbols of colonial capitalism and prompted the reaction amongst our founding fathers exemplified by the belief that India lives in villages. Perhaps even the strong advocates of modern industrialisation failed to understand that wealth could only be generated by healthy and thriving city. Perhaps the sheer number of rural voters swayed our policy makers in their decisions. Perhaps we still lack the foresight to equip our cities for the future.

Whatever the reasons, Indian towns and cities have suffered a singular lack of attention and it is a tribute to their resilience that they continue to fuel the engines of whatever industrial and commercial progress that has been achieved over the last five decades. Used, abused, exploited, overburdened and neglected, India's cities and towns with their pre-British grandeur, colonial cantonments and polluting industrial estates continue to provide attraction to the rural villages as a strong magnet.

After independence, Indian policy makers had two choices in the development strategy. In one scenario, existing inevitable surplus would be used predominantly for agrarian development to generate growth and create employment in rural area, which in turn would generate surplus for self-sustained industrialisation. This alternative appeared the natural choice given the country's demographic picture in 1947. Instead our planners chose the other option utilising the vast store of India's human and material resource to develop industrial sector which would modernise Indian agriculture, develop infrastructure and make the country self-sufficient in all major requirements. This was the strategy adopted and most clearly spelt out in Second Five-Year Plan and in the Industrial Policy Resolutions of 1948 and 1956. Thus, contrary to popular belief, India had cast its lot with city-based industrialisation as the road to self-realisation.

The ground realities were vastly different that turned good intentions into shreds. The first government of the country inherited a truncated country, ravaged economy by colonial exploitation and long intense freedom struggle and traumatic partition. Poverty, hunger and deprivation were everywhere and the first priority of the government was naturally to feed, clothe and shelter its citizens. In 1947, of the population of 350 million, nearly 50 million lived in towns and cities whereas 86 per cent lived in rural villages and constituted the bulk of the nation's poor. Urban areas at that time were believed to be self-sufficient and it was both natural and imperative in order to maintain law and order that the country's meagre resources be made available to rural areas: unfortunately, this initial prioritisation soon led to two nations within the country – the rural Bharat and urban India.

The inability of successive governments to reconcile the needs of the cities (the chosen vehicle of growth) and villages where bulk of population lived haunted Indian planners for a long time. It was only after the census of 1981 that the country's demographic reality and inescapable urban future stared in the face and a new realism began to emerge. By then a lot of damage had been done by well-intentioned people who took the easy road to revive the dying villages with the last breath of the dying cities. Huge investments and subsidies did not reduce rural poverty but spread it to urban areas through migration of rural poor.

Meanwhile, during the fifties and sixties, industries were encouraged to be set up in already industrialised metropolitan areas but little or no provision was made for the upgradation of urban services and infrastructure. The combined allocation for housing, urban and regional developments speak for themselves. Since the Second Five-Year plan in 1951, this sector received only around 2.5 per cent of plan allocation till the Eighth Plan. Thus, although there was a clear decision to industrialise the nation, there was no matching concern to urbanise it. The economic benefits of industrialisation were appreciated but its social impacts were neglected. The situation has hardly changed. Speaking as recently as in January 2000, the Minister for Urban Development, Government of India, stated: "Though 90 per cent of Government revenues and 60 per cent of GDP emerged from cities, they got at the municipal level only 0.6 per cent of the

GDP. Over the years, the percentage of Plan allocation for urban development schemes has been declining. In 1953, the allocation for urban development was 8 per cent of the total Plan outlay. It decreased to a bare two per cent as of now".

In the beginning, it was the 'pull' factor, which led to migration from rural areas as urban centres needed their labour and skills. However, as it became evident that the vast investment of resources in rural development had not really closed the gap but created in its stead a 'push' factor resulting in the second wave of migration.

This migration which still continues causes the cities to bulge round the seams, creating in its wake urban slums, deprived and dilapidated fringe areas, growing urban poverty and the like. Unlike in the western developed countries, urbanisation in India is still increasing and spreading its tentacles to new areas creating ever-increasing fringe as well as other centres.

If this trend continues, as it appears it would, then by the middle of the 21st century, five emerging truths will reveal themselves tellingly before the nation: (1) India would emphatically have won the race, it would have desperately liked to lose, namely, it would have usurped the status of the most populous state even surpassing China. (2) The oft-repeated truth of the past incessantly drilled into every mind that India lives in villages would have been falsified. Textbooks would be rewritten to say that India lives predominantly in towns and cities. (3) With such a shift of population primarily of the poor, rural India will cease to have the monopoly over poverty. (4) If a radical appraisal of urban policies continues to elude us, the urbanisation of poverty will inexorably lead to the poverty of city administration. Emaciated cities saddled with loads of vital responsibilities that enable daily life will be reduced to the pitiable situation of being asked to service brimful multitudes with empty coffers.

Finally, if national and state macro planning for industrialisation for wealth creation and infrastructure investment was skewed, Indians would not spread evenly into hundreds of towns – an inordinately large bulk would be sucked into a handful of magnetic mega and metropolitan cities that would offer them hope of sustenance. The great Indian challenge of the 21st century would be to avoid the occurrence of any such calamity.

This is the story of cities considered as a single unit but the story of any sizeable township anywhere in India is the tale of two cities, one a formal planned town, and the second unplanned twin, which would include the urban fringe of the cities. As the unplanned fringe twin grows, its demand outstrips its meagre resources and soon it becomes a drain on the other twin, leading to all-round impoverishment. Situation worsens as immigrants migrate from rural areas to the cities already having inadequate services without adding to its resources.

Unable to buy residential land at market price, they squat and settle on any part of land available. In many ways an informal settlement negates the foundation in which formal settlement rests, and the laws, plans and regulations on which the cities stand – development plan, zoned lands or demarcated lands for the kind of usage they can be put to. The formal city conforms to the zoning. Houses are built on land meant for housing. In the informal city or in the fringe around the city, land is priced high out of such zones. Lack of purchasing power forces settlers to build on lands that are un-zoned, open or unfit for construction, and hills, river lands, lands on the vicinity of railway track etc. spoiling the scenic beauty, disrupting the green belt.

Since a resident of the formal city builds in permissible zones, he does so with proper plans and hires professionals for the same. In contrast, in fringe areas, since permission is not given or even not necessary, he does not build in permissible zones, with proper title, material etc.

The formal city resident has a right to utilize city infrastructure as pays taxes and the infrastructure in such a city is already planned. The informal settlement in the fringe areas, on the other hand, is not planned and a resident cannot take advantage of its infrastructure, particularly, because he does not pay taxes. In such an anomalous situation, politicians have golden opportunity to distribute favours of water, electricity etc., regularising settlements etc.

Police Commission of which I was a member had studied these fringe areas and found that unemployment and underemployment is high in these areas leading to increasing criminalisation.

In many cases youth from the rural areas migrate and live in these fringes. They are separated from their families. They do not have decent and normal social and family life and are under continual stress. They live in the most unsanitary conditions which breed drug addiction, diseases such as AIDS etc. Terrorism, dissatisfaction and discontent breed on empty stomachs, hands without work and mind without occupation. Indeed, a large variety of problems plague the fringe areas, which need to be studied and understood.

India's cities and towns have quite evidently not been prepared for an influx of the kind experienced by them, the rapid growth witnessed by them as well as rapid impoverishment and inadequacies of the infrastructure. The situation has unleashed political, administrative and financial problems of monumental proportions. Further, the immigrants constitute a non-tax-paying segment. In spite of this, cities have to be left liveable – a great challenge which urban planners are ill-equipped to face.

The urban poverty, the uninhabitable fringe areas etc. are clearly the contribution of rural areas, which does not aspire for planned development, informalises the formal city and ruralises the urban areas. Even it increases class conflicts and undermines the city's civil order. The existing laws do not help either.

Bewildered by the revelations of the 1981 Census, an initiative was taken by the Government of India in the form of the appointment of the First National Commission on Urbanisation in 1985 under the chairmanship of an eminent architect. A lot was expected from it and which it really delivered. For the first time since independence, some stood back and looked at what had become of the nation's dreams, and just how far we have wandered away from our tryst with destiny since fateful midnight hour of 15th August 1947.

Confronting the demographic demon that refused to go away, the Commission in its comprehensive 1988 report avers that the sheer magnitude of the numbers has made our attitude to urban centres both confused and equivocal. On the one hand, we see them as heroic engines of growth not only creating skills and wealth for the nation but also generating employment for the migrants from rural areas. On the other hand, these urban centres are held guilty of generating the most brutal and inhuman living conditions with large section of citizens living in desperate squalor.

The Commission submitted its report in 1988. It was very well received, and to be fair, the government of the day did incorporate the broader approach in framing 74th amendment to the Constitution in 1992 and launched an Urban Poverty Alleviation Programme. Let us see how it is implemented.

There is a great and urgent need for critical assessment of the whole scenario of urbanisation including urban fringes, urban poverty etc., and to recommend to various statutory bodies involved as to how to solve some of the problems. I do hope that this seminar will come out with studied and worthwhile solutions to the staggering problems of the fringe areas, urbanisation, urban poverty etc.

With these words, I have great pleasure in inaugurating the seminar.

3

Managing the Urban Fringe of Indian Cities

VINOD TEWARI

Urbanisation in India, accompanied by unabated movement of rural people towards the cities in search of means of livelihood, rapidly changing land use structure and concentration of economic activities in large urban areas, has created an unprecedented challenge to urban planners and managers due to its massive scale and complex nature. The process of urbanisation, which has been causing rapid population growth and spatial spread of cities, is not supported by judicious planning, efficient management and good governance. Almost all urban areas in the country have serious shortage of power, water supply, sewerage, developed land, housing, transportation, communication and other facilities, as the provision of urban infrastructure and services, required to support large concentrations of population and related activities, is lagging far behind the pace of urbanisation.

Spatially, the cities have been expanding, in a haphazard manner, beyond their administrative boundaries into the surrounding rural areas mainly due to the absence of a regional approach in city planning, lack of co-ordination in the plans of multiple planning agencies, ineffective implementation plans, and lack of resources for plan projects. As a result, the peripheral or the fringe areas of Indian cities, today, are characterised by largely unplanned shift from primarily agricultural to mixed urban land uses, scattered urban development, environmental degradation, slow incremental development of roads, and inadequate provision of other infrastructure and services. These traditional zones, which are the future of intermediary areas of cities, are going through an unprecedented phase of physical expansion and social, economic and environmental transformation.

The fringe areas usually fall into administrative jurisdictions of gram panchayats in the rural hinterland of the city. The municipal body of parent city has little or no say in the development that takes place in the fringe. On the other hand, the agencies administering the fringe assume that the city's infrastructure would be used and will take care of the essential infrastructure required for the development that takes place in the fringe. However, this does not happen and the fringe development causes severe burden on its infrastructure. In the recent past, the urban fringes of several metropolitan cites, like

Delhi, Bangalore, Hyderabad and Pune, have witnessed the advent of retail malls, multiplexes, IT parks, biotech parks, special economic zones etc. without a corresponding development of the supporting infrastructure. Inadequate resources and low capacities of municipal bodies have further aggravated the complexities of management and governance of the cities in general and their fringe areas in particular.

In order to have sustainable development in the fringe and a systematic and orderly spread of urban areas, the cities need to be managed by using innovative planning approaches, new strategies and policy instruments, decisive actions, detailed socio-economic and spatial data structures, and co-ordinated efforts of all stakeholders. Reforms in several areas, including provision and delivery of municipal services, tax assessment and administration, levying of user charges, urban legislation, municipal accounting and financial reporting systems, personnel systems and assets management, are needed to facilitate and strengthen municipal management and governance structures.

The Urban Fringe Development

Conceptually, the urban fringe is the area that lies immediately outside the designated limits of a city/town. It has strong linkages with the city and bears an urban reflection on its physical, occupational, socio-economic and demographic characteristics. The urban fringe, also called the rural–urban fringe, the city edge, the city periphery, the city's outskirts, the city's outlying areas, etc., essentially consists of the spill over urban land uses and activities that could not be accommodated in the city itself, due to various cost and other constraints, into the surrounding areas. The activities are normally seeking relatively inexpensive land close to the city to take advantage of its market and other infrastructure facilities. Land values, taxes and service charges are relatively higher in the city than in the fringe area, and therefore many industrial activities get located in the fringe. Village settlements, new residential layouts carved out from the agricultural land, commercial and industrial activities, vegetables and flower cultivation etc. are intermingled in a haphazard manner giving rise to an unplanned development and mixed land use pattern in the fringe.

The extent of the fringe and nature of development are strongly correlated with the population size of the city; the larger the city, the greater is the intrusion of urban activities in the surrounding rural areas. While the fringe of a small or medium town may extend up to a kilometre or two from the town boundary, in the case of a metropolitan city it could go up to 50 to 60 kilometres. The nature and complexities of the development in the fringe areas increase with the size of the city and more so when the fringes of two or more cities overlap.

An analysis of the city region of Bangalore, when it was a 1.6–million city, using a number of population and land use indicators of fringe development, like population density, population growth, sex ratio, non-agricultural workers, and area under fruits and vegetables and commuting patterns showed that the influence of the city in its region extended up to 20 kilometres (Prakasa Rao and Tewari, 1979). There was a clear distance decay effect in the intensities of the variables that characterised the fringe. The types of development included scattered industrial development along transport corridors, townships of some major public sector industries, a few educational institutions, a satellite town, vegetable, fruit and flower cultivation etc. With the emergence of the city as a major global city, the fringe development patterns have changed completely today with the emergence of express ways, farm houses, IT parks, biotechnology parks, recreation facilities and clubs, and luxury housing complexes.

Urban fringe development is a continuous process, partly in response to the agglomeration economies and partly arising out of the inefficiencies of management and inadequacies of the city. The policies of de-industrialising the city have also resulted in many industries getting relocated in the city region or the new industries to come up at the city periphery. Urban activities in the fringe, first, start along the transport corridors taking advantage of the access to the city. Typically, the fringe development is triggered off when an educational institution, or an industrial estate, or a housing layout, is located along a transport corridor near a city. The intermediate areas, facilitated by transport infrastructure, are then filled up by residential and commercial land uses. The generalised process can be described as that of institutional and industrial leapfrogging and residential and commercial infilling, first along the major transport routes and then in interstitial areas. Thus, the fringe is an area that, by definition, is in transition – from a rural agricultural state to an urban industrial/commercial state.

In this transition process, the village settlements located in the fringe get engulfed by urban land uses and activities, the occupations of population of the settlements change due to the conversion of their agricultural land to non-agricultural uses, and the composition and lifestyle of the population changes due to inmigrants, mostly low-income group, seeking inexpensive housing or space for petty business in these areas. The demand for housing provides incentives to the villagers to upgrade their housing from *kutcha* to *pucca* structures using poor building material and add new floors to the structures without any consideration of the structural safety and amenities. The population densities in these settlements increase and these areas become potential slums for the future city.

The agricultural lands in the fringe get converted to non-agricultural uses and often purchased by the rich and influential people for speculative purpose. Due to high land prices in the city, many urban activities and low/middle income group people look for land outside the city limits. This demand is met by the speculators who hold the land in the fringe. They start selling the land plots by parcelling their holdings unauthorisedly and without any services attached to the plots. While some buyers use the land for housing and other activities, others hold the plots without using them in anticipation of infrastructure development or further rise in land prices. Thus, most development that takes place in the fringe lacks basic amenities like open spaces, proper roads, water and sanitation facilities, and education and health services.

In the case of metropolitan cities, the fringe areas often cover not only village settlements but also towns and cities. The National Capital Territory of Delhi, for example, has a metropolitan city, Faridabad (2001 population: 10,89,180) besides a number of large cities, viz., NOIDA, Gurgaon and

Ghaziabad in its city region. The demand for land in the fringe of metropolitan cities for relatively expansive land and higher quality of life has also been responsible for planned land mostly by builders, in pockets of the fringe areas of these cities. Delhi, for example, has seen planned residential and high-tech industrial development in its fringe areas. However, these developments have put an enormous pressure on the city and have poor transport linkages with the rest of the area.

The Management Issues

The main issues involved in urban fringe management are as follows:

- Checking unplanned development
- Controlling avoidable urban sprawl
- Protecting prime agricultural land from conversion to non-agricultural uses
- Protecting the social and economic interest of the rural population
- Dispersing the activities of the parent city to other towns/cities in the region
- Providing basic infrastructure and services in the fringe areas
- Maintaining environmental quality

In the context of urban fringe development, one of the major management issues is how to anticipate the development trends and plan for an orderly growth and spread of the city. The scattered fringe development that takes place in the absence of any plan is inefficient, wasteful, and leads to a situation where any planned development later becomes impossible. Most such unplanned developments are irreversible, as they remain unchecked for a very long period due to the weaknesses prevailing in the land use control and regulation systems. The scattering of the activities necessitates movement of people and goods to longer distances and services that are highly uneconomical.

The scattered, leapfrog and ribbon development in the fringe leads to an urban sprawl of predominantly low-density land uses that are not functionally related. Such a sprawl, in advance of urban infrastructure, is a result of poor or non-existent planning. No one takes responsibility for planning and investment in functional spaces and infrastructure. Developers and landowners controlling the market build what is easiest and fastest.

The sprawl leads to conversion of prime agricultural land and natural features like lakes and tanks to inefficient non-agricultural uses. Preservation of prime agricultural lands in the fringe of expanding cities is necessary for maintaining open space and environmental quality.

The land use changes force the rural population of the fringe to change their livelihood activities and occupations. Though income from their land that normally fetches higher price than the agricultural land away from the fringe provides short-term security to the local people, they face problems of finding alternate means of livelihood. Lack of education and skills required for non-agricultural occupations often pushes a large number of them into poverty, and sometimes towards crime.

Providing infrastructure and services in the fringe is expensive and commercially unviable due to scattered development. No agency or developer pays attention to providing infrastructure services, as any cost recovery is uneconomical. Poor quality infrastructural development, therefore, occurs on piecemeal small-scale basis, area by area, rather than in a planned manner with a regional perspective. Such a state of affairs is neither in the interest of local bodies and other public authorities nor in the interest of the individuals.

Poor infrastructure and services and absence of functional open spaces cause urban degradation and slum-like conditions in many fringe areas. Irrigation tanks and lakes are often used as garbage dumps and eventually converted to residential or other urban uses. Lack of planning and environmental infrastructure, like protected water supply, sewerage and solid waste management, further adds to the degradation and environmental problems.

Planning and Management of the Urban Fringe of Delhi

Metropolitan Delhi has a complex structure of municipal administration. The National Capital Territory of Delhi (NCTD) includes areas that are administered in tandem by the Central Government, government of NCTD and three municipal bodies, viz., Municipal Corporation of Delhi, New Delhi Municipal Corporation and the Delhi Cantonment Board. The areas surrounding the NCTD include municipal towns of the neighbouring states, formal housing development, unauthorised housing development, slums and squatter settlements, planned industrial, commercial and institutional areas, unplanned/unauthorised industrial and commercial areas, agricultural lands and rural villages. The fringe extends almost up to 50 kilometres in the neighbouring states of Uttar Pradesh, Haryana and Rajasthan.

While the government of NCT-Delhi, Delhi Development Authority and Municipal Corporation of Delhi are responsible for planning the city, the task of regional planning has been entrusted to the National Capital Region Planning Board (NCRPB). The National Capital Region (NCR) covers an area of 30,242 km^2 including 1,483 km^2 (4.4%) of NCT-Delhi, 4,493 km^2 of Rajasthan state, 10,853 km^2 of Uttar Pradesh and 13,413 km^2 of Haryana state. The area includes the fringe of NCT-Delhi as well as a number of other towns falling in the region. Thus, the region has a very complex administrative structure with overlapping fringes, towns and rural areas from three other states, and obviously, very difficult to plan. The NCRPB was constituted as per the NCRPB Act of 1985 that sought "*to provide the constitution of a Planning Board for the preparation of a plan for development of the National Capital Region and for coordinating and monitoring the implementation of such plan and for evolving harmonised policies for the control of land uses and development of infrastructure in the National Capital Region so as to avoid any haphazard development of that region and for matters connected therewith and incidental thereto*".

The need for planned development of Delhi and its region was felt in the early 1950s itself and the first plan was prepared in 1956 by the Town Planning Organisation. This was followed up by the Master Plan of Delhi 1962, for the perspective year of 1981, which defined the NCR and recommended setting up a statutory National Planning Board and development of the region in accordance with a regional plan. In 1973, a regional plan was prepared by the Town and Country Planning Organisation that reiterated the need to regulate the growth of Delhi and decentralisation of economic activities.

The first plan of the NCRPB, the Regional Plan 2001, approved in 1988, visualised a goal of "balanced and harmoniously developed region leading to dispersal of economic activities and immigrants to Delhi, thereby leading to a manageable Delhi". The plan contained an interrelated policy framework with regard to re-distribution of population, integrated settlement system, regional land use pattern, environmental protection, economic activities and infrastructural facilities for a sustainable development of the city and its region.

According to the NCRPB Act, each participating state is required to prepare a sub-regional plan for the sub-region of the state included in the NCR. While the Regional Plan 2001 was notified in 1989, the sub-regional plans prepared by the states of Uttar Pradesh and Rajasthan were approved in 1992 and 1994 respectively. The plans of Delhi and Haryana are still awaited. The NCRPB Act also provides for preparation of functional plans to elaborate one or more elements of the Regional Plan by the NCRPB with the assistance of its Planning Committee. Such plans were prepared in regard to transport, power, telecommunication and industry.

Though the exercise of preparing the Regional Plan 2001 was quite elaborate and time-consuming, it failed to achieve its objectives due to weaknesses in the implementation and lack of resources. A review of the plan, conducted in 1999, pointed out the weaknesses in the plan and its implementation based on piecemeal and ad-hoc decisions. The review suggested a number of measures with regard to location of economic activities, offices, institutions, investment in infrastructures, implementation of the principal of common economic zone, and amendments and modifications in the plan enabling legislation. Based on the review, the NCRPB is now preparing another plan for the year 2021. For this purpose eight study groups were constituted with experts, non-officials and senior officers from various government agencies as members with regard to the following aspects of planning:

1. NCR policy zone, demographic profile and settlement pattern
2. Regional land use and rural development
3. Physical infrastructure including transport and communication
4. Utility and service infrastructure including power, water supply, sewerage, solid waste, drainage, irrigation etc.
5. Social infrastructure including education, health, shelters, recreation, law and order etc.
6. Environment including tourism, heritage, pollution, disaster management etc.
7. Institutional framework
8. Economic and fiscal policy including resource mobilisation, funding etc.

The exercise of preparing the Regional Plan 2021 based on the recommendations of the study groups is in progress and a draft report has been prepared for the discussion in the NCRPB. This plan is aimed "to promote growth and balanced development of the National Capital Region" (NCRPB, 2002) through:

1. Providing suitable economic base for future growth and by identification of regional settlements capable of absorbing the economic development impulse of Delhi.
2. Providing efficient and economic rail and road transport networks integrated with land use pattern.
3. Minimising the adverse environmental impact.
4. Improving efficiency of existing methods of resource mobilisation and adopt innovative methods of resource mobilisation and attract private investment.
5. Developing selected urban settlements with infrastructural facilities.
6. Providing a rational land use pattern in order to protect and preserve good agricultural land and utilising unproductive land for urban land uses.
7. Promoting sustainable growth with social justice and empowerment.
8. Improving quality of life particularly of the poor and deprived.
9. Promoting effective people's participation in the process of development through decentralisation.

The 2021 plan framework for the development of the NCR is envisaged through four policy zones: The NCT-Delhi, Delhi Metropolitan Area (excluding NCT-Delhi), rest of the NCR, and Highway Corridor Zone. As per the plan, no new major economic activities, except those necessary to sustain the local population, should be permitted in the NCT-Delhi. The opportunities in the Delhi Metropolitan Area excluding NCT-Delhi should be maximised to enable it to compete with the NCT-Delhi in terms of economic activities, transport systems, housing and other infrastructure and quality of environment. The rest of the NCR should have a policy of accelerated development of both urban and rural areas. Planned and regulated development has been proposed along the national highway converging at NCT-Delhi.

The Regional Plan 2021 will be augmented by Sub-regional Plans, District Plans and Master Plans of Townships and Area Development Plans. The responsibility of its implementation will be on the government of NCT-Delhi, the various central ministries and the participating state governments. Private sector will be encouraged to participate in the financing, execution and management of commercially viable projects envisaged as part of the overall investment programme.

Constraints in Effective Planning and Management of Urban Fringe

All planning exercises become futile in the absence of enabling environment for implementation of the plans, and lack of financial resources, appropriate institutional mechanisms, and capacities of implementing agencies. Some of the constraints faced in the management of urban fringes in the country are:

- Lack of comprehensive urban policy
- Weaknesses in the legislations governing land acquisition and development
- Outdated municipal and town planning acts and planning practices
- Lack of information base needed for regional planning
- Delays in preparation of regional plan

- Absence of district planning committees and metropolitan planning committees as required by the 74th Constitution Amendment Act
- Weak implementation of plans
- No monitoring/review of plans
- Gap between demand and supply of land and its acquisition and development
- Inadequate financial resources
- No involvement of private sector
- Weak municipal bodies and their management systems and practices

Suggestions for Managing the Urban Fringe Development

To improve the management of urban development in the fringes of Indian cities, the following suggestions deserve attention:

- Formulation of comprehensive urban development policy including urban land policy
- Modifications in municipal, town planning, land acquisition, and other enabling laws
- Speeding up the regional planning process
- Constitution of metropolitan planning committees (MPCs) and district planning committees (DPCs)
- Improving coordination among agencies involved in the planning and development process
- Introducing municipal reforms for making the municipal bodies credit-worthy
- Developing partnerships with private sector
- Using innovative methods for raising financial resources
- Developing information systems for planning, implementation and monitoring of regional plans
- Building capacities of municipal functionaries and municipal bodies

References

National Capital Region Planning Board (2002): *National Capital Region: Regional Plan 2021* (Draft), NCRPB, New Delhi.

Prakasa Rao and Vinod Tewari (1979): *The Structure of Indian Metropolis: A Study of Bangalore,* Allied Publishers, New Delhi.

4

On Encounter between Urban Fringe and Neoliberal Capitalism

D.N. DHANAGARE

My attempt would be to probe the *modus operandi* that neoliberal capitalism penetrates the urban space with and engulfs the urban fringe using politics as its surrogate. But first it should be useful to reflect on how one understands neoliberal capitalism. This paper is divided into three parts. The first part will discuss the notion of neoliberal capitalism; the second part will elaborate what is called as the encounter between the neoliberal capitalism and the urban fringe; and finally in the last part some remedial measures would be suggested to rectify the collateral damage that metropolitan structure, its political economy, along with its neoliberal artillery, does to the fringe areas of the urban spaces.

I

The very concept of neoliberal capitalism suggests that it shares some common features of the classical form of capitalism – the ways in which it broke out during the romance of the Industrial Revolution (particularly in its second phase) in Western Europe. It flourished in England first and later in North America. However, the qualifying adjective 'neoliberal' to the well-known concept of capitalism clearly implies that it qualitatively differs from the classical model of capitalism in certain ways. It might be worth our while to examine certain critical distinctions between the two manifestations of capitalist political economy that are not necessarily two stages of its historical development.

1. First and foremost is the fact that the classical form of capitalism focused on profit-making through ever-enlarging system and forces of production and continuous reproduction of profits by capturing more and more markets. In this process, imperialism and colonialism were the systemic by-products that served as instruments in establishing supremacy of the process and product both. Nevertheless, the classical form was not oblivious or totally apathetic to its social welfare functions that were treated as systemic

obligations. Neoliberal capitalism, on the contrary, has gathered momentum and has also accelerated its pace more recently since the end of the Cold War. It is only thereafter that the bipolar world order turned into a uni-polar hegemonic system headed by the USA. This new brand – called neoliberal capitalism – prides itself in undermining commodity production *per se*, or avoids direct involvement in commodity production; rather it prefers to rely chiefly on profit-making through financing activities. Hence, finance capitalism is the other side of the coin that we recognize today as neoliberal capitalism. It is concerned more with profits through financing, and with outsourcing actual production, and is concerned neither with employment generation nor with welfare of the worker. Its latest incarnation is to be seen in the predominance of credit network that involves essentially management of cash flows in money market globally.

2. Secondly, both the varieties of capitalism – wedded to the *laissez faire* principle – profess principle and practice of 'free market competitive economy' to be left unfettered by the state. However, it needs to be emphasised that the classical capitalism still viewed the state as a safety-valve institution for rapprochement between 'profit' and 'social welfare' when required. The neoliberal variety of capitalism, however, assiduously seeks an unbridled pursuit of profit, and tends to undermine the state in the euphoria for globalisation – or global economic regime to be precise. So, it perceived 'social sector spending' as a drain on resources and wants to consign social service sector to private investments. No doubt, in both the forms of capitalism, appropriation of labour surplus is a common feature though it was more visible in earlier type of capitalism; in the neoliberal epoch, labour exploitation tends to be camouflaged by systems of casalisation, and contractualisation of labour and more so by the system of outsourcing. For instance, 'Corporate Social Responsibility' (CSR) is the buzzword these days for multi-national corporations (MNCs) that are spreading their tentacles not only over countries but also over continents. It is significant to note that while claiming all concessions including tax holidays and similar other benefits from the state, these corporate sector companies are seen blatantly violating national labour and industrial laws with impunity. This is doubly true with the post-colonial economies and nation-states. It is quite ironical that at the same time the MNCs at times overzealously finance voluntary agencies, NGOs and similar other civil society initiatives including providing funds for international seminars or workshops on CSR! Such acts of benevolence of neoliberal capitalism indicate their anxiety to seek respectability besides legitimacy.
3. It is true that in the days of classical form of capitalism 'conformism' was rewarded and aberration was penalized. Neoliberal capitalism on the contrary advocates 'reformism' – particularly institutional reforms, what is often called as 'structural adjustments' that turn out to be even more oppressive and atrocious than 'conformism'. Neoliberal capitalism puts pressures on nation-states to reform their age-old institutions, especially those of banking, marketing, and insurance, as well as reforms in existing laws. Hence, ardent advocates of free market economy introduce stringent

conditions of 'environment safety', 'reform in labour laws and laws of copyright (Intellectual Property Right)', 'record of human rights', 'prevention of child labour' and the like. Reforms thus become pre-conditions for entering any collaborative undertaking or a financing agreement. All this is done in the name of economic reforms of the neoliberal variety.

4. Metropolitan cities and urban areas are the new spaces in which neoliberal capitalism has found fresh pastures for financing activities. There is an ever-expanding market for shelter (housing) as also for meeting demands of consumer goods through retail marketing. Builders/architects, urban development planners, retail traders and businessmen, bankers and politicians, i.e., elected representatives of the people, all form a nexus to tap service sector chiefly housing and marketing sector. This nexus that is tightening its grip over the urban space and through its financing network tends to control the state. The urban fringe is the new player – stakeholder in some sense, in urban development, that in the ultimate analysis remains at the receiving end as we shall see shortly.

II

The Urban Fringe

In any discussion on the urban fringe, the focus is always on the 'centre', i.e., city or metropolitan city and its megapolis culture rather than its 'periphery' – namely the rural hinterland that actually feeds the towns and cities with goods, raw materials and services in day-to-day life. We tend to express concern primarily for the wanton expansion of the city limits, unplanned growth of the fringe habitations and for the encroachment of urban spaces by rural–urban migrants within or immediately outside the city limits. Decision-making in a democratic functioning being tardy offers enough leeway to those who flout DPs (Development Plans) of cities to get the irregular constructions duly regularised in exchange of political support in elections. Most city dwellers look at the fringe as a threat to the quality of their life while urban planners and administrators look at the problems of the fringe mainly with a view to managing the mega-cities with better efficiency without letting production of goods and services adversely affected. In doing so, *'growth'*, and not *'development'* of the fringe is permitted to the extent it does not, at least apparently, harm the civic services and urban comforts.

Most civic bodies – whether corporations, improvement trusts or municipalities – lack resources for development of their infrastructures: such as roads, housing, power water and sanitation. It is not always clear as to what happens to the revenues these civic bodies collect from the city tax-payers. City authorities are often seen approaching the World Bank, IMF, UNDP or Asian Development Bank and similar other international funding agencies for securing loans for repairs of their water distribution schemes or for laying underground drainage system or for modernising its transport system, starting Metro service. It is very unlikely that such funds-starved metropolitan civic bodies would spare their scarce resources for the development of the fringe. Instead, what is preferred is a shortcut that allows an unplanned growth of the fringe in such a way that the 'so-called symbiotic' relationship between the core and periphery, i.e., between the downtown areas of the cities and the urban fringe transforms the latter into a permanently 'parasitic' dependency on the city.

The process of such a transformation gets completed, at least in so far as a particular fringe area is concerned, when it is officially included in the limits of the city corporation area. Such an inclusion creates a façade that the problem of the fringe is solved. On the contrary, the real problem of the urban fringe begins after its incorporation into the limits of a city by the corporation. Faced with revenue deficits all the time city administration too welcomes this inclusion for obvious reason that it fetches additional revenues. The hitherto unplanned growth, i.e., unapproved structures in the fringe, or construction of a hotel restaurant or a multiplex on plots of land otherwise reserved for school or park, or for setting up a workshop where a welding machine is used day and night within a residential area gets regularised. This extraordinary liberal treatment is often given by imposing a laughingly nominal fine on those who breach law. The growth (or fate?) of the 'fringe' thus gets consigned to the builders lobby regardless of whether or not the fringe is or is not included in the city limits. Civic bodies only too willingly complete the rituals of regularisations because at least a section of the beneficiaries is primarily interested in getting their own representatives to the civic bodies. A sizeable chunk of recent migrants from the erstwhile fringe now manage to get entry in the electoral roll. Local self-governing bodies in the villages (*panchayats*) in proximity with cities are rarely seen resisting absorption of the fringe within the city limits. *Panchayats* have neither the will nor money power to assert their autonomy. One of the reasons of their inability to do so is that at least some of the sitting members and office bearers anticipate wind-falls from a formal absorption of the fringe in the city limits. Land prices shoot up even before this process of incorporation of the fringe is completed. The only immediate development of the fringe is then visible in the forms of multi-storeyed residential apartments, new shopping malls on any vacant plot of land regardless of whether or not it is certified as 'non-agricultural land' by revenue authorities and construction plans approved by civic authorities. The concept of 'developed plots' gets a safe burial as buildings are raised without even checking whether basic minimum facility of water and sanitation would be available or not. The best strategy for any builder of a mega-project is to invite city-mayor or deputy mayor to lay the foundation stone of the project!

In such a view 'from above', the fringe is perceived as a pathological appendage of the mega-city – a source of all nuisance and social problems by those very people who create them. In this perspective the city, metropolis or large towns are taken as irrevocable, unassailable and as an inescapable reality in any discussion on the fringe. This perspective of the fringe from 'above' is almost always predicated on certain premises or assumptions that need to be subjected to closer scrutiny.

(i) One of such premises is that the problems of the fringe and the cities are largely due to demographic crisis resulting from population explosion. The truth element of this assertion need not be contested beyond a certain point in so far as the Indian scenario is concerned. Nonetheless, all over the world metropolitan centres and their fringes have been coping up with the problem of rising numbers and have managed with a reasonable degree of success without allowing one to impinge on the other. Cities like London, Paris, and Amsterdam, New York or Tokyo have all grown in size in geographic and demographic terms. However, none of them has reached the point of crisis in relation to their fringes and hinterlands as most metropolitan cities in India have. Even with growing numbers, fringes can be managed well provided their 'development', not just 'growth' is planned systematically keeping in view the fringe as an independent, though semi-autonomous, entity. 'Semiautonomous' because the links of the fringe with the market and places of work as well as for other services located in metropolitan centres cannot be simply wished away.

(ii) Another assumption is that rural–urban migration is an irreversible process. It is true that in the decades ahead the rate of rural–urban migration in India is likely to shoot up noticeably. At present, India has about 34 per cent of her total population living in urban areas. In fact, Indian society is yet to face the kind of urbanisation process that Europe and North America have gone through after the two (or three) phases of the Industrial Revolution. The rural–urban migration can be contained only by a properly planned development of the fringe in relation to the rural hinterland more than as an integral part of the city. Problems like massive poverty, poor health facilities, absence of work opportunities, shelter and even minimum amenities like drinking water and sanitation are rife in Indian villages, barring exceptions. Consequently, the urban fringes keep swelling in size almost endlessly. Fringes keep reproducing themselves as rural migrant population gravitates nearer or around those fringes that await their inclusion in the corporation limits. Till then "free-for all" rule prevails. This migration can indeed be checked to a considerable degree if the developmental focus is turned on the villages, the rural hinterland. In coming years and decades, water schemes and factories, roads and hospitals, schools and telephone exchanges, decent and affordable shelters with toilet facilities – all these amenities have to be developed only in the hinterland after proper feasibility studies are conducted. Planning has to be done to turn villages into towns of manageable size and with viable resources. That is possible only by adopting an alternative model of urban development, and by planning industrial development accordingly so that the need of the rural population to migrate is obviated, if not in the immediate future, at least in the next 20–25 years.

(iii) Problem of the fringe is further predicated on the assumption that the existing cities must expand and this expansion is inevitable as well as uncontrollable. That in a democratic society no one can be prevented from moving into a city and from spreading his bedroll, if he has one, on a pavement of his choice. There is no reason why even in a liberal democracy, restrictions cannot be imposed on illegal construction, or encroachment of a vacant plot whether in the city limits or in a fringe area. There are cities in the world that do not allow any construction of further buildings or apartment blocks within their existing limits. Until the 1970s, Paris civic authorities, for instance, did not permit any construction of a building with more than five or six floors (including basements). Utilisation of urban space or land use in the countryside cannot be left to the sweet will of builders' lobby, greedy professional politicians and spineless urban planners whose developmental blue-prints undergo changes under pressure from neoliberal capitalists as well as the swelling corporate sector. Land use has to be monitored and regulated strictly in accordance with established norms and law that in turn ought to reflect welfarism to the core. What is required is a leadership that has greatest good of the greatest numbers that is enshrined as a value in the Constitution. A leadership with 'political will' and the one that is prepared to face onslaught from the neoliberal capitalist lobby could alone face the challenge of developing the urban fringe. Such a determined leadership will ensure that vested interests – nexuses of builders, professional politicians and, slum lords, who get elected to the civic bodies are cut to size, are brought under the rule of law, and their nefarious activities, that are injurious to the public good, are curbed. They manage electoral support from those very latest migrants whom they had helped to settle down and occupy space illegally and by promising them both safety as well as regularisation in due course. Such migrant parasites constitute a perennial vote bank for the new leaders for whom their own interests in political power and pelf are prior to real welfare of the people whom they represent. When attractive offers are made to the slum-dwelling migrants by builders, these very leaders have no qualms in getting slum areas vacated, if needed by forcible eviction, or in setting a slum on fire so that a new shopping complex could be raised in its place. Such professional politicians in the garb of real wheelers-dealers must not be allowed to sabotage a planned development of the fringe as independent and autonomous centres of economic-industrial and socio-cultural activities more in relation to the rural hinterland.

(iv) It is often assumed that development of the urban fringe quintessentially means development of industries and residential areas at the cost of agricultural land. This assumption is predicated on the premise that decline of agricultural economy with the rise of industry is almost axiomatic. Without such an indefensible logic the policy of setting up Special Economic Zones (SEZs) by acquiring thousands of acres of agricultural land would not have been pushed to extremes in India by the state. Nothing could be more misleading than to accept this assumption uncritically as valid in the Indian context. There is certainly a trade-off between agriculture and industry in a political economy. Nonetheless, it would be erroneous to think that development of the fringe would necessarily mean its final and irrevocable estrangement from the ties with the farm. In India, even today, as many as 65 to 70 per cent of the population is rural and 61 per cent of the total working population depend on agriculture. The fact that such a major part of economy, i.e., farm economy contributes only 31 per cent of the GDP suggests that all is not well with the farm sector. It is not being suggested here that such a stagnated farm sector ought to be preserved (as National Parks!) at any cost as it is at its presently low level of performance. Nevertheless, while developing the urban fringe its ties with the farm need not either be written off or severed totally. A centrifugal model of development that concentrates more on the hinterland rather than on the city centre is called for. In such a development model agro-industrial centres can be set up between the fringe and rural hinterland in a manner that will generate employment, improve the purchasing power of the rank and file, reduce burden on farm, prevent unplanned and unsustainable rural–urban migration, sustain rural ecology and environment, and create new self-contained centres and towns so that city-dwellers, especially new entrepreneurs, are enticed to move out of the hustle and bustle of the metropolis. This calls for a paradigm shift in industrial policy that will not play into the hands of the nexus between neoliberal capitalist forces, the builders' lobby and the political class. Hence, the need to ban any further industrial development in cities that are already sitting at the mouth of the pollution volcano cannot be overemphasised.

(v) Generally, it is assumed that any fervent plea for preserving the farm sector has emotional and nostalgic streaks, and that in the age of globalisation, clinging to farm economy is anachronistic as well as irrational. Far from it, an overwhelming majority of the working population in India is engaged in agricultural and allied occupation. Even then, only the best and fertile lands must be reserved exclusively for farming. Less productive lands can be identified for non-agricultural developmental activities, including SEZs to attract multinational corporate companies to set up their units on promise of fabulous tax and other concessions. Only such city development deserves full state support where it minimizes displacement, and uplifts quality of life in the fringe areas. For instance, notwithstanding her rapid integration with world market China sustains a kind of 'dual economy', as its farm sector is still an important component. Only a well integrated as well as decentralised plan of fringe development and its equally spirited implementation is required so that the development of the urban fringe (in relation to the rural hinterland) becomes sustainable.

(vi) Very often 'fringe' is understood more as a spatial and geographical reality. It is seldom borne in mind that talking about a 'fringe' is basically talking about society, human groups, their interrelationships, cultural practices most of which are inherited from tradition. Even migrating population carries some of these cultural attributes and transplants them in the new urban/fringe setting. In spite of the growing pressure of modernisation communities, castes and ethnic groups keep yearning for preservation of their tradition. Their time-tested collective wisdom has stood them in good stead. Sometimes traditions are even reinvented. Humans as cultural beings, and not Robots, live in fringes and rural hinterlands. It is human groups with diverse identities that come together to form what is known today as the urban fringe. Technical and rational solutions may be necessary, but not sufficient, to deal with the problems of the urban fringe. Pragmatism coupled with sensitivity may hold the key in dealing with the problems of development of a fringe.

III

For a balanced development of the urban fringe, following remedial measures can be suggested:

1. After a careful assessment of available resources, the coping capacity of a metropolis has to be determined in quantitative terms keeping focus on the quality of life. Cities must not be allowed to grow beyond their physical capacity. This is precisely where social commitment of capitalism as was honoured in Europe despite its imperialist history must serve as a role model, rather that transnational corporate capitalism that believes in unbridled profit maximization through pontification of neoliberal reforms and structural adjustments. The developing world must not leap into the trap of neoliberal capitalism.
2. The fringe has to be developed in relation to the hinterland and not as an integral part of a metropolis. Autonomy and independence of the fringe should be protected so as to prevent cultural erosion and or invasion by neoliberal capitalism.
3. As a matter of a conscious policy decision, resources will have to be allocated in a just and fair manner in favour of the fringe and the hinterland on a priority basis.
4. Instead of including the fringe in the city limits, new local authority should be created for managing the fringe and the hinterland.
5. Industries and factories will have to be established/or relocated between the fringe and the rural hinterland, not either in the fringe or between the metropolis and the fringe. SEZ projects must not be permitted to bulldoze the hinterland much against the wishes of the people. At any rate the state must not act as an agent of neoliberal capitalist forces and MNCs and help the latter in acquiring agricultural lands by invoking provisions of the Land Acquisition Act.
6. An alternative development model has to be tried for the fringe so that appropriate technology and industry are harmonized with the farm sector taking into account the local, regional human as well as natural resources. People themselves need to be involved in evolving that model. Its prerequisite is a governance structure that is founded on the trilogy of transparency, accountability and people's participation in decision making.
7. Ideas of decentralised and sustainable development will have to be propagated through the voluntary effort of NGOs while the state ought to play a more proactive role and provide all possible encouragement/incentives for any move away from the core of the metropolis, especially for those investing in the development of the fringe and rural hinterland.

5

Expansion of Urban Capital and Marginalisation of Fringe

An Antipode of Urban Development

HANUMAN SINGH YADAV

The concentration of productive forces and accumulation of capital, in the megacities in India under the new dynamics of capitalism, have created inherent contradictions in the economy. These contradictions are manifested in the crisis and antagonisms specific to the city and its fringe. The most important of these are rural–urban antagonisms, which Marx regarded as the territorial division of labour, and the contradiction of capital versus the urban labour and rural peasantry. The new economic order and the functional relationship of extended structure of city and fringe, as built environment (production, circulation, exchange and consumption) display the unity of contradictions between urban processes and predicament of the fringe. Harvey (1981) argues that this *"urban process, in relation to the theory of accumulation, implies the creation of material physical infrastructure for built environment which helps in the surplus value"*.

Present paper attempts to analyse the changing character of urban fringe of Bhopal city under the contemporary new economic order. The first part elaborates the theoretical context of relationships of urban phenomena of capital accumulation under capitalist mode of production that carves out the spatial and economic organisation of the fringe. The second part discusses the urban process that eases the accumulation and expansion of urban capital in the city as a result of investment in 'built environment'. The third part provides an elaborate analysis to the structural change in the fringe shaped by urban process under the influence of capitalism.

The city and fringe cannot be separated as two dichotomous spatial units having any antagonism rather they produce dialectical unity under the capitalist urban development. The traditional definition of urban fringe confines itself to the physical location of the area as "the extended urban space with distinct characteristics of partly assimilated into urban complex and still partly rural." The area is predominantly rural but it, socially and economically, does not belong to it. The urban context refers to the physical character (land use) of the area and the people living in the area reveal the social characteristics. Most studies prior to the 1970's confined to the physical demarcation and the land use pattern of the fringe. The area is designated with a variety of names as "*institutional desert*" (Wehrwein, 1942), "*geographical no-man's land*" (Golledge, 1960), "*area of great differentiation*" (Wissink, 1962) and the main characteristic features are segregation, selective immigration, commuting, collapse of hierarchy and rural–urban continuum (Pahl, 1965 and 1968).

Marxist geographers have all through rejected the orthodox empirical evidences of spurious correlation between different indices of superstructure. The explanation to the phenomenon of urban process, within the city or cities as system (Berry, 1962 and 1967), where production/consumption interlock, or urban centres as geometric shapes of points and lines in locational context (Haggett, 1967), or casual-effect relationship with economic development (Sjoberg, 1960 and Berry, 1962), are not of much significance because of banal arguments, devoid of consideration of dialectical principles of political economy. They even do not refer to the mode of production and class relations in the social production under capitalism. The core idea of the Marxist literature, on urban process under the capitalist mode of production, is centred around the accumulation of capital via surplus value, antagonistic relation between the labour and capital, ownership of means of social production, and investment of capital in the built environment. Urban process under capitalism is necessarily exploitative where the production is controlled by capitalist class, which is actually carried out by the class of wage labourers (Clark and Dear, 1981). The over accumulation of capital under the "*primary circuits of capital*" of Karl Marx, results into the flow of capital investment in built environment so as to complete the "*secondary circuit of capital*" to create fixed capital for production and consumption funds (Harvey, 1981). The part of this circuit, which goes to real estate and land development, takes the form of "*property circuit of capital*" (Walker, 1981). This investment creates spatial differentiation in the super-structure and is the end product of division of labour.

The economic order that emerges at the urban fringe is not divorced from the urban process/development discussed above. It produces the dialectical unity of city and its fringe. The dynamics of commodity producers (the classes) and the territorial relation of profit maximisation (accumulation of capital) under the capitalist mode of production bind the city and the fringe. This is because the land use system and employment structure at the fringe (both as part of the superstructure) are the end product of class relation and division of labour. The prime objective of capital investment in the fringe is maximisation of profit from land market. Hence the superstructure of city and fringe demonstrates the inherent contradiction of capitalism in the form of urban crisis, class antagonism and city–fringe dichotomy. The property sector investment at the fringe is more prominent because of higher return as rent and appreciation of land values.

Bhopal, the capital of Madhya Pradesh, has grown exponentially in the recent past, with a unique process of urban development under the capitalist mode of production. It has crossed the two million-population marks in the current census. The capitalistic crises are clearly visible in the form of problems and predicaments of working class especially in the post globalisation era of WTO regime. The analysis of development of urban economy under the influence of new economic policy reveals that, the job market has refused to absorb any additional labour. Speculative capital has grown without generating employment, the service sector has expanded to a disproportionate level, hierarchy of services has almost collapsed, and specialised IT based and super specialised management consultancy has over powered the traditional production. The influence of accumulation of fast growing capital is visible in the property sector, in real estate and land development with a tendency of concentration of money capital in few hands and fewer sectors. Urban process has accelerated the pace of accumulation of capital in the city and its expansion over the fringe areas. Withdrawal of government has almost undermined the public utility sector to facilitate the uncontrolled growth of private sector for the exploitation of the labour market as well as the exchange of goods and services. This process has resulted into the deprivation of the poor from productive assets and income of wage labour.

Urban development has proved to be counter-productive and an antipode to the general process of development. The urban process must have incorporated the mechanism to improve the conditions of the poor and marginalised sections of society. Rather, it has gone in the reverse direction to enhance the problems and predicament of people.

The characteristic features of the fringe of Bhopal City are the manifestations of the urban process, which the city experienced over the last two decades under the structural adjustment of the economy. The clearly distinguished changes emerged at the fringe are summarised under the social and economic traits of economy. The newly emerging social production in the city has generated enormous surplus value for over accumulation by the primary circuit of capital of Marx. This accumulated capital found way of reinvestment in the built environment in real estate and land development in the city and the fringe. The neo-capitalist class has invested large amounts and purchased agricultural land in the name of farms and farmhouses. This helped the bourgeois class in two ways, first it legalised the unaccounted money as agricultural income and secondly it is expected to provide dividends as enhanced land value, with the expansion of the city limits.

The fringe has gone through a structural change in the ownership of productive forces. The farm size at the fringe falls under the small and marginal category. The speculative land value has tempted the farmers/peasants to sell the agricultural land and to use the money, so received, in a more productive manner as the urban entrepreneurs do. This has changed the pattern of ownership of productive assets in the fringe and the productive forces are transferred from poor peasant to the capitalist class in the city. The villages altogether became landless villages. This change in the ownership brought money to the villages at the fringe and as a consequence it has changed the division of labour and production consumption behaviour of the entire villages.

The change of ownership in the property sector, division of labour, and production pattern, immediately affected the income-employment pattern and almost all small marginal farmers have no option other than to join the army of landless labourers or to become sharecroppers on the same land they sold. The consistency in income got affected in two ways. The land they sold is further fragmented by change of ownership and uniform desired land use in agriculture came to an end. Productivity declined, even a large part of land is left unused. Secondly, the urban labour market did not provide any job to these unskilled and uneducated workers. The rate of unemployment in the fringe experienced explosion of marginal workers and even non-workers.

Another striking phenomenal change in the fringe is brought by the flow of liquid money capital in the hands of poor small and marginal farmers. The money flow to the villagers was to the magnitude of Rupees 2 to 15 lakhs, in the hands of the poor of yesteryears. Being uneducated and poor entrepreneurs, the confusion prevailed in the money management, which most of them could not utilise in a rational manner. Some intelligent farmers could retain their land, as well as use the money, so received, also in buying more land elsewhere. The consumption behaviour of fringe people has not been beyond the influence of speculated urban market. This money allowed them to behave like urban rich and as consequence the consumption behaviour of these people had a quantum jump. Almost all households fell in competition to have an urban like house, equipped and furnished with modern utilities. The capital goods found way to these villages as cars, motorcycle, colour television, refrigerator, coolers and air conditioners, even mobile phones. The general consumer behaviour has seen a sea change.

The economics of this process suggests that, the money takes the full circle, and it reaches back to the bourgeois class of city. The money, which flew to the fringe, is taken back in the city in a very short span of time. The ownership of productive forces is transferred for higher returns to the urban rich. On the other hand the productive forces, which were providing the livelihood to the poor are replaced by reoccurring expenditure oriented unproductive assets, which were neither needed by them nor can be utilised for living. This conclusion, not only confirmed to one single city, rather it is the generalised urban processes under capitalism that is operating in the same manner and is neutral to space, time and scale.

References

Berry, B.J.L. (1962): Some Relations of Urbanization and Basic Patterns of Economic Development, in Forrest R. Pitts, ed., *Urban Systems and Economic Development*. Eugene: The School of Business Administration, University of Oregon, 1–15.

——. (1967): *Geography of Market Centers and Retail Distribution*, Prentice-Hall Inc. Englewood Cliffs.

Clark, G. and M. Dear (1981): The State in Capitalism and the Capitalist State, in M. Dear and A.G. Scott (eds), *Urbanisation and Urban Planning in Capitalist Society*, Methuen, London, 45–61.

Golledge, R.G. (1960): Sydney's Metropolitan Fringe: A Study in Urban-Rural Relations, *Australian Geographer*, 7:243–255.

Haggett, Peter (1965): *Locational Analysis in Human Geography*, Arnold, London.

Harvey, D. (1973): *Social Justice and the City*, John Hopkins Press, Baltimore.

——. (1981): The Urban Process under Capitalism: A Framework for Analysis, in M. Dear and Alien J. Scott (eds) *Urbanisation and Urban Planning in Capitalist Society*, Methuen, London.

Pahl, R.E. (1965): *Urbs in Rure;* London School of Economics, Geographical Paper No. 2.

——. (1968): Sociological Models in Geography, in R.J. Chorley and Peter Haggett (Eds) *Socio-Economic Models in Geography*, Methuen, London .

Sjoberg, Gideon (1960): *The Pre-industrial City*, Free Press, New York.

Walker, Bruce (1981): Income Distribution, City Size and Urban Growth: A Rejoinder, *Urban Studies* 1981 18: 121–122.

Wehrwein, G.S. (1942): The Rural–Urban Fringe, *Economic Geography*, 18: 217–28.

Wissink, G.A. (1962): *American Cities in Perspective: With Special Reference to the Development of their Fringe*, Assen, USA.

6

Land Dispossession and Changes in Rural Livelihoods

Case of Periurban Delhi

CHINMOYEE MALLIK AND SUCHARITA SEN

The Context

The restructuring of capital at the global scale, more intensively observed in the last two decades in India and many other developing countries, have seen an emergence of new economic spaces in and around large metropolitan cities. This process has reorganised the means of production in the periurban areas in a way that has been both negotiated and contested. The major manifestation of this reorganisation has been in terms of urban land intrusions on agricultural land and thus involves direct land transfers from land-utilisation of one category to the other.

Scholars have argued that changes in land use and livelihood are *"co-produced, where shifts in one are reflexive of shifts in the other"* (McCuskur and Carr, 2006: 791) and that land use and livelihood change must be studied as an intertwined process viewed in the light of power relations and social processes. That land forms the basis of rural livelihoods in the developing realms and that incidence of poverty is highly correlated with landlessness has been a well documented fact (Mearns, 1999; Hanstad, 2004; Cotula et al., 2006). Land, besides being a productive asset stands as a symbol of status of the households (Mearns, 1999). Livelihood, on the other hand, is the outcome of how the individuals manage the complex combination of capabilities, assets and activities (Tacoli, 1999). It encompasses the way in which a living is obtained and hence is not just the net results in terms of income received or consumption attained (Ellis, 2000). Chambers and Conway (1991: 6) has conceptualised livelihoods as comprising of *"the capabilities, assets (stores, resources, claims and access) and the activities required for a means of living"* thereby linking assets that people possess and the options that emanate from such asset. It has been argued that with increased access to assets, vulnerability and livelihood insecurity declines (Moser, 1998).

Dispossession of land, which is central to rural livelihood, stands out as one of the most important issues in the periurban areas (Tacoli, 1999; Anguilar and Ward, 2003). Those dependent upon land-based livelihoods are posited with the challenge of sustaining themselves in a locale which goes through a transition which requires adjustments in terms of the means of livelihood. Those capable of taking advantage of the emerging opportunities of work created as a result of urbanisation could be drawn within the folds of non-agricultural work, while others would be marginalised from productive work and will negotiate a deterioration of livelihood. The extent of access to livelihood assets plays a decisive role in enabling the periurban population to translate the spatial characteristics of the periurban interface (PUI) into opportunities rather than constrains (Allen, 2003; Tacoli, 1999; Hanstad et al., 2004).

This paper seeks to look into the impact of land acquisition, following urban expansion, upon the livelihood status of the affected households in a village lying in North West Delhi. The paper attempts to explore the extent to which land dispossession affects the livelihoods of the people engaged in land-based activities. It also tries to see whether education has played any role in enabling the affected people in securing alternative livelihoods.

Hypothesis of the Study

The central thesis of the paper is that there exists a strong and positive link between access to land and sustainability of rural livelihoods. It may however may be hypothesized that this link may not to be so significant in a periurban locale where nearness to the mega-city perhaps have imbibed an undertone of urbanity such that the villages in the fringe areas have already reached a stage to move on the trajectories of livelihood that have scant links with land. So, the paper hypothesizes that in the PUI land acquisition may not pose as a very serious threat to the sustainability of rural livelihoods although access to assets, especially land asset is of significance as a tool enabling the sustenance of rural livelihoods in the fringes.

The paper has been organized into six sections. The first section is introductory in nature and presents the background of the study. Section II delivers the hypothesis of the paper. Section III reflects upon the methodological concerns and the data used. Section IV provides the general characteristics of the sample; section V elaborates upon the analysis and results and section VI tries to summarise and conclude the discussion attempting to point towards the possible policy interventions.

Methodological Issues, the Data and Limitations of the Study

Two villages have been selected from the periurban Delhi for the field survey (Figure 1): Rani Khera, Delhi and Manesar, Gurgaon.

The DDA data for land acquisition from the villages around Delhi for the different projects have been compared with the census data to see what proportion of the village land had been taken possession of before and after 1991. It has been observed that there are around 8 villages where maximum acquisition took place before 1991 and another 8 where it happened mostly after 1991. The sample villages fall in the latter category.

Figure 1 *Study Area for Field Survey*

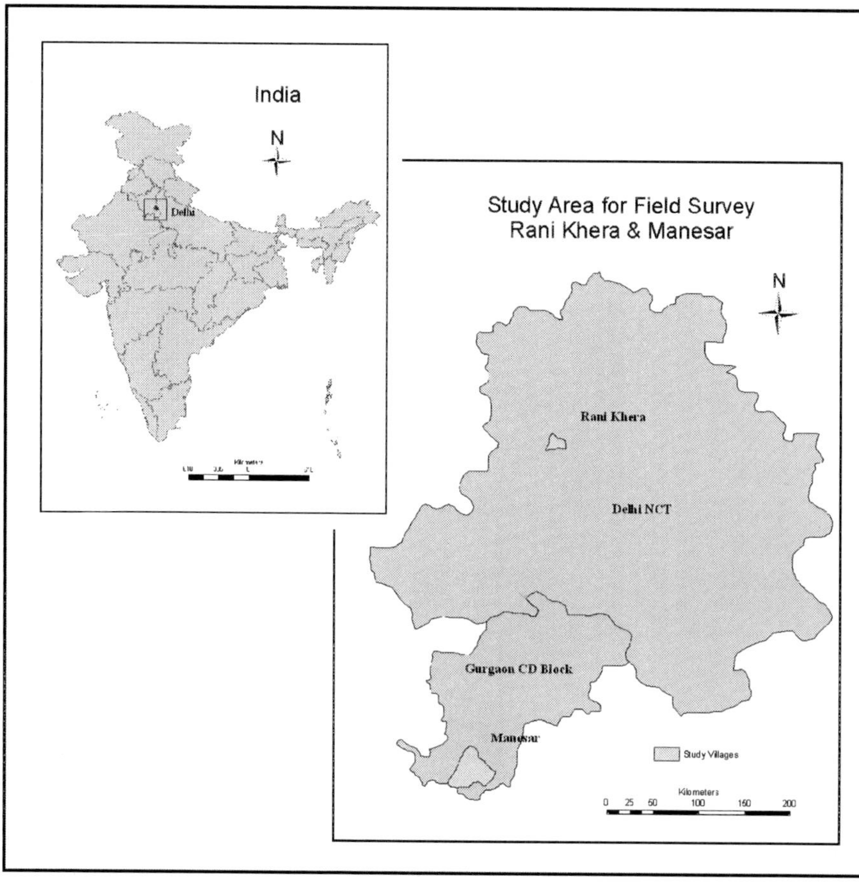

It must be mentioned at this juncture that there exists a multitude of terminologies to refer to the areas surrounding the cities. The terms like urban fringe, rural–urban fringe, periurban areas, periurban interface (PUI), peripheral areas and the related terms used to denote the vicinity of cities have been used interchangeably and quite loosely. Also the term livelihoods have been used here in a very limited sense generally denoting occupation.

The paper is based on an exploratory field survey conducted during April 2008 where both households as well as individuals have been the level of analysis. The sample consists of 30 households selected purposively such that at least some of the family members of the household had been engaged in agricultural work prior to land acquisition. Although the study is based upon small sample size and hence does not employ rigorous statistical analysis, it has been able to bring out significant issues that pave the pathway for further research.

General Characteristics of the Sample

The sample consists of 30 households of whom Jaths (24) are the principal land-owning households in the village. There are 6 landless households who used to cultivate by leasing-in land. Out of the 30 surveyed households, 21 of them (70%) have been affected by the recent DDA land acquisition and 3 households (10%) have not suffered from any loss of land (Table 1).

Table 1 *General Characteristics of the Surveyed Households*

Household Characteristics	*Attributes*		*Count*	*Per cent*
	Caste	Jath	24	80
		Jimmer	2	6.7
		Kashyap	4	13.3
		Total	**30**	**100.0**
	Religion	Hindu	30	100.0
	Access to Land	Land Owned	24	80.0
		Landless	6	20.0
		Total	**30**	**100.0**
	Category of Household	Partially lost land	18	60.0
		Never owned land	6	20.0
		Never lost any land	3	10.0
		Completely lost land	3	10.0
		Total	30	100.0
Individual Characteristics		**Age-Sex Composition**		
	0–14	Male	37	28.7
		Female	15	17.6
		Total	52	24.3
	15–59	Male	75	58.1
		Female	58	68.2
		Total	133	62.1
	Above 60	Male	17	13.2
		Female	12	14.1
		Total	29	13.6
	Total	**Male**	**129**	**100.0**
		Female	**85**	**100.0**
		Total	**214**	**100.0**
		Education Level (above 15 years)		
	Households Owning Land	Illiterate	20	15.4
		Up to Primary	3	2.3
		Up to Secondary	47	36.2
		Higher Secondary and Above	60	46.2
	Landless Households	Illiterate	9	33.3
		Up to Primary	3	11.1
		Up to Secondary	14	51.9
		Higher Secondary and Above	1	3.7
	Total	Illiterate	29	18.5
		Up to Primary	6	3.8
		Up to Secondary	61	38.9
		Higher Secondary and Above	61	38.9
		% of Persons in Non-Farm as Primary Occupation (above 15 years)*		
		Households Owning Land	30	19.0
		Landless Households	4	10.5
		Total	**34**	**17.3**

Source: Field Survey, 2008 – *pertains to pre-acquisition period

It has been noted that majority of the land owning households (62.5%) cultivated the owned land for self-consumption only while the landless households leased in land for raising crops for marketing them (Table 2). It may also be mentioned at this juncture that the land-owning households have larger number of their members into non-agricultural pursuits than the landless households (Table 1). Therefore, it may perhaps be concluded that the dependence on land is much more crucial to the landless households than the landed gentry. It is a well documented fact that access to education enhances one's capabilities and empowers him to enjoy a beneficial edge in the labour market. It may be noted that the level of education among the landless households is remarkably lower than that observed among the land owning households. While only one person has opted for higher education from among the landless households, this figures as 60 (46.2%) for the land owning households (Table 1). On the other hand, the landed households exhibit a much better scenario in terms of educational attainment.

Table 2 *Land Ownership and Principal Use of Crops*

		Principal Use of Crops				
		*Not applicable**	*Self Consumption*	*Marketing*	*Self Consumption and Marketing*	*Total*
Households Owning Land	Count	2	15	1	6	24
	Per cent	8.3	62.5	4.2	25.0	100.0
Landless Households	Count	0	0	4	2	6
	Per cent	0.0	0.0	66.7	33.3	100.0
Total	Count	2	15	5	8	30
	Per cent	6.7	50.0	16.7	26.7	100.0

Source: Field Survey, 2008.

* These households lease-out their land and thus the question pertaining to principal use of crop is not applicable for them.

Analysis and Results

Changes in Access to Land

Following repercussions have been noticeable following land acquisition by DDA,

- The average size of holding among the surveyed households has decreased from 11.6 bighas to 6.2 bighas within a span of one year (Table 3).
- The number of landless households has increased from 6 to 9 within this one year.
- The number of households owning land above 10 bighas has been reduced from 12 to 8 owing to DDA land acquisition (Table 3).
- While, all the surveyed households had access to land before land acquisition, 9 of them (30%) have been reported as completely losing the same (Table 4).

Table 3 *Change in the Size of Ownership Holding (2007–2008)*

		Landless	*Small (0.1–5)*	*Medium (5.1–10)*	*Large (above 10)*	*Total*	*Mean Size of holding (Bigha)*
Before Land Acquisition (2007)	Count	6	6	6	12	30	11.6
	Per cent	20	20	20	40	100	
After Land Acquisition (2008)	Count	9	8	5	8	30	6.2
	Per cent	30	26.7	16.7	26.7	100	

Source: Field Survey, 2008.

Table 4 *Change in the Nature of Access to Land (2007–2008)*

		Owned	*Leased in*	*Owned but leased out*	*Owned and leased in*	*No access*	*Total*
Before Land Acquisition (2007)	Count	20	6	2	2	0	30
	Per cent	66.7	20	6.7	6.7	0	100
After Land Acquisition (2008)	Count	19	0	1	1	9	30
	Per cent	63.3	0	3.3	3.3	30.0	100

Source: Field Survey, 2008.

Therefore, it can be inferred that the DDA land acquisition has been instrumental in not only downsizing ownership holdings, but has also displaced some of the households from land-based activities. Thus, the farmers have been confronted with shrinking land base hindering livelihood from land. It is therefore expected that the affected farmers shall seek alternative means of sustenance. It has been noted by many scholars that as agriculture has failed progressively in providing productive additional rural employment, there has been a thrust towards diversifying rural livelihood opportunities to accommodate the rural population seeking rural non-farm work. It has, however, been observed that rural non-farm work is highly heterogeneous and access to different non-farm jobs vary considerably with education levels and possession of other assets.

Change in Primary Occupation

Broadly it may be noted that following land acquisition, 15 out 36 persons who reported agriculture as their primary occupation have been displaced such that the share of workers having agriculture as primary occupation has declined from 18.4 per cent to 10.7 per cent within just one year (Table 5). While a marginal increase in the share of workers in non-agriculture has been observed, there has been an increase in the share of non-workers from 7.1 per cent to 12.2 per cent within one year. In terms of absolute numbers, out of the 15 people who were displaced from agriculture as primary occupation, only six of them have been able to secure alternative employment in the non-agricultural sector while the remaining nine have become jobless.

Table 5 *Change in the Shares of the Broad Primary and Secondary Occupation Categories (2007–2008)*

Occupation Categories	*Occupations Before Land Acquisition (2007)*				*Occupations After Land Acquisition (2008)*			
	Primary Occupations		*Secondary Occupations*		*Primary Occupations*		*Secondary Occupations*	
	Count	*Per cent*	*Count*	*Per cent*	*Count*	*Per cent*	*Count*	*Per cent*
None	14	7.1	97	49.5	24	12.2	112	57.1
Agriculture	36	18.4	86	43.9	21	10.7	70	35.7
Non-Agriculture	34	17.3	10	5.1	40	20.4	11	5.6
Students	55	28.1	2	1.0	55	28.1	2	1.0
Housewife	57	29.1	1	0.5	56	28.6	1	0.5
Total	196	100	196	100	196	100	196	100

Note: Population above 5 years of age has been taken as often children are also engaged in agriculture as secondary occupation.

Source: Field Survey, 2008.

Table 6 *Change in Primary Occupation and Educational Level (2007–2008)*

Change in Occupation		*Educational Levels*				
		Illiterate	*Primary*	*Secondary*	*Higher Secondary and Above*	*Total*
Not applicable	Count	2	0	0	0	2
	Per cent	100.0	0.0	0.0	0.0	100
Cultivator to Wage labourer	Count	0	0	2	1	3
	Per cent	0.0	0.0	66.7	33.3	100
Agricultural Worker to Non-Farm Work	Count	1	0	4	1	6
	Per cent	16.7	0.0	66.7	16.7	100
Agricultural Worker to Unemployed	Count	1	1	4	1	7
	Per cent	14.3	14.3	57.1	14.3	100
Continuing with Earlier Agricultural Occupation	Count	3	0	10	5	18
	Per cent	16.7	0.0	55.6	27.8	100
Total	Count	7	1	20	8	36
	Per cent	19.4	2.8	55.6	22.2	100

Source: Field Survey, 2008.

It is important to note the role of education in affecting the occupational shift of the people who reported agriculture as their primary occupation. It has been revealed that 5 out of the 6 agricultural workers who got absorbed into non-agricultural pursuits have above secondary education.

However, majority of the agricultural workers who became unemployed (61.4%) and all the cultivators who turned towards wage labour also reported being secondary and above educated (Table 6). The role of education as a

Box 1

Perspectives from Manesar

Focus group discussions were conducted in Manesar Village of Gurgaon, lying on NH 8. It was a small village which has now turned into an industrial and commercial hub. The IMT Manesar Industrial area has boosted up the commercialisation of the area.

It has been reported that 99 per cent of total agricultural land in the village has been acquired for industrialisation with the result that agriculture is almost non-existent and the livestock economy has been demolished. A lot of money has been injected into the village economy in the form of compensation money that has given spurt to conspicuous consumption and immoral activities. The Yadavs were the chief land owners and consider it below their dignity to do anything other than cultivation and prefer to remain idle than going for service.

The village headman Gajraj stated "... kheti nahi hai, par hum Yadav apas mein majduri nahi kar sakte, jo so kam nahi karte. Apna prestige hai ... sab Baith ke tash khelte hai ..." (Agriculture is no more ... but we Yadavs cannot afford to do anything and everything. We have some prestige ... we prefer playing cards).

Alternative Occupations following Land Dispossession

Social stratification has influenced the capability of the individuals to change their occupation. The higher castes diversified their livelihoods in the following ways:

- Compensation money has been used to build and extent houses that accommodate "paying guests" or are rented out;
- Invested in shops and cars for hiring out as an alternative to farm income.

The lower castes were traditionally tied to land as labourers also were compelled to shift towards non-farm income sources. They lacked financial capital and managed to find place in menial and petty non-farm work like:

- wage labourers, and
- petty vendors and shops

Voice of the Commons

'Land acquiring agency, public or private, must ensure compensatory employment for at least one of the family member of the household whose land is being taken away or those who were tied to land in any form for their livelihoods'.

capability-enhancing element has not emerged clearly. However, it may be possible that access to productive assets and social network has enabled some of the affected individuals to secure productive non-farm occupation.

However, majority of the agricultural workers who became unemployed (61.4%) and all the cultivators who turned towards wage labour also reported being secondary and above educated (Table 6). The role of education as a capability-enhancing element has not emerged clearly. However, it may be possible that access to productive assets and social network has enabled some of the affected individuals to secure productive non-farm occupation.

Change in Secondary Occupation

With respect to agriculture as secondary occupation, it has been observed that:

- Out of the 86 members who reported being in agriculture, 16 got displaced such that the share declined from 43.9 per cent to 35.7 per cent within one year (Table 5).
- Out of the displaced agricultural workers, only one has been accommodated in non-agriculture while the remaining 15 persons have become idle such that the share of workers having no secondary occupation increased from 49.5 per cent to 57.1 per cent (Table 5)

Looking at the educational level of the affected people, it has been observed that of those who shifted from self cultivation to wage labour as a secondary occupation, 75 per cent of them are illiterate and those who have lost subsidiary (secondary) course of income about half of them are educated up to primary level (Table 7). The only one person who has shifted to non-agriculture has more than the level of higher secondary education. Thus a direct correspondence between educational achievement and occupational shift has not been observed with respect to agriculture as secondary occupation.

Table 7 *Change in Secondary Occupation of Agricultural Workers and Educational Level (2007–2008)*

Change in Occupation		*Level of Education*				
		Illiterate	*Primary*	*Secondary*	*Higher Secondary and Above*	*Total*
Cultivator to Wage labourer	Count	3	0	1	0	4
	Per cent	75.0	0.0	25.0	0.0	100
Agricultural Worker to Unemployed	Count	6	2	11	0	19
	Per cent	31.6	10.5	57.9	0.0	100
Agricultural Worker to Non-Farm Work	Count	0	0	0	1	1
	Per cent	0.0	0.0	0.0	100.0	100
Continuing with Earlier Agricultural Occupation	Count	8	5	21	28	62
	Per cent	12.9	8.1	33.9	45.2	100
Total	Count	17	7	33	29	86
	Per cent	19.8	8.1	38.4	33.7	100

Source: Field Survey, 2008.

Occupational Shift and Category of Household

The nature of shift of workers who were in agriculture has been different for the different categories of households. While some of the agricultural workers from households affected by land acquisition have exhibited occupational shift, those hailing from the households that never lost any land are continuing with agriculture as primary and secondary occupations (Table 8 and 9). Such a phenomenon points towards the fact that land continues to be a very significant source of livelihood and that urbanisation has not offered enough opportunities which may act as a pull factor for shifting away from agriculture. Had there been any such pull factor operative, some of the members of the households unaffected by land acquisition would have shifted out of agriculture voluntarily.

Table 8 *Category of Household and Change in Primary Occupation (2007–2008)*

Category of Households		*Change in Primary Occupation*					
		*Not applicable**	*Cultivator to Wage labourer*	*Agricultural Worker to Non-Farm Work*	*Agricultural Worker to Unemployed*	*Continuing with Earlier Agricultural Occupation*	*Total*
Never lost any land	Count	0	0	0	0	4	4
	Per cent	0.0	0.0	0.0	0.0	100	100.0
Partially lost land	Count	1	0	1	3	14	19
	Per cent	5.3	0.0	5.3	15.8	73.7	100.0
Completely lost land	Count	0	1	2	0	0	3
	Per cent	0.0	33.3	66.7	0.0	0.0	100.0
Never owned land	Count	1	2	3 #	4	0	10
	Per cent	10.0	20.0	30.0	40.0	0.0	100.0
Total	Count	2	3	6	7	18	36
	Per cent	5.6	8.3	16.7	19.4	50.0	100.0

Source: Field Survey, 2008.

* This includes those individuals who left agriculture due to old age and has no relation to land dispossession.

Out of these 3 in non-farm, 2 are into petty non-farm work like vegetable vending and construction wage worker.

For agriculture as primary occupation, worse affected have been the households who completely lost land and those who were tenant cultivators. A shift towards wage work from self cultivation as primary occupation is exhibited by members from these two categories of households (Table 8). Shift towards non-farm work has been more for the land owing households than the tenants. It re-iterates the proposition that even for diversification towards non-farm work, access to land plays a vital enabling role (Hanstad, 2004; Mearns, 1999; Cotula et al., 2006). It has also been argued that land owners diversify their livelihoods to accumulate, while the landless and near landless diversify to survive (Ellis, 1998). It is probable that access to land facilitate the land owning households' shift towards non-farm work, although induced by a push factor. For the landless households shift is principally towards petty non-farm work like vegetable vending. The most remarkable shift has been towards unemployment. About 40 per cent of the agricultural workers from landless households have become idle which constitutes 15.8 per cent of the household that partially lost land.

Table 9 *Category of Household and Change in Secondary Occupation (2007–2008)*

Category of Households		*Change in Secondary Occupation*				
		Cultivator to Wage labourer	*Agricultural Worker to Unemployed*	*Agricultural Worker to Non-Farm Work*	*Continuing with Earlier Agricultural Occupation*	*Total*
Never lost any land	Count	0	0	0	5	5
	Per cent	0.0	0.0	0.0	100.0	100
Partially lost land	Count	0	2	0	56	58
	Per cent	0.0	3.4	0.0	96.6	100
Completely lost land	Count	0	1	1	0	2
	Per cent	0.0	50.0	50.0	0.0	100
Never owned land	Count	4	16	0	1	21
	Per cent	19.0	76.2	0.0	4.8	100
Total	Count	4	19	1	62	86
	Per cent	4.7	22.1	1.2	72.1	100

Source: Field Survey, 2008.

With respect to agriculture as secondary occupation, once again it is the livelihood of the landless households who are hard hit due to land acquisition. About 19 per cent of the agricultural workers from landless households have taken up agricultural wage work as secondary occupation and 76.2 per cent of them have no alternative secondary occupation (Table 9).

Table 10 *Use of Compensation Money*

Households	*Not Applicable**	*Consumption*	*Investment in Agriculture*	*Investment in Asset Creation in Non-Agriculture*	*Financial Investment*	*Multiple Response*	*Total*
Count	9	1	3	2	4	11	30
Per cent	30.0	3.3	10.0	6.7	13.3	36.7	100

Source: Field Survey, 2008.

* This category includes the landless households and those households which were not affected by land acquisition.

Although the preceding analysis reveals that the land owning households have not been affected drastically due to land dispossession and that they already had alternative sources of income other than agriculture, all of the households negotiating reduced access to land perceive deterioration in their livelihood. Also, none of the households were satisfied with the rate of compensation provided by the government. Some of the households have sold off all their land to private agencies at a much higher price before DDA could notify

Box 2

Perspectives on Compensation

Although the issue of compensation has not been explored in details, the issue of differences in public-private compensation rate has come up through informal discussion with the respondents in Rani Khera as well in Manesar. The important observations may be summed up as follows:

- Households selling land to private agencies did so willingly whereas majority of those giving away land to government did so under compulsion. Moreover, when government agencies notify any land for acquisition, the owner does not have any choice either in terms of giving up the land or negotiating for the compensation amount. There were some households in Rani Khera who sold some portion of their land to private agencies before DDA could serve notification to acquire their land.
- The difference in the rate of compensation offered by private and public agencies seems to be the key factor in causing these behavioural discrepancies. While the private agencies offered one crore thirty lakh rupees for one acre of land in Rani Khera village and two to five crore rupees in Manesar, government agencies provided only twenty-five thousand rupees per acre as compensation.

The land owners, whose land has been acquired by the government, thus perceive that not only are they losing their traditional means of livelihood, but they are also unjustly compensated for the loss of land asset perpetrated by the state. The common consensus in the affected village is that the state rather than working to improve the living standards of the people, is leading to its deterioration by acquiring their most valued livelihood enhancing asset.

their land for acquisition. Most of the households have used the compensation money in more than one way (Table 10). It is only the land owners who are compensated while it has been observed that the livelihoods of the tenant farmers are affected more severely.

Concluding Remarks and Policy Directions

From the preceding discussion it has been revealed that land and livelihood are not mutually exclusive and that one influences the transformation of the other, sometimes through an indirect route. The study has revealed that although the villagers have been exposed to prolonged urban influences, land continues to be an integral part of their lives. Their proximity to urban area has not de-linked their livelihoods from land-based activities. At this juncture, two issues have been focused on: firstly the role of asset ownership or lack of it in combating challenges arising out of land dispossession; and secondly the role of education in enabling them to shift in favour of non-agricultural occupations in the context of land-use change. Asset ownership has emerged as a very significant enabling factor for diversification of livelihood towards high-return non-farm activities in response to land dispossession. It has also been observed that not only the land-owning households are more educated than the landless households; the former's dependence on land for sustenance has been less than the latter even before land acquisition. Although the link between education as a factor enhancing capability to get absorbed in non-agricultural activities has not been explicitly established, the difference in the nature of occupational shift of the agricultural workers hailing from landed and landless households point towards the fact that access to land rather than educational endowment of the workers has played a more important role in determining the direction of occupational shift following land acquisition. This study has revealed that state perpetrated land acquisition and the compensation policies fail to take cognizance of the most disadvantaged groups comprising of the tenant cultivators and the agricultural labourers which is corroborated by the findings of other scholars. These two groups already lack asset ownership and through the land acquisition drive essentially lose their livelihoods. They are not compensated for their economic displacement.

The policy interventions must address these issues regarding land acquisition and related compensation policies in the peripheries of large cities. In particular the aspects need to be taken into account by the relevant policy makers:

(a) Compensation net must cover the tenant cultivators as well as all those who lost livelihoods following land acquisition. For this to be successful formalisation of tenancy needs to be undertaken in those peripheral areas which are expected to be affected recently. So, before state perpetrated land acquisition is undertaken the direct as well as indirect stakeholders are to be identified so that the compensation policy may be targeted.

(b) The target population in the safety net programmes, specifically those promoting self-employment opportunities can be tied up with the compensation package for land acquisition and should be flexible enough to include affected agricultural workers within their purview.

(c) The compensation provided to the land owner must be in accordance with the prevailing market price such that they are more competitive and less exploitative.

References

Allen, Adriana (2003): Environmental Planning and Management of the Peri-urban Interface: Perspectives on an Emerging Field, *Environment and Urbanization*, 15 (1): 135–147.

Anguilar, Adrian G. and Peter M. Ward (2003): Globalization, Regional Development and Mega-City Expansion in Latin America: Analyzing Mexico City's Peri-Urban Hinterland, *Cities*, 20, (1): 3–21.

Chambers, Robert and Gordon R. Conway (1991): Sustainable Rural Livelihoods: Practical Concepts for the 21st Century, IDS Discussion Paper 296.

Cotula, Lorenzo, Camilla Toulmin and Julian Quan (2006): Policies and Practices for Securing and Improving Access to Land, *International Conference on Agrarian Reform and Rural Development (ICARRD)*, Issue Paper No. 1, http://www.icarrd.org/en/icard_doc_down/Issue_Paper1.pdf

DFID, Natural Resource Systems Programme (2005): 'A Synthesis of Peri-Urban Research of Kumasi, Hubli-Dharawad and Kolkata Peri-urban Interfaces', Final Report of Project R8491, Development Planning Unit, University College London, http://www.ucl.ac.uk/dpu/pui/research/previous/synthesis/final%20report_interfaces.pdf

Ellis, Frank (1998): Household Strategies and Rural Livelihood Diversification, *The Journal of Development Studies*, 35 (1), October: 1–38.

Ellis, F. (2000): *Rural Livelihoods and Diversity in Developing Countries*, Oxford University Press, Oxford

Hanstad, Tim, Robin Nielsen and Jennifer Brown (2004): *Land and Livelihoods: Making Land Rights Real for India's Rural Poor*, Livelihood Support Programme, Working Paper 12, Rural Development Institute (RDI), USA, ftp://ftp.fao.org/docrep/ fao/007/J2602E/J2602E00.pdf

McCusker, B. and E.R. Carr (2006): The Co-production of Livelihoods and Land Use Change: Case Studies from South Africa and Ghana, *Geoforum* 37: 790–804.

Mearns, Robin (1999): Access to Land in Rural India: Policy Issues and Options, World Bank Policy Research Working Paper No. 2123, http://papers.ssrn.com/sol3/papers.cfm?abstract_id=636208

Moser, Caroline O. N (1998): The Asset Vulnerability Framework: Reassessing Urban Poverty Reduction Strategies, *World Development*, 26, (1):1–19.

Tacoli, Cecilia (1999): Understanding the Opportunities and Constraints for Low-Income Groups in the Peri-urban Interface: The Contribution of Livelihood Framework, Paper produced for the Research Project on Strategic Environmental Planning and Management for the Peri-Urban Interface, Development Planning Unit, University College, London, www.ucl.ac.uk/dpu/pui

7

Planning and Managing the Urban Fringe of Indian Cities

Issues and Options

G.R. DIWAN

Land is the basic platform of any development activity. In a democratic country like India most of the land is in private ownership. Per capita land availability in India is very low (compared to other countries) due to population pressure. It is around 0.3 ha. Urban fringe is an area of town or city on its outer edge or periphery. It may bẹ or may not be within the urban boundaries depending upon the extent of the civic area limits at a time.

Urban population in India has been growing rapidly and is around 32 per cent at the moment (350 million in total of 1,100 million) more than three times the corresponding figure of 1971.

Normally gross land area with the jurisdiction of urban area as per Census of India has been termed as urban land. It is further classified as 'developed land' and 'undeveloped land'. But these terms have acquired a definite legal meaning as defined under the Urban Land Ceiling and Regulation Act. 1976. India is the seventh largest country in the world occupying 2.40 per cent of total world area. In terms of population it is the largest contributing about 15 to 16 per cent of the world population (1,100 millions in 6,500 to 7,000 millions).

According to Urban Land Ceiling Act 1976 urban land means:

(i) Any land situated within the limits of an urban agglomeration and referred as such in the master plan; or
(ii) In a case where there is no master plan, or where the master plan does not refer to any land as urban land, within the limits of an urban agglomeration and situated in any area included within the local limits of a municipality (by whatever name called), a notified area committee, a town committee, a city and town committee, a small town committee, a cantonment board or a panchayat, but does not include any such land which is mainly used for the purpose of agriculture.

This Act however failed and has been scrapped by many states though not yet in Maharashtra.

Major cities in India have been experiencing spontaneous periurban growth on surprisingly large sites and mostly outside the legal framework. This periurban growth is usually so called unauthorised within or outside the civic limits.

Beyond the city limits there may be some *urbanisable* land. So a fringe area may be even partially rural at some time but may be likely to be urbanised over a period of time. It has been noticed that in the absence of adequate development control measures this land is vulnerable to have haphazard growth particularly along the highways and communication corridors, which get choked up for smooth traffic and need bye-passes for diverting the traffic outside the developed area. Many planners, administrators and research scholars feel that this is the lacuna of the present development control system in operation in many large cities, which has in fact denied the opportunity for a majority of population in economically weaker sections to acquire affordable shelter. There is a wide gap between the requirements of affordable land by the poor and the supply of serviced land in the cities at affordable price which is naturally fulfilled by unplanned or so called unauthorised development for regularisation. This is why a new Gunthewari Act has been now brought into force in Maharashtra and also being considered in some other states. Such irregular and unauthorised colonies in the fringe area lack infrastructure and the burden of providing the necessary infrastructure is eventually passed on to the adjacent civic body who find it most difficult to provide the same when the colonies are regularised (now under Gunthewari Act). The disparities in provision and infrastructure in such unauthorised colonies and the other authorised one continue to create problems to the civic body. It is seen that such unauthorised developments which are vote banks are given lot of concessions and the effective date for regularisation of such colonies are fixed and extended on political considerations when elections are due; normally people know that such irregular developments are connived at by the civic bodies and the Government, and most of them are eventually regularised. This encourages lawbreakers to go for developments without the legal permissions.

Major Issues of the Fringe Area Development

(i) Urban fringe areas where vast lands may be under agricultural and other non-urban uses attain a greater demand by virtue of their proximity to urban use. Thereby land market takes the central role in transferring agricultural use and value of such land to potential urban use and higher values.

(ii) Land values in fringe areas are comparatively lower than in the core areas of cities, and as such speculators and profiteers enter into speculative transactions of lands in urban fringe resulting in artificial rise in land values in the fringe tempting land owners to sell the land for non agricultural use at higher values than for agricultural use.

(iii) Present planning system and development control system has certain negative or restrictive aspects and hence they are not so effective in practice. They need to be replaced by more positive management policies.

(iv) Fringe areas have a specific and distinctive role particularly in regard to metropolitan containment and decentralisation strategies and have definite distinct character with linkages between city and the surrounding region.

(v) In planning a fringe area it is important to identify its typology and development potential. The future of the fringe area lies in between the urban rural continuum.

(vi) At present the decisions about the extension of civic limits in fringe areas are made mostly on political considerations, and are not based on certain surveys analysis of ground reality situation. This is quite clear from the recent instances of extension of municipal limits of Pune Corporation area. Limits once extended three years back cover some 35 villages were altered to exclude some villages. Similar changes occurred in 1970 when the village panchayats of Pimpri Chinchwad area were converted into a new urban civic body.

(vii) *Changing Pattern of Urban Fringe and Land Use Changes – Fringe Area and Green Belt*. It is observed that space extensive users mostly get located in fringe areas. Expansion of urban population into fringe areas was made possible by the development of automobile transportation and the improvement of roads and highways. Fringe areas have attracted improvement of roads and highways. Fringe areas have attracted people to live in the countryside away from the congested part in natural surroundings. This is how a continuous urban growth takes place outside the city limits. This is known as 'Fringe Area Development'. Mostly it occurs on highways and railway lines of communication in a linear fashion, some time leapfrogging the existing development. Normally no building construction is allowed in the green belt except for agriculture and allied activities sports and recreation.

It is noticed that large areas of green zone are converted into development zone for expansion of city. De-zoning of lands from green to residential uses has been a regular agenda of civic bodies and State Government. The State Government has already regularised residential constructions in eight out of twelve agricultural zones in the Pune city. Individual farmhouses and holiday homes are being permitted in green belts.

(viii) Fringe settlements have obviously comparatively large growth of population due to their vicinity to city limits. The physical expansion of urban areas bears serious impact of these activities. Concept of standard urban area and urbanisable area and has been used in Urban Land Ceiling Act.

(ix) In some of the states like Maharashtra regional plans are being prepared for Metropolitan regions/District regions but the enforcement of the provisions of these plans is weak/loose. This is because civic bodies have no effective jurisdiction beyond the master plan of their area and in practice the village panchayat officers do not bother to see the statuary provisions of regional plans while permitting development in urban fringes with the result that large unauthorised haphazard development takes place in the first belt of the green zones for example at villages Dhakawadi, Kothrud, Warje, Wadgaon BK, Dhayari, Hingane, Manibaug etc. on the earlier boundaries of Pune civic limits now included in the extended Corporation limits. This shows the ineffectiveness of statuary regional plan in fringe area just outside civic limits.

(x) *Management Objectives for Fringe*: Promoting appropriate fringe area development after considering its potential and strategies evolved in the light of overall planning considerations, sound population projections and suitable and pragmatic planning norms.

(xi) *Organisation for Fringe:* It may be the existing civic body or a new development agency or a private cooperative agency, company as in Magarpatta. This will depend upon the prevailing local condition and the most suitable strategy option tested at time for example for Navi Mumbai and Pimpri Chinchawad New Town Development Agency like CIDCO & PCNTDA were appointed, while for Magarpatta scheme a private company was allowed to carry out development on the basis of a plan approved for this part of fringe area.

(xii) *Most Effective Land Assembly Policy under Prevailing Conditions in Many Big Cities:* The review of prevailing land assembly policies indicates that there is no strategy without limitations. Local conditions are the only guide. In view of growing resistance to compulsory acquisition of land it may be perhaps limited only to development land of EWS.

The Towns Planning Scheme methodology or land pooling and redistribution technique can be advantageously adopted as a substitute for wholesale land acquisition. In fact most of the earlier fringe areas or areas ripe for development in big cities of Maharashtra and Gujarat are developed by making town planning schemes. Pune and Ahmedabad have developed on the basis of large areas under Town Planning Schemes. The Town Planning Scheme process has been extensively used by Ahmedabad Urban Development Authority by suitably amending the cumbersome procedure under earlier Town Planning Act. Maharashtra needs to also use it for major extensions of cities and towns by making similar suitable amendments to the M.R. and T.P. Act.1966 to expedite the procedure for preparing Town Planning Schemes. It is necessary that there should be some kind of urban civic body for the fringe zone to take up planned development of the area, well integrated and dovetailed within the overall framework of the total plan of the larger region including the urban fringe. Urban fringe has to be recognised as an integral part of a bigger region for planning and management. The technique of Town Planning Scheme is most acceptable to owners as it is participatory.

References

ITPI Journal volume 127, 145, 147.

Planners Newsletter ITPI No. 35 of 1992.

Report of Government of India Committee on Urban Land Policy 1995.

8

The Concept of Urban Fringe and the Basis for Delineation

SANDEEP PARKHI

Land is the means of life without which man could have ever existed and on which his continued existence and progress depends. This scarce resource is subject to competing claims for various land uses and plays the most significant role in the process of urbanisation. The process of urbanisation involves the spatial expansion of cities due to the phenomenon of natural growth of human population, which is an inevitable process. The demand for land starts from the core of city and moves over a period of time towards the peripheral or fringe areas due to saturation. It is accentuated by functional disposition of land in these areas and is a manifestation of the ever-expanding urban sprawl.

The net effect of the socio-spatial processes has an impact upon the lifestyle of citizens influencing inter-relationships of journey to work, access to facilities etc., and is most tangibly revealed in patterns of land use. This change on the edges of cities is of great importance since a large area of land is involved and day-to-day life of more people is affected.

The physical changes that occur at periurban areas are associated with the transfer of land from rural to urban purposes. It could be considered a more fundamental alteration than many other land use changes, and is accompanied with a sharp increase in land value. The change at the urban periphery denotes different phenomena of urban growth, accordingly the growth of peripheral areas have achieved strategic locations in terms of residential use. Thus the phase-wise development of the fringe areas, depending upon the impact of urban centre, has become an integral part of the physical growth structure of cities. The urban fringe, which represents the first phase in the outward development of the town in terms of its nearness to the urban fabric and which experiences the impact of the urban centre, plays a key role in the urban growth phenomenon. In this process of urbanisation, the fringe is undergoing an accelerated transition from rural to urban land uses.

Fringe

"It is this countryside, the green belt or rather the greed belt, where the farmer sells land rather than crops, where the developer takes the public resource of the city's hinterland and subdivides to create a private profit and a public cost! Certainly here is the area where public powers are weakest – either absent or elastic – where the future costs of streets, sidewalks, sewers, schools, police and fire station are unspoken." Ian L. McHarg (*Design with Nature* 1971: 22).

The term fringe suggests a border, which lies at the periphery of urban areas. It is the annular belt – physically undefined, adjoining a city or a town – which is mostly a mix of urban and rural characteristics. It is, therefore, an area of transition between well-recognised urban land uses, i.e., the main city, and the area devoted to agriculture. Wissink (1962) identified fringe areas as suburbs, satellites of growth of the urban city centres (School of Architecture, 1992). Fringe area in its broadest sense is the transitional zone where the city expands in near future, which shares the rural and urban characteristics with a lower economic status than the urban centres (Kumar, 1998: 239).

Urban Fringe

The urban and rural settlements, however small or large, interact with each other ideally in a two way process. Space use in the urban fringe can be characterised as a continuously changing pattern where rapid residential expansion with low to average densities is observed. A supply of infrastructure and services that tries to keep pace with the inhabitants but is still unsatisfactory can also be seen[1]. The term *"urban fringe"* is used co-terminus to the periphery of towns and cities, where the process of sprawling has started or taken place. It refers to an annular belt adjoining a city, which is in the process of conversion to urban area (Kumar, 1998: 15).

Figure 1 *Schematic Representation of Fringe Definitions*

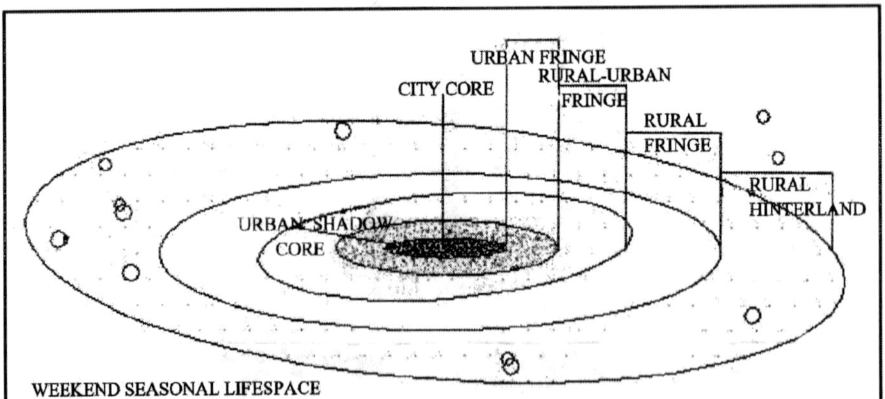

Pune – From *Kasba* to I.T. Development of Fringe

The origin of Pune City dates back to 2000 years. Pune is known as the queen of the Deccan, because of its old historical associations, its picturesque surroundings and because of its importance as a great cultural, social and political background in the whole of the Deccan plateau. Pune's history goes back to seventh century A.D. The earliest known remains are the Shiva caves at Shivajinagar area in the city core. The origins of dominant human settlements lay in a small village located in the southern part of the city, which is today's congested city core – Kasba Peth. The dominant phases of growth can be stated as follows:

1. TILL YEAR 1820: The Brahmin area south of river Mutha, Kasba, developed into a peth (coherent to ward) under the Peshwa rule. By this time, many other similar wards grew and the peths soon became specialised in certain specific economic activities.
2. DEVELOPMENT BETWEEN 1820 TO 1890: This was the phase when the settlements started expanding towards the south of the city and some development towards north along the west banks of river Mula. During the same period, Pune Cantonment and Khadki Cantonment were established. The construction of Khadakwasla dam in 1880 and Bombay – Pune railway line in 1856 were some of the development projects taken up by British.
3. DEVELOPMENT BETWEEN 1890 TO 1950: The city developed considerably equally in all directions with development along both the riverbanks as well as the newly established traffic corridors towards Mumbai, Satara, and Ahmednagar. The first major step towards an urban planning strategy was the implementation of town planning schemes during this phase of development in the city.
4. DEVELOPMENT BETWEEN 1950 TO 2001: The city has been undergoing a rapid phase of expansion, especially with the growth of periurban areas. The floods of the Panshet dam disaster of 1961 washed away many houses of the right bank of river Mutha, thus forcing many people to move away from the core of the city. Government organised housing was developed in the areas away from the low-lying city core. The inclusion of 36 villages to the Pune Municipal Corporation (PMC) limits was a major event in terms of physical expansion of the city. The development of Software Technology Park in the fringe area boosted development in the western part of the fringe. The main trunk roads like NH-4, NH-9 and others have become the major areas of dominant development of housing. The task of preparation of development plan for the same has been taken by PMC.

From its embryonic form covering a small area around the Kasba Peth, Pune like other towns, has grown in size by successive annexations of peripheral areas. In 1960 and 1962 small pockets and parts of villages Katraj Dhankawadi, Lohegaon, Dapodi, Sutarwadi etc. were added, increasing the area within PMC's ambit to 138.85 sq. km. Simultaneously, a significant number of small-scale industries developed outside the corporation limits. These units are the suppliers of components to the industrial giants in the nearby area. Also a notable construction activity took place in the fringe area during the last two decades because of pressure of urbanisation in the city and availability of houses at an affordable price. This development was very haphazard and thus to control this development and give better facilities to the dwellers corporation, the decision of including this fringe area under the jurisdiction of PMC was taken. Today the city is known as the educational and cultural capital of the state of

Maharashtra. It also serves as an important defence establishment, as the headquarters of the Southern Command, the largest in India, is situated here (Hemlata Dandekar et al., 1998). On account of the presence of the cyber city on the outskirts of the city, Pune is also emerging as a strong contender in this field just parallel to Hyderabad or any other IT development centre in India.

Urban Fringe: Operational Definition

Interpretations from legislations, different research works, and studies, help to define the urban fringe as:

1. The area that is left after excluding the area under urban land (urban land as per ULCR Act is land within the limits of land within municipal or relevant acting local body limits/any land situated within the limits of an urban agglomeration and referred to as such in the master plan, provided use of land does not include use for agriculture) from the total area within the region.
2. The peripheral zone adjacent to an urban centre, involved actively in the expansion of urban activities.
3. An area notified either by the State or Central Government as a part of the total urban agglomeration with a population more than one lakh.
4. A village or a group of villages forming a continuous spread lying within or outside the municipal limits of the urban centre but lying within the revenue limits.

Delineation of Urban Fringe

The integration of peripheral villages in the municipal limits over a regular interval of time with the increasing rate of urbanisation is not a new experience in Indian cities. However the basis of integration of villages remains a debatable issue till date followed with the political and other interventions. The delineation of urban fringe and the integration of the same can facilitate a scientific merger of peripheral villages in the Master Plan, avoiding too many controversies and interventions in the statutory process. On the basis of the analysis of the available information, previous studies and attempts of delineation, the following is an example for the delineation of urban fringe of Pune, so as to provide a technical basis for merger of villages in India.

Examples of Delineation and the Determinants Used

M.W. Rodehaver (1947) described fringe as the area of transition between urban land uses and the area devoted to agriculture. In his study of Madison fringe of Wisconsin state, he delineated the urban fringe on the basis of ecological, social, cultural and demographic aspects. The determinants used were:

1. The percentage of non-farming families to the total number families in an area under consideration.
2. Per square mile density on non-farming population.
3. Per acre assessed value of land and buildings.

Following Martin (1953) the delineation an urban fringe should be done on the basis of the characteristics of land use pattern and then further evaluated on the basis of points to be given to each area within the study area. Golledge (1960), noted six characteristics to demarcate an urban fringe, namely

1. Intensive cultivation by mobile population with sparse to moderate density,
2. Pattern of land use,
3. Smallness of the farm – bigger farmlands shall lie outside the urban fringe boundary.
4. Rapid residential extension,
5. Lack of various basic services,
6. Abundant provision for speculative buildings.

Hind-Smith (1962) delimited the urban fringe on the basis of four indices,

1. Land subdivided but yet not developed or recorded by planning board,
2. Farm lands for sale for urban purposes as indicated by developers,
3. Land in non-farm ownerships, either idle or tenant farmed,
4. Farmland assessed at higher than normal farmlands as shown by local assessors (Thakur, 1991: 7–15).

U. Singh (1966: 41–48), defined the urban fringe of Kaval in Uttar Pradesh using the following factors:

1. Change in land use pattern as regards the city core,
2. Change in built form as regards the city core,
3. Occupational structure,
4. Housing typology,
5. Distribution of industrial and non farming activities,
6. Limiting basic services,
7. Distribution of educational activities,

Types and patterns of streets.

From the Census of India, 1961, urban fringe can be delineated as a part of urban agglomeration, which includes a continuous urban spread and normally consists of its adjoining urban outgrowths, which is co-terminus to the urban fringe.

As per the Urban Land Ceiling and Regulation Act 1976, the urban fringe is a peripheral area notified either by State or Central Government and is as part of urban agglomeration with a population of more than one lakh and stipulated as five kilometre around the city.

The International Urban Research Unit and the United States Bureau of Census have suggested that the projection of non-agricultural workers should be considered as the sole criterion for the delimitation of the urban fringe (Thakur, 1991: 23).

Delineation of the Urban Fringe of Pune

The following determinants stipulated to delineate the urban fringe of Pune are based broadly with due consideration to demographic aspects, the residential land use and the density, the occupational structure and the likely chances of speculation in land prices. The villages, which satisfy the following determinants, are hereby considered as a part of the urban fringe thereby delineating the urban fringe of Pune as mentioned in the Table 1.

Table 1 *Determinants to Delineate the Urban Fringe of Pune*

Determinants / *Village name*	*1*	*2*	*3*	*4*	*Villages forming the urban fringe*
Sector C		✓			
Balewadi		✓			
Baner		✓	✓	✓	1
Sus		✓			
Mhalunge		✓			
Sector D					
Bavdhan Bk		✓	✓	✓	2
Bavdhan Kd	✓	✓			
Kothrud	✓	✓	✓	✓	3
Warje	✓	✓	✓	✓	4
Shivane	✓	✓	✓		5
Kondhwa Dhawade					
Kopre		✓			
Sector E					
Hingne Kd	✓	✓	✓		6
Wadgaon Kd		✓			
Wadgaon Bk	✓	✓	✓		7
Nanded		✓			
Narhe		✓			
Dhayari		✓	✓		
Kirkatwadi		✓			
Khadakwasla		✓	✓		
Sector F					
Dhankawadi	✓	✓	✓		8
Katraj	✓	✓	✓	✓	9
Ambegaon Bk	✓	✓	✓		10
Ambegaon Kd					
Kondhwa Kd	✓	✓	✓		11
Kondhwa Bk	✓	✓	✓		12
Sector G					
Undri					
Pisoli					
Mohamadwadi		✓	✓		
Hadapsar	✓	✓	✓		13
Manjri Bk		✓	✓		
Mundhwa	✓	✓	✓		14
Sector H					
Wadgaon Sheri	✓	✓	✓		15
Kharadi	✓	✓	✓		16
Lohagaon		✓	✓		
Dhanori		✓	✓		
Kalas		✓	✓		

Determinant 1: Percentage of workforce engaged in non-agricultural activities – Villages, which exhibit a value above 20 per cent as per 1991 Census are categorised for selection of urban fringe.

Determinant 2: In the cases where the population density is observed to be above 400 persons/sq. km. in the year 1996 is considered for the delineation of urban fringe.

Determinant 3: Villages displaying a value above 5,000 persons as per Census 1996 are categorised in the delineation of urban fringe.

Determinant 4: The land price is an important determinant in the delineation of urban fringe as it is the immediate repercussion of the demand for land. The villages, which satisfy a value above Rupees 200 per sq. ft. in year 2000 are selected for the categorisation under the urban fringe (please refer annexure). The application of these determinants for the delineation of urban fringe of Pune is expressed as follows:

From the above representation, it can be seen that, out of the 36 villages that have recently been integrated, 16 villages score 3 or more to be a part of the urban fringe of Pune. These delineated areas (villages) forming the urban fringe can be considered as an example of the strong basis for the integration in the municipal limits.

Recommendations

The following is a set of brief recommendations, described with the purpose of providing a guideline to understand the importance of the urban fringe and its delineation in the process of statutory planning for Indian cities.

- The identification and delineation of urban fringe should be taken up as one of the primary activities in the process of formulation of Development Plan.
- The basis of delineation should have a technical basis, and the other interventions that can hamper and delay the process such as political interests; real estate sector should be adequately taken care of, during the process.
- The delimited urban fringe should be considered for the integration in the new municipal limits as a part of urban area.
- The development plan for newly added villages should not be prepared in isolation, but comprehensively formulated with the Development Plan for the old as well as new limits.
- The publication and implementation of Development Plan in the scheduled time frame should be made more stringent and its violation should be adequately taken care of in the State Government Notification for preparation of Development Plan.
- A statutory authority for the administration of the fringe should be set up under the municipal corporation to monitor unauthorised development and violation of D.P. provisions in the fringe areas.

The development of urban fringe has become an integral component of physical structure of cities, which is a result of the inevitable spatial expansion. The need for an orderly and planned administration of the areas in expanded limits that form the fringe areas especially the urban fringe is increasing with the increasing urban sprawl. In the conventional Indian city administration systems, the surroundings villages around urban centres are integrated in the administrative limits during Development Plan revisions. However, the underlying dilemma in this schism is the number and the basis for integrating villages in the municipal limits. It is crucial to understand that adopting a scientific basis for identification and integration of villages in the new administrative limits has to be practised as a regular system.

This article describes different concepts of urban fringe and gives an example of delineation of urban fringe, which can be considered as the basis for the integration of villages in the municipal limits in case of Pune city. The haphazard growth is an immediate repercussion of the unregulated development in the periphery of cities.

Note

1. http://impulskulak.ac.be/south_africa/Mod4_fringe/tables/box16.htm

References

Dandekar, Hemalata and Shishikant Sawant (1998): Housing Needs in New Suburbs of Indian Metropolis, Case Study of Kothrud Pune, *Economic and Political Weekly*, Nov.14.

Golledge R. (1960): Sydney's Metropolitan Fringe: A Study in Urban-Rural Relations, *Australian Geographer*, 7:243.

http://impuls.kulak.ac.be/south_africa/Mod4_fringe/tables/box16.htm

Kumar, Bimal (ed.) (1998): *Urbanisation and Land Use: Conflict at the Urban Fringes*, A.P.H. Publishing Corp., New Delhi, p. 15 and p. 239.

Martin, W.T. (1953): Rural Urban Fringes, *Am. Sociological Rev.*, 18: 248.

McHarg, Ian L. (1971): *Design With Nature*, Natural History Press, New York, p. 22.

Rodehaver, M.W. (1947): *Rural Soc.*, Vol. 12.

School of Planning and Architecture (1992), Background Material for Workshop on *"Planning Issues in Metropolitan Fringe Areas"*, New Delhi, Jan., p. 103.

Singh, U. (1968) Urban Fringes in Kaval Town, *Applied Geography*, NGSI, Varanasi, pp. 41– 48.

Thakur, Binda (1991): *Land Utilization and Urbanization: The Rural Urban Fringe*, Deep and Deep Publications, New Delhi, pp. 7–15, p. 23.

Wissink. G.A. (1962): *American Cities in Perspective, with Reference to the Development of their Fringe Areas*, Van Gorcum, Assen.

Annexure
Land Prices in the 36 Villages in the Fringe Area

Village	*Land Value Rs/sq. ft.*	*Village*	*Land Value Rs/sq. ft.*
Balewadi	150	Katraj	300
Baner	300	Ambegaon Bk.	170
Sus	80	Ambegaon Kd.	100
Mahalunge	100	Kondhwa Kd.	120
Average-Sector C	**157.50**	Kondhwa Bk	190
Bavdhan Bk.	280	**Average-Sector F**	**195.00**
Bavdhan Kd.	100	Undri	30
Kothrud	450	Pisoli	100
Warje	375	Mohamadwadi	75
Shivane	170	Hadapsar	180
Kondhwa Dhav.	150	Manjri Bk.	100
Kopare	100	Mundhwa	65
Average-Sector D	**232.14**	**Average-Sector G**	**91.70**
Higne Kd.	180	Wadgaon Sheri	195
Wadgaon Kd.	150	Kharadi	150
Wadgaon Bk.	210	Lohagaon	175
Nanded	50	Dhanori	80
Narhe	45	Kalas	50
Dhayari	180	**Average-Sector H**	**130**
Kirkatwadi	65		
Khadakwasla	120		
Average-Sector E	**125.00**		

Annexure Source: Real Properties, July 2001, vol. 52, p. 45

HYPERLINK "http://www.punebestproperties.com" , http://www.realpropertiesmag.com

9

Conundrums, Visions and Devices of Urban Form

CHRISTOPHER CHARLES BENNINGER

Urban form and pattern has been the subject of urbanism since the ancient *shastras* provided guidelines for laying out a city. Images of what a city should be have ranged from the practical to the romantic! The vision of an ideal Arcadia is a thread running through history, back to the Greek gymnasia in periurban, rustic gardens, away from the polluted thinking and degraded form, of inner cities. The idea of "the garden" as an escape from worldly chaos can be seen in imperial Roman estates, Moghul Gardens, and in the vast gardens which hinted at an urban design schema in the palatial royal estates at Versailles, Karlsruhe and elsewhere (Moore, 1997). The urban fringe has been the subject of both ridicule and nostalgia in painting, literature and urban theory (Museum of Modern Art, 1999).

In the Nineteenth Century the Garden Cities Movement attempted to draw "the gardens" into the city and to modulate a neat transition to the rural countryside. Urban planning theory was actually a theory of "escape:" Escape from the city and the realities of contemporary urban life (Howard, 1903). Frank Lloyd Wright tried to "even grain" the transition of urban fabric almost to nil, reflecting the industrialised people's fascination with the countryside as a vehicle to escape reality! Broadacre City, as Wright fancied his dream, was an automobile dependent, spread out fabric of orchard plots, peopled by households very much like the multi-millionaires who were his clients (Wright, 1946). Ayn Rand hallmarked this individualistic philosophy, in her now classic demand, "Never say we, always say I" (Rand, 1940).

Le Corbusier's Radiant City levitates the city on stilts above an undisturbed rural landscape that flows under the detached urban form (Le Corbusier, 1931). Thus, the European abstraction of nature is an antagonistic one. It sees humans and nature in opposition, to be separated. The American construct integrates man and nature (McHarg, 1970). At a more mundane level, "Green Belts" create a counter intuitive no-man's land, where a jumble of illegal and unrecognised development occurs. Ironically these jungles of neglect are referred to as the "breathing lungs" of the city, trying to imagine an anthropolis with its lungs hanging somewhere off on the side! Thus, in theory, law and practice, the fringe of the city is an ambivilous realm of the poetic ideal, and the reckless concrete jungle.

The modern movement, like the Modern Era, saw a marriage between a program of social objectives, technological applications and art (Frampton, 1988)! Early Twentieth Century urbanism from Ebenezer Howard to the CIAM (International Congress of Modern Architecture), was a statement about the social structure and the social organisation of the city, equally as it was about efficiency and city form (Charter of Athens, 1933, published by CIAM 1943). There were considerations for social justice and for creating social opportunities (Giedion, 1962). The planning principles of the CIAM were largely misused in post-war Europe to create numbing, bland milieus of boring landscapes of gridded streets and International Style "look-a-like" structures. In the rush to rebuild cities, poetry and the lyrical were neglected (Jacobs, 1968). As cities expanded, axioms were applied as formulae (Mumford, 1948). Team Ten, the children of the Modernists and the fathers of the Post Modernists, searched for abiding themes that make cities work for people. The public domains, and the movement STEMs, were amongst their central concerns (Tzonis and Lefaivre, 1994). Those who followed them seem to have thrown the baby out with the bath water, favouring urban designs devoid of public domains, cut off from open-ended stems, shut in with "gates" and entrance filters, lacking in any social theory of mobility, accommodation, or opportunity systems! Young urbanists were foolishly advised to go to American suburbia and to learn from its artefacts, as if it were the Florence of the Twentieth Century (Venturi and Brown, 1974). Post Modernism ushered in the era of the big, personal, egocentric statement ... as if everything were a Bilbao Museum or the Sydney Opera House! *"Never say we, always say I."*

Out of the void of Post Modernism, which has been too individualistic and idiosyncratic to focus on something as complicated as "the city," came the New Urbanists (Duany, et al., 1996). The New Urbanism is neither "new," nor in any sense "urban." Like the New Economy which follows Ayn Rand's motto, the New Urbanism is a mechanism for personal "opportunity," created to appear as a vehicle for the public good. These isolated, inaccessible, resort-like elite communities have their roots in Seaside, Florida and in The Walt Disney Corporation's Celebration adjacent to Disney World in Orlando. Both concoctions reflect the malaise of the late Twentieth Century (Kundera, 1992). A kind of virtual reality replaces the actual. Disney "do-overs" make the New Urbanism projects into antique villages. The concept is to create stage sets (usually modelled from the mythical 'small American town') of make believe streets and structures, much like Disney Lands and Worlds! The strategy is attracting buyers into the resale market. Instead of "communities" these are investment opportunities (Benninger, 2001). They are created as places to "park money" and not to live in! These so called urban communities have no jobs, no low-income housing, no workshops nor any other aspect of a diverse urban fabric. They are inhabited by white, Anglo-Saxon elite, who rather than embrace urbanism want to escape it! Moreover, these are gated communities with security guards at the controlled entrances! The past two decades have witnessed the demise of the "public domain," with the rise of privately guarded, controlled and accessed spaces! Shopping centres like Crossroads in Mumbai require a credit card as a 'visa' for entrance! Economic profiling is taking over the apartheid of race profiling.

Urban planning, land regulation and development reflect the most civilised ambitions of any society. Therefore they also mirror the ugly realities of societies! Urban sprawl and "strip development," plague India and the USA alike. The automobile takes command! Loans for cars are cheaper than loans for houses in most countries, and easier to get! Roads are subsidised, and petrol bills, insurance and car payments are all tax deductible! The government is paying a small minority to congest the roads and pollute the air of everyone! Public policy nurtures spread and sprawl. At least in India prohibitive taxes stave off petrol consumption and automobile purchases! Yet, consumer loans and tax breaks attempt to make up the difference! The automobile has had a greater impact on urban form than any other technical or policy intervention. Our policies on the automobile are our policies on the city pattern!

To a great extent urban form is a play-off between greed and regulation. In the New Economy where one is never to say "we" and always say "I," the plan is one to satiate desire, and not to resolve social stresses and find solutions to problems. Those who stand to benefit from a particular urban shape or form, usually take on the "burden" of responsibility to shape that form. Opportunities lie out on the fringe, where land is bought cheap, developed and sold expensive! The urban fringe is the Babylon of this new economic frontier.

A small university town, Gainesville Florida, with a population of 125,000, has an urban area slightly larger than the city of Paris! Why? The elected city and county commissioners are all land traders and developers, who personally benefit from the city services and amenities, which will spread over vast tracts of urbanising land.

All of the above has made city management relatively impossible, with land prices spreading horizontally out from the urban core, over an ever-urbanising space (Knos, 1958). Artificially low FARs (Floor area ratio) help "push" development out, by making habitable land more rare and costly! Land use planning stimulates a system of "bids and prices," which direct users to compete for land in different zones (Alonzo, 1964). Low FARs make the cost of laying storm and sewage drains more costly, extending fire fighting, water supply, telephone and optic fibres more costly, and they make the maintenance of law and order improbable. Fleeing high prices, residential development leapfrogs from one pocket of development over the next, forcing urban systems to stretch far beyond their capacities. Low FARs, vehicle subsidies and land use planning contribute to this sprawl and spread, where densities are too low to support efficient public transport, walkable compact communities, or even basic public health infrastructure (Sabhiki, 2002).

Instead of master plans and development plans, we must start with a public Charter of Intelligent Urbanism (Benninger, 2001). This would lay out a kind of "covenant" of principles, or themes, around which the fixed components of the city structure can be decided upon. A Structure Plan includes the "non-negotiable" parts and components of the city. These parts range from "urban corridors" along which future movement of people, goods, water, and waste will move. It includes the establishment of high-density nodes and hubs that gather enough people to support express transport halts, amenities and services all at a walkable distance from compact neighbourhoods. The Structure Plan includes a very basic set of regulations on uses that are compatible to each other, and on the shapes, safety and hygiene of the urban fabric nurtured.

The Structure Plan is basically the physical arrangement and interpretation of Intelligent Urbanism principles, impaled as physical themes over a spatial arrangement moulded by the geo-climatic context. Local area plans, such as Town Planning Schemes, and private layouts, are kind of mini-master plans that plug into the Structure Plan, though a participatory and transparent process of incremental and disjointed planning. This 'process of planning' makes cities into channels for people to realise their dreams. Without such a process of policy, planning and participation, development is bound to be motivated and dominated by vested interests. It is bound to lack environmental protections, social facilitation, or the promotion of efficient infrastructure. The plans that we are producing and the cities we are creating are barriers to the nations' and to the peoples' development. These are not artefacts for the public interest, or in the interest of the public. Only a hand full of land traders will benefit.

Selected Readings

Alonso, William (1964): *Location and Land Use,* Harvard Univ. Press, Cambridge, Mass.

Benninger, Christopher C. (2001): Charter of Intelligent Urbanism, *Ekistics,* Volume 69, No. 412: 39–65, Athens.

Corbusier, Le (1933): *The Radiant City,* Orion Press, NYC.

Duany, Andres and Elizabeth Plater-Zyberk (1991): *Towns and Townmaking Principles,* Rizzoli.

Duany, Andres, Elizabeth Plater-Zyberk and Jeff Speck (2000): *Suburban Nation: The Rise of Sprawl and the Decline of the American Dream,* North Point Press, New York.

Frampton, Kenneth (2006): *The Evolution of 20th-Century Architecture: A Synoptic Account.* Springer, New York.

Frampton, Kenneth (2007, 4th ed.): *Modern Architecture: A Critical History (World of Art),* Thames & Hudson, London .

Giedion, Sigfried (1962, 4th ed.): *Space, Time, and Architecture.* The American Association of Architectural Bibliographers .

Howard, Ebenezer (1902): *Garden Cities of To-morrow* (in Letchworth, the first English garden city was founded in 1903).

Jacobs, Jane (1961): *The Death and Life of Great American Cities,* Random House, New York.

Jacobs, Jane (1969): *The Economy of Cities,* Random House, New York.

Kundera, Milan (1988): *The Art of the Novel,* Faber and Faber, London.

McHarg, Ian L. (1969): *Design with Nature,* New York, Natural History Press (Second edition 1992).

Moore, Charles (1988): *The Poetics of Gardens,* MIT Press, Cambridge, MA.

Mumford, Lewis et al. (1948): *What is Happening to Modern Architecture?* Museum of Modern Art, New York.

Mumford, Lewis (1961): *The City in History: Its Origins, Its Transformations, and Its Prospects*, Harcourt, Brace & World, New York.

Rand, Ayn, (1940, 1953 revised edition): *The Fountainhead,* Caxton Press, Christchurch.

Rand, Ayn (1957): *Atlas Shrugged,* Random House, London.

Sabhiki, Ranjit (1996): The Collapse of Planning, published in *Form, Modernism and History*, GSD, Harvard University.

Tzonis, Alex and Liane Lefaivre (1994): Lines of Vision Lines of Fire. The Role of Analogy and Image Cognition in Designing the Renaissance Bastion, *Das Bauwerk/The Building and the Town.*

Tzonis, Alexander, Lefaivre, Leone (1995): *Architecture in North America since 1960,* Thames and Hudson, London.

Venturi, Robert and Denise Scott Brown (1972): *Learning from Las Vegas*, MIT Press, Cambridge MA.

Wright, Frank Lloyd (1958): *The Living City*. Horizon Press, New York.

10

Engaging the Peripheries

In Search of India's Future Cities

RAJEEV KATHPALIA

This paper is in two parts. The first part is a brief overview of urbanisation in the Indian context and its impact on the urban fringe. The paper believes that cities have not grown more formless than they were during the last forty, hundred or thousand years. The formation of mega-cities and mega-regions does not necessarily mean an increase in entropy, but can lead to an ever-greater informedness and organisation. That cities are growing increasingly complex, increasingly rich in internal and external linkages, increasingly comprehensive and concentrated, increasingly transparent yet incomprehensible. The second part examines the problem in the context of this multivalent, multi-layered "rich" city and the challenges posed to planners and architects within this framework. The engagement with the complexity and contradictions inherent in this approach are illustrated by actual examples of planning and architectural work being done by the author in the fringe.

Urbanisation

Cities everywhere are makers of wealth, magnets for the industrious, motors of invention. In developing countries, more than half of the GDP originates in cities. Urbanisation is a companion and stimulus of development. As the process has accelerated, however, cities in Asia, Africa, the Near East, and Latin America have all collided with the challenges of congestion and pollution, and with concentrated poverty and uncontrolled sprawl, with problems that at the least impede productive growth and, at worst, stifle it.

It is significant to note that in 1960, less than 22 per cent of the developing world's population was urban, and the proportion averaged 34 per cent by 1990. Thirty years on, it is expected to exceed 50 per cent, and the total number of residents in such cities by 2020 is due to reach four billion, more than twice today's total. Cities in the developing world are thus expanding at a rate of 62 million inhabitants annually, which is equivalent to adding a country the size of France or Egypt every year. It is projected that India would cross the Rubicon of being 50 per cent urban sometime before the year 2020. Half a billion people would populate our cities.

While these cities continue to be the generators of employment and income leading to rapid growth in population, the supply of serviced land and housing has been very slow.

Peripheries

Till very recently the Urban Land Ceiling and Regulation Act (ULCRA), planning proposals for reservations, limited provision of land for urban use, their provision at inappropriate places, and rising land values have all led to spilling over of growth beyond Urban Development Authority limits. Low land prices in the peripheral urban lands, their proximity to developed areas, and easy accessibility through private transport have added pace to this development.

In this context it may be worthwhile considering that in the state of Gujarat six corporation cities accommodate 50 per cent of its urban population. A rapid appraisal of peripheral urban development around the city of Ahmedabad on its western side shows that a population of barely 20,481 persons in 1991 is expected to reach 6,41,000 persons by 2011 in an area covering 59 sq. km. Thus one of the most significant issues confronting all our burgeoning cities today is of peripheral urban development.

At the peripheries of our cities, builders and developers buy cheap agricultural land outside of the cities' urban administrative controls. This extremely cheap un-serviced land is converted to non-agricultural use, plotted and sold to the growing population desperate to have a home of their own. Often the only value addition they do is to build a type design for either a small house or flat on this land. No value addition in terms of physical or social infrastructure is made by the builder.

Eventually the city catches up with this periphery and then the city authority has one more development to service by an already over stretched infrastructure network. Not only does it lack resources to do this but the social infrastructure of educational, health, recreational facilities that go with this growing population is missing. In the absence of an overall plan to guide the development, it takes place in a random and haphazard manner. Large scale violations of building regulations take place due to lack of monitoring. This leads to a growing series of slums on the edge of our cities, giving rise to disease and the inherent degradation that goes with it. Finally giving rise to potential health, social and environmental time bombs waiting to explode.

The popular perception common to all our cities is that they grow indiscriminately by a variety of ills, whose numbers and variety on the one hand, and proportion of extreme cases of incurable diseases, on the other, increase steeply with city size.

Among the ills, those most frequently causing concern include: pollution of all kinds, loss of contact with nature, traffic congestion, alienation (social and psychological), complexity of city life and related difficulties of orientation and choice, inaccessibility (or accessibility only after unbearably long delays) of essential city functions, increase in crime and terrorism and the resulting insecurity, loss of balance between action and dreams, ideals, values and many others, that may differ from city to city.

The Problem: The City Doomed

For over forty years now architects and urbanists have been saying that the city is disintegrating and vanishing owing to new modes of transport and communication. The four urban functions of working, living, leisure and transport which Le Corbusier once so elegantly deployed in his model of the city, can no longer be separated from one another either spatially or socially. Living and transport have become practically identical (viz. Paul Virilio's account of the rail commuter who meets his friends and acquaintances in the train and merely passes the night in his dormitory-city home). What was once a place, the city, has now ceased to be a clearly localizable spatial unit and has transformed into what might be termed an 'urban field', a collection of activities instead of a material structure. The contemporary urban experience is splendidly symbolised by the mobile phone: wherever your mobile works is the city, and anywhere else is the countryside.

Grumbling about the disintegration of the city always contains an implicit reference to what the city used to be. There are two idealised archetypes, which have some currency. The first is the medieval variant, the city as a tangle of narrow streets and little neighbourhoods, *pols, mohallas,* surrounded by specialised bazaars and streets, grouped around a temple square or mosque and often supported by the palace or citadel – business, religion and politics – entirely surrounded on the outside by a wall marking the boundary between town and country. The other archetype is that of the late nineteenth century, colonial city with its cantonment, civil lines and railway station. The semi-industrialised boulevard-and-parks city, in which the former impenetrability and rigidity of the urban mass has been broken open, and the boundaries between inside and outside, and between politics and business have not so much been erased as blurred. The medieval city is associated with a pre-architectural era: no architect or town planner was ever involved in shaping it (exceptions like Jaipur are rare). The nineteenth century city belongs to the heyday of planning and targeted architecture – the former being military in character, the latter scenographic. The street pattern of the medieval city follows the logic of the labyrinth, and that of the nineteenth century city the logic of the grid. And so on. Once the ideal has been invoked, it becomes possible to portray the decline in vivid colours; to depict how the urban fabric has been torn and fragmented by the introduction of railways, cars, air transport, TV, computers, the Internet; how the antithesis between the market square and the town perimeter has been replaced by one between the city centre and the suburbs; and how nondescript satellite towns then arose, all looking the same but all pretending to be different, while the original centralised city has turned either into an authentic ghetto or a simulated open-air museum.

The "Rich" City

The best model of the world is the world itself. Reducing the world to a few images, slogans, formulas or lines of development does not make it easier to understand. 'The city' never existed in history; there were only 'cities'. A city is not a machine for the production of goods, people and urban experiences; the only kind of change a machine is party to is wearing out or breaking down, after which we replace the faulty parts or consign the whole thing to the scrap heap. That's not how it happens with cities. A city is an unstable system, a living system, which is in a state of dynamic flux, which continually reorganises and rearranges itself, which expands and shrinks. One of the actors or 'agencies' in this process of self-organisation is the urban population, including the city's architects, urbanists and local government officials. Other 'agencies' include technical developments, the mass media and migrations. People do not change because they wish to do so, but because they allow themselves to be changed and, in doing so, themselves modify the broader process of transformation in which they are being swept along.

Cities have always been places for strangers to visit and live; their presence made it possible for the inhabitants to define themselves. The word 'culture' denoted a collection of images, customs, assumptions and peculiarities that were the concrete expression of the inhabitants. A city, a region or a country could be recognised by its building style, costume, festivals and mentality. To paraphrase Johan Huizinga, the culture is where the local population 'enacts' its identity. My city has residents from most of the other states of India and of many different nationalities; some of them concentrated in particular neighbourhoods but mostly dispersed around the urban area. The name of my city is irrelevant, for much the same applies to cities all around the world. All those sub-groups and nationalities, are not always distinguishable to outsiders, 'enact' their own culture. Sometimes they do so in order to distinguish themselves from one another, but often it is to reinforce connections or indeed similarities. They each have their own festivals, religious occasions, video shops, eating places, community representatives, music, TV channels, street habits, child-raising methods and preferred foods; and these continually cross and intersect with the cultural networks other communities have woven within the city web. Nobody has a single culture any longer, but all participate in a multiplicity of 'cultures'. What was once a homogeneous, low-information monoculture has now become a high-information, heterogeneous cultural process; the continual transformation process of temporary coalitions, collisions, hybridisations and migrations that we call 'city life'.

The rule for participation in a culture is that you have to change so as to adapt yourself to existing cultural forms, over and over again; and you have to change the given cultural forms so that you fit in, over and over again. We are no longer present in a single place but we are continually co-present in many different places – not as soon as we step outside the house and enter the city context, but for example as soon as we turn on the computer or the TV. The low-information home has similarly turned into a high-information node in a network of data and commodity flows. Within a radius of 100 metres around my house, you not only will find a Panjabi, Udipi, Saurashtrian, Chinese and Continental restaurant, but also a "*shakh bhajiwalla*" where in June you can buy lichees from Muzzafarpur, strawberries from the foothills of the Himalayas, and mangoes from Ratnagiri et cetera. The homes of the poor of Nepal, Bangladesh, Bihar, Eastern UP, Bengal and Orissa have moreover become just as information-rich as their counterparts in Gujarat, and their occupants' imagination is equally stimulated to visit this city as ours is to go to their part of the country, migration in one case, and business and tourism in the other.

As Arjun Appadurai has observed, the power of imagination, charged as it is by the mass media, has become one of the major social and political factors of our times. On the one hand, the media stimulate people to move somewhere else, in search of a better life. On the other hand, those same media make it possible for migrants, having settled elsewhere for the while, to maintain contact with their home base – although within one generation the land of origin itself has become a place of the imagination. A city is not really just a network of intersecting information and commodity flows – that would be too meagre a representation. The city is still localised as a place or a region, but 'locality' now means the feeling of being somewhere, of having a place in a context where your life has some relevance. A city produces a series of 'localities'. It no longer is a single public domain but is a concatenation of a series of diaspora-related public domains in which numerous 'cultures' or 'contexts' are settled but linked via the media to similar cultures and contexts elsewhere. 'India' is located not only in India but in the Gulf States, in London, in the Caribbean and in my street. 'America' is to be found all over the world, although less and less often in the United States. A 'culture' is a translocal, unstable system that blossoms forth, now here and now there, produces localities, goes into decline, metamorphoses, subsides once more and recovers. Instead of 'cultures', it might be better to speak of 'cultural systems'.

The Challenge

The design challenge for planning and architecture in this context is, instead of trying to create a single public domain, to create an atmosphere for the establishment and coexistence of a diversity of public domains. Transcontextualize. You cannot design a city, but you can help a city organise itself as a living structure – not by breaking down all barriers to the streams of information and commodities, but by allowing specific obstacles, channels, retardations and accelerations to be designed for individual streams, and thus to be informed by the city itself.

Thus the questions that arise are: Can India's future cities give choices to all their citizens at all levels, economic and social, to attain their needs? Can this happen across the historic city, the colonial city, postcolonial city and the newly emerging peripheries?

11

The Problems of Urban Fringe

KIRAN KALAMDANI AND ANJALI KALAMDANI

The paper starts with some of the key statements by the early urban thinkers and observers of the urban development in the 20th century. It tries to assess the directions taken by planning in the Indian context, its shortcomings, and some of the problems as seen by the authors that relate to the urban fringe. It is felt that the urban fringe cannot be separated as a distinct element and the solutions offered at various levels are often applicable to other parts of the Indian city. The authors' experience is largely conditioned through living and working as an Architect, Urban Designer and Conservationist in the cities of Pune and Pimpri-Chinchwad.

Introduction

Patrick Geddes in India:

> *"Town planning is not mere place making, nor even work planning. If it is to be successful it must be folk planning ... to find the right places for each sort of people, places where they will really flourish. To give people in fact, the care that we give when transplanting flowers, instead of harsh evictions and arbitrary instructions to 'move on' delivered in the manner of officious amateur policemen."*

This early piece of advice given by one of the forefathers of Town Planning has been consistently ignored in the Indian scenario, which has been seen as the domain of primarily the Politician or Bureaucrat, followed by the Statistician, Physical Planner and sometimes, the Economist. Aspects relating to people and human concerns have been conspicuous by their absence, so also attention to details and planning as an iterative process (read Urban Design) has seldom been the Agenda for thought and action on cities.

In the word of Richard Sennet, in *The Uses of Disorder* ... "*Town planning has too often been driven by the motor of capitalist profit and fuelled by the desire to police whole communities ... to create a city of order and surveillance rather than one of pleasure and opportunity.*" He argues for a city, which offers excitement and risk rather than conformity.

Figure 1 *Pune Metropolitan Area*

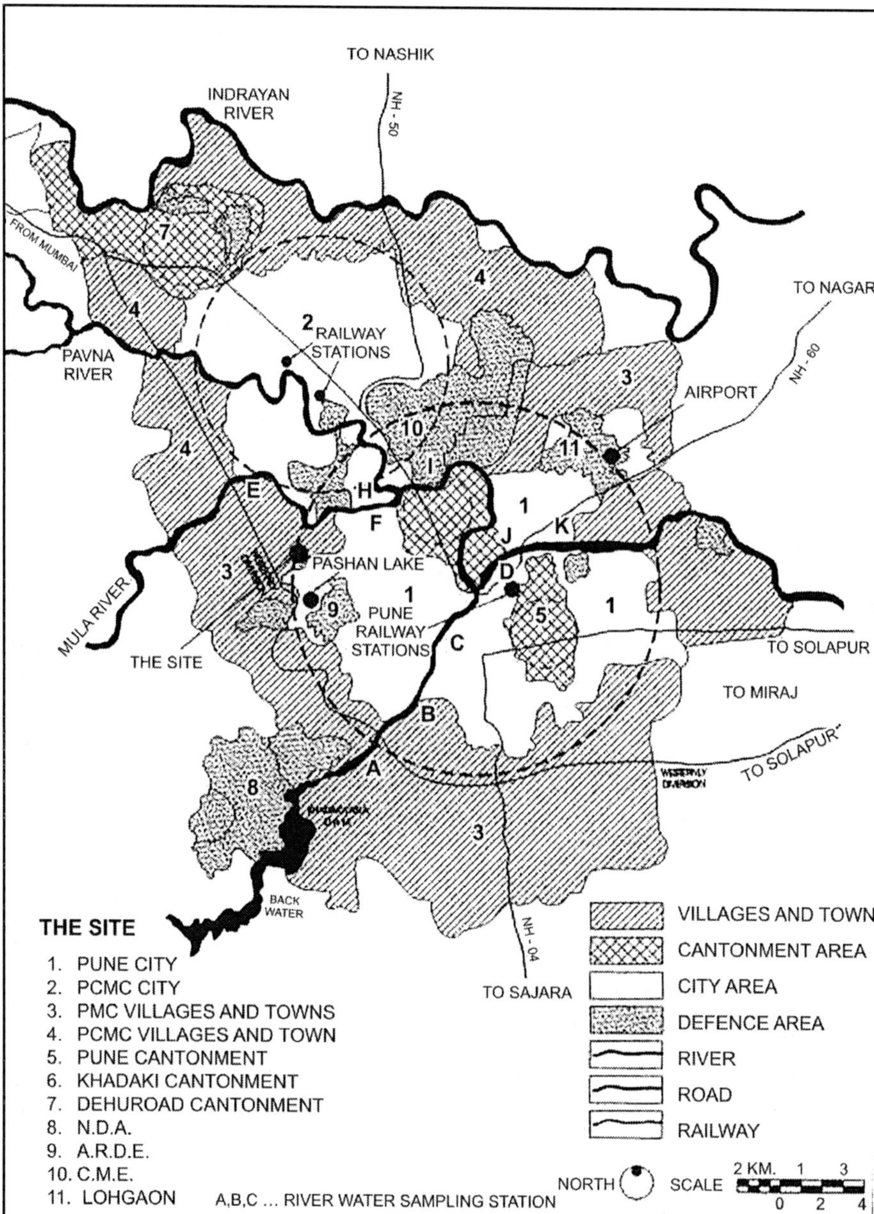

As we move towards the suburb and fringe of the city, which is characterised by a low-key urban experience, we are reminded of the words of Rudyard Kipling (1896) "... *Half your trouble is the curse of America ... sheer, hopeless, well-ordered boredom; and this is going someday to be the curse of the world.*" Kipling put his finger, at the early date, upon the weakness of the suburban way of life.

Meaning and scope of the fringe may be seen as follows:

1. Distance between buildings is more than 200 m.
2. The degree of enclosures of streets and open public spaces falls below 1:4.
3. It is characterised by large open spaces of agricultural or other urban uses.
4. It functionally interacts intensely with the core city as well as the rural hinterland.
5. Fringe could vary from 1 km. to 10 km.

In the Indian context, some of the problems of the fringe are enlisted below:

1. Highlands, farmlands, factories are located, which pre-exist and have to be contended with.
2. Security problems – the fringe is easily accessible to dacoits and in degrading employment situation, disparities prompt such actions.
3. Large land pools by private developers create islands of affluence – clubs, affluent societies, farmhouse plots, institutions, hospitals etc.
4. Small farmhouse plot holders find it impossible to grow fruits and vegetables and easier to sell land to private developer. Long and narrow farmlands having rich alluvial soils are sold to the private builders who built virtual wall-like buildings, one flat deep, which generate a peculiar and ungainly urban element.
5. There is little or no concern to enlist heritage sites of cultural or natural interest, ensure its conservation regardless of ownership and use this factor as a positive resource in improving the quality of life.
6. There is no recognition of the human and local geography. Fertile lands suited for agriculture are used up for buildings and subhuman, water-logged and low-lying areas are given residential uses.

Some Solutions

1. Be proactive – generate lots of ideas! Planners employed by the establishment and freelancers have been fighting shy of putting force visionary ideas and standing by them.
2. If only 5 to 10 per cent of a plan gets implemented, envision and think of a 1,000 per cent better plan – but backed with the power and resources to implement it. Typically, the 600+ master plans generated for Indian cities have shown a pathetically low rate of implementation, since plans were not related to available resources. Yet we have adopted a westernised system of planning without having the resources to implement it. A state in India has the resources equivalent to a county in England, which explains the reason for not being able to police and implement similar plan.
3. Poverty is of the mind – planning is reduced to physical and scenarios. See the city and regions as flows of people, money, goods and power resources. The Indian urban scenario and the dynamics of it is an unprecedented phenomenon in world history. The speed and accuracy at which planning needs to move always fall short of the necessary.
4. Often change is about perception (formed out of generalisation) than accurate information. Information is the key – accurate and up-gradable databases are needed – involve people who are inclined towards such tasks, e.g., NGOs, voluntary organisations, academic institutions etc.

5. Make small implementable projects – short term – that the local authority can implement and have a major impact from the minds of the people, e.g., project for Revitalising Environs of Shanivar Wada, Pune.
6. Very often a top down approach is adopted leading to non-acceptance of the solution (e.g., de-linking of villages that were earlier merged with the PMC limits). Instead a bottom up approach, which first takes stock of the ground realities and issues affecting those related to the areas, needs to be adopted. The final solution may meet the top down and bottom up approach somewhere around the middle. Such an approach might have a greater chance of success.
7. People as resource – it is very often seen that if people are convinced about the benefits of planning resulting in measurable changes in economy, health and an overall quality of life, there will be less resistance to planning than is normally encountered. Typically, government departments are known to do bare minimum of 'public participation' as stipulated in the Law books. The use of various media in highlighting scenarios were no planning has resulted in subhuman living conditions as against those in planned quarters, cannot be underestimated.
8. In a recent initiative of the Union of International Architects and a group in the city of Lieda near Barcelona have launched a movement of the intermediate cities. The fact that a large portion of the world's population will be living in smaller cities in the present century, which are neither state capitals nor economic capitals, has been recognised. Consequently, their problems and solutions as derived through experience can be shared and networked to increase the collective wisdom on such cities. Some of the solutions are offered below for the enlightenment of the reader.
9. The earlier system of pooling land, preparing town planning schemes and constituting plots is conspicuous by its absence. A complete lack of any control has yielded hundreds of acres of look-alike urbanism without identity, character or quality. There is need to outline the basic character and create distinct or identifiable areas in the fringes, which are meaningful and legible to the inhabitants.
10. Mapping the human geography, pathology, areas conducive to farming, habitation, aquifers, sacred groves and such aspects that have never been on the planners agenda need to be identified.

References

Bellet, Carme and Josep M. Llop, (Ed.) (2000): *Intermediate Cities and Sustainability,* published by UIA, City of Lieda, March.

Hughes, Jonathan and Simon Sadler (Ed.) (2002): *Non-Plan-Essays on Freedom Participation and Change in Modern Architecture and Urbanism,* Architectural Press.

McHarg, Ian L. (1969): *Design with Nature,* New York, Natural History Press (Second edition 1992)

12

Politics in Pune's Urban Planning

PANKAJA KULABKAR

Pune's proximity to Mumbai, pleasant climate, historical past, rich culture and growing industrial base has attracted people from several parts of the country to the city. Planning for this ever-expanding city has become a challenge. The past and the current trend show that getting an urban plan implemented in Pune is probably a bigger challenge. Politics is often put forth as the reason for non-implementation of plans. This paper focuses on just one proposal of the current development plan of Pune, viz., reservation of hills, and explores the role of politics in its implementation.

The current development plan of Pune came into effect in 1987. The Pune Municipal Corporation (PMC) is the body responsible for its implementation. Figures regarding reserved sites of this plan that have been implemented have varied from 5 per cent (Paranjape, 1991) to 8–10 per cent (Sardesai, 1998). However, they all indicate that implementation has been far from satisfactory. Past record of earlier plans of Pune also has not been encouraging. Politics has often been put forth as the reason for inadequate implementation. The current plan of Pune (1987–2007) is soon to expire and its review is due, for according to the Maharashtra Regional and Town Planning Act (MRTP) 1996, a plan is to be revised every twenty years.

At this juncture the paper seeks to contribute to the plan's review process by examining the role of politics in the implementation of one proposal of the plan viz., reserving hills of Pune for afforestation and recreation.

Politics is considered in this paper as a process in the public realm wherein actors seek to further their respective interests. The paper raises several questions: Who are the key players involved in the implementation of this plan proposal? Do these players have an interest in the implementation process? What are the interests? What is the impact of these interests and what are the activities of players on the implementation process? These are some of the questions addressed in the current paper.

Methodology

This paper is based on the doctoral thesis submitted to the University of Birmingham in 2000. Several sources of data are used which include documents and studies, newspaper articles, in-depth semi-structured interviews, and observations. A total of 114 key informants were interviewed in Pune, Mumbai and Delhi. Informants included NGOs, planners, commercial developers, citizens, politicians, bureaucrats, academics, media, architects, engineers, landowners, bank employees and industrialists.

Data collected was analysed with the help of framework, which has been laid out in the following paragraphs. This framework has been built on several elements of Grindle's (1980) model that deals with politics of implementing urban policy and developing countries. This framework has been used while analysing implementation of the plan proposal selected for this paper.[1]

Analytical Framework

The analytical framework developed by this study consists of three stages. The *first stage* is concerned with decisions related to the objectives and the content of the plan, the *second* with decision related to the strategy of implementation, and the *third stage* is where benefits of implementation become apparent. The following paragraphs discuss how issues related to decisions taken in each of the stage might influence implementation of the plan.

First Stage: Plan Formulation

Planners and the body responsible for sanctioning the plan (usually the State Government) are the likely actors involved in this stage.

Type of Benefits

Plan proposals offer benefits, which may be classified as "collective" or "divisible". Since "collective benefits" accrue to the people in the neighbourhood as a whole, the implementing body is likely to get collective support of this neighbourhood and there are chances of the proposal being implemented as envisaged in the plan. However, it is important that people perceive them as benefits. On the other hand "divisible benefits" like housing accrue to individual members of the community and may lead to conflict and competition among individuals. The level of conflict may depend on how highly individuals value these benefits. Those enjoying more power may stand to gain the most, and the implementation process may take a direction very different from what was stated in the plan.

This distinction between "collective" and "divisible" benefits may also help the researcher to predict the mobilisation efforts of actors involved in the implementation process. If actors perceive implementation of a particular plan proposal as benefiting an individual (or set of individuals) rather than a large section of the city's population, it may be easier for those disapproving of the proposal to mobilise the support of others against the implementation of this proposal.

Time Scale

The time scale of the plan may also affect the implementation process. Plans in India usually have a span of twenty years. A municipal body is usually responsible for implementing a plan. A municipal body has two wings: the executive and the legislative wing. While a single tenure of councillors is five years that of the commissioner (head of the executive wing) is three years. It is not surprising therefore, that a municipal body with such tenure is not keen to implement a plan that has a span of twenty years. While the above is true about the development plan as a whole, it may not necessarily be true in case of individual plan proposals. Some plan proposals may have a short time span and the municipal body may be more willing to implement them as compared to others.

Clarity of Goals

Problems in interpreting a proposal's objectives may stand in the way of initiating implementation of a plan proposal. Clarity in a plan's goals facilitates an implementing body to design projects in the process of implementing proposals. While clarity may reduce differences in interpretation of the goals, it does not necessarily remove differences. Differences in interpretations may be influenced by interests of actors. Actors might seek to influence the implementing body towards their respective interpretations.

Realism of Goals

Planners in India appear to be divided on what needs to be considered while recommending proposals. For some planners, the foremost concern ought to be the ability of implementing bodies in achieving the goals. According to this view, to prevent mismatch between goals and the capacity of the implementing body, planners ought to seriously consider the financial resources of the implementing body. The other view is that planners need to give precedence to the present and future needs of the citizens rather than the resources of the implementing body. According to this view, if planners did not reserve adequate lands for the future, an implementing body would never be able to find the required land even if it did find the resources to acquire and develop it. While both these arguments hold merit, those planners closest to power (for example those consulted by the sanctioning body) may be able to influence plan preparation towards their respective interpretation.

Second Stage: Strategy of Implementation

Various ways in which issues related to this stage of planning might influence plan implementation are:

Resources Invested

Resources may be said to include the following: Finances, land, requisite skills, time, information, intelligence and enthusiasm of leadership and political support. Resources might also give one level of government power upon the other. An implementing body is heavily dependent on the respective State Government for the supply of funds and skills for designing and implementing a plan. This dependence on the State Government may give the latter considerable leverage in implementing plans.

Availability of resources may also influence which proposal an implementing body chooses to implement and the manner of implementing it.

However, availability of resources may not necessarily be the reason for not initiating implementation. It may be used to disguise some other reason like political non-acceptability of a plan proposal.

Characteristics of the Project

Once the decision to implement a plan proposal is taken and a project is designed to implement it, the nature of the project may affect implementation through following ways:

- Level of participation of actors,
- Nature of "political activity" of these actors,
- Number of organisations involved which may require coordination if more than one organisation is involved,
- Time span of the project.

Implementation also depends on whether crucial elements of a project are systematically worked out which in turn depends on willingness and ability of an implementing body to work out the details.

Third Stage: Implementation

The following related to this stage might influence the implementation process:

Actors: Power, Interests and Strategies

Actors are described in this study as those (individuals or bodies) involved in implementation. They must seek to protect and further their *interests* related to implementation, which may range from self-interest to altruistic, like the desire to work to improve the city's environment. In order to further their interests, actors seek to influence implementation. Ability of actors to influence the process depends on their *power*. *Power* has been considered in this study as the ability of actors to make others act in ways in which they would not have acted otherwise.

Power of actors is likely to depend on *resources* they possess and their willingness to use them for political purpose. They need to employ them in an effective manner so as to reach their respective objectives. In other words, they need to use an appropriate strategy for protecting and furthering their interests. The strategy of actors is likely to depend on the following: first, perception of actors about their interests (for example how important are these interests to them); second, perception about resources at their command (whether they think they have adequate resources to influence implementation); third, their perception of how best to further their interests through resources available to them.

In the context of urban planning in India we would expect the following actors:

- Planners (different from the development control officers),
- Municipal body (including both the politicians and the bureaucratic staff),
- The municipal body may not be a 'homogenous' actor. State Government (the Chief Minister, ministries and the bureaucratic staff), State Government too may not be a homogenous actor. Since city planning is beyond the jurisdiction of the Centre, Central Government may not be a probable actor in the context of urban planning in India.

- Politicians (other than those at the municipal and the state level which have been included in the above two categories),
- Landowners,
- Commercial developers,
- Beneficiaries as perceived by the plan,
- Citizens (who may not be direct beneficiaries of the proposal),
- It is likely that there would be differences among citizens, and therefore citizens as actors might not be homogenous.
- NGOs and professional organisations (like the chamber of commerce, association of architects, association of engineers),
- Media,
- Judiciary.

Institutional Characteristics

This refers to characteristics of bodies involved in implementation and the overall political system. Implementation is likely to be influenced by the organisational structure of these bodies. For example, the level of co-operation between the two wings of the municipal body is expected to affect the implementation process. Relationship between the State Government and the municipal body is also likely to affect implementation, which in turn may be influenced by the relevant legislation. Though implementation process may be formally entrusted to the local body, it may be controlled at the state level. Implementation of a project, therefore, is expected to depend on whether and to what extent the local body has the financial and the political support of the State Government for the project.

Level of openness of a political system is also relevant since it influences how far information is allowed to various actors, and whether their participation is encouraged in the implementation process.

Compliance and Responsiveness

If a plan proposal is to be implemented, compliance of both wings (legislative and executive) of the municipal body is required. In addition, a municipal body needs to have the support of the State Government, politicians at the local and the state level, beneficiaries and other actors in the city depending on the nature of the proposal under implementation. This may be achieved through either one or a combination of the following: persuasion, negotiation and bargaining, using intermediaries, using one's good offices and reputation, patronage, posing threats and releasing minimum information to the public. Effectiveness of these measures also depends on the level of resistance to the plan proposal. While a municipal body may resort to these measures to ensure compliance of actors concerned, actors not happy with the proposal may simultaneously seek to subvert the process. The consequences may be a stalemate as far as implementation of the plan proposal is concerned.

If a plan proposal is to have support of beneficiaries, it also requires being responsive to the needs of the people. In principle planning legislation in India incorporates this element in the planning process through measures like making it obligatory on the part of the planning authority to invite objections and suggestions from the public prior to the plan receiving the approval of the sanctioning body. It however needs to be seen whether this requirement of the planning legislation is followed in spirit.

Pune, Development Plan and PMC

Pune, which is located 115 miles (175 km.) southwest of Mumbai, has a proud history. Capital of Maratha rulers during the eighteenth century, it was also the second capital of the Bombay Presidency under the British. Pune situated near the Sahyadri Mountains has been traditionally known for its salubrious climate. However, the growing population (2.5 million as per the 1991 Census) and increasing traffic has rendered it the sixth place in terms of air pollution (MASHAL, 1996:165:179).

Hills are a prominent characteristic feature of Pune's landscape and cover an area of 913.70 hectares of land within the jurisdiction of PMC. Citizens frequent those that are within easy access. Temples adorn some of these hills and people throng them during religious festivals and some on a regular basis for exercise and pleasure.

Around 41 per cent of these hills are privately owned (Kardaley, 1998; MASHAL, 1996: 89). Some of the hills that were once lush green have turned barren over the years and slums have encroached particularly upon those parts, which are close to water bodies. Planners kept the hills of Pune free from any construction and reserved them for recreation (like play grounds and jogging tracks) and afforestation. Planners had taken advantage of the hills while laying down the planning norms (Keskar, unpublished). Instead of the usual 0.6 hectares per 1,000 population, only 0.24 hectares of land were retained as open areas. Planners assumed that this reduced level of open space would be compensated by the hills (Keskar, unpublished). Response of various actors to planner's recommendation regarding hills will be examined in this paper.

The process of preparing the plan under study began in 1976. The draft plan was prepared and published by the Directorate of Town Planning (DTP) on behalf of the PMC in 1982 and objections from the public were invited. DTP submitted the plan along with the objections to the State Government in 1984 and the State Government sanctioned the plan in 1987. The plan came into effect in the same year.

In the context of Indian planning, reservation is an instrument by which sites are kept aside for public purposes like play grounds and hospitals. Owner of such lands cannot develop or sell them. The planning authority is expected to take over possession of these areas and develop them as mentioned in the plan. Landowners usually perceive themselves to be as disadvantaged when their lands are reserved. While it is true that the planning authority is expected to pay the landowners market value of the land, given the existing property tax structure, landowners would rather sell their lands to a private party than to the planning authority. It is therefore not uncommon for landowners to try and get their land deleted from reservations. This was also seen among landowners owning parts of hills of Pune.

PMC concerned with implementing the plan consists of two wings, the executive and the political wing. The Municipal Commissioner is at the head of the executive wing and normally has a term of three years, unless removed earlier from the office. On the other hand is the political wing consisting mainly of councillors who have a single term of five years. The PMC with a leadership of such a short span has been vested with the responsibility of implementing a plan that has tenure of twenty years.

Attempts to Modify Proposal

A newspaper (*Sakal*, Jan. 18, 1988) reported that since 1982 when the draft plan was published, several hill owners petitioned the State Government to get their lands de-reserved and that they may be permitted to construct on their land. A professional organisation of developers in Pune also requested the State Government to permit 10 per cent FSI[2] constructions on hills (PBAP, unpublished). It was clear from the past record that PMC was unable to afforest the hills and to prevent encroachment. Allowing construction on the hills would not only benefit the owners but would get them interested in stopping encroachment and in planting trees on the area within their possession (PBAP, unpublished; PBAP, 1998).

State Government took up the matter with PMC. The then Municipal Commissioner told the State Government that PMC was in favour of permitting construction on hills at a modest level (*Sakal*, Jan. 18, 1988). In fact in 1993 PMC sent a proposal to the State Government requesting it to permit construction not beyond 4 per cent Floor Space Index (FSI) upon hills for recreational purposes. This was to accommodate "swimming pools, sports and games centres, health clubs, cafeteria, canteens and amusement parks" on hills. PMC justified its proposal on grounds that it did not have funds to acquire these hills and afforest them, not to stop encroachments upon them. Those who would own and maintain the constructed property were expected to plant trees in the area within their jurisdiction that was left vacant after construction. This was expected to check hills from growing barren and being encroached by slums. Moreover, construction for recreational purposes was supposed to provide recreational facilities required in the city (Express Citizen's Forum, 1998).

State Government sanctioned PMC's proposal for allowing 4 per cent FSI construction on hills on June 5, 1997. Two months before the approval a newspaper had reported the State Government to be of the opinion that 4 per cent FSI construction would not be attractive to commercial developers and that 20 per cent FSI would be a better proposition (*Sakal*, April 10, 1997). The Municipal Commissioner subsequently invited representatives of local NGOs for discussion on the issue and the latter were reported to have strongly opposed 20 per cent FSI construction on the hills (Kamble, 1997).

However, soon after the State Government sent a directive (No TPS-1893/1945/CR 54/93/ID-13 dated June 27, 1997) to PMC. In this directive State Government instructed PMC to proceed with the modification procedures so that 20 per cent FSI construction was allowed on the "green belt, hill top and the hill slope zone" in Pune. PMC was asked to publish the notice within sixty days of the directive being issued. Viewing the delay from PMC the State Government went ahead and published the notification in the Government Gazette and invited objections from citizens.

Resistance to Modification

The above directive took the NGOs (ECONET, Parisar, Social Civic and Environmental Forum, Vanarai, etc.) by surprise and they strongly opposed the move. They argued that permitting such a high percentage of construction upon hills amounted to violating planner's recommendations. The modification furthered the interests of developers and landowners at the cost of the city's environment. It was also questioned if the Government had considered the financial costs involved in providing basic amenities to settlements on hills if 20 per cent FSI residential construction were allowed in accordance to the State Government's directive. Moreover, what was to happen to the slums that had come up on the hills?

NGOs also resented the manner in which the State Government had proposed an increase amount of construction on hills. In spite of the fact that it was such a vital issue, the State Government had not thought it necessary to explain its stand to citizens through press conferences. Instead it had chosen to merely carry out the technical obligation of publishing the notification. Moreover, the State Government had merely mentioned in the newspapers that people were to file their objections within one month of the notification being published in the Gazette. It did not specify the date of the Gazette. Were people expected to read up all the Government Gazettes to find the appropriate one (Kardaley, 1998)?

NGOs lobbied the PMC and citizens. They wrote articles in newspapers, held workshops to inform people about the repercussions of construction and encouraged people to file objections to the State Government's proposal. The Express Citizens Forum (ECF), an organisation formed by the Pune edition of the English language daily newspaper, *The Indian Express*, joined the NGOs. Convener of this forum is the editor of the Pune edition of the newspaper, and its membership includes academics, planners, artists, filmmakers, industrialists, retired senior bureaucrats and environmentalists. Conveners of several NGOs are members of the ECF. Partnership between ECF and NGOs facilitated mobilisation of citizens. The Indian Express covered arguments both for and against reservation and gave space to measures taken by forces opposing reservation. ECF also took the State Government to the court. However, the court dismissed the petition on grounds that it was premature.

Interestingly, the State Government soon withdrew its move for 20 per cent reservation. There could be several possible explanations. The State Government had seen the strength of the combined resistance of NGOs and the media to its attempt to de-reserve sites in earlier cases like in survey no. 33. In survey no. 44, NGOs had successfully brought pressure upon the State Government by seeking the Central Government's intervention apart from mobilising the citizens. Another possible factor was the Prabhat Road case, for which the State Government had de-reserved a school site in a prime locality in Pune so that this land could be developed for commercial purposes by the Chief Minister's son-in-law.

Analysing Implementation of Proposal

Actors who played a prominent role in the implementation process were: commercial developers, PMC, State Government, landlords and the media.

Their *interests and strategies* (mentioned in Table 1) and the various issues mentioned in the analytical framework help in understanding the events that have unfolded in the process of implementing the proposal.

Table 1 *Summarising Findings*

First Stage: Plan formulation	
Type of Benefits	• C.B. offered by *original proposal* helped NGOs and media to mobilise citizens only after original proposal threatened by modification
Time Scale	• L.T.S. of *original proposal* discouraged PMC to implement it, while S.T.S. of modification procedure and implementation of *modified proposal* (4%FSI) appealed to PMC • L.T.S. of *original proposal* discouraged NGOs and media to campaign for its implementation prior to modification threats
Clarity of Goals	• Not significant
Realism of Goals	• PMC considered goals unrealistic
Second Stage: Strategies to implement	
Resources invested	• PMC's leadership reluctant to implement proposal and did not invest any resources
Characteristic of project	• One modification attempt stalled and other successful but too early to comment. Characteristic of project therefore irrelevant
Third Stage: Implementation	
Actors	**Developers, PMC, State Government, landlords, NGOs, media**
Power	• Developers: monetary strength, contacts • PMC: power to initiate modification and vote on proposal • State Govt.: power over PMC and plan implementation • Landlords and developers: monetary strength • NGOs: reputation • Media: reputation, power to reach large numbers
Interest	• Landlords and developers: expected to benefit financially from modification • PMC: reluctance to implement original proposal, successfully mobilised by developers and landowners, wary of opposition from media • State Government: successfully mobilised developers and landlords. Alleged that some ministers in State Government own hills in Pune • NGOs and media: protect Pune's environment
Strategies	• Landlords and developers: mobilised PMC and State Govt. • PMC: mobilised support within PMC and of State Govt. • State Government: invoked MRTP Act and gave minimum information to public
Institutional characteristics	• Both wings of PMC agreed to oppose State Government's modification • State Government invoked MRTP Act to intervene, gave least information about modification to public
Compliance and Responsiveness	• PMC responsive to NGOs objection to modification and resisted State Government's directive

Key: C.B. =Collective Benefits, L.T.S. =Long Time Scale, S.T.S. =Short time scale, PMC = Pune Municipal Corporation

Planners had denied construction on the hills. Hills were reserved for afforestation and recreation and citizens had free and equal access to them. The original plan proposal therefore offered collective benefits to the citizens. In contrast, changes sought in the proposal opened up avenues of financial rewards to owners and commercial developers. The modifications ushered in divisible benefits since only those who owned and developed the hills were likely to benefit. Citizens in general were losers because constructions could be expected to pose constraints on their access to the hills.

In spite of the fact that the proposal offered collective benefits to citizens, PMC did not take it up for implementation. Inadequate resources were often the explanation offered by PMC. There is little evidence that PMC *ever invested its resources* or even seriously estimated the total costs involved in implementing the proposal. Why was PMC reluctant? This may be explained in terms of the *long time span* of the proposal. Implementation of the proposal implied taking into possession the sites, cordoning them and putting them into use as recommended in the plan. This was likely to take considerable time. Moreover, the proposal did not seem *realistic* to PMC. While planners seem to have thought that implementing the proposal was well within the capacity of PMC, the latter thought otherwise. A few councillors owned some of the sites and "political costs" would be involved if these were to be acquired. Implementing the proposal certainly did not appear tempting to PMC.

PMC was in favour of construction on the hills and yet had objected to 20 per cent construction proposed by the State Government. It probably anticipated opposition from the environmental group in the city. Moreover if 20 per cent residential construction were to be allowed on the hills, basic services would have to be provided to the residents involving high costs.

One might have expected citizens, environmental NGOs of Pune and the media to exert pressure upon PMC to implement the proposal of reserving sites of afforestation and recreation. This does not appear to have taken place. Several explanations may be offered. Citizens were not aware that the hills were reserved in the plan. Even if they were, and they disliked slums encroaching, encroachments did not stop their access to the hills. Therefore, there was no strong desire on their part to pressurise PMC to implement the proposal. They responded strongly on perceiving a change in the collective benefits offered by the proposal. NGOs along with the media launched a crusade against permitting construction on hills. They wrote articles in the newspapers, held workshops to inform people about the repercussions of permitting constructions, mobilised people to file in their objections to the modification of the proposal and also took the State Government to the court. The partnership between NGOs and the media proved to be most effective in citizen mobilisation. Citizens were aware of the activities of NGOs through newspapers. The *Indian Express Forum*, the forum of the daily *The Indian Express* was actively involved in opposing the modification. Measures taken by NGOs in opposing modification were covered in detail particularly by this newspaper.

The same State Government that had approved the original plan's recommendation of reserving hills had now proposed 20 per cent construction. What brought about this change? This appears to have been partly a result of successfully mobilisation by landlords and commercial developers who have been advocating modification in the original proposal. Increasing population has exerted pressure on land in Pune and the vast expanse of hills constitutes an attractive potential for construction. Modification in the proposal that allowed construction on the hills had financial prospects to land owners and developers.

The move to allow 20 per cent construction was stalled. While 4 per cent construction on hills still stands there are no major projects to implement it and, therefore, *characteristics of the project* are not relevant here. Also not so relevant in this case are *clarity of goals*. In spite of the fact that the proposal had clearly stated that the hills be reserved for afforestation and recreation, there were attempts to change the proposal. The move to modify proposal does not seem to have been inspired by lack of clarity or differences in interpreting the proposal.

Two *institutional characteristics* played a significant role: the State Government provided minimal information to the public when involving MRTP provisions for a speedy implementation of its proposed modification, and both wings of the PMC agreed to oppose the State Government's proposed modification. As to the public, the point made earlier regarding following planning legislation in spirit may be recalled. PMC's *responsiveness* to objections from NGOs contributed to the stalling of the modification proposed by the State Government.

Conclusion

Implementation of hills has been a story of non-implementation of the original proposal, efforts at modifying the proposal, success in getting one modification passed and failure in the other. Should the future plan continue reserving hills of Pune for afforestation and recreation? Given PMC's reluctance to implement the proposal and resistance from landlords to their sites being reserved, should there be a change in the overall time span of plans and reforms in the property tax? If residential construction were to be permitted on the hills, how would PMC cope with the concerns that NGOs have expressed? It is hoped that questions like these raised by this paper would be attended to by authority while revising current plan.

While landowners and commercial developers were seen in this paper to be resourceful in mobilising different levels of government, NGOs and the media strongly opposed the modification proposed by the State Government. The NGO-media partnership has proved to be effective and a force to be reckoned with in Pune. Such networking and partnership ought not to be lost sight of by academics, practitioners and policy-makers.

Given the not too different implementation record of urban plans in other cities of India and the alleged role of politics in plan implementation, similar studies may be undertaken in other parts of the country. While analysing implementation in other cities, the framework developed in this study might be found useful.

Notes

1. This framework was also used by the author while comparing the role of politics in the implementation of the hill slopes along with two other proposals of the Pune development plan (Kulabkar, 2002).
2. The FSI according to the MRTP Act, 1966 is the "quotient or ratio of the combined gross floor area to the total area of the plot".

Select Bibliography

Express Citizen's Forum (1998): The Press Note, *The Indian Express*, May 19.

Grindle, M. (ed.)(1980): *Politics and Policy Implementation in the Third World*, Princeton, Princeton University Press.

Kamble, M. (1997): Tekdya Vachvinyasathi Ladhyachi Garaj, *Kesari*, August 18.

Kardaley, P. (1998): 'He Kay Gaudbangal Hai', *Vanarai*, February.

Keskar, J.G. (unpublished): Draft for Discussion: Evaluation of the Pune Development Plan

Kulabkar, P. (2002): The Politics of Implementing Urban Plans in India: The Case study of Pune's Development Plan, *IDPR*, 24(1).

MASHAL, (1996): 1st Annual Report on the State of Environment, Pune, Pune Municipal Corporation.

Paranjape, K.G. (1991): *Pune Action Plan: Report of the Working Group appointed by Government to recommend an Action Plan for improvement in the civic services in Pune and the Pimpri-Chinchwad region*, Government of Maharashtra.

PBAP (1998): Newsletter published by the Promoters and Builders Association of Poona, February.

PBAP (unpublished), Objections and suggestions presented to the special officer regarding notification of the Urban Development Department No. TPS 1893/1045/CR54/93/UD-13.

Sakal, Shaharantil Tekdyanchya Vaibhavas Dhoka, Jan. 18, 1988.

Sakal, Arakshit Dongar Jaminivar Bandhkamas Parvangicha Vichar, April 10, 1997.

Sardesai, P.G. (1998): Pune ani parisaracha niyogan, tekdya va paryavaran, *Kesari*, February 25.

II

Fringe Development in Germany and France

13

Recent Developments of Urban Fringes in Modern Society

An Evolutionary Perspective

GERHARD BAHRENBERG

When talking about urban fringes one can distinguish three forms. The urban fringe of traditional cities, i.e., cities of agrarian societies before industrialisation, was a strict border marked by the city wall. During industrial growth cities expanded into their rural hinterlands and their walls were demolished. But even then one could observe a distinct border between the city and its rural surrounding separating the built-up area and the agriculturally used land. It was only during suburbanisation and the termination of urban growth that this border weakened and the urban-rural dichotomy became obsolete. It is my impression that this sequence does not apply to Indian cities since at present they are subjected to urban growth and suburbanisation simultaneously. Nevertheless, I believe the following arguments taken from the history of settlement structure in western countries apply also to the Indian urban situation.

The History of Suburbanisation

Suburbanisation, i.e., the emergence of suburbs, has a long tradition. It began in Europe in the 17th/18th century in England and was exported from there to North America (Fishman, 1984, 1987; Holzner, 1996). It was the economically successful middle class, namely traders and bankers, later also industrial entrepreneurs who turned their weekend cottages in the rural villages surrounding the cities into permanent residences and commuted each day into the city by coaches/carriages. This kind of suburbanisation, insignificant in quantitative terms, did not attract much attention since it was overshadowed by the enormous growth of the industrial cities. Suburbanisation attracted the attention of the disciplines interested in settlement structure only in the 20th century, and in Germany only since the late 1960s when it started to bring about a decline in the population of the cities. Consequently, suburbanisation was defined as the relative growth of population and/or number of jobs in urban hinterlands at the cost of the cities. The population growth of urban hinterlands results firstly from the negative migration balance of the city with its rural hinterland (residence oriented migration), and secondly, from interregional migration to the hinterland. The hinterland profited from this work-place oriented migration even when the immigrants started work in the city.

The observation of residential suburbanisation and commuting population led to new terms for describing the settlement structure: the city region consisting of the city (which became the so called core city) and the suburban hinterland. This terminology reflects that both parts – core city and the suburban hinterland – built a unit in functional terms resulting in the growing traffic (commuting) between them. The suburban hinterland could not survive without the city since the city provided jobs and necessary services for the suburban population. On the other hand the city also profited from suburbanisation. The increasing demand for larger residential units could not be met within the city borders. And the supply of land in the suburban areas relieved the urban land and housing market.[1]

Table 1 shows the amount of residential suburbanisation in German cities during the last 30 years taking the City of Bremen as an example. One should note that whereas the hinterland population reached 70 per cent of the city's population in 1970, 1999 was the first year in history when the population of the city was smaller than the population of the hinterland. It is also evident from Table 1 that the amount of population redistribution within the city region (i.e., city plus hinterland) is much higher than the population change in the city region as a whole.

Table 1 *Suburbanisation in the Region of Bremen*

		Population	
		1970	*1999*
Bremen City		5,90,000	5,40,350
Hinterland		4,15,951	5,47,546
Region of Bremen		10,05,951	10,87,896
Difference City – Hinterland		1,84,049	-7,194
Total migration balance between Bremen City and its hinterland	Period 1965–2000		-64,745
		City	*Hinterland*
Development of Employment	Period 1970–1987	-23,964	32,924
Proportion of 'net suburbanisation'			59%

Proportion of 'net suburbanisation' means the rate of change not due to population suburbanisation.

Source: Statistical Bureau of the City of Bremen; Personal Communication (2002) and Bahrenberg (1997).

Suburbanisation of population was immediately followed by the suburbanisation of work-places. One can distinguish two elements. Firstly, the growth of population in suburban areas resulted in a higher demand for locally supplied, so called household oriented services like schools, shopping facilities, medical and administrative services etc. Secondly, the improved transport infrastructure in the former rural areas surrounding the city together with the availability of cheap land improved the attractiveness for enterprises marketing their goods and services at a regional or even national level. In a study on the suburbanisation process in Bremen we came to the conclusion that in the time period 1970–1987 approximately 50 per cent of the loss of employment in the city of Bremen and of its growth in the suburban hinterland of Bremen could be attributed to each of these two factors (see Table 1 and Bahrenberg, 1997, p. 19).

The list of enterprises having been established in suburbia contains not only traditional elements like spacious shopping centres, leisure parks, multiplex-cinemas and other establishments of the entertainment industry that need a market area of up to several hundred km-radius. In addition, it comprises standardizable administrative functions like computing centres and insurances as well as control centres of firms; in the suburban area of Munich for instance Microsoft, Cisco, 3Com, Texas Instruments, Infineon which – by the way – are located in different suburban communities. Only part of these enterprises was relocated from the city, the rest (for example Cisco, 3Com and Microsoft) were established as respective German headquarters (Kagermeier, Miosga and Schußmann, 2001, p. 168/169).

The loss of former typical CBD functions of the core city and the growing importance of the former suburban areas can best be observed in the United States where it found it clearest expression in the so called *edge cities* (Garreau, 1991). These edge cities need at least 4,65,000 sq. m. office space, 56,000 sq. m. retail space and have to have more jobs than inhabitants to be classified as *edge cities*. In the meantime they accommodate even nationally distinguished theatres and galleries (Holzner 1996, S. 99p.). In other words, edge cities are typical Central Business Districts and resemble them also because of their high-rise skyline. But, in contrast to CBDs, their density of land use is much lower, and they are not integrated into the city fabric, as spatial and urban planners would stress.

The growing autonomy of suburbia, the weakening linkage between the city and its suburban hinterland and, as a result, the replacement of the traditional radial transportation pattern of the early suburbanisation by a non-directional, more tangential and even a random or chaotic one with its highest density within and between the former suburban areas,[2] and the side by side existence of rural areas with agricultural land use, highly concentrated urban functions and traditional suburban residential areas has provoked notions like *'cityland'* (Holzner, 1996), *'betweencity'* (Sieverts, 1997) or simply 'Metropolitan Areas' (see Figure 1). They express, that "the city as a specific unit beyond the randomness of administrative territorial organisation does not exist anymore" (Häussermann and Siebel, 1987, p. 10).

These 'metropolitan areas' are neither urban nor rural. And "*unlike all cities of the past, this new city has no defined centre or periphery; no core, no manufacturing or commercial districts, and no hinterland. Instead, urban functions spread out along highway 'growth corridors' in low-density settlements that combine urban, suburban, and rural elements in a seemingly random and endless collage*" (Fishman, 1994, p. 92). One can observe a spatial form of societal order whose characteristic feature is the rapid weakening of the (spatial) centre-periphery gradient plus the disappearance of a territorial border. Today the city is everywhere and nowhere. And cities can be observed as a spatial form, if at all, only in the case of small and medium sized towns. By the way the author prefers the term *'cityland'*. Cityland does not describe the suburban areas as a third type of settlement structure. Instead it expresses exactly the weakening of the urban-rural dichotomy and the fact, that the suburban hinterland is not a uniform residential area it used to be during the early suburbanisation period but a mosaic of cells of different densities and land use without any centre. And the (former) core city is just one cell within the patchwork[3]. It seems to me that such a patchwork structure without significant spatial centre-periphery differences is the most important characteristic feature of modern society. The arguments will be presented in the following chapter.

Figure 1 *The Structure of Metropolitan Areas*

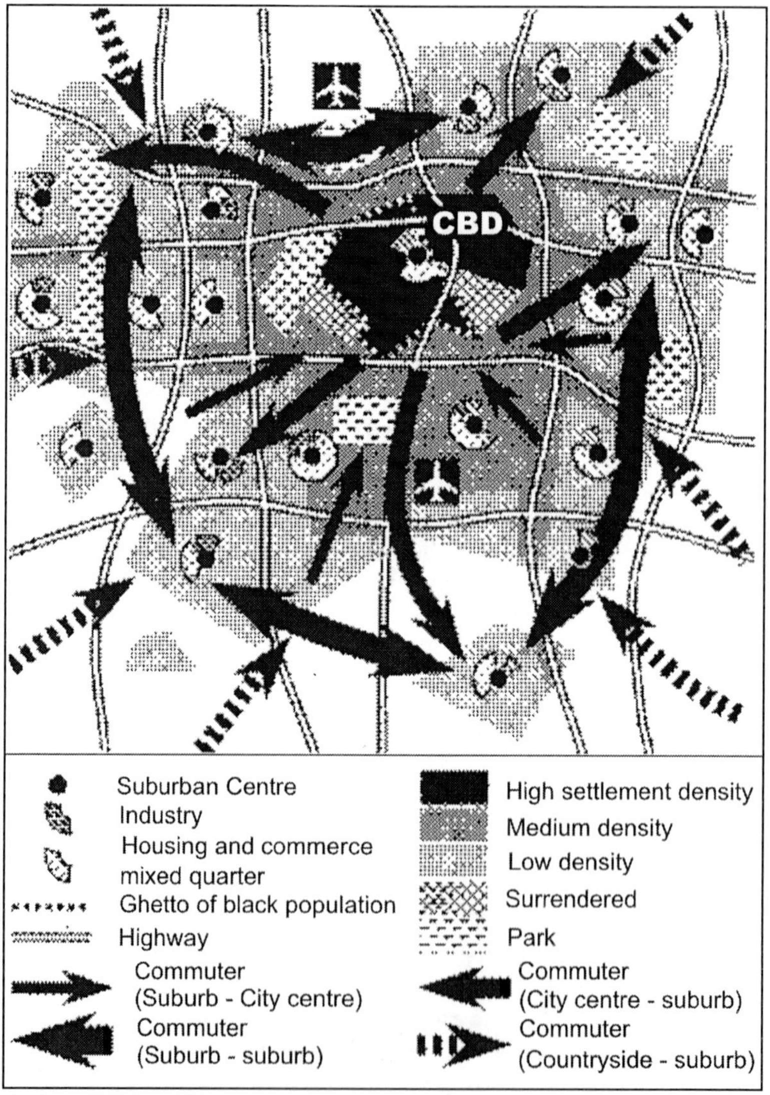

Source: Holzner 1996, p. 104

Society, Space and the City

If one talks about cities one has to deal with an ambiguity: In urban and regional sociology, the term city refers to specific *social* features, for instance *"a specific way of living, a civilised behaviour, tolerance towards strangers, the 'small' family, the utopian hope for emancipation"* (Siebel, 1999) or its function as an inclusion/integration machine for immigrants. Such normative concepts cannot convince since they can easily be balanced by negative definitions emphasising the social disorder and disintegration in cities as compared to rural villages. In contrast, urban geography tends to concentrate on physical/spatial characteristics of cities as the size and density of population or built environment while talking about cities. To my knowledge the only approach to integrate the sociological and geographical point of view is 'Central Place theory' since it combines central services/functions, 'the market' (social dimension) with 'central location of the market place' (physical/spatial dimension). Unfortunately the Central Place theory is adequate only for the description of agrarian societies and cannot be applied to modern society. The simple reason is that – apart from some special cases – a 'market' does not need a 'market place' anymore; the financial market is the most prominent example.[4] In generalising this observation I would like to stress that since Max Weber society – in contrast to population and/or community – is being conceived as the set of interconnected social actions, i.e., human actions having preceding and succeeding actions.[5] The important term is *interconnectivity* since it excludes actions in a situation such as Robinson Crusoe's on his island.

In Palaeolithic hunter-gatherer and early Neolithic societies, physical presence of different actors was a necessity for interconnectivity. And it is no surprise that cities, making possible a significant division of labour for the first time in history, emerged only and soon after the invention of sedentariness. Since then cities became the centres of societal development because they were the places where interconnectivity of human actions could most easily be realised. Accordingly, cities became the centres of innovation, i.e., the places where almost all societal innovations were invented and diffused. This applies especially to transport and communication technologies. To name just three extremely important and often overlooked innovations: (1) font (script) developed in the city (!) states of Sumer, and the first communication medium allowing interconnectivity to overcome time distances (and to provide society with a memory); (2) printing, the first medium of telecommunication since it additionally permitted to overcome spatial distances; (3) generalised symbolic communication media like money, truth, law etc. being the basis for the development of societal function systems like economy, science, and the legal system.

Despite all innovations in transport and communication technology, the cities of agricultural societies remained small in size (apart from centres of large empires) (Table 2). For instance 4,000 cities existed in medieval Germany but only 16 of them had a population size bigger than 10,000 inhabitants. The largest city was Cologne with a population just above 50,000. The limits to urban size were due to the high costs in terms of time and money to overcome spatial distances. Only the emergence of railroads changed this situation significantly. Now cities could grow up to several million inhabitants (with the side effect of increasing urban-rural disparities).

Table 2 *Population (estimated) of Selected Cities*

Ancient Times		
Jericho	(7000/8000 B.C.)	1, 000
Sumer	(approx. 3000 B.C.)	20,000
Uruk	(approx. 2500 B.C.)	50,000
Athens	(4th Century B.C.)	1,00,000
Rome	(Augustus)	10,00,000
Byzantium	(5th Century A.D.)	10,00,000
Medieval Times in Germany		
	City Size (Population)	*Frequency*
	<1,000	2,800
	1,000–2,000	900
	2,000–10,000	250
	10,000–20,000	6
	20,000–50,000	9
	>50,000	1
(Urban Functions: 'Agriculture' (Gardening), Processing Trade, Long Distance Trade)		
Pre-industrial Metropoles		
Venice	(Medieval Times)	1,00,000
Naples	(18th Century)	4,00,000
Paris	(18th Century)	7,00,000
London	(18th Century)	8,00,000
Industrial Metropoles (approx. 1890)		
London		5,6 Mio.
Paris		4,0 Mio.
New York		3,0 Mio.
Berlin		1,5 Mio.

Source: Schmitz, S. (2001), p. 30, Sieferle, R.P. (1997), p. 110.

From economic geography/regional economics we know that the enormous growth of the industrial city was due to internal economies of scale and external localisation and urbanisation (!) economies and – one should add – to the externalisation of the costs of high density (bad living conditions, noise, and environmental pollution). What seems to be more important in our context is the enormous spatial centralisation of social actions that resulted from the emergence of railroads. Transportation on rails privileges the nodes within a linear network. This feature is the most important disadvantage of railroads. Consequently the rise of the automobile and new telecommunication technologies (radio, television, telephone, and internet) resulted in the decline of the railroad.[6] By using these technologies it became possible to avoid the costs of density without any reduction in the participation of social actions. As a consequence one can observe a steadily increasing degree of spatial decentralisation in social actions. Suburbanisation is just one small facet of this universal trend in modern society.

Management

The critiques against suburbanisation are manifold, mostly fundamental and well meant. From the point of view of political ecology, suburbanisation is criticised mainly because of the so-called 'wastage of space' (conversion of agricultural land into urban land use) and the increasing daily trip lengths between the different activity locations of the population leading to higher fuel consumption and thereby reinforcing climate change (greenhouse effect). Urban sociologists often point at the increasing socio-spatial segregation connected with suburbanisation: Since it is mainly the middle class that leaves the core city, the proportion of elderly, poor people, singles, and immigrants increases in the core city creating severe financial problems for the local authorities. Most of these arguments are not very valid. And what is more important: they didn't show any results in terms of reducing suburbanisation, because in a democratic political system one cannot see any appropriate and acceptable measure, in order to restrict or even stop suburbanisation processes.

The argument of increasing social-segregation with suburbanisation refers to a problem closely connected with changes in the settlement structure. The political system (together with the legal system) is the only subsystems of society with territorial borders. This poses a problem insofar as the other subsystems of society (health care, education, science, economy, love etc.) do not care about territorial borders; they even do not perceive them when their communication crosses them. During urbanisation these problems of the political system were solved at the local level by adjusting the territorial borders of local authorities to the dominant activity spaces of the individuals; that is by incorporating former independent rural villages into the city when they became a virtual part of the city in functional terms. The period of enlarging the political territory of cities ended in Germany during the late 1960s/early 1970s. Further incorporations were not possible since the suburban areas were strong enough to resist successfully analogous efforts of the core city. As a result local authorities in Germany's metropolitan areas began to take suburbanisation for granted and – although competing for business and residential population – started to cooperate in areas that were formerly in the responsibility of communal authorities. They built so called 'special purpose associations' in fields such as wastewater treatment, waste disposal and provision of drinking water, electricity and gas, thereby realising economies of scale. It is important to note that the co-operation in these areas is not restricted to the provision of the physical infrastructure but extends to the complete supply of a particular service.[7] During the last twenty years, one could also observe the emergence of metropolitan, intercommunal transport authorities (in Germany the local authorities (communes) carry the responsibility for local public transport). Firstly the new authorities started harmonising ticketing and fares. Later on, they began to co-ordinate the different time schedules of the communal services. Nowadays they start to even take on themselves the responsibility for public transport planning in the complete metropolitan area.[8]

The most recent step in the co-operation of different local authorities is the establishment of new 'metropolitan authorities' at – what is called in Germany – the district level of the political-administrative system. Among other aims they are responsible for regional planning and can thus strongly affect the land use planning (zoning) of local authorities, for instance shopping centre development. To be sure this process is totally different from the traditional incorporation of former independent rural communities into the city during industrialisation and the early period of suburbanisation since the independent local authorities are members of the new metropolitan authorities and do not loose their political autonomy but rather delegate deliberately specific responsibilities to the new political-administrative body. What is most important is the fact that this body is not dominated by the former core city. Virtually this means a strong trend towards spatial decentralisation at the local and regional level of the political system.

The Future of Cities

What does this process mean for cities? Obviously cities are no longer the 'laboratory of modern society' as the so-called 'Chicago School of Sociology' maintained. Recent developments of society can no longer be best observed in cities. And participation in meaningful societal communication doesn't presuppose living in cities. People are well aware of this fact since only a small proportion wants to live in cities in the future (see Table 3).

Table 3 *Actual and Desired Residential Locations of Metropoles' Residents in Germany, Results of a Survey in Large German Cities on behalf of Renault Germany*

Residential location	*2002*	*2007*	*2022*
City	58%	45%	28%
Suburbia	40%	41%	41%
Rural area	1%	13%	25%

Obviously, the societal need for cities is rapidly declining – at least as far as the traditional functions of cities are concerned. In other words: Society whose primary form of differentiation is functional differentiation doesn't need spatial centres of communication. Of course the chances of spatial decentralisation are different for different societal subsystems. In subsystems such as education or health care, social interaction, that is for communication among individuals being physically present plays and will play an important role (Kuhm, 2001, p. 15). Accordingly, these functional systems are to some extent dependent on the existence of spatially concentrated physical infrastructure. But the need to concentrate the physical infrastructure of several functional systems at a single location is rapidly declining.

Of course this doesn't mean the end of cities. They will continue to exist first of all because of the persistence effect of physical structures. But their societal function will change. An indicator may be the rapidly increasing city tourism. Its destination is not the urban fringe, where all recent developments take place, but the old traditional city centres. These old cores can be uploaded with important symbolic values for society. City centres are the places where society can present itself and its history. This is the reason why Germany invests such a lot of money in the reconstruction of its former and present capital Berlin. And this construction includes even the old Berlin castle in the centre of the city which is going to be totally reconstructed according to its original look.

Notes

1. This and other benefits for the city from suburbanisation are often overlooked in the German literature on suburbanisation which in general prefers a 'critical' view on suburbanisation. For a rather rare exception see Hammerschmid and Stiens (1980).
2. Similar observations albeit less clearly can be made on German agglomerations (Albers und Bahrenberg 1999).
3. This term stems from Kagermeier, A., Miosga, M. und Schußmann, K. (2001).
4. If one wants to buy or sell shares at the Frankfurt Stock Exchange one doesn't need to be physically present in the building of the Frankfurt Stock Exchange. One can do one's business as well from Hongkong, Bremen, Pune or from any other place in the world.
5. Choosing social action as the basic operation of society poses severe theoretical problems since action is too restricted (cf. Stichweh, 2000). Therefore 'action' has been replaced in present societal theory by 'communication' as the three-component unit of information, utterance and understanding (see Luhmann, 1995). For our purpose the difference between action and communication is not that important.
6. One should stress that the increasing wealth of the population that resulted from the spatial concentration of economic activities in cities was another important prerequisite: At the beginning of automobilisation one had to have an income well above the average in order buy a car. Nowadays the percentage of car ownership per household reaches almost 100 per cent.
7. By the way this tendency is reinforced by privatisation of the services in question.
8. As an example one can mention the transport association of the Bremen region. It comprises 34 transport companies, 5 counties (with roughly 30 communes) and 5 cities.

References

Albers, K. and G. Bahrenberg (1999): Siedlungsstruktur und Verkehr in der Stadtregion. Eine Analyse der Entwicklung 1970–1987 am Beispiel des Berufsverkehrs in der Region Bremen. Universität Bremen, *ZWE Arbeit und Region, Arbeitspapiere 37.*

Bahrenberg, G. (1997): Suburbanisierung – Auflösung der Stadt in die Region? in T. Krämer-Badoni and W. Petrowsky (Ed.): *Das Verschwinden der Städte.* Dokumentation des 16. Bremer Wissenschaftsforums der Universität Bremen, 14.-16. November 1996 (= Universität Bremen, ZWE Arbeit und Region, Forschungsberichte 8: 13–25.

Fishman, R.L. (1984): Origins of the Suburban Idea in England, in: *Chicago History* 12: 26–35.

Fishman, R.L. (1987): American Suburbs – English Suburbs – A Transatlantic Comparison, *Journal of American History* 13: 237–251.

Fishman, R.L. (1994): Die neue Stadt des 20. Jahrhunderts: Raum, Zeit und Sprawl. The New City of the 20th Century: Space, Time and Sprawl, in B. Meurer (Ed.):

Die Zukunft des Raums – The future of space, Frankfurt am Main, New York, Campus Verlag, pp. 91–105 .

Garreau, J. (1991): Edge cities are the crucible of America's urban future, *Architecture* 46/47: 114–115.

Häussermann, H. and W. Siebel (1987): *Neue Urbanität*, Frankfurt am Main: Suhrkamp.

Hammerschmid, A. and G. Stiens (1980): "Stadtflucht" in hochverdichteten Regionen – Gefahr oder Erfordernis? – *Informationen zur Raumentwicklung*, No. 11: 585–598.

Holzner, L. (1996): Stadtland USA: die Kulturlandschaft des American way of life, *Petermanns geographische Mitteilungen*, Ergänzungsheft 291, Gotha: Perthes.

Kagermeier, A., M. Miosga and K. Schußmann (2001): Die Region München – Auf dem Weg zu regionalen Patchworkstrukturen, in: K. Brake, J.S. Dangschat and G. Herfert (Ed.): *Suburbanisierung in Deutschland. Aktuelle Tendenzen*, Opladen: Leske und Budrich pp. 163–173.

Kuhm, K. (2001): Telekommunikative Medien und Raumstrukturen der Kommunikation. Paper presented at meeting of the section "Wissenschafts- und Technikforschung" of the Deutsche Gesellschaft für Soziologie. Berlin. Manuskript, 20 p.

Luhmann, N. (1995): *Social Systems*, Stanford, Cal.: Stanford University Press.

Siebel, W. (1999): Ist Urbanität eine Utopie? *Geographische Zeitschrift* 87: 116–124.

Sieverts, T. (1997): *Zwischenstadt*. Braunschweig und Wiesbaden, Vieweg.

Stichweh, R. (2000): Systems Theory as an Alternative to Action Theory? The Rise of 'Communication' as a Theoretical Option, *Acta Sociologica* 43: 5–13.

14

Urban Fringes in France (1968–2002)

JEAN STEINBERG

France knows "periurbanisation" or "rurbanisation" for over thirty years. This represents an increasingly important spreading of urbanisation, which is not a continuous "oil patch" but resembles rather a "leopard skin" where the agglomerations are scattered in a more or less preserved rural territory.

Urban fringes are different from the densely urbanised suburbs without breaks made by agricultural and forest spaces. The constitution of suburbs was the principal type of growth in French towns before periurbanisation, although the housing estates of the years 1920–1939 were characterised by an intermediate style between suburbs and fringes. Since the 1970s, town and country interpenetrate more and more, not only around big cities, which leads us to think that the French periurbanisation is different from other forms of urban growth in the world.

This phenomenon of periurbanisation continues to grow more than thirty years after its birth, as the results of the last population census of March 1999 show. The first part of this paper will present definitions about urban outskirts and the French specificity. The second part will show the evolution of periurbanisation between 1968 and 1990, according to the size of the programs, their structure and the distance from the hearts of cities. Finally, the third part analyses the impact of metropolisation upon periurbanisation, the prospects opened by inter-municipality and the preoccupation about the environment for the years 1990 to 2002.

Periurbanisation, a French Character

Some Definitions

Urban outskirts have several names: "faubourg", "banlieue", peri-urbanisation, rurbanisation, suburbs, favelas, etc. The "faubourg" is an old urban extension beyond the town walls (for instance Faubourg St. Antoine in Paris). The "banlieue", resulting from the industrial revolution in the end of the 19th century, became a dense urbanisation in which green and agricultural spaces are very few.

Periurbanisation (or rurbanisation) correspond either to the old meaning of suburb, or to a new suburb, or to something entirely different. It is in fact a discontinuous urban growth, generally joined to old towns and villages on the outskirts of the agglomeration, which keep in their space great parts of agriculture, forest and leisure. This urbanisation is generally separate from the agglomeration, but the neighbouring fringes become new suburbs by contact.

French periurbanisation is little more than thirty years old: dating back to the first public exposition of individual houses (Villagexpo) in 1967. After a big start during the last years of the "Trente Glorieuses" ("The Glorious Thirty", 1945–1975) -until 1975 – the phenomenon continued to develop less rapidly in the following years. However, the census showed that periurbanisation spread very widely in the rural environment, as far as hundred kilometres from Paris, extending beyond the Île-de-France region, upon which it is named "franges franciliennes" (Francilian Fringes).

International Comparisons

The French periurbanisation has few equivalents in the world and it is consequently highly original. For in the developed "new countries" of North America and Australia, suburbia exhibit intermediate forms of urbanisation between suburbs and fringes, characterised by the dominance of individual houses and abundance of green spaces.

In Russia, in particular around Moscow, since more than ten years a green suburb is growing beyond the crown of housing schemes with *datchas* which at the beginning were cottages for well-to-do people (the sovietic nomenklatura), but which are scattering as housing estates of main or second homes.

In developing countries, there are no equivalents to French periurbanisation: the planned outskirts or spontaneous urbanisation, as favela or barriada, are the endlessly spreading of towns and metropolises rather than really discontinuous urbanisation.

In Europe, the English model and those of some countries of Scandinavia are close to the French experience. On the other end, Mediterranean Europe has always densely built towns with few outskirt developments: Italy, Spain in particular.

Conditions for the Phenomenon to Appear

They correspond exactly to the wishes of the urban population at the end of the sixties: reaction against concrete jungles, beginning of ecologist action with a new return to nature, growing wealth of population. We can thus distinguish the following elements:

- Industrialisation of the building industry extends now to individual housing: It is possible to build groups of several hundreds of houses, as in the USA (American builders Levitt or Kauffmann and Broad, and also the French Bouygues or Phenix).
- In the beginning of the seventies, the private car is common, and it allows the spread of the population everywhere in the fringes.
- At the same time, the highway network is developing and, because of the interchanges, it becomes possible to live far from the centre of the town without loss of time during commuting.

- The passion of the French people for individual housing is not declining even after more than thirty years: It is a true social phenomenon which concerns all the sections of the population, not only the middle classes, the principal target of periurbanisation, but also the well-to-do classes, for instance in the west of the Île-de-France, and even the lower income classes spread out more and more towards the "Francilian Fringes" in the nearest Paris Basin.
- Despite the creation of new towns, the fact that these were specialised in social and collective housing has either pushed the richer segments of the population out of these towns, or the people were more attracted by the purchase of individual housing. Fifteen years were necessary for the housing market to find its balance.

The Periurbanisation, Evolution between 1968 and 1990

The Decrease of the Program Size

The golden age of periurbanisation took place during its first years, between 1968 and 1975. The decrease was linked to the end of the "Trente Glorieuses" and to a bad control of speculation. During the early period, some periurban areas knew a much higher growth than nascent new towns, for instance the West Fringe of Seine-et-Marne department in comparison to the new towns Marne-la-Vallée and Sénart. Programs having more than 1,000 houses were built there.

The action of the minister of Equipment in the 1969–1972, Albin Chalandon, was inscribed in the same dynamic: In order to open the market as much as possible, and to favour the access to individual housing to anybody, Mr Chalandon created the "Concours International de la Maison Individuelle" which generated the construction of several thousands of low cost houses with three or four rooms in periurban areas. Of course, these modest quality and comfort houses brought with them some problems (manufacturing defect, bad thermal isolation, etc.).

Since 1975, the economic crisis settled into France and thus big programs of individual housing declined strongly. Also, the governmental aid to individual persons replaced the earlier aid for building activities in 1978, which strengthened this trend. The programs went down from several hundred units to a few tens; the mean in the 1980's is near to one hundred houses per program. It is a trend, which is not specific to the fringe but concerns the whole French building industry, in particular in the new towns. With economic constraints, there is a greater will to realise "tailor made" programs, which exclude big size operations.

The Spreading into the Rural Space

The reduction in the size of programs since 1975 did not cause the decline or the arrest of the fringe spreading into the countryside. On the contrary, there was in fact an inverse movement, which was the acceleration of the urban explosion around existing towns. As mentioned earlier, periurbanisation is reaching distances of several tens of kilometres for the principal French towns

(Lyon, Bordeaux, Toulouse, etc.) and one hundred kilometres for Paris (the boundaries of Parisian Region are widely crossed).

The reasons are the same than those that created the phenomenon: generalisation of cars, development of road network, etc. Besides, it is possible to access the land and property market at much lower costs in the periurban areas than in the towns and in the fringes close to them, which lead modest families to settle in these faraway areas. These families have moreover the tendency to underestimate the expenses caused by settling down in the periurban areas (pay back of loans, transport costs, etc.).

The types of fringes that proliferated after 1975 differ from those before 1975 in two points:

1. "Turnkey" programs created by big builders are decreasing and are executed less and less in rural spaces, which is linked up to the reduction of their mean size.
2. Isolated constructions in agricultural or forest areas are completely vanishing because of the increasingly strict planning control.

The result of this is a "normalisation" or a rationalisation of periurbanisation: Except a few cases, housing estates amenities and activities settle around already inhabited spaces, villages or important hamlets, thus giving importance to natural and agricultural spaces. Agriculture, contrary to fringes close to the suburbs, can continue its normal activity, and it is not subjected to the conflicts, which is the rule where urbanisation is widely overlapping on its territory. On the other hand, struggles between new rural people and farmers take place in the agglomerations and often lead, in municipal elections, to the replacement of the former by the latter.

A Social Diversity of Fringe which looks like the Diversity of French People

In the first years of periurbanisation (1968–1975), programs were intended to cater to the middle and executive classes, which were most interested in individual housing and had means of access to property. In fact, since a long time, well-to-do classes of the French society were interested in the "country", in the form of principal or secondary housing (for instance in the north of Lyon, on the side of the Saône, or in the far Parisian suburbs). In the Île-de-France region, there is a remarkable tropism towards the west: in Paris, first with Haussmann's planning, then the nearest suburbs, and more and more faraway until the rural spaces. People of the upper classes prefer to stay in old manors and some gated communities, as in the USA, which are strongly guarded.

At the other end of the social scale, the lower classes could take an interest in the fringe only when, since the 80's, the programs were developed far from agglomerations, thus offering land and property at lower cost. In these areas, there are mainly small size programs, of less than 50 houses. These are most often small municipal or private housing estates, and also individual buildings, plot by plot, in particular at the periphery of existing villages; sometimes the owner himself is the builder. With an economic crisis and unemployment, the population of the faraway fringe suffered because they were in debt, especially since living in the fringe is very expensive (transport for instance). In the fringe of the Parisian Region, there exist some pauperisation areas, which, since several years, create great economic and social problems.

Activities and Amenities in the Fringe

The residential areas represent about half of the urbanised surfaces in periurban districts. The other half is made up by different economic activities, amenities and collective services. Besides agriculture, industrial and tertiary activities are scattered over the fringe, but it is true that they are more numerous close to the old suburbs and especially in the metropolised districts, where the main "zones d'activités economiques" and the technology parks are found. Many boroughs planned small areas of economic activity, which provided an important number of jobs in different branches (metallurgy, mechanics, press, food production). In the tertiary sector, there are commercial centres and leisure parks.

Regarding the amenities that are following the local growth of population, there is definitely nearly always a more or less important delay in relation to the needs of the population of the fringe: It is the famous "vicious circle" of periurbanisation, which often leads to a "flight ahead" by the territorial councillors: the need for amenities set population growth going which starts again a new demand for amenities and so on.

Despite the large efforts made in this direction, periurban activities and amenities are not enough to satisfy the local demand, as regards jobs and services. The periurban areas are characterised by the continual need to resort to the metropolis, or to the main urban agglomeration, which leads to a great mobility of the periurban population, for work, shopping, school and leisure. Commuting constitutes one of the main criteria of fringe definition: The boroughs in which the majority of the active population doesn't work on the spot are evidently part of the fringe. From one census to another, one observes an important growth in the overall mobility of the population. This is not only due to the process of periurbanisation, but also to the evolution in the behavioural pattern, which concerns the whole French society.

Metropolisation and New Regulations

Periurbanisation Continues

Even if a policy of renewal and new development concerns again some old parts of big cities, in particular Paris, where the Schéma Directeur of 1994 confirms the need for renewing the old industrial estates, it is true that the census of March 1999 shows the continuation and extension of the periurban phenomenon. The new delimitation created by INSEE[1] of Zonage en Aires Urbaines (ZAU) which replaces the "Zones de Peuplement Industriel et Urbain" (ZPIU) clearly testify that.

An urban area is a group of boroughs constituted by an urban pole (town-centre and its suburbs) and by rural boroughs or urban units in which more than 40 per cent of the active resident population is working in the urban pole or in boroughs attracted by the pole: the census of 1999 established that 45 million inhabitants of France live in urban areas and 48 millions in a space with urban dominance (out of a total of 60 millions). These are divided into 354 urban areas.

It is not really the crude population growth, which generates periurbanisation in the rural environment, even if it always exists to some extent and if it concerns only the villages, because the urban boroughs have a tendency to stagnate or to lose population. It is above all a matter of a continued growth in mobility of the new rurals: in 1999, only 39 per cent of the active population was working in their residential borough against 45 per cent in 1990. This may be the main factor of periurbanisation in the 2000's: this element certainly explains the important increase in population in the big urban areas in comparison with the ZPIU of 1990.

Thus the urban area of Paris has more than 10 million inhabitants, the urban area of Lyon and Marseille more than 1.5 million, of Bordeaux and Toulouse more than 8,00,000, of Nantes 6,00,000 and of Grenoble 5,00,000 inhabitants.

If we take into account the other elements of mobility (purchases, leisure, school moving), this strengthens the scale of periurbanisation in so far as these flows are not mainly orientated towards the centre of the urban pole, but cut across the space in all directions, because secondary poles more or less supplied with activities and services have emerged: for instance the new towns or the "towns of the crown" in the Île-de-France (Meaux, Melun, etc.).

Metropolisation Induced Economic Inequalities

One of the main effects of metropolisation results from the fact that the new economic activities are concentrated in the great cities to the detriment of smaller towns. Thus, periurban areas of French million towns would be more favoured than those of other agglomerations: This means that the first would have a balance between housing, services and activities, while the second would be only concerned with housing and services directly linked to it.

On the whole, the reality corresponds to this image, but with slight differences: Thus, in the Île-de-France metropolitan region, we can distinguish areas with a higher and lower degree of periurbanisation. For instance, a great quarter northwest of the Department Seine-et-Marne is going to be metropolised, mainly close to Roissy-Charles-de-Gaulle airport and in the new town of Marne-la-Vallée, and a little in the old town Meaux. All the remaining parts of this Department, except the new town Sénart, represent a fringe in which agriculture dominates, besides some industrial and tertiary activities preceding the metropolisation. Certainly, Val d'Europe district in Marne-la-Vallée is a particular example of metropolisation, for the two Disneyland parks, the new urban centre and the regional shopping centre have increased its importance.

In the provinces, there are examples of beginning metropolisation in Lille-Est, Marseille-Nord, Lyon-Est, Bordeaux-Ouest, Toulouse-Sud-Est and Nice-Ouest. All the others periurban sectors do not contain tertiary or secondary activities (or very few) in the forefront of planning or renewal. Thus, we can speak of economic inequalities, but which are relative as far as the fringe is never completely without activities, for instance agriculture and food production.

Future Prospects: The New Law "Solidarity and Urban Renewal" (SRU)

We were seeing the change in the situation since the beginning of 90's: a significant growth in population mobility as part of metropolisation in some fringes. Facing this trend, the law of December 13th 2000 concerning the "Solidarity and Urban Renewal" (SRU) searches to promote a more consistent, more sustainable development of urban areas that shows more solidarity. In fact, this law takes again several elements contained in the previous laws: law Voynet (25/6/99) and law Chevènement (12/7/99). In particular, the question that refers to the promotion of sustainable development and inter-municipality.

The SRU law creates new urban planning documents, which replace the one created by the Land Use law of 1967. The "Schémas de Cohérence Territoriale" (SCOT) replace the Schémas Directeurs. They are prospective documents, which have to represent a clear project outlay held by a pluri-municipal structure. The "Plans Locaux d'Urbanisme" (PLU) replace the Plans d'Occupation des Sols (POS); they have to express the project stemming from the SCOT in a more flexible and more overall structure than the POS.

The Chevènement law created communities besides inter-municipality through boroughs and agglomeration: As in the new towns Syndicats d'Agglomération Nouvelle, professional tax is put in common, thus avoiding the inequalities between rich municipalities which have numerous activities and the poor which have few of them.

These new regulations seem well adapted to problems of the fringe: the lack of inter-municipality and the lack of consistent planning projects, financial inequalities between boroughs, degradation of rural and natural environment, etc. But it is necessary to test their application in the long run, and of course it is too early at this moment to comment: Unexpected effects are always to be feared, even with laws apparently well conceived!

Those results of the Schéma Directeur of 1994 of the Parisian Region proposals which accompany the operating of planning itself are relatively positive: struggle against pollution and risks, protection of the environment, in particular of green and agricultural spaces. On the contrary, land policy and town planning seem to have made little progress in the fringe: for instance, the function of relay which had to be played by the new and medium towns of the Parisian periphery did not operate, and periurbanisation continued more or less anarchical. Thus, the balance between the pro and contra is much divided, and we must be careful in our predictions of the outcome of the planning scheme. By all means, the planning of the fringe will stay for a long time; a bet on the outcome of the effects of the new regulations is difficult to win.

Conclusion

French periurbanisation concerns an increasingly greater part of the territory and of the population because, even if the residential migrations are going to decrease (the inhabitants of central parts of the towns going to settle in the far suburbs), the socio-demographic transformations of periurban towns and villages will play a dominant role: less and less persons are working near their home and in local activities (agriculture in particular), but more and more commute not only towards the centre of the metropole, but also towards the centres of peripheral activities.

Urban aspects of France have been deeply and for a long time modified. Even if periurbanisation suddenly stopped, which is actually not the case, its effects are not going to cease. Are the planners really equal to the fringe problems, or are they not overtaken by it?

Note

1. Editorial note: INSEE (Institut National de la Statistique et des Etudes Economiques), the French National Institute for Statistic and Economic Studies. Criteria for ZPIU of 1962 (Zones of Industrial or Urban Population) around an urban centre were 1. Industrial communes, defined as rural communes with several industrial, commercial or administrative units with 20 or more salaried people, and a cumulative total of 100 employed people, or 2. Rural non-industrial communes with few agricultural workers but an important share of people working outside the commune in the urban centre, the "dormitory communes".

Bibliography

Ascher, F. (1995): *Métapolis ou l'avenir des villes,* Editions Odile Jacob, Paris.

Bauer, G., J.M. Roux (1977): *La rurbanisation ou la ville éparpillée,* Le Seuil, Paris.

Dezert, B.A. Metton, J.Steinberg (1991): *La périurbanisation en France"* Sedes, Paris.

Dubois-Taisne, G. et Y. Chalas (sous la direction de) (1997): *La ville émergente,* L'Aube, Paris.

Veltz, P. (1996): *Mondialisation, villes et territoires. L'économie* d'archipel, PUF, Paris.

III

Urban Fringe of Different Indian Cities

15

The Fringe Areas of Kolkata Metropolis

Nature, Problems and Prospects

CHITTARANJAN PATHAK

Concept and Paradigm

The Urban Fringe areas emerge as the spatial counter part of the urbanisation and sub-urbanisation processes. In the earlier stages of such processes, urban places grow through rural–urban migration to the central part of the urban places. They grow in population and urban functions. They grow vertically through the processes of concentration while horizontal expansion remains a slow process. The urban places grow from small towns to medium size town and to a large metropolis in course of time and space. As the size increases and very high density is achieved at the core, horizontal expansion begins with spill over population and incompatible functions find their new locations in the periphery. These peripheral locations are sub-urban in nature, and are termed as *fringe* areas. They may be under-bound or over-bound to the urbanised tracts depending upon the flexibility or rigidity of administrative boundaries of the urban areas. If such location and relocation of functions and people in the urban periphery take place in unplanned manner, this could be termed as urban sprawl. The urban character declines from the urban limit towards rural areas. If the spatial process of urban growth measured in terms of change in population density, land use changes, addition and alteration of non-agricultural functions and occupations, and other development indicators are continuous in time and space, it may result in urban-rural continuum. The density of population declines to the fringe areas from the city core. The land use changes from agricultural use to non-agricultural ones; so is the case of occupational pattern of the residents. Such changes are brought about by the extension of the transport infrastructure network in linking such areas with the urban core both spatially and functionally. With the de-concentration process starting at the urban core, the fringe areas grow at faster rate than the core in people and functions. The rate of change of such urban dynamics is influenced by the supremacy of the urban core in attracting the people and functions from the hinterland areas. From the physical characteristics point of view, the fringe areas are different from both the rural areas and the urbanised areas. Their distinctiveness shall also change over time. Today's fringes may be integrated with the urban core and the new fringe will come up and will expand territorially. This spatial process is not going to stop but may be thwarted or accelerated depending upon disadvantageous factors or spatial dynamics.

The fringe areas are qualitatively and quantitatively different from both urban and rural areas. Their distinctiveness could be studied from the point of view of land use pattern, population dynamics, the social and economic characteristics and ambient environment. Their nature, problems and prospects vary from country to country and also from city to city because of the varying location and situational factors.

The Urban Fringe of Kolkata Metropolis

In this paper we shall take up the case of urban fringes of Kolkata Metropolis. The fringe area had been emerging since the period Kolkata exerted push back forces towards the migrants since when farther growth in population and functions could not be accommodated in the city core. Result was the development of urban-rural continuum.

A short history of the urbanisation process in and around Kolkata deserves a reference. The very siting of Kolkata around three villages – Sutanuti, Govindapur and Kolikata – was on the defensive eastern bank of the river Hooghly surrounded by waterlogged marshy areas in 1690 by Job Charnock of British East India Company. It is a colonial city of the colonial government set up as a trading cum-mercantile town and grew to a capital city of the British colonial empire. Predating the location of Kolkata, both the banks of the river Hooghly 45 km. south to 80 km. north were dotted with a number of trading river ports for performing river-borne trade and commerce. The river was the main artery of water transport. These trading ports attracted the location of agro-based and engineering industries and flourished during the colonial period, each growing towards each other along the road and railway axially to connect the city of Kolkata. Their growth was supported by the vast hinterland of agricultural produce such as jute-hemp, paddy and sugarcane and strengthened their economic base. The resultant spatial pattern of urban growth along the river Hooghly is the Kolkata conurbation. These nucleated towns; each growing towards each other formed the super-urban fringe of the Kolkata Metropolitan Urban Agglomeration – a zone in transition. While town-planning activities were limited to the administrative boundaries of the municipal towns, the fringe areas were left to the natural processes of unplanned growth resulting in a most problematic area.

The *'chance directed and chance erected'* city structure of Kolkata has grown with unplanned and haphazard urban fringe areas. During the post World War II period followed by the partition of Bengal, Independent India experienced with an unprecedented urban growth around Kolkata because of large-scale migration of refugees from across the eastern border. A large number of refugee colonies have emerged on the fringe areas of the towns in the conurbation. These indiscriminate locations of settlements in the rural periphery of the towns with indiscriminate business functions in the residential areas on the adjoining areas of the old towns and cities and petty industries have complicated the urban fringes structurally. These settlements are primarily residential in character, provided shelter to a large number of commuters to the metropolis for job and other opportunity. Their commutation has been facilitated by the axial layout of suburban rail and road and river transport corridor linking the towns and the fringes to the Metropolis. The Kolkata Metropolitan Urban Agglomeration is characterised by hundreds of municipal towns in the conurbation and the Kolkata-Howrah Metropolises each joining each other to form a megalopolis in the making. The resultant pattern is urban-rural continuum. The cities and towns of the conurbation are no longer isolated units but functionally and spatially linked settlements with the Metropolis.

Planning Process in the Kolkata Metropolitan Region

Calcutta Metropolitan Planning Organisation (CMPO) was set up in 1961 to look into the planning problems of Calcutta Metropolis. The CMPO published its perspective plan namely: "The Basic Development Plan – 1966–86." This was followed by the "Master Plan for Comprehensive Traffic and Transportation Plan" and a "Plan for Water Supply, Sewerage and Drainage" for the metropolitan area. The CMPO also recommended the setting up of CMDA in 1970 to prepare the Action Plan for the whole metropolitan area.

The CMDA delineated the metropolitan planning area, which has been revised in 2001.The present CMA has been delineated according to West Bengal Metropolitan Planning Committee Act of 1994 with statutory boundary in 2001. The CMA (now KMA) covers the whole of Kolkata conurbation and is composed of three Municipal Corporations of Kolkata, Howrah and Chandan Nagar, thirty-four Municipalities, and twenty-three Panchayat Samities consisting of seventy non-municipal urban areas, and fourteen urban outgrowths (Census towns). The KMA area has changed to some extent since its inception in 1970s. For the preparation of a perspective plan for Kolkata – 2011, the State Planning Board (SPB) modified the CMC in 1990. The present CMA (KMA) area has been delineated for the preparation of a perspective plan – 2025 for integrated development of the entire area including the fringe areas. The Table 1 shows the composition of the CMA (VISION–2025). The population figures in the table related to the Census of 1991. The population of CMA is going to increase from 14.96 million in 2001 to 17.70 million in 2011, 20.70 million in 2021 and by 2025, it will reach 22.04 million.

Table 1 *Composition of CMA (KMA), 1991*

	No. of Units	*Area in sq. km.*	*Share percentage of Area*	*Share percentage of Population*	*Population in 2001 (in millions)*
Municipal Corporations	3	271.31	15.20	43.85	6.07
Municipalities	38	607.75	34.05	41.62	6.55
Non-municipal urban areas (Census towns)	70	178.34	9.99	6.34	
Outgrowths	14	14.03	0.78	0.37	2.33
Rural areas	22	713.61	39.98	7.82	
Total		1785.04	100.00	100.00	14.96

Structural Modification of Kolkata Metropolis and its Fringe Areas

Independent India inherited a dualistic urban structure of Calcutta metropolis with anglicised planned areas on the south side and the unplanned and congested north with primarily the indigenous people and migrants from its hinterland. The planned part with military cantonments, civil line and better residences was occupied by the people of European origin. The northern part was not only congested residential-cum-commercial establishments with narrow winding roads, lanes and bye lanes; this area even housed some palatial buildings of the rural zamindars. Such buildings bear the testimony of rural prosperity enjoyed by the landlords. The concept of urban fringe was unknown and the process of concentration agglomerated a high density of urbanites within the city. The city boundary was defined by a sharp break in population density and administrative boundary.

Since the partition of Bengal followed by a flux of refugees from Bangladesh Kolkata grew very fast primarily settling the migrants in the urban fringes. Up to 1951 the density gradient of population from the core was quite steep and there was a clear break of the high-density profile on the periphery. Since 1961, there has been a de-concentration process set in with the expanding urban horizon. The urban fringes have emerged with the resettlement refugee colonies. The city core with high population density could hardly afford to absorb the new migrants. As a matter of fact, the spill over process started towards the fringe areas as the city planners made provision for housing with infrastructure facilities in the fringe areas. Thus, the urban fringes faced a quiet revolution of sub-urbanisation process, and structural modifications. The fringe areas have experienced changes in population density, land use and physical, social and economic environment.

Urbanisation, Population Growth and Density Pattern in CMA

The Table 1 shows the aerial spread of the CMA in 1991. A total population of 12.52 million of CMA has been distributed over 1,785 sq. km. with an overall density of 7,012 person per sq. km. The Kolkata Municipal Corporation (KMC) accounts for 11.07 per cent in area and 35.15 per cent of KMA's population. Other two municipal corporations of Howrah and Chandan Nagar extend over 4.13 per cent in area and 8.71 per cent of KMA's population. 38 municipal towns sharing 34.05 per cent area accounts for 41.62 of KMA's population. 70 non-municipal urban areas occupy only 9.99 per cent area supports 6.34 per cent of its population. A vast rural fringe of these urban areas share 39.98 per cent of land, but only 7.81 per cent of KMA's population.

The density is highest in the KMC with three times of the average density. The average density in the municipalities is 8,573 per sq. km. The Table 2 has recorded the population dynamics of KMA. The population growth during 1981–91 was 20.95 per cent. Highest growth rate was during 1961–71, i.e., 26.58 per cent. All the settlements in the KMA are growing in population but least growth was in KMC (6.61%). This has been reflected in the declining share of KMC's in KMA's population.

Table 2 *Population Growth, Density Pattern and Level of Urbanisation in CMA, West Bengal and India: 1971–2001*

Year	*Population in million*			*Level of Urbanisation*			*Decennial Growth in CMA in %*	*Population Density in CMA per sq. km.*
	India	*W.B.*	*CMA*	*India*	*W.B.*	*CMA*		
1971	548.16	44.31	8.53	19.87	24.75	93.60	21.81	4760
1981	685.15	54.48	10.40	23.73	26.47	93.17	21.91	5804
1991	846.30	68.08	12.53	26.10	26.50	92.19	20.45	7012
2001	1027.20	80.22	14.96	27.78	28.03	—	19.39	8379

The level of urbanisation in West Bengal is 27.50 per cent (1991) with 18.7 million urban people of which 61.71 per cent or 11.54 million reside in KMA in area of 900 sq. km. KMA mainly has accounted for high level of urbanisation in West Bengal. When KMA's urban population is excluded the level of urbanisation would come down to only 12.91 per cent. More than a quarter of KMA's populations are migrants (25.92%). About 40 per cent of the migrants to KMA are from West Bengal and 33.7 per cent from other states (Table 3). A limited number of migrants could be accommodated in the KMC, the majority, however, had to go outside of the Metropolis. Because a decentralised urbanisation process has started in West Bengal, the KMA's share of West Bengal urban population is going to decline to 50 per cent by 2025 against its share of 64 per cent in 1991.

Table 3 *Migrant Population in CMA in 1991*

Source	*Calcutta City*	*CMA*
West Bengal (other places)	27.91%	40.35%
Other States in India	45.78%	33.70%
Outside India	26.28%	25.92%
Unclassified	0.03%	0.03%
Total migrants	100.00%	100.00%

Total migrants to Calcutta in 1991 were 7,13,000 and to CMA 26,17,000 persons

Population Density Changes in Kolkata and in its Fringe Areas

In this paper we have examined the population density changes in Kolkata and its fringe areas, land use pattern, physical, social and economic characteristics and environmental factors. We shall also examine the town planning provisions extended to the fringe areas in respect of designing and development of new urban areas to decentralise the urban functions and housing the spill over population and the new migrants towards Kolkata.

The prevailing push back forces at the metro core area would divert the urban-ward migration stream to the urban fringes. The nature of absorption of the migrant people either from the rural areas or the displaced people from the city core is reflected in the density changes in them. The rate of growth in population density is much higher in the fringe areas than in the city core. The density changes during 1961–71 were the highest. The rate of density change was still high during 1971–81 and 1981–91 but lower than that of the decade 1961–71. If the present trend continues, there will be quantitative change in the fringe areas but may result in a degraded environment as the provision for infrastructure such as water supply, drainage, transport and communication facilities for health and sanitation and other social amenities take a long time to provide unless the town planning measures are introduced immediately. As the residents look for employment and living in the metro-city, they will continue to commute. The urban fringes need to be transformed into work places too, without which there will be increasing pressure on the suburban transport network. Figures 1 to 4 have illustrated population density pattern of CMA for 1981–2001 for both the urban and rural fringe areas giving density changes and population growth.

Figure 1 *Population Growth Rates: 1991–2001 – Panchayat Samiti Area representing the Kolkata Urban Fringe*

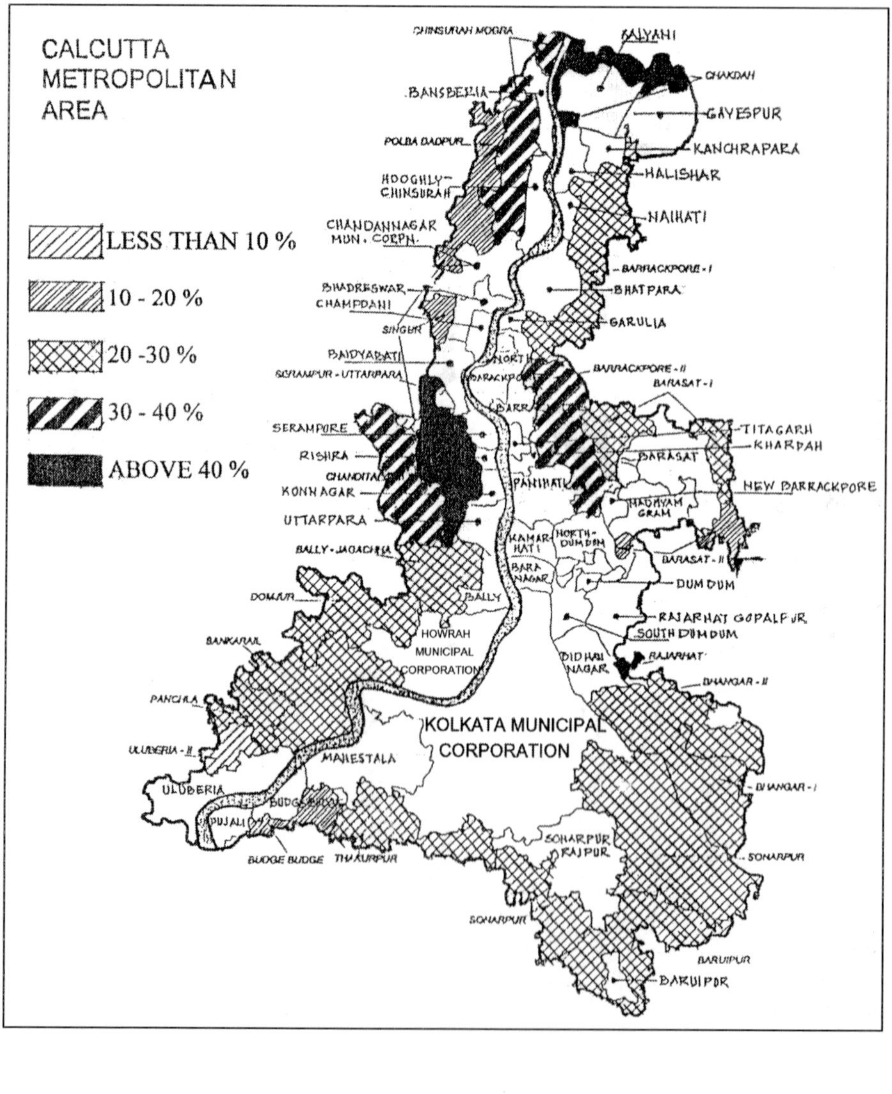

Figure 2 *Density Pattern: 2001 – Panchayat Samiti Area*

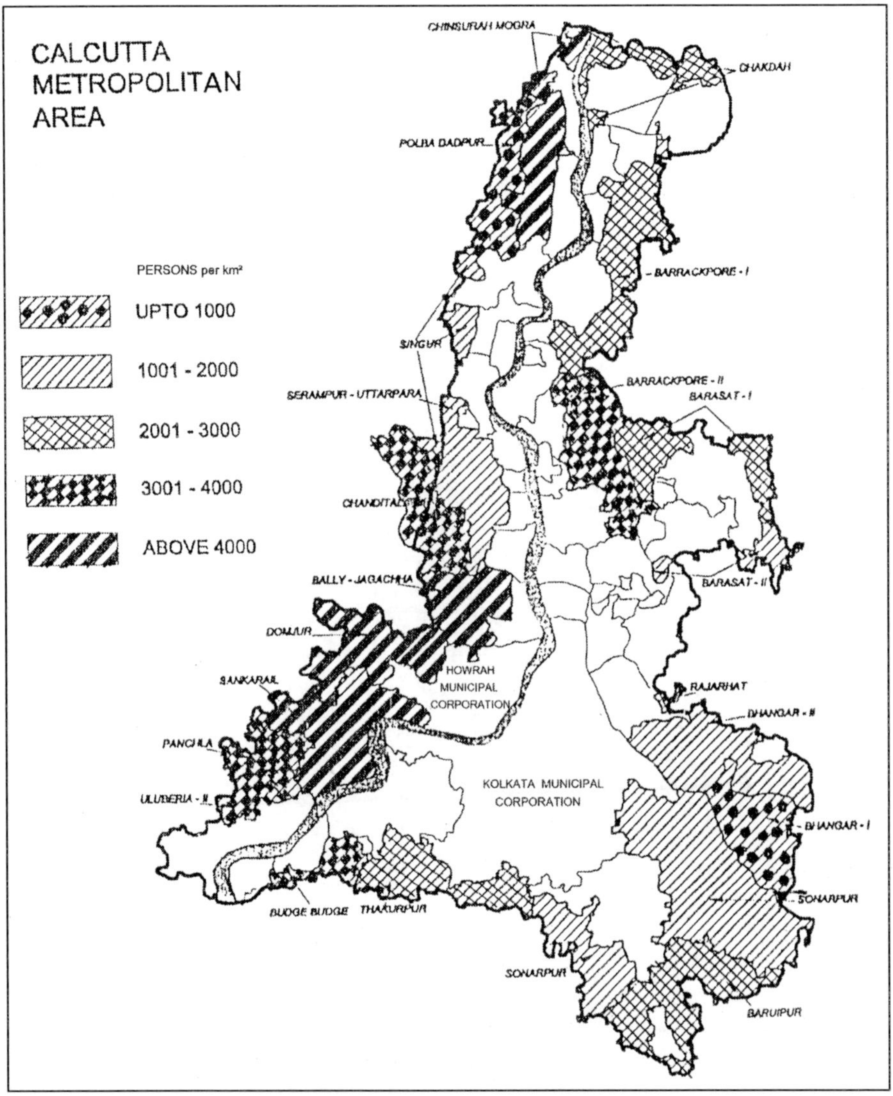

The spatial pattern of urbanisation in KMA could be explained by the urban sprawl. "The built-up land in CMA stretched in a linear pattern on both banks of Hooghly from south to north has changed to ribbon development pattern along the major transportation corridor. The recent trend of urban sprawl in urbanising the fringe areas, the ribbon development has formed a corridor and may expand beyond the present CMA boundary, and the CMA may not be able to accommodate future urbanisation in spatial terms. The built up land has been increasing at an annual rate of 10 sq. km. since 1960" (VISION–2025). The urbanisation pressure is so high that urban sprawl will engulf the good agricultural/plantation fringe lands.

Figure 3 *Growth Rates: 1991–2001 – Municipal Corporation and Municipalities*

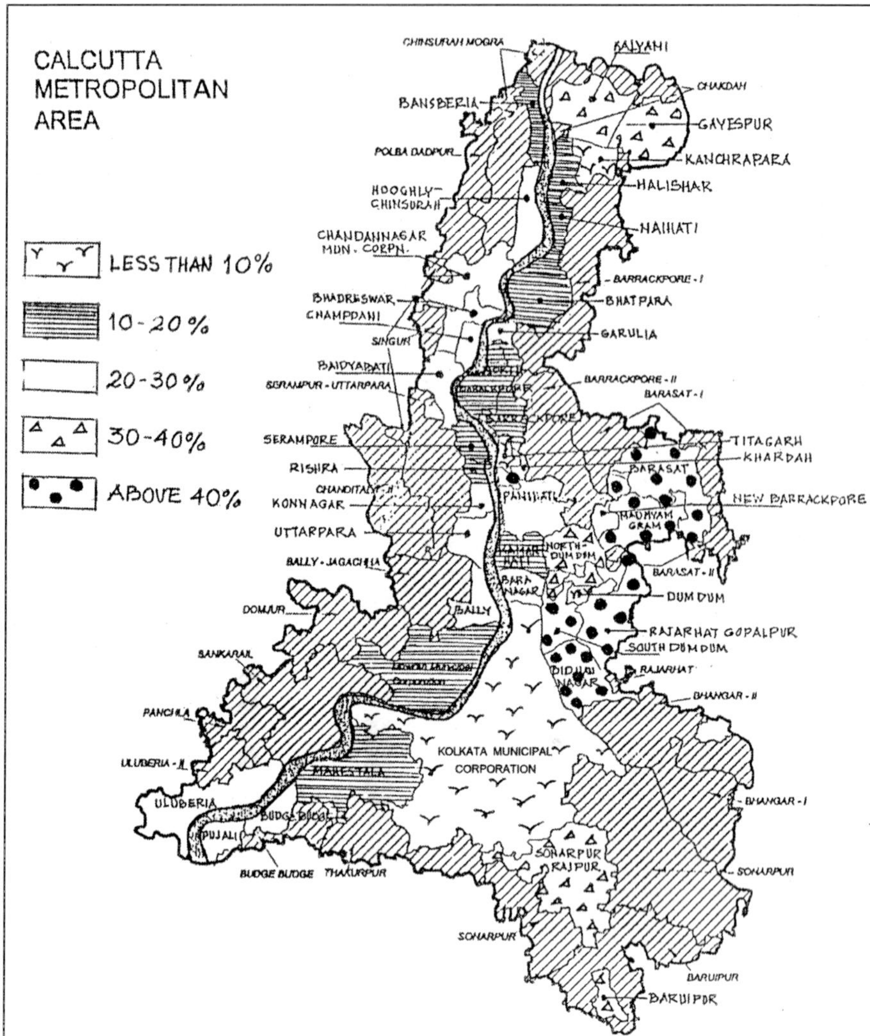

"The Mega-city of Kolkata serves as the hub of several functional networks including imports and exports, telecommunications, international airlines, and international finance. This determines its extensive global linkages. In the borderless economy of today, it is the acquisition and accumulation of functions that determine the centrality role of a mega-city like Kolkata in the world economy" (VISION–2025).

Economic Profile of KMA

There has been continuous decline in industrial growth in and around Kolkata since 1980s; still 80 per cent of West Bengal industries are located in KMA. The industrial structure is composed of coal and steel based engineering industries, jute and cotton textile industries, chemical, paper and paper products. While these traditional labour intensive industries are in doldrums, a hundred hectare electronic and information technology complex has come up in the Salt Lake City (Bidhannagar) only 6 km. east of Kolkata with lot of promise. Rajarhat Township has been planned on the northeast of Kolkata fringe for a 400 ha light industrial complex. In the north of the KMA, Kalyani Township and industrial area has been planned forty years back but yet to grow fully. Here is an example of lack of economic growth although infrastructure has been provided. It has been constrained by the absence of a structure plan.

There has been steady growth of the informal sector, which was facilitated by the tertiary and quaternary sectoral growth. The extended suburban rail and road network has been integrating the urban fringe to the urban economies.

Land Use Development Pattern in the Fringe Areas

The phenomena of urban sprawl with all its characteristics are seen clearly in the metropolitan fringe areas. Cheaper land price and low rent in the periphery attracts the migrants as the core area of the metropolis has already been

Figure 4 *Density Pattern: 2001 – Municipal Corporations and Municipalities*

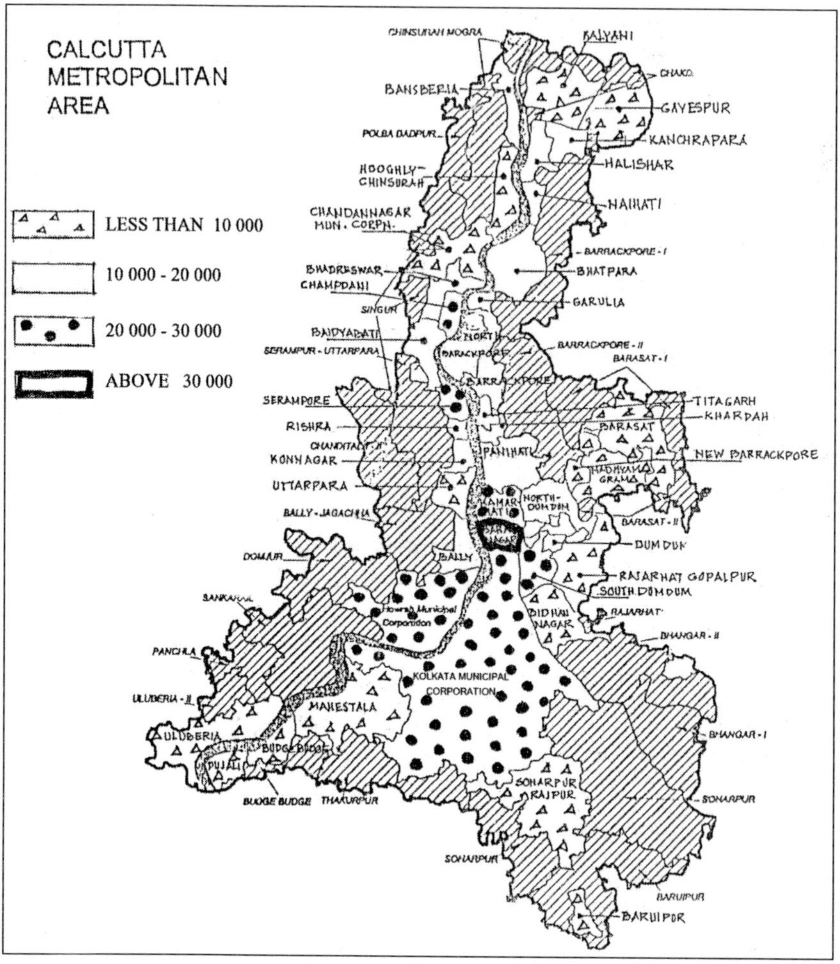

saturated. It is true that the old city houses a large number of slum dwellers, farther scope for slum development in the city core has been restricted. The new migrant could only occupy the footpaths or unhealthy canal sides or railway yards. The new home seekers could settle in the fringe areas and commute to the city for employment. These settlements develop like dormitory suburbs without having any near-by work place. The main advantage of the peripheral settlements development is the availability of buildable land with price lower than the urban areas and with suburban rail transport to the city. These new commuters cycle or walk to the nearest railway station and then take the rail or trunk roads to reach the place of work The level of land development and accessibility in the fringe area is poor and unplanned. Although having lot of greenery and abundant low-lying water bodies, the fringe areas could hardly be maintained and become mosquito infested. The ambient environment is far from being conducive to healthy living even though population density is quite low.

The planned settlements of Bidhannagar (Salt Lake City) and Rajarhat township in the eastern fringe, Garia and Sonarpur townships in the south-east, Kalyani in the north and Kona-Dankuni township in the west have been emerging as decentralised concentration of urban development in the fringe as satellite towns, the rest of the fringe has been left for unplanned occupation by the settlers. The land use-zoning plan has to be implemented in the fringe area for integrated urban-rural development. The spontaneous uncontrolled and unplanned settlement development will lead to haphazard urban sprawl. Already a large number of people have settled indiscriminately; a development plan cannot be prepared easily *ab initio* and has to incorporate the existing land uses. The development plan has to be superposed. This has made the task of town planning more difficult.

Conclusion

There is a great similarity in respect of unplanned fringe character of Kolkata Metropolis with that of other metropolises of India. Historically however, the emergence of Kolkata conurbation as a poly-nuclear urban agglomeration is different from others. There was a sharp break in the urban-rural continuum until India's Independence when a high rate of urbanisation and large scale migration from Bangladesh and intense push force operating in the rural hinterland of the metropolis agglomerated a large number of people in and around Kolkata. Most of the rural fringe areas with low lying land and good for agriculture or dumping ground of urban solid waste disposal have been changed to semi-urban or suburban development. The traditional paddy cultivation in the urban fringe has been replaced by commercial horticultural cropping pattern feeding the Calcuttans with much cheaper fruits and vegetables. Both the solid wastes and the city sewage water are recycled to produce good varieties of crops, even the sewage water is used for irrigation and sewage water pond fisheries. Once the fringe lands are stabilised, settlement comes up threatening the very survival of the water bodies. These developments have far-reaching ecological and environmental consequences.

Since the inception of CMDA in 1970s, there have been various efforts to organise planned urban development in the fringe areas. Some of them are planned as townships: Kalyani in the north, and Kona-Dankuni in the west but could not take off until recently. The Bidhannagar and Rajarhat in the east and northeast and Garia-Sonarpur in the southeast respectively have been growing very fast. The east of Kolkata has drawn the attention of the town planners who bring out the adverse environmental impact of urban development there, but are required to plan the location of urban settlements in the east of Kolkata as they are helpless and follow the trend. The desired pattern of urban development should develop on the west bank of the river Hooghly with greater accessibility to the rest of India but the east of Kolkata has been urbanising fast where land development is a costly affair. The low-lying areas and water bodies are to be reclaimed for making the land buildable. Such development is not sustainable environmentally and may upset the ecological balance, as large quantity of ground water has to be tapped for meeting various needs of the people.

The townships in the fringe areas could relieve the urbanisation pressure on the metropolis but has increased the commutation to it. To release the pressure of commutation and on the suburban transport network, the fringe towns need to be planned for the location of economic activities, create employment opportunity and transform them from dormitory towns to self contained urban settlements and reduce the friction of space between the place of work and place of residence.

Acknowledgements

The author is grateful to Dr Chand Moni Basak of CMDA for preparing all the illustrations and for compiling the tables for this paper.

References

CMDA (1990): Plan for Metropolitan Development – 1990–2015, August.

CMDA (2001): Perspective Plan of CMA-2025, VISION–2025, Executive Summary.

Dept. of Environment, Govt. of West Bengal (1997): Calcutta Environment Management and Action Plan.

Ghosh, Santosh (1998): *Metropolitan Planning and Governance in Asia and Pacific: Case Study on Calcutta Area* (A UNCRD Research Project).

Pathak, C.R. (1991): Rural–Urban Continuum in the Context of Metro-Region, *Proceedings of 39th Town and Country Planning Seminar on Metropolitan Decentralization*.

Som, Nishit (1991): *Metropolitan Land Use in Future: A Perspective Plan for Calcutta: 2011*, Supplementary Volume 2, State Planning Board, Calcutta.

South Asian Foundation for Human Initiatives (1999): Socio-economic Survey of Calcutta, Environment Improvement Project.

16

Dynamics of the Rural Segment around a Planned City and the Need for a Broader Framework

A Case Study of Chandigarh (U.T.)

K.D. SHARMA, PIPPA DEODHAR AND BHAWANA BALI

Ever since its recognition as a major feature of expanding modern cities, the urban fringe as a land use zone, social entity and a functional region has been a theme for a number of studies. Initially, the focus was on its definition and demarcation. In more recent years its management and planning has emerged as a major area of concern.[1]

It is commonly accepted that the characteristics acquired by the urban fringe are a response to the processes and demands generated in the cities, which in turn are closely associated with the nature and size of the city. The former would include the functions specific to a city and the latter the population and physical size. In recent decades, urban planning has emerged as a strong determinant of both, particularly in the case of planned cities. In such cases, the city plans also include a framework for future expansion, accompanied by the requisite legal sanctions and institutional support for the plan proposals.[2] The urban fringe development and its characteristics, in a context in which the direction of future development of a city is predetermined, the processes of development specified and, legal sanctity provided to the plan proposals, form an interesting theme of study. It is expected that such a study would help in a better understanding of the processes and characteristics of urban fringe in cities where a planning and management framework already exists. It is also suggested that such a study would help in the identification of measures for a better management of the urban fringe in planned as well as evolved cities. For this purpose, the rural segment of Chandigarh Union Territory, which surrounds Chandigarh, a completely planned city, has been studied.

Objective, Sources of Data and Methodology

The paper describes the changes that have taken place in the characteristics of population, land use, and settlements in the rural segment of Chandigarh

Union Territory during 1971–2001. It also relates these changes to the planned expansion of Chandigarh city. An attempt is also made to suggest a strategy for a more effective management of the developments taking place in this rural segment.

The paper is based on published data from the Census of India, unpublished data from revenue records of the Chandigarh administration and primary data and observations from the field. The paper comprises of three parts. Part 1 describes the genesis and development plan of the city. Part II deals with the characteristics of the rural segment forming the fringe of the city and Part III takes up the policy and management issues and suggests measures for a broader framework for city planning.

I

Freedom for India in 1947 was accompanied by partition of the country and emergence of the two dominions, India and Pakistan (East and West). It also divided the province of Punjab between India and Pakistan. The region comprising West Punjab in which Lahore, the historic capital city of the province was located, went to Pakistan. This left the Indian part of Punjab without an administrative centre. The Punjab Government decided to build a new state capital rather than locate the administrative functions at one of the already existing urban centres.[3] As many as eight sites were examined before the selection of the present site of Chandigarh.[4] The present plan of the city was prepared by Charles-Edward Jeanneret, better known as Le Corbusier and his team.[5] The Chandigarh project was formally declared open on Oct.7, 1953 by the then President of India, Dr Rajendra Prasad. It was the second planned state capital of independent India, the first being Bhubaneshwar, whose foundation stone was laid in April 1948 by the then Prime Minister of India, Pandit Jawaharlal Nehru. The third planned state capital is Gandhinagar, whose Master Plan was approved in 1966 and it was declared the capital of Gujarat in 1970.[6]

The site of Chandigarh has the Shivalik Hills backed by Himalayan ranges in the north, and two seasonal streams, Sukhna *choe* and Patiali Rao *choe* to the east and west respectively. These natural barriers define the control on the expansion of the city to the north, east and west. The future expansion of the city was thus to take place only to its south.[7]

The plan proposals for Chandigarh brought into practice such modern town planning concepts as zoning, modular structure and traffic separation. Chandigarh was planned to develop on a cross-axis, with the administrative complex located on the northern side and the city-centre at the junction of the two main roads. The industrial and educational zones were to form the eastern and western parts of the city respectively. The city was planned to develop on a formal gridiron pattern formed by east-west and north-south running streets defining individual sectors, the basic functional unit of the city (Figure 1). The city, planned for a population of 5 lakh persons, was to develop in phases. Under Phase I, thirty sectors were to be developed for a population of 1.5 lakh people, and additional 17 sectors were to be developed for a population of 3.5 lakh people under Phase II. The target population of each sector was specified in the plan. Evidently, the Phase II sectors located in the southern part were planned as high-density residential areas. The plan proposals included architectural and building controls and zoning regulations. These were provided legal sanctity through suitable legislation.[8] The legal sanctity to the Chandigarh Project was provided by the Capital of Punjab (Development and Regulation) Act passed by the Indian Parliament in 1952 and endorsed by Punjab Government in December 1952. To regulate and control development around Chandigarh the Punjab Legislature passed the Punjab New Capital (Periphery Control) Act 1952. The Act was initially applicable within a radius of 8 km. around Chandigarh. This limit was later extended to 16 km.

The present political-administrative set-up, in which Chandigarh emerged as Union Territory, and the city became the administrative headquarters of the Union Territory and the states of Punjab as well as Haryana came into existence on Nov. 1, 1966, due to the reorganisation of Punjab state. It influenced the city in two ways, (i) a proliferation in the administrative function of the city resulted in an increase in the demand for housing and created a larger employment base, particularly in the informal sector, and (ii) the emergence of a clearly demarcated rural segment to be administered by the U.T. administration and over which the city was to expand. A total of 54 villages had comprised the pre-urban landscape of the present Union Territory of Chandigarh. Due to acquisition of land for development of the city, their number was reduced to 34 in 1971. In the following decades this rural segment has decreased consistently due to urban expansion in the Union Territory (Figure 1).

The introduction of meticulous planning and building controls and the massive scale of their execution made the coming up of Chandigarh a landmark development in town planning in India. The success of the city can be judged from its growth trends. The population of city was 38,377 in 1957.[9] The first census, after the establishment of the city, in 1961 recorded its population as 89,321 people. In 2001 the population of the city had increased to 8,088.796 people. The area of the city increased from 38.68 sq. km. in 1961 to 79.34 sq. km. in 2001.

Corbusier had visualised Chandigarh as a "city offering all amenities to the poorest of the poor citizens to lead a dignified life".[10] Interestingly, the presence of large number of construction workers in the city and other segments of the informal sector, an integral part of urban economies in developing countries, could not find a place in the plan proposals.[11] Added to this was the problem of people displaced due to the acquisition of land for expansion of the city. This resulted in the coming up of hutments at different locations in the city and its fringe. Although policies for providing alternate sites for rehabilitation, construction of resettlement colonies, EWS housing have been followed consistently by the Chandigarh Administration, only 47.56 per cent of the dwellings in labour colonies comprised authorised settlements in 1998.[12] The present pattern of distribution of such settlements resembles the one commonly found in the fringe areas of large evolved towns, that is, a concentration on the peripheries.[13]

The rural segment of Chandigarh U.T. represents unique situation in which the villages are included in U.T. administratively but many of their functional aspects are influenced by the adjacent location of two cities other than Chandigarh, namely Mohali and Panchkula (Figure 1). The former had a population of 1,23,284 and the latter 1,40,992 people in 2001. The layout of Mohali forms a continuation of the Chandigarh city plan in the south. Administratively, it is located in Ropar district in the state of Punjab. Panchkula city adjoins Chandigarh U.T. on the eastern side. It is the district headquarters of the district of the same name in the state of Haryana.

II

Changes in Area and Number of Villages

A fundamental characteristic of the rural segment of Chandigarh U.T. has been a continuous reduction in its real/actual extent. Of the fifty-four villages, which comprised the area presently constituting the U.T., seventeen villages covering approximately 8,500 acres (34.34 sq. km.) of land were acquired in 1949 for Phase I of the development of Chandigarh city.[14] In the 1951 Census the entire population of 24,261 people living in the area now comprising the U.T. was recorded as being rural. At the end of the next decade, i.e., in 1961 the rural population figure was 20,619 people and the number of villages 37, which included six uninhabited villages. By 1971 three more villages had been acquired completely for the development of the city reducing their number to 34, out of which 8 were uninhabited. Of the total area of 114.00 sq. km. in 1971, the rural segment comprised 56.40 sq. km. Over the next thirty years it decreased consistently and covered 34.66 sq. km. in 2001, a decrease of 21.74 sq. km. In 2001 the number of villages had decreased to 24, all of which were inhabited (Table 1).

Table 1 *Chandigarh U.T.: Changes in the Area and Population of the Rural Segment (1971–2001)*

Attribute/Year	*1971*	*1981*	*1991*	*2001*	*Remarks*
Area (km^2)	56.40	45.67	36.00	34.66	Loss of 21.74 km^2 to city expansion since 1971
No. of Villages	34	29	25	24	Ten villages acquired for city expansion since 1971
Uninhabited Villages	8	3	—	N.A.	All villages inhabited since 1991

Changes in Rural Land Use

Although the process of acquisition of rural land has been a continuous one, it was never uniform, either in terms of area acquired or the number of villages affected, e.g., during 1986–87 only 46.13 hectares of land was acquired, and the number of villages affected was 14. In comparison, during 1996–97, the area acquired was 228.26 hectares and the number of villages affected was 12. In some cases, the entire area of a village was acquired resulting in a reduction in the number of villages; in others the acquisition was partial resulting in a change in the total area of villages. During the period 1966 when the U.T. came into existence, and 1997 for which latest revenue data is available, the number of villages having an area of less than 81 hectares increased from seven to seventeen, while the number of medium sized villages, having an area between 81 and 405 hectares, decreased from 18 to nine.[15] The change in the number of villages over the decades is given in Table 1. Almost the entire acquisition of rural land has taken place on the southern side of Chandigarh city, the direction earmarked for its expansion. As in the case of fringe development in other cities, a very high proportion of acquired land (79.66%) came from Net Area Sown and Land Not Available for Cultivation (19.30%). This was followed by Culturable Waste Land and Fallow Land. There was no acquisition of area under forest (Table 2).

Table 2 *Chandigarh U.T.: Change in Area under Rural Land Use (1966–97)*

Land Use Category	*Area in ha 1967*	*Area in ha 1997*	*Absolute Change (% Change)*	*Per cent in Total*
Net Sown Area	3,957.16	2,021.06	–1,936.10 (–48.83)	79.66
Fallow Land	68.80	61.92	–6.88 (–10.00)	0.28
Culturable Waste Land	47.35	29.14	–18.21 (–38.46)	0.74
Land Not Available for Cultivation	1,117.78	648.74	–469.04 (–41.96)	19.33
Forest	75.27	75.27	0.00 (0.00)	0.00
Total Area	5,266.36	2,836.13	–2,430.23 (–46.14)	99.98

Source: Estate Office, Chandigarh U.T.

The acquisition of land has resulted in a reduction in the Total Geographical Area of individual villages. However, the basic pattern of rural land use continues to persist, with the highest proportion of land being under Net Area Sown, reflecting the compulsions of the rural agricultural economy. Interestingly, while there has been a decrease of 3.88 per cent points in the proportion of Net Area Sown as compared to 1966, the area under Fallow, Culturable Waste Land, and Land Not Available for Cultivation has registered a marginal increase.[16]

This is related to the apprehension of acquisition of land in the immediate future in case of Fallow Land and Culturable Waste Land, and an increase in the use of land for non-agricultural uses, particularly construction for housing and other activities.

Changes in Population Attributes

There has been a consistent increase in the rural population of Chandigarh U.T. since 1971 (Table 3). Since the number of villages during this period has declined, two implications of the increase in population have been (i) a decrease in the number of uninhabited villages and (ii) a restructuring of the existing villages in terms of their population size. While there were eight uninhabited villages in the U.T. in 1971, all villages have been inhabited since 1991. Interestingly, the smallest populations of three and one person in 1971 and 1991 respectively were recorded in villages, which did not have a legally demarcated *abadi* area as per revenue records, and referred to persons who had illegally built hutments over village land.[17] In terms of population size, the number of villages with a population of more than 2,000 people increased from only one in 1971 to 12 in 1991. In comparison, the number of villages with a population of less than 1,000 people decreased from 18 to 7 during the same period (Table 3). The villages registering large populations are located mostly along the southern margins of Chandigarh city, a location that provides their residents easy access to different employment centres in and around Chandigarh. However, the growth of population in individual villages has not followed a consistent trend over the decades, and has been influenced by such factors as development of specific functions and their location in Chandigarh city, e.g., expansion of Industrial Area in the eastern part of the city; relocation and rehabilitation sites provided by the Administration mostly on the western margin of the city; security of tenure for a longer period and, housing made available by the local village residents.

The trend of growth of rural population and its socio-economic attributes in Chandigarh U.T. present an interesting phenomenon and are suggestive of the impact of development of Chandigarh city as well as the character that the rural population has acquired over the decades. A comparison of different population attributes since 1971, given in Table 3, suggests that the decade 1981–1991 was crucial in determining the present characteristics of the population residing in the rural fringe of Chandigarh city. This is the decade during which the Phase II sectors (Nos. 31 to 47) developed at a fast pace, generating considerable employment in construction and the informal sector. It was also during this period that an area of about 141 hectares was acquired for ongoing and proposed development of the city, creating greater pressure in the rural areas. Further during this decade the rural population of U.T. registered an almost dramatic change in its characteristics, viz., it increased by 130.06 per cent (an absolute increase of 37,417 people), the highest ever; its sex ratio declined by 56 females/1,000 males, the maximum decrease ever; the percentile increase in the proportion of literate population (3.55 percentage points) was the lowest ever; the growth rate Scheduled Castes population (107.54%) was highest ever (significantly the proportion of this segment in the total population declined indicating a higher contribution of non-Scheduled Castes segment); and there was a phenomenal growth in the proportion of working people by 165.43 per cent.

The overall trends of change in the attributes of rural population in Chandigarh U.T. can be summarised as, a higher rate of growth as compared to its urban counterpart in spite of a decreasing areal extent; a decline in sex ratio by 62 females/1,000 males while urban sex ratio improved by 54; an increase in proportion of literate population by 45.71 per cent points as compared to the urban figure of 17.56; a marginal decrease by 0.32 percentage points in the proportion of Scheduled Castes population as compared to an increase by 5.74 percentage points in the urban segment during 1971–1991; and an increase in the proportion of working population by 8.3 percentage points as compared to the figure of 3.87 for the urban segment.

Table 3 *Chandigarh U.T.: Changes in Population Attributes of Rural Segment (1971–2001)*

Attribute/Year	*1971*	*1981*	*1991*	*2001*	*Remarks*
Villages with population of +2,000 persons	1	7	12	N.A.	Highest village population in 1971, 5,255 persons, and 10,270 persons in 1991
Villages with population of less than 1,000 persons	18	12	7	N.A.	Lowest village population 03 persons in 1971 and 01 persons in 1991
Population (% growth)	24,311	28,769 (18.34)	66,186 (130.06)	92,118 (39.18)	+6,7807 (278.91% growth) Comparative urban value 247.21 per cent since 1971
Sex Ratio (Females/1,000 males) (Change)	683	688 (+5)	632 (-56)	621 (-11)	(-) 62. Urban sex ratio improves by +54 since 1971
Per cent Literate population (percentile change)	30.52	44.72 (14.20)	48.27 (3.55)	76.23 (27.96)	Percentile gain of 45.71 percentage points since 1971; comparative urban figure 17.56 percentage points
Per cent Scheduled Castes population (% growth)	21.68	23.68 (29.20)	21.36 (107.54)	N.A.	Decrease of 0.32 percentage points; comparative urban figure +5.74 during 1971–1991
Proportion of workers (% growth)	35.11	35.84 (20.84)	41.36 (165.43)	43.41 (46.09)	Increase by 8.3 percentage points since 1971; comparative urban figure 3.87

Changes in Residential Housing

One of the major impacts of increase rural population can be evidenced in the changes in rural residential housing attributes. In the study area the number of rural census houses increased from 8,308 to 26,428 during 1971–2001 (Table 4). In this case also the decade 1981–1991 is notable for registering the highest increase (from 7,099 to 21,816 census houses). A similar trend can be identified for the increase in the number of census houses put to residential use, which increased from 5,499 in 1971 to 19,716 in 2001 (Table 5). The increase during 1981–1991 was from 5205 to 16,577 residential houses. There was, however, only a marginal decrease in the number of persons per residential census house during 1971–2001 (Table 4). Thus, the total housing stock as well as the number of houses put to residential use has increased. However, there have been significant developments reflecting the changing character of residential housing, e.g., the proportion of households living in rented accommodation has increased by 23.90 percentage points, while those of living in owned houses decreased by 26.09 percentage points during 1971–2001 (Table 4). The proportion of households living in one-room houses has increased from 60 per cent in 1971 to 71.30 per cent in 2001. The highest proportion of households living in one-room houses was recorded in 1991 (81.35%). Taken together these attributes suggest an increasing trend towards renting out residential accommodation while total residential stock has increased. It also suggests an increasing presence of migrant population comprised of small families or single member households. At present, about 80 per cent of the total census houses are being used for residential purposes, 8.3 per cent as shops and offices and 3.1 per cent for residence-cum other uses (Table 5).

Table 4 *Chandigarh U.T.: Changes in Rural Residential Housing Attributes (1971 and 2001)*

Housing Attribute	*1971*	*2001*	*Change*
Number of Census Houses	8,308	26,428	+18,120
Persons per Residential Census House	4.87	4.67	–0.2
Households owing a house (%)	59.17	33.08	–26.09 percentage points
Households in rented houses (%)	40.82	64.72	–23.90 percentage points
Households living in one room house (%)	60.00	71.30	–11.30 percentage points

Source: Housing Report and Tables, Series 25, Part IV, Chandigarh, 1971; Press Release, Directorate of Census Operations, Chandigarh, 2003.

An analysis of data regarding the increase in the occupied residential houses at the individual village level shows that, except for the villages, which were partially or completely acquired, all the villages have registered an increase since 1971. As in the case of other attributes, the maximum increase was during 1981–91. Interestingly, the highest increase during the entire study period was recorded in five villages, viz., Palsaura, Kujheri, Nizampur Burail, Hallo Majra and Nizampur Kumbra, all of which are located on the southern margins of Chandigarh city (Figure 1). This further corroborates the observation regarding the impact of location of these villages in close vicinity to the areas of employment, despite the constant threat of being uprooted as the city plans are executed in the near future.

Table 5 *Chandigarh U.T.: Rural Census Houses by Different Uses (1971 and 2001)**

Sr. No.	*Uses*	*1971 (Number)*	*Per cent in Total Census Houses*	*2001 (Number)*	*Per cent in Total Census Houses*
1.	Residential	5,499	66.39	19,719	80.1
2.	Residence-cum-other uses	N.A.	—	761	3.1
3.	Hotel, Lodge, Guesthouse etc.	69	0.83	16	0.1
4.	Shop, office	1	0.01	2,054	8.3
5.	Factory, Workshop, Workshed	94	1.13	147	0.6
6.	Place of Worship	37	0.44	80	0.3

*Only broad categories, comparable in 1971 and 2001 have been given. Source: As in Table 4.

Changes in Built-up Area

The increase in the number of residential houses also implies an increase in the built-up area in villages, whether through infilling or expansion. Conventionally, as well as legally, the limits of the *abadi* area in a village is confined within the *lal lakeer* (red coloured line), a term probably derived from the colour of the line that defined the village settlement area in the village property ownership maps. It is also referred to as *lal dora.* Usually, the *abadi* area thus

Figure 1 *Chandigarh (UT) Location Map*

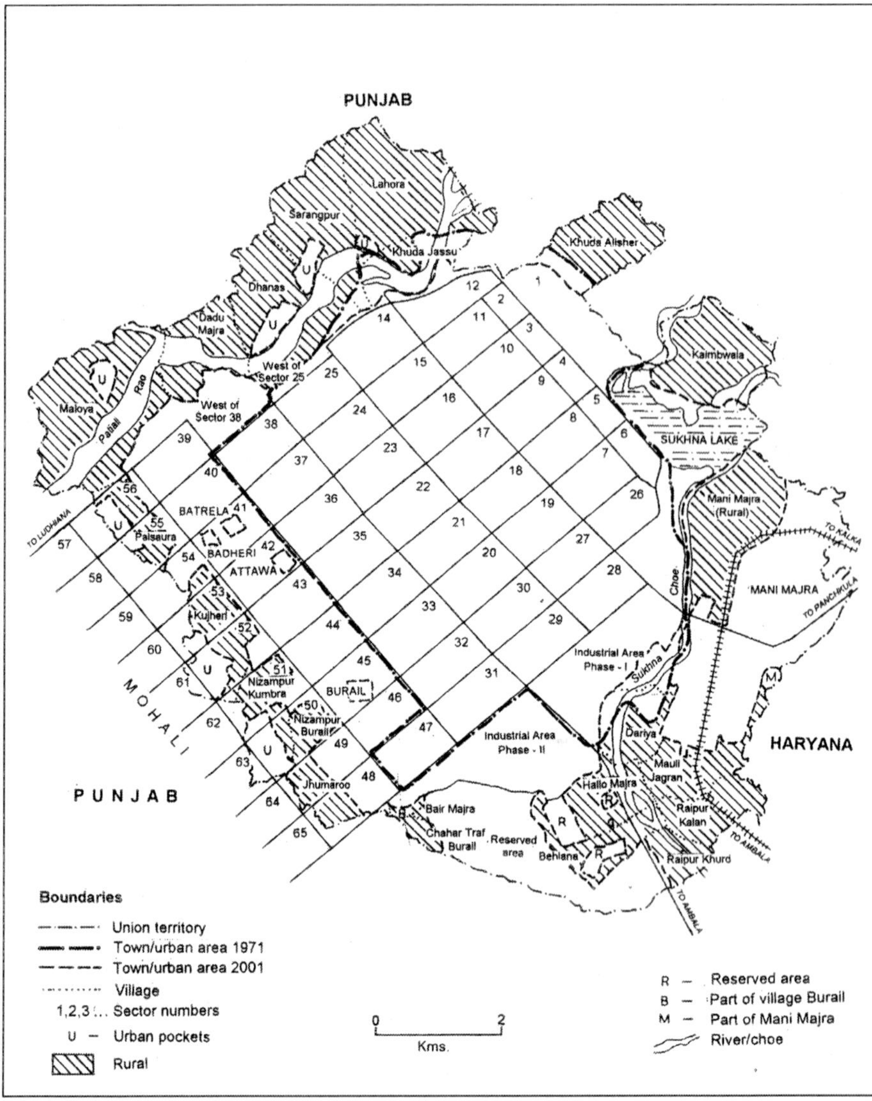

demarcated did not have a common formal shape. The consolidation of landholdings at a later stage resulted in the emergence of an almost common shape of the *abadi* area, generally square or rectangular, defined by a street/path called *phirni* (circumambulatory path), which encircles the *abadi* area. The *phirni* separates the agricultural land from the *abadi* area. All construction for non-agricultural purposes outside the *phirni* is illegal. Within the area enclosed by the *phirni* the ownership of land inside the *lal lakeer/dora* is on the basis of traditional occupancy, and between the *lal dora* and *phirni* land ownership is registered formally in the land records of the village. This threefold division is reflected in three types of built-up areas, old *abadi* within the *lal dora*, extended *abadi* between the *lal dora* and the *phirni*, and new *abadi* outside the *phirni*. The first two are legal and generally experience infilling and accretion respectively; the third is illegal and involves dispersal and expansion in the built-up area.

The changes in the built-up area, which form the most conspicuous element of the landscape of the rural–urban fringe, should be understood in terms of the following:

1. The development of the built-up area in terms of infilling, accretion, dispersion and expansion processes within and outside the legally demarcated area for *abadi*.
2. The coming up of built-up area in villages which do not have a formally demarcated *abadi* area as per revenue records, but the census shows some population, which lives in illegally built structures on village land.
3. The villages where only non-*abadi* area was acquired and the *abadi* became a part of the city as it expanded, and
4. Development that have taken place in the fringe due to policy decisions.

Out of the 27 villages, which formed the rural segment of Chandigarh U.T. in 1971 comparable data regarding *abadi* area from revenue records is available for only 16 villages till 1997. Of the remaining eleven villages, four did not have an *abadi* area.[18] The remaining seven were acquired for city expansion and their *abadi* included in the city limits at different points of time.[19]

In 1971 the built-up area in the 16 villages, for which revenue data are available, was confined mostly within the *lal dora* comprising the present old *abadi*. The total area covered was 83.12 hectares. During 1971–1997 the built-up area has expanded outside the *lal dora*, between it and the *phirni* (extended *abadi)* as well as outside the *phirni* (new *abadi*). In the extended *abadi*, the ownership of land is legal, and the process involved is accretion, expansion and dispersion. In 1997 the total area under different types of *abadi* was 146.16 hectares, an increase of 63.04 hectares (growth by 75.74%). At present, of the total *abadi* area 83.12 hectares (56.87%) are under old *abadi*, 52.74 hectares (36.08%) comprise extended *abadi*, and the remaining 10.30 hectares (7.04%) are under new *abadi*.

The nature of constructions and their functional use in the extended and new *abadi* areas is almost similar to the one found in the fringe areas of other cities. In the extended *abadi* there is a predominance of single room barrack like rectilinear structures, which are rented mainly by single member or small migrant labour households. In the village located on the southern periphery of the city, where the demand for housing is highest, these structures are two or even three stories high. Basic amenities like water and sewerage are shared. Interspersing such structures are garbage dumps, cattle sheds/ponds, and other houses inhabited by the local village inhabitants or rented by others. On the inner as well as outer flanks of the extended *abadi* commercial development has taken place. Compared to the old *abadi*, which forms the core, the extended *abadi* encircles it, has better construction and access because in most cases the *phirni*, which encloses it, can be used by motorised vehicles. As mentioned earlier, the *phirni* also demarcates the limit between the legal and the illegal ownership of land.

It is the new *abadi*, located outside the *phirni* that contains the tubercular landscape – an amalgamation of built-up area, open spaces, manufacturing units, godowns and bulk material markets, dumping sites, housing of different types and labour colonies – features typical of the urban fringe areas. Some of the developments in the fringe of Chandigarh city are related to policy decisions of the administration directly or indirectly. In this case, the role of policy decisions is even more basic because the entire rural segment of Chandigarh U.T. is covered under a clearly defined future plan, viz., the development and expansion of Chandigarh city.

Housing for the Poor and other Developments

The impact of policy decision on the developments in the urban fringe of Chandigarh can be best illustrated in terms of the policy for housing the poor. It has already been pointed out that the meticulously prepared development plans for the city failed to make any provision for the workers in the informal sector. The policy adopted by the administration for housing the lowest level workers in the city formed an appreciable effort initially. With the passage of time however, it turned out to be a contributing factor in the problems associated with the management of the fringe.

The large-scale construction activity associated with the coming up of the Chandigarh brought a large number of construction workers to the city. They built clusters of thatch huts adjoining the major construction sites. A system of parallel construction, that being constructed by the government, and the other by those who were doing it, continued for the first few years. However, as the major construction works were completed, the labour settlements came to be viewed as setting a precedence of encroachment on public land. In 1958, the Capital Project Office (CPO) decided to remove all non-plan settlements. A demand for alternative sites was raised and the settlements were shifted to peripheral locations in different sectors. The temporary status of these settlements, relocated by the administration, meant that practically no infra-structural facilities were provided. This first initiative, taken to check the setting of a precedent for encroachment on public land, itself became one for a continuous process of removal and relocation of illegal settlements, mostly on the fringe, in the coming years. Since the 1970's a policy of establishment of rehabilitation colonies has been followed. The difference between the two is in the tenure status, the former has the status of temporary lessees of the government; the latter are illegal squatters on government land.[20] Also, the former are provided with infra-structural facilities.

Currently the administration is in the process of providing alternative sites to residents of various colonies who were *bona fide* residents of the city as per the electoral rolls of the city for 1996. At present there are eight major rehabilitation colonies and fourteen unauthorised colonies in different villages in Chandigarh U.T. Their distribution shows a concentration of unauthorised colonies in villages located to the south of the city (Figure 2). This area is already earmarked for the development of the remaining sectors of Chandigarh.

Among the other functions that have developed in the rural fringe of Chandigarh due to policy decisions are the bulk material market in marble and other stones for construction, furniture and re-cycleable products (*kabari*), and LPG godowns. It must be pointed out that the location of each of these acts as a morphological and functional nucleus and attracts further growth, invariably illegal.

Figure 2 *Chandigarh (UT) Location of Landuses in Rural Segment 2002*

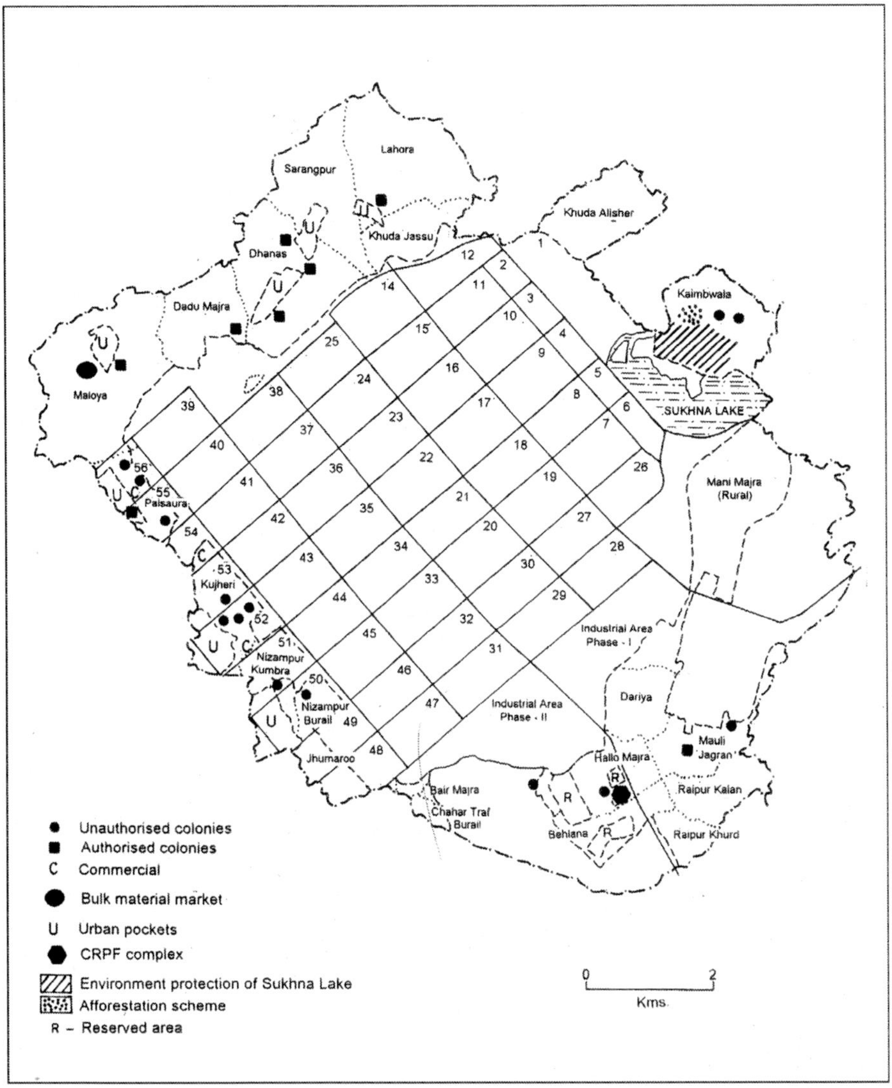

Although housing the poor continues to be a major concern, the U.T. administration has plans for taking up some institutional projects also in different parts of the fringe of the city. Major among these are the Afforestation Scheme on the northern, an I.T. Park, a Race Course and extension of the Industrial Area on the eastern and a Botanical garden on the western margin of the city. All of these will cover a larger area and represent a less intensive use of land as compared to the development on the southern margin.

There is another important aspect of the impact of policy decisions. The village *abadi* areas, which were not acquired and became a part of the city subsequently, have generally retained their rural character structurally as well as functionally. The major structural change in most cases has been emergence of shops and other commercial establishments along *phirni*, which encloses the *abadi* and the major streets inside it. These establishments have a distinct orientation towards the urban market. The former village *abadi* with its characteristic housing and functions appears like a carbuncle in an otherwise meticulously planned and laid out city. Specifically the case of four former village *abadi* areas viz., Attawa, Burail, Badheri and Buterla can be cited.[21] Another interesting situation is of location of pockets of land in different parts of the rural segment of Chandigarh U.T., which were acquired and developed by the administration for various purposes. They were treated as part of the urban area of Chandigarh city without physical contiguity till 1991 and came under the jurisdiction of the Municipal Corporation of Chandigarh after its formation in 1996. An interesting development related to this event is the inclusion of the authorised rehabilitation/relocated colonies along with many of the unauthorised labour group of colonies within the jurisdiction of the municipal administration and accords them an urban status, although as a slum and an encroachment on municipal land.

III

The existing attributes of the rural segment of Chandigarh U.T. and their development since 1971 bring out their striking similarity to the general characteristics of the urban fringe found around other cities also. This is somewhat surprising since the causative force in the case of Chandigarh U.T. is Chandigarh, a completely planned city with clearly laid out plan for its future growth over the area constituting the rural segment in the U.T. This raises the necessity of looking at the policies for future growth of the city and the management of the rural segment over which this growth is to take place. It would appear that while the future plan for growth of the city was quite clear and specific, it suffered from two flaws (i) ignoring the lowest level population from its scope – a limitation realised at a very early stage of development of the city. This was attempted to be overcome by evolving a policy for housing the poor in later years, and (ii) a completely deterministic urban-centric perspective, i.e., assuming that the components comprising rural landscape would naturally be succeeded or subsumed by the expanding urban monolith. So far as management of the rural segment till it came under the urban development process was concerned it was to be done through legislation – Periphery Act, Anti-encroachment Act, etc. – enacted for this purpose. The following discussion would try to establish that although the policy for urban development as executed through the plan of the city and the framework for management of the rural segment were salient efforts by themselves, both proved to be inadequate in dealing with the ground realities, partly due to systematic compulsions and partly because of the failure to recognise that policy decisions themselves act as an input into the ever changing equations in the dynamics of urban growth and its associated fringe development.

Policy Issues

Two major spheres where the existing policy framework has been found lacking are housing for the poor and, location of land use/functions not provided for in the city plan. In 1975 the U.T. administration introduced a scheme for offering bare sites EWS housing units, tenements and sites under Sites and Services scheme for housing the poor. In March 1980 a survey conducted by U.T. administration reported 8,485 slums dwelling units. Since the total allotment of alternative sites by the Administration between 1975 and 1980 was 11,804, a complete coverage of demand was deemed to have been achieved.[22] However, this scheme probably resulted in an additional incentive for more population to settle in and around the city, in the hope of acquiring a house site. This also resulted in the emergence of a dual structure of labour/housing colonies, authorised and unauthorised.[23] (Figure 2). Needless to say, there are wide gaps in the level of available living space and infrastructure between the two. An idea about the magnitude of the problem posed by unauthorised land uses is provided by the following information from the recent anti-encroachment drive:

(i) 4,500 huts were removed from a colony in Korsan village (Sector 49). The area cleared of encroachments was 43 acres, i.e., approximately 17 hectares.[24]

(ii) 2,000 huts, 50 cattle sheds and 13 *anganwari* centres removed from colonies in Palsaura village (Sectors 55,56). Out of a total 50 acres (approximately 20 hectares) encroached upon, 20 acres, i.e., 8 hectares was cleared. About 300 families affected in this process had been uprooted from Korsan village only a year ago.[25]

(iii) A furniture market located on land meant for development of Sectors 54 and 55 was removed and 30 acres (approximately 17 hectares) of area cleared.[26] An additional 29 acres (approximately 17 hectares) were cleared from an adjacent location after removing dairies, *kabari* shops; saw mills and plant nurseries.[27]

(iv) Structures from farmhouse, being used for commercial purposes, located on the fringe of the U.T. were removed.[28]

(v) The Chandigarh Estate Office estimates suggest that out of about 623 hectares of land currently under illegal occupation only 101 hectares have been cleared of encroachments.[29]

These encroachments had developed over a number of years. Some of these came into existence after their initial locations were cleared to pave the way for expansion of the city some time ago. This raises the issue of management of the fringe over which future expansion of the city is already planned.

Management Issues

In the case of Chandigarh the management of the urban fringe should ideally involve managing the area that has been acquired for urban development and monitoring the area is yet to be acquired but has already been designed for this purpose. It seems that there are problems in both these spheres, e.g., there is invariably a time gap between the acquisition of land and handing over its possession to the concerned department/agency for carrying out developmental work.[30] Another time gap exists between taking possession of the land and start of the development work before allocation is made to the actual user. It is suggested that monitoring of such lands would help in at least partially checking the process of illegal/unwanted developments.

The need for a similar strategy is even stronger for the yet to be acquired lands. Since these are designed as rural, the concerned departments comprise a different segment of the administrative set-up. This however, should not pose a difficulty in evolving a strategy for monitoring compliance to the designated use of land because even in the rural context, the use of agricultural land for non-agricultural purposes is illegal. However, such illegal uses of land become a problem area only when the concerned piece of land is required to be used for urban development/expansion. Is it that the element of illegality is unacceptable only in one context? Ideally the answer should be in the negative, but the ground reality is different, and reflects the conflicts and dichotomy in attitudes, nature of development, level of living and uses of land, between the urban and rural segments. One of the possible strategies for resolving, partially if not wholly, this situation could be the adoption of a more comprehensive framework for urban planning.

Need for a Broader Plan Framework

It has already been pointed out that the existing framework for development of Chandigarh city has a strong urban-centric element, a feature common to the development plans of other cities also. This element makes the existing or evolving characteristics of the rural segment an anathema. It is axiomatic that the urban fringe will present a dichotomous context in terms of its structural and functional characteristics, although many of these represent the urban influence. Specifically, in the case of Chandigarh the contrasts are striking in terms of developments in village *abadi* areas, the use of agricultural land for commercial and residential purposes, the levels of living and provision of infrastructural facilities. This is particularly so on the southern margin of the city, the area earmarked for future expansion of the city since its inception.

From the implementation of the Phase II of the development of the city, the Chandigarh administration followed a policy of partial acquisition of land. The unacquired area constituted the rural segment of U.T. and underwent development as a rural area. This represented an anomalous situation, i.e., the area continued to develop and was treated as rural although its future urban character had already been specified. It is in this context that the need for a broader framework for city planning is suggested as a means for resolving such situations and reducing the level of dichotomy between the existing and the prospective urban land.

Some of the specific measures that may be included in such a framework could be as follows:

1. Provision for rural pockets wherever the village *abadi* area is not to be acquired. The existing by-laws related to construction of building and their use in urban areas should be extended to such pockets. Similarly, the standards for provision of infrastructural facilities in urban areas should be adopted for such pockets also, in place of their current coverage under different rural development schemes.
2. The location of such urban oriented activities as milk dairies, bulk material markets, saw mills, godowns etc. should be specified.
3. The location of housing schemes for the poor – migrant as well as persons displaced in the process of land acquisition – should be specified. This

measure should be undertaken keeping in mind the numerical and locational adequacy because of the basic role played by housing in determining the population as well as functional characteristics of the urban fringe.

The measures outlined above are suggestive rather than comprehensive. The strategy is to pre-empt the chaotic growth and intermixing of the uses and activities. The key element in this strategy is the identification of the morphological and functional nuclei in the rural segment and placing these within the plan proposals for future expansion of the city. It is believed that such a framework by being selectively permissive rather than exclusively restrictive would help in resolving many of the conflicts between the existing rural and prospective urban uses. However, adoption of such a framework would itself require resolution of some of the systemic conflicts, e.g., the agency to be entrusted with the task of looking after the designated rural pockets and other such locations; the legal framework under which the by-laws and standards applicable in urban areas can be extended to the existing rural area earmarked for inclusion in the city in the near future; what should be the time frame for taking over the development work once an area is acquired etc. Till such time as the suggested strategy is adopted and related issues resolved enforcement of the existing laws and constant monitoring of the rural fringe need to be undertaken more rigorously.

Conclusions

The development of the rural segment in Chandigarh U.T. and the characteristics it has acquired during the study period has followed a pattern observed in the case of other cities also. This is somewhat surprising because the plan framework of Chandigarh city was meticulously drawn and backed by suitable legal measures. Interestingly, although the gaps in the plan proposals were sought to be filled through subsequent policy decisions, the inherent curmudgeonly equation between the city and its fringe is evidenced in this case also. One of the possible factors for this has been a strong urban-centric focus of the plan proposals. It is suggested that a broader plan framework, which places some of the key functional and morphological elements of the existing rural landscape within the prospective plan for urban expansion, and is thereby more permissive than restrictive, will help in resolving many of the conflicts and in diluting the levels of dichotomy between the city and its fringe. However, adoption of such an approach does not, in any way, undermine the need for a rigorous implementation of the existing laws and monitoring of the urban fringe.

Notes

1. Some of the important studies are:

   Wehrwein, G.S. (1942): The Rural–Urban Fringe, *Economic Geography,* 18: 217–28.

   Andrews, R.B. (1942): Elements in the Urban Fringe Pattern, *J. of Land and Public Utility Economics,* 18: 169–83.

Firey, W.I. (1946): Ecological Considerations in Planning for Urban Fringes, *American Sociological Review*: 411–23.

Myers, R.B. and J.A. Beegle (1947): Delineation and Analysis of the Rural–Urban Fringe, *Applied Anthropology*, 6: 14–22.

Blizzard, S.W. and W.F. Anderson (1952): *Problems in Rural–Urban Research: Conceptualization and Delineation*, Pennsylvania

McKain, W.C. and R.G. Burnight (1953): The Sociological Significance of the Rural–Urban fringe from the Rural Point of View, *Rural Sociology*, 18: 109–16.

Kurtz, H.A. and J.B. Eicher (1958): Fringe and Suburbs: A Confusion of Concepts, *Social Forces*, 37: 32–37.

Golledge, R. (1960): Sydney's Metropolitan Fringe: A Study in Urban-Rural Relations, *Australian Geographer*, 7: 243–255.

Whiteland, J.W.R. (1967): Fringe Belts: A Neglected Aspect of Urban Geography", *Trans. Inst. Br. Geogr.*, 41: 223–33.

Pryor, R.J. (1968): Defining the Rural–Urban Fringe, *Social Forces*, 47: 202–15.

Johnson, James H. (1974): *Suburban Growth: Geographical Processes at the Edge of the Western City*, John Wiley, London.

Mookherjee, Debnath (1963): The Concept of Urban Fringe and its Delineation, *Geog. Rev. India*, 25: 47–57.

Jadhav, R.S. (1967): Land use planning in the Rural–Urban Fringe of Poona, *National Geogr. J. India*, 13: 158–67.

Ganguly, M. (1967): The Nature of Fringe Areas of Calcutta", *Geog. Rev. of India*, 29: 53–59.

The Indian Inst. of Public Administration (1968): *Administration of the Urban Fringe*, New Delhi.

Ramchandran, R. and Bina Srivastava (1974): The Rural–Urban Fringe with Particular Reference to the Delhi Metropolitan Area, *Indian Geogr. Jl.* 49: 1–9.

Nangia, Sudesh (1976): *Delhi Metropolitan Region: A Study in Settlement Geography*, K.B. Publishers, New Delhi.

Gopi, K.N. (1978): *The Process of Urban Fringe Development: A Model*, Concept Pub., New Delhi.

Kabra, K.N. (1980): *Developing an Urban Fringe*, The Indian Institute of Public Administration, New Delhi.

Desai, A. (1986): Problems of Changing Land Use Pattern in the Urban Fringe, in Yadav C.S. (Ed.) *Rural–Urban Fringe*, Concept Pub., New Delhi.

Bimal Kumar (Ed.) (1998): *Urbanization and Land Use: Conflict at the Urban Fringe*, A.P.H. Pub. Corp. New Delhi.

2. Some these are the Controlled Area Authority, Periphery Act, Development Authority etc.
3. For a detailed discussion on this aspect see Kalia, R. (1987): *Chandigarh: In Search of an Identity*, Southern Illinois University Press, Carbondale and Edwardsville.
4. Evenson, Norma (1966): *Chandigarh*, University of California Press, Berkeley, p. 7

5. For an account of the search for an architect/planner for Chandigarh see Kalia (1987) op. cit. and Evenson (1966) op. cit.
6. For a comparative study of the plans and growth of the three state capitals, see Deodhar Pippa Maryann (2000) *Growth of Modern Planned State Capitals in India: A Study of Chandigarh*, Unpublished Ph.D. Thesis, Punjab University, Chandigarh.
7. Fry, Maxwell (1953): Chandigarh: A New Town for India, *Town and Country Planning*, 21:219.
8. Lamba, N.S. (1960): Zoning and other Tools for the Development of a New City (Chandigarh), *Journal of Institute of Town Planners, India*, Jan-April, pp. 134–35; Chandigarh Administration (1972) *Chandigarh*, Souvenir of Indian Independence, Silver Jubilee, 14–15 August 1947–1972.
9. Evenson, Norma (1966), op. cit., p. 58.
10. Le Corbusier (1959): For Establishment of an Immediate Statute of the Land, Mimeographed, Town Planning Department, Chandigarh, p. 2.
11. As early as 1955 Maxwell Fry wrote "... there were vast masses of people who were not included in the project estimates. We tried to make provision for them, but in a certain sense we failed. There was no economy on which we could do it, even with the smallest house." Fry, Maxwell (1955): Chandigarh: The Capital of the Punjab, *Jl. of the Royal Institute of British Architects*, Series 3, p.92; also see Madhu Sarin (1978): A Raw Deal for Labour, *Design Incorporating Indian Builder*, March, pp. 21–24, and Sarin Madhu (1982) *Urban Planning in the Third World: The Chandigarh Experience*, Mansell Publishing Ltd., London.
12. *Chandigarh Newsline*, 19 January 1999, 3: 1.
13. Krishan, Gopal (1999): *Inner Spaces-Outer Spaces of a Planned City: A Thematic Atlas of Chandigarh*, Chandigarh, Map 15 and Deodhar, Pippa Maryann (2000), op. cit., p. 264.
14. Kalia, R, (1987) op. cit., p. 13.
15. Bali, Bhawna (2000): *Dynamics of Rural Component of Chandigarh Union Territory (1971–1991)*, Unpublished M.Phil. Dissertation, Punjab University, Chandigarh, p. 106, Table 3,2.
16. Ibid. p. 108, Table 3,4.
17. Ibid. p. 136.
18. These are Chahar Tarf Burail, Jhumroo, Nizampur Kumbra and Nizampur Burail. See Figure 1.
19. These are Attaa, Badheri, Burail, Buterla, Korsan, Shahpur and Bair Majra (See Figure 1). Out of these Attawa and Burail were identified as Census Towns, and Badheri and Buterla as Out Growth in 1981 as well as in 1991 within the Chandigarh Urban Agglomeration. With the formation of Chandigarh Municipal Corporation in 1996 these were merged in the city. According to 2001 Census there is no Urban Agglomeration and Chandigarh U.T. has only one city, i.e., Chandigarh.
20. Sarin Madhu (1982) op. cit., p. 159.
21. See note 19 above. A field survey of Attawa, a Census Town till 1991 brought out the following observations: i) keeping of milk cattle in residential houses for commercial dairying purposes, an activity banned by the administration is quite common and a carry over from the past, ii) almost all the major streets running

through the *abadi* have commercial ribbon development. iii) There are more than 250 shops in the settlement. Major items in which these shops deal in are general merchandise, electrical repair and goods, building material, auto repair and parts, bamboo and other wooden material and *kabari*. According to the 1991 census the settlement had a population of 4,554 people. A similar field survey of Badheri, and Out Growth of Chandigarh UA in 1991 with a population of 3,753 persons, identified an almost similar pattern of location of commercial development with about 400 shops, the main items being general provisions, electrical repair and goods, printing press and related items, hardware, confectionary and tailoring.

22. Dubey, V.P. et al., (1999): Socio-economic Profile of Slum Dwellers in Chandigarh, *Man and Development*, Vol. XXI, (3) p. 126.
23. A survey of all the colonies in 1998 reported that 77 per cent of the total households in authorised colonies and 88 per cent of total households in unauthorised colonies in and around the city were of migrant families, Ibid, Table 3 pp. 30–31 and Table 16, p. 142.
24. *Chandigarh Tribune*, 19 June 2003, 1–5 and *Chandigarh Tribune*, 20 June, 5: 6.
25. *Chandigarh Bhaskar* (Hindi), 27 June 2003, 1: 3.
26. *Chandigarh Bhaskar* (Hindi), 4 July 2003, 1: 1.
27. *Chandigarh Bhaskar* (Hindi), 5 July 2003, 8: 1.
28. *Chandigarh Bhaskar* (Hindi), 3 July 2003
29. *Chandigarh Bhaskar* (Hindi), 16 July 2003, 1: 5.
30. During the approximately last ten years the Chandigarh Administration acquired 9,448 hectares of land. Out of this possession only 5,852 hectares could be handed over to the Engineering Department for carrying out development work till date. *Chandigarh Bhaskar* (Hindi), 19 July 2003, 1: 6.

17

Evaluation of Master Plans and Changing Character of Fringe Areas of Jaipur Urban Complex

H.S. Sharma and R.N. Mishra

The princely city of Jaipur has pride of its being one of the few planned cities of the world. Jaipur is known as Pink City of India. It is the first planned city of the medieval period. The walled city of Jaipur was founded in 1727 A.D. by Maharaja Jai Singh-II. Its map was prepared by a Bengali engineer named Vidyadhar Bhattacharya. The original walled city was planned in rectangular blocks on an area of 6 km^2 in 1727; it had increased to 65 km^2 in 1941 and to over 300 km^2 in 1991. The urbanised area has increased from 4,047 hectare in 1971 to about more than 12,141 hectares in 2001 (Figure 1).

The city presents a great administrative and environmental complexity and has encountered in the process of expansion a wide range of geo-environmental problems like shrinking of agricultural land, gullying and destabilisation of stabilised sand dunes due to urbanisation, deforestation, depletion of ground water resources, problem of solid waste disposal, increasing nitrate and fluoride in the ground water, air and noise pollution and unplanned growth in the fringe areas.

Geomorphic Background

The city is located on a sandy triangular plain conjectured to be on a bed of a dried-up lake. This sandy plain is enclosed on three sides by hill ranges. The eastern and north-western portions of this sandy plain are undulating and dissected into many rain-fed nallahs. The hills form a northeastern continuation of the Aravallis belonging to the oldest orogeny. The average height of these hills is about 500 m above sea level. The town, which was designed as a small capital city within a fortified area of 6 km^2 in 1727, has since undergone radical changes during the past 275 years. After becoming the state capital in 1949 this small beautiful city had to equip itself to bear this great responsibility and provide accommodation for large number of immigrants expected to come to the city from all over the country. Its population has increased from 1.758 lakhs in 1947 to 23.24 lakhs in 2001.

Figure 1 *Urban Sprawl: Jaipur City*

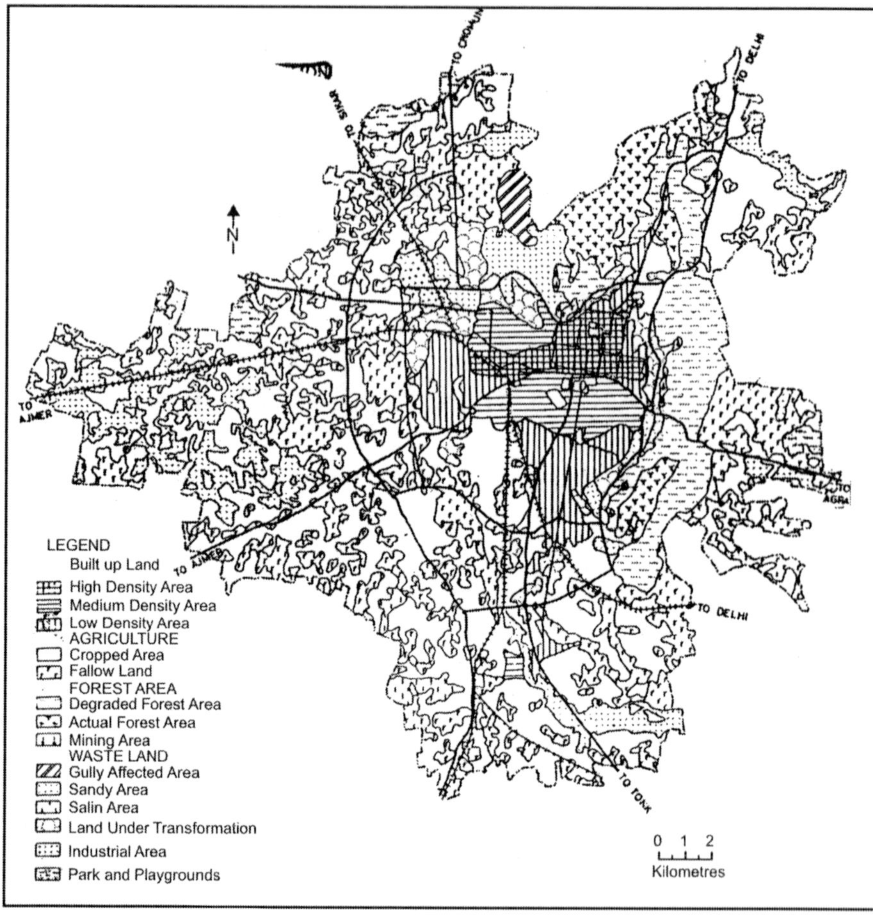

Objective of the Study

The objectives of the present study are to evaluate the Master Plan of Jaipur Region and to identify deviations in the Master Plans 1971–91 and 1991–2011. Further an attempt is made to study the changing character of land use in the fringe areas and the unplanned growth over the last three-four decades.

Methodology

The research is based on the study of the Master Plans proposed by the Urban Improvement Trust and Jaipur Development Authority. The data on land use of the urban complex have also been generated with the help of satellite data and old maps from Man Singh-II Museum. The study is further supported by field observations in and around the city.

Jaipur Master Plan (1971–1991)

A Master Plan is a basic tool in city planning, which provides a broad framework for future development of the city in the right direction. Jaipur Master Plan was prepared under the Urban Improvement Act 1959 and its first draft was published in December 1972, and the final Master Plan was approved by the Government in 1976. This Master Plan was prepared to show the problems related to physical, social, economic and infrastructural developments and also to serve as a guide line for the future growth of the city up to the horizon year 1991. The entire urbanised area had been divided into nine planning districts, which were supposed to be more or less self-contained communities in matters of employment, housing, commercial, recreational and other community facilities. The planning districts delineated in 1991 are given below:

Table 1 *Planning Districts: Jaipur, 1991 (Area in Acres)*

A.	Walled City District	3,850 acres
B.	Bani Park District	2,700 acres
C.	Ashok Nagar – Tilak Nagar District	3,300 acres
D.	Gandhi Nagar District	3,050 acres
E.	Jhalana District	5,000 acres
F.	Sanganer District	5,250 acres
G.	Civil Lines District	8,180 acres
H.	Jhotwara District	6,470 acres
	(Urbanisable Area)	38,400 acres
J.	Green Belt District	57,000 acres
	Notified Urban Area	96,300 acres
	approximately	i.e., 385 km^2

Table 2 *Land Use Master Plan Proposals 1991 versus Actual Development 1991 (Area in acres)*

Land use	*M.P. Proposals 1991*			*Actual 1991*		
	Existing 1971	*Proposed Development*	*Total Area of Development*	*Total*	*Development in right places*	*Development in wrong places*
Residential	5,000	12,200	17,200	15,880	12,014	3,866
Commercial	340	1,260	1,600	950	684	266
Industrial	710	3,750	4,460	2,490	1,767	723
Governmental	210	230	440	390	287	103
Recreational	330	670	1,000	530	487	43
P. and S.P.	1,680	900	2,580	2,120	1,751	369
Tourist Facilities	—	200	200	—	—	—
Circulation	1,730	4,290	6,020	2,910	2,909	1
Total	10,000	23,500	33,500	25,270	19,899	5,371

Source: JDA Reports.

The analysis of Master Plan proposals 1991 and actual development clearly indicates that when the Master Plan was being framed, the area of about 10,000 acres was already developed. The Master Plan proposed an additional 23,500 acres for urban development during the plan period. However the actual area that has been developed during these 20 years was about 45,270 acres. This means that an overall development to the extent of 65 per cent has been achieved. Table 2 shows the Master Plan proposals 1991 versus the Actual Development 1991.

Table 2 shows that about 610 acres new area has been developed under commercial use. It is important to note that not a single newly proposed sub-city centre or district centre has been developed. The entire commercial activity has been generated along the roads in the form of rows of shops. Three new industrial areas were proposed at Viswakarma, Sanganer and Jhalana areas. In all about 4,460 acres of land was proposed for industrial use in the Master Plan. Out of the actually developed land of 2,490 acres in 1991 only 1,767 acres were developed at the locations proposed by the Master Plan, while the rest did not follow the plan. Out of the total developed land of 25,270 acres in 1991 only 19,899 acres were developed according to the Master Plan.

Situation in Fringe Areas

With an objective to control the peripheral areas, which were prone to urban expansion, the Master Plan proposed a peripheral control belt extending about 1 to 1.5 km. beyond the proposed urban development area. In this area urban activity was to be fully checked and only rural activities were allowed to continue. Here an industrial township known as Kanakpura-Bindayaka Township was proposed. However, in the peripheral areas and green belt zone co-operative housing societies purchased land and started their developments, particularly along major arteries such as Sikar Road, Agra Road, Ajmer Road, Jagatpura Road and Tonk Road. Jaipur Municipal Corporation has been given the complete responsibility to maintain the heritage and character of the walled city of Jaipur. The study shows that this was not a very effective agency in this regard. Physical factors such as relief, drainage, wind direction and hydrology play a dominant role in the development pattern of the settlement. In Jaipur natural hills in the north and east provide a strong physical barrier restricting urban development in these directions. The Amani Shah nallah running in north-south direction in the western periphery has long been acting as a physical barrier in the west. Thus the expansion of the city was open mostly towards the south. Therefore, most of the development outside of the walled city has taken place in the southern direction. The drainage of the city is mostly carried out by the Amani Shah Ka nallah and Jagatpura nallah. It may be noted that not much thought has been given to the drainage system. As a result new developments and residential colonies developed even over the beds of these drains. The striking example is Jawahar Nagar nallah, which flows southward through Jawahar Nagar, the university area and then turns southwest to join Amani Shah nallah. Virtually this nallah has become non-existent within the university area and beyond. As a matter of fact, during the 1981 flood this nallah caused maximum damage to the university, Bajaj Nagar and O.T.S. areas.

Master Plan (1991–2011)

Jaipur Master Plan (1971–1991) shows that the planned and rational development of Jaipur urban areas envisaged in the plan could not be achieved and the development of the city during the last two decades has been totally neglected and there was an utter negligence of the Master Plan proposals. So to avoid this situation, a detailed study of the existing situation has been done and a new Master Plan for the horizon year 2011 was prepared by the Jaipur Development Agency. This master plan has covered the entire J.D.A. region covering an area of 1,464 km^2 comprising 6 towns and 385 villages of fringe areas (Table 3 and Figure 2 and 3).

The policy document of the Master Plan 2011 has identified 32 urban nodes, of which 20 urban nodes fall under urbanisable area of Jaipur city for the year 2011 and the remaining 12 nodes have been distributed all over the region, guiding growth potentials to satellite towns and inner ring towns (Figure 4). Each of the urban nodes has been identified with the activities that strengthen the vocational aspect of the area and meet the needs of the increasing population. Each of these urban nodes will be in continuation with various urban facilities. These urban nodes have been classified in the following categories:

(i) Predominantly Commercial Node
(ii) Predominantly Industrial Node
(iii) Predominantly Public and Semi Public Node
(iv) Predominantly Recreational Node.

The following predominant activities have been identified in the urban nodes falling in the urbanisable areas of Jaipur City 2011.

Figure 2 *Jaipur City Region: Present Developed Area*

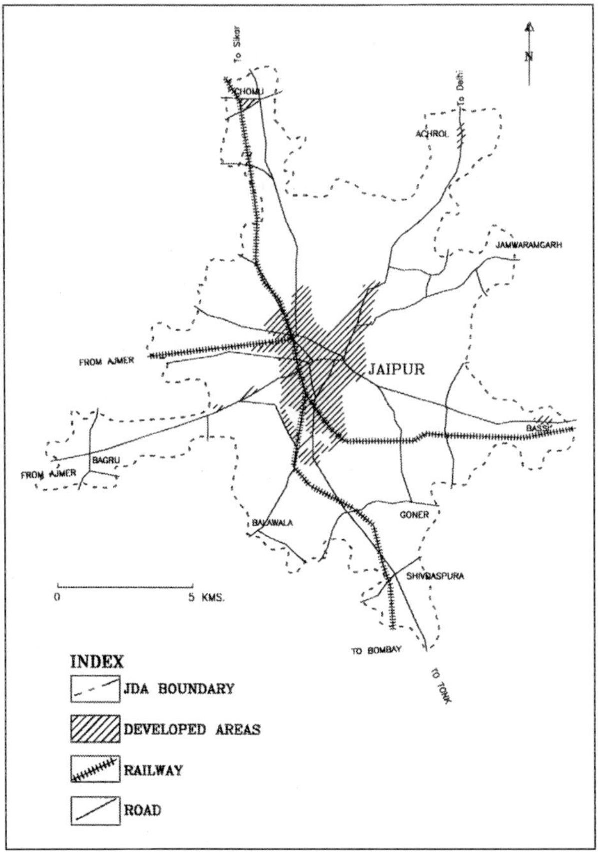

Figure 3 *Jaipur City Region: Urbanisable Limit*

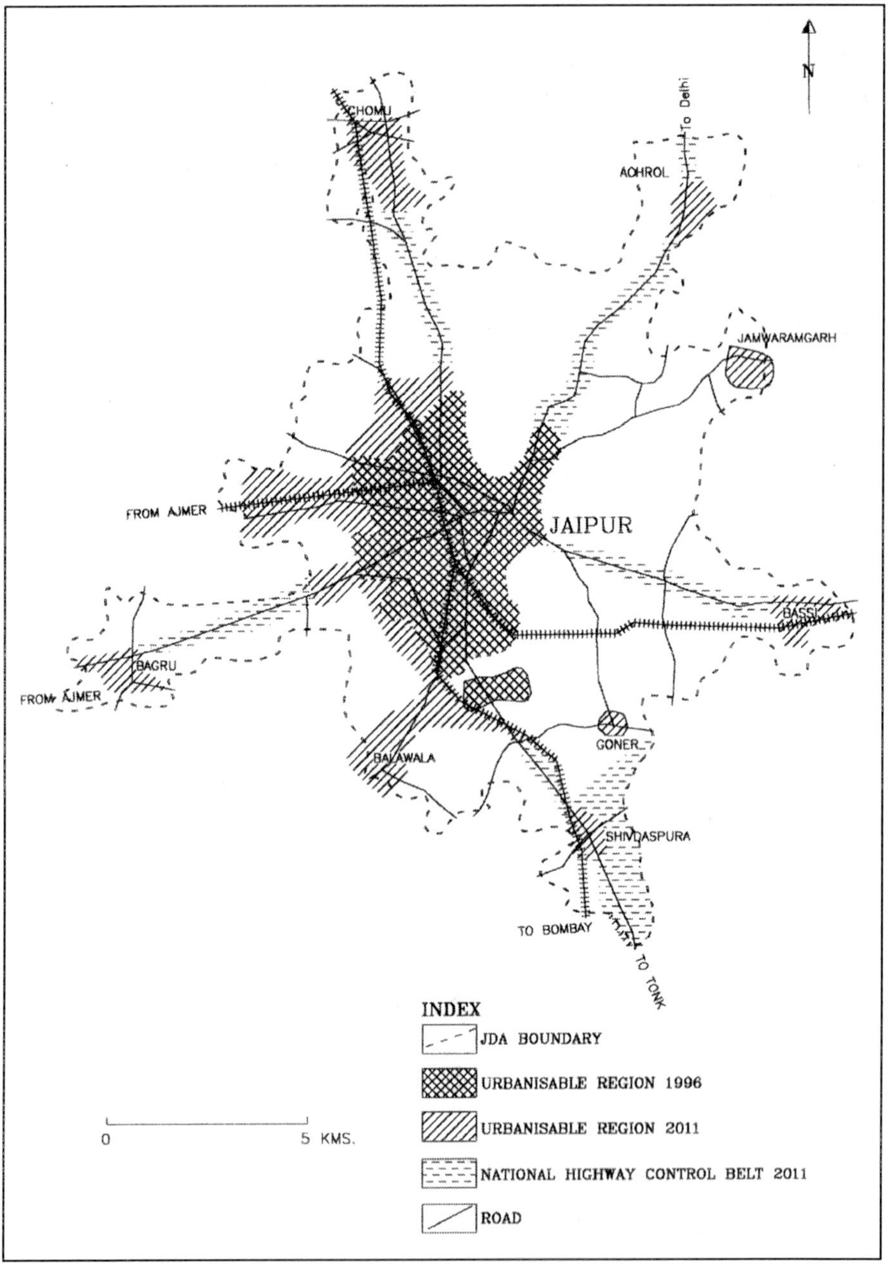

Figure 4 *Jaipur City Region and its Environs*

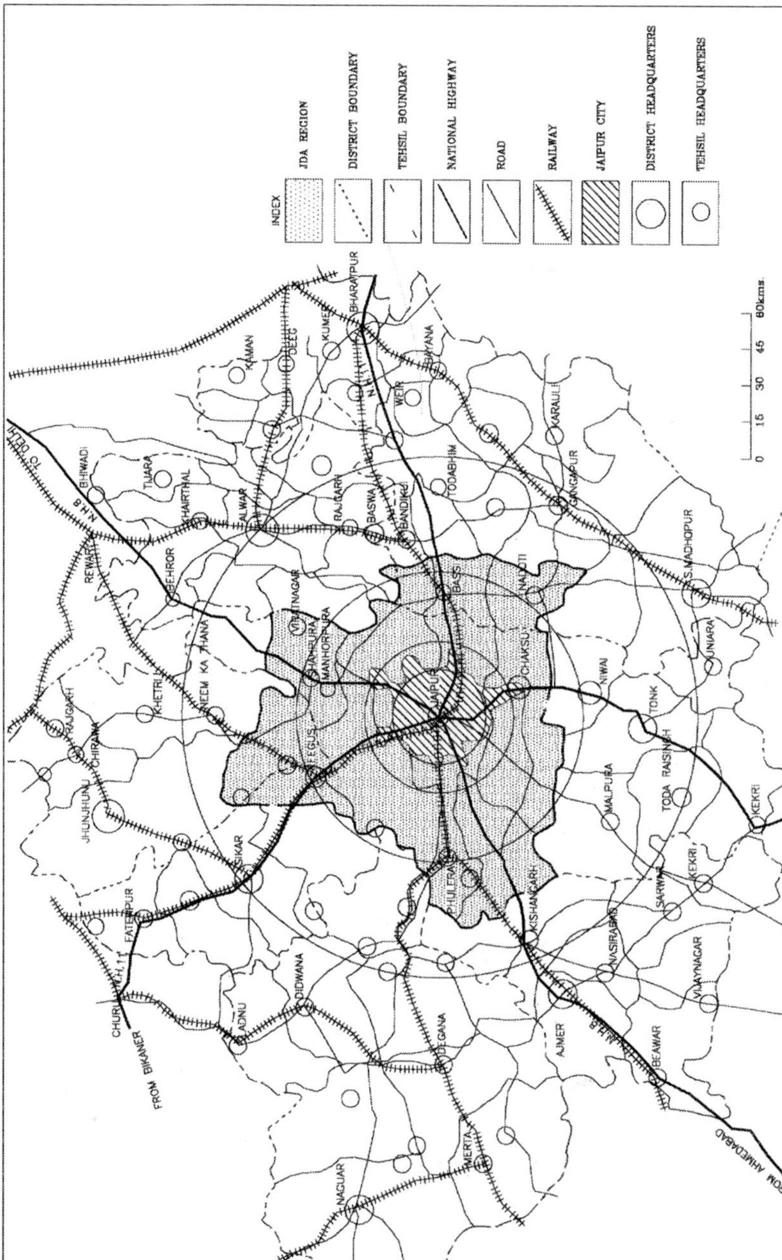

Source: JDA Jaipur

Table 3 *Land Use 2011*

S. No.	*Land use*	*Area (in acres)*	*Area (in hectares)*	*In per cent*
1.	Residential	34,150	13,825	44.8
2.	Commercial			
	(A) Retail Commercial Business	2,875	1,165	3.8
	(B) Whole Sale Business, Ware Housing and Godowns	1,615	654	2.1
	(C) Special Markets	605	245	0.8
3.	Industrial			
	Manufacturing	4,600	1,862	6.0
4.	Mixed Land use	2,555	1,034	3.3
5.	Governmental			
	Govt. and Semi Govt. Offices	14,85	602	2.0
6.	Public and Semi Public			
	(A) General Inst. Education, Medical	6,060	2,453	8.0
	(B) Social, Cultural, Religious and Historical Monuments	490	198	
	(C) Other Community Facilities	190	77	0.6
	(D) Public Utilities	1,105	448	0.2
	(E) Cremation and Burial Grounds	160	65	1.5
7.	Recreational			
	Park, Open spaces and Play ground/recreational and stadium	8,550	3,461	11.3
8.	Circulation			
	(A) Railway Station and Yards	430	174	0.6
	(B) Bus and Truck Terminals	490	198	0.6
	(C) Roads	8,840	3,580	11.6
	(D) Air Port	1,950	789	2.6
	Total Developed Area	76,150	30,830	100.0
	Nurseries and Orchards	351	142	
	Govt. Reserved Areas	1,549	627	
	Water Bodies	1,731	701	
	Regional Park	884	358	
	Urbanisable Area	80,665	32,658	

A.	**Urbanisable Areas in Jaipur**		
1.	Banipark Node	:	Public, Semi Public
2.	Vidhyadhar Nagar Node	:	Commercial
3.	Vishwakarma Industrial Area Node	:	Industrial
4.	Harmada Node	:	Commercial
5.	Kanakpura Node	:	Commercial
6.	Bindayaka Node	:	Industrial
7.	Bhankrota Node	:	Commercial
8.	Prithvi Raj Nagar Node	:	Institutional
9.	Mansarovar Node	:	Commercial
10.	Sitapura Node	:	Industrial
11.	Vanasthali Marg Node	:	Commercial
12.	Subhash Nagar Node	:	Commercial
13.	Jhotwara Node	:	Industrial

14.	South Sector Node	:	Institutional
15.	Amargarh Node	:	Commercial
16.	Jhalana Node	:	Institutional
17.	Malviya Nagar Node	:	Commercial
18.	Gopalpura Node	:	Commercial
19.	Bhogpura Node	:	Commercial
20.	Secretariate Node	:	Institutional
B.	**Urbanisable Areas in Inner Ring Towns/Satellite Towns**		
1.	Chommu Node	:	Commercial
2.	Jaitpura Node	:	Industrial
3.	Bagru Node	:	Commercial
4.	Sheodaspura Node	:	Commercial
5.	Bassi Node	:	Commercial
6.	Ramgarh Node	:	Recreational
7.	Achroal Node	:	Recreational
8.	Kanota Node	:	Commercial
9.	Hirawala Node	:	Industrial
10.	Goner Node	:	Recreational
11.	Kukas Node	:	Recreational
12.	Balawala Node	:	Industrial

In the new Master Plan a separate zone has been identified as Ecological Zone, which includes hills, forests, water bodies, settlements etc. Such zones have been identified on both sides of National Highway. No urban activity of major construction shall be permitted in these zones.

The detailed study of Master Plan 2011 brings out some shortfalls. They are listed below:

1. Master Plan document to JDA region has saved itself from delineating Jaipur Metropolitan Town, even Chaksu town, which is only 35 km. away on Kota Road, has been left out.
2. Jaipur is a principal town of the state and the most important town between Delhi and Ahmedabad. It is attracting people not only from Rajasthan, but also from all over the country. Considering the above fact, the planning of Jaipur city should have been done in the context of a broad regional perspective, as a state capital. But this aspect has not been taken care of in the Master Plan.
3. The plan has suggested the development of certain nodes, but these nodes have not been clearly identified in terms of area and location. If such nodes are to be developed, they should be located separately and all the facilities to be provided in these nodes should have been mentioned. The areas of these nodes should have been specified.

Reasons for the Non-implementation of the Master Plan and the Unplanned Growth in Fringe Areas

The detailed analysis of the implementation of the Master Plan (1971–1991) reveals that none of it has been implemented properly. There is a wide gap between the envisaged and the actual development that has taken place during 1971–1991. There has been a gross violation of the plan due to number of factors like:

- Shortfalls in the planning concept,
- Implementation mechanism,
- Geographical factors,
- Demographic factors,
- Land Acquisition problems,
- Changes in land use,
- Cooperative Housing Societies land conversion rule 1981,
- *Katchi Bastis*,
- Administrative and managerial failures.

The old town of Jaipur was undoubtedly designed as an ideal capital city for its Kingdom. It was strategically located almost in the centre of the territory surrounded by hills. The design of the town was unique and provided for all the activities related with the town, such as palace and administrative complex, residential areas for businessmen, public and labourers in different parts of the city. The shopping arcade was provided along the main road with a veranda for shoppers, however, the rulers of Jaipur could not visualise the growth of the town to the present scale.

The planning of Jaipur was never conceived by the city managers in its regional perspective. Even the Draft plan prepared by JDA for 2011 A.D overlooks this aspect. Once the city was made a state capital, the regional plan for the well identified state capital should have been prepared, in which the neighbouring towns of Ajmer, Sikar, Sawai Madhopur, Dausa, Kotputli, Shahpura, Bassi, Dudu etc. should have been included. This approach should have provided a broad planning perspective. Thus the planning policies for development of various activities in the region should be formulated and a number of activities like large and medium sized industries, wholesale markets, warehousing etc. which need not be essentially located in Jaipur, could be located in the neighbouring towns. With a well conceived regional plan document, the entire state capital region needs to be developed including the rural segments, so that people can live in their villages and can come to the city during working hours with efficient means of transport.

It may be noted that the Master Plan proposed to develop 17,200 acres of residential land, which was more than the 12,000 acres that existed in 1971. Thus even assuming an average density of 50–100 persons/acre the above additional residential area has a capacity to accommodate about 10 lakh people. Taking note of re-densification within existing developments, the Master Plan has a capacity to accommodate about 20 lakh people. This is quite evident from the fact that the entire population of 15.18 lakh in 1991 was residing in about 16,000 acres. The Master Plan proposed vast areas at a density below 50 persons/acres, which is a very low density and is an under-utilisation of the valuable urban land.

The zoning regulations are provided generally in the Master Plan. They prescribe various urban spot uses permitted in the different land use zones. In case of Jaipur Master Plan, such zoning regulations were not provided. Zoning provides definite guidelines for implementing agencies to approve or reject the spot locations to be developed in different land use zones. It also prescribes the building height, road width for various spot uses. In case of Delhi Master Plan, such zoning regulations were prescribed and were made a part of the Master Plan document. But in the case of the walled city no definite planning parameters were identified.

Thus in the absence of any zoning regulations the development proposals for spot uses was left totally to the whims of the administrators. As a result, mixed land uses developed in contravention to the master plan proposals. A number of multi-storied commercial complexes can be seen in Jaipur all over the city and within the walled city in particular.

The first Master Plan of Jaipur was prepared in 1971, which actually came into operation in 1976. During this period the rapid growth of population created many problems like *katchi bastis*, encroachment, mixed land uses, encroachments on public lands and roads, lack of community facilities and public services.

Physical factors such as relief, drainage, wind direction, hydrology play a dominant role in the development pattern of the settlement. In case of Jaipur, the natural hills in the north and west provide strong physical barrier, as it restricts urban development in these directions. The Amani Shah Nallah running in the north-south direction in the western periphery has long been acting as a physical barrier in the west. Thus the city expansion was mostly open towards the south. Therefore most of the development outside the walled city has taken place in the southern direction.

One of the important reasons for the failure of the Master Plan was that, the planners did not take care of the physical conditions in the post independence period. Four streams, namely Amani Shah nallah, Ganda nallah, Jawahar nallah and Jagatpura nallah, mostly carry out the drainage of the city. It may be noted that not much thought was given to the drainage system. As a result new developments and residential colonies were developed over the beds of these drains. The burning example is Jawahar Nagar nallah. This nallah has virtually become non-existent within the university area and beyond. Thus during 1981 floods this nallah caused maximum damage due to flooding the university area, Bajaj Nagar, and Jaipur Dairy plant area. In case of other nallahs the culverts were designed with a very small opening and the development took place on the beds of these nallahs, resulting in a severe damage during the1981 floods.

Jaipur city is gifted with beautiful scenic hills in the north and the east side of the city. But these hills were not preserved in spite of the Master Plan proposals. The stone quarrying continued along these hills till recently. As a result, the hills, which would have provided pleasant scenic views to the city, are now barren and rocky.

The location of the industrial areas was decided without taking into consideration the direction of the wind. Most part of the year, i.e., from November to February the wind blows from the north and northeast. The industrial areas which are located in the north cause air pollution by bringing dust, industrial smoke and other poisonous gases along with the wind from the north.

Many a good plan fails due to non-availability of land with the development agencies. The main reason for non-implementation of the plan proposals has been observed to be non-availability of land with the Local Authorities. Jaipur

Master Plan was based on the concept of bulk acquisition of land. Liberal planning standards were adopted envisaging that bulk land will be developed by local authorities. However, large chunks of land could not be acquired. After the approval of the Master Plan in 1976, the U.I.T., Jaipur took up two large areas for bulk acquisition. One was located towards the south of the city from Bajaj Nagar to Aerodrome and the other towards the west, southwest direction known as sector No. 1. These areas covered most of the urban lands required for the development in the near future. However, legal complications delayed the acquisition process and only few fragmented pockets could be acquired, which were not suitable for taking up any comprehensive schemes. The land conversion rules of the Revenue Department made it further difficult to acquire any pocket of land already in possession of co-operative housing societies. The practice of back dated agreements was followed by speculators for the purchase of land. Therefore, the plan that was based on the concept of 'PUBLIC OWNERSHIP' was implemented, where most of the land was privately owned. The private developers/co-operative housing societies did not adhere to the planning standards proposed in the Master Plan. This has resulted in poor quality development in such areas. There is a vast difference between the schemes developed by the Local Authorities and those developed by the co-operative housing societies with respect to the provision of facilities to the areas, road network and infrastructure. Therefore, the qualitative aspect of the development in general is poor.

Due to the non-acquisition of the land, a number of important proposals could not be implemented. Such as:

1. Sub-city and district centres,
2. Railway complex,
3. University sub-centre and colleges,
4. Truck stands and bus stands,
5. Ring roads,
6. New office complexes,
7. City level parks,
8. Planned residential areas.

Change in the Land Use Cases

The Master Plan of Jaipur was approved in 1976, but there was no provision in the act for a change in the land use or modification in the Master Plan. Therefore, the State Government itself has changed the land use in a number of cases. The main changes were from the green belt to residential areas and other urban uses. These were bulk areas covering about 3665 acres.

In the case of spot level cases JDA has changed as many as 65 cases. The details of those are given below in the Tables 4 and 5.

It may be noted that there has been a change in the land use even in the land reserved for public facilities, parks and open spaces. The change of land use from industrial to residential is also dangerous, because these areas are very close to industrial developments. Green belt area was severely affected including the virtual disappearance of the green belt in the south. Green belts and open spaces have been mostly converted into residential or industrial land use.

Table 4 *Cases of Changes in Land Use*

S. No.	Land use in Master Plan	Change in Land use	Total Cases
1.	Residential	Other Uses	10
2.	Commercial	Other Uses	3
3.	Industrial	Other Uses	8
4.	Govt. Offices	Other Uses	—
5.	Govt. Reserved	Other Uses	3
6.	Public facilities	Other Uses	9
7.	Parks and open spaces	Other Uses	6
8.	Green belt	Other Uses	19
	Total		58

Table 5 *Changes in Land Use*

S. No.	Master Plan Land Use	Changed Land Use	S. No.	Master Plan Land Use	Changed Land Use
1.	Green Belt	Institutional	2.	Nursery/Orchard	Institutional
3.	Tourist Facility	Commercial	4.	Commercial	Residential
5.	Truck Stand	Commercial	6.	Industrial	Residential
7.	Industrial	Residential	8.	Green Belt	Industrial
9.	Educational	Residential	10.	Public Facilities	Residential
11.	Parks/Open Spaces	Residential	12.	Governmental	Residential
13.	Park	Residential	14.	Green Belt	Residential
15.	District Centre	Residential	16.	Educational	Residential
17.	Residential	Commercial	18.	Residential	Commercial
19.	Residential	Commercial	20.	Residential	Commercial
21.	Industrial	Residential	22.	Residential	Commercial
23.	Residential	Commercial	24.	Residential	Commercial
25.	Govt. Offices	Public Facility	26.	Residential	Commercial
27.	Residential	Commercial	28.	Park/Open Spaces	Public Facility
29.	Social Cultural	Commercial	30.	Residential	Commercial
31.	Open Space	Residential	32.	Open space	Social Cultural
33.	Green Belt	Residential	34.	Educational	Residential
35.	Educational	Residential	36.	Educational	Residential
37.	Industrial	Residential	38.	Green Belt	Residential
39.	Green Belt	Educational	40.	Green Belt	Residential
41.	Green Belt	Residential	42.	Green Belt	Residential
43.	Green Belt	Residential	44.	Green Belt	Residential
45.	Green Belt	Residential	46.	Green Belt	Residential
47.	Green Belt	Residential	48.	Green Belt	Residential
49.	Green Belt	Residential	50.	Green Belt	Commercial
51.	Green Belt	Residential	52.	Green Belt	Industrial
53.	Green Belt	Urban Use	54.	Educational	Residential
55.	Industrial	Residential	56.	Industrial	Residential
57.	Industrial	Residential	58.	Ware Housing	Residential

Land Conversion Rules 1981 and Co-operative Housing Societies

The State Government framed land conversion rules in 1981, in which agricultural land may be converted for commercial and residential purpose in the urban area. These rules affected the Master Plan most adversely. As a result the land speculators, irrespective of the Master Plan proposals, purchased all the vacant land within the urban area including the green belt, in the name of the cooperative housing societies. Thus JDA as well as the government could do nothing to stop such development and the entire urban land was passed on to the land speculators purchased directly from the farmers.

Jaipur has experienced a typical aspect of co-operative housing societies where a large portion of land within the urbanisable limits is presently in the possession of private entrepreneurs operating in the guise of cooperatives. These cooperative housing societies have illegally converted agricultural land, subdivided it into residential plots and sold them to their members. The acquisition and subdivision of the land in the name of cooperatives has made it almost impossible for the authorities to acquire land for housing schemes.

As many as 1,100 cooperative housing schemes have been submitted to the JDA for conversion. Although, on the one hand, these cooperative housing schemes have been able to add to the quantum of housing stock, and it is estimated that over one lakh plots have been provided by these societies spread all over the city, on the other however, they did not initiate the required development. The plots were usually subdivided and sold with no provision for water supply, sewerage, drainage and electricity. Even access roads are not developed properly. The development of the area was supposed to be taken up by the societies themselves, which never happened. As a result JDA had to take up the task of development at a very low charge, which is much lower than the cost of actual development in case of JDA schemes.

As per JDA records pertaining to the extent of built-up plots in the approved and unapproved schemes located close to the existing built-up areas and along the roads, it has been found that over 60 per cent of the schemes have more than 50 per cent of their plots lying vacant. The approved schemes numbering over 400 accounting for over 40,000 plots and huge number of unapproved schemes together account for an estimated one lakh vacant plots.

The cooperatives are spread all over the city with concentration in the south and the west of the walled city. Presently several schemes in the name of cooperatives are coming up in the east side of the walled city, beyond the Aravalli ranges along the National Highway (NH-11). The land has already been illegally subdivided and sold. Even big pieces of land have been sold for the purpose of farmhouses, which are going to create scarcity of land for urbanisation in the near future, though a huge chunk of prime land within the urbanisable limits will be lying vacant.

Development of *Katchi Basti*

A general description of the slums would reveal the relationship between poverty, shelter and its environment. Slum settlements show the non-availability of formal housing for the poor in urban areas due to various reasons, such as an increase in land prices and very low affordability of urban poor to pay for the formal housing. The problem of housing for the urban poor is most critical in big metros, and Jaipur is no exception, resulting in the dependence of urban poor on non-formal housing, which is illegal and substandard according to normal accepted norms.

The type of housing illustrated here is known by different names in different parts of the country. For example *jhuggi-jhorpi* in Delhi, *jhopar patti* in Mumbai and *katchi basti* in Jaipur.

Although there is no formal or official definition of *katchi basti*, generally these *bastis* have been taken as slums with illegal occupation of public/private land with uncontrolled, unplanned and haphazard development. They have mostly used rejected building materials and have no civic amenities provided by the municipal corporation like electricity, water, drainage system etc. The area is generally overcrowded and unhygienic for residential purpose.

In the pre-independence period *katchi bastis* have had a very strong correlation with the social factors. Most of the *katchi bastis* were located on the outskirts of the city and inhabited by the people of lower castes like sweepers, beggars, *khatik* and dhobi etc. These were in the form of clusters of shabby houses and straw huts with very unhygienic conditions and were an outcome of the practice of untouchability in those days. In 1942 some new housing schemes were developed outside the walled city. As a result, families were relocated and started living in different locations by building *katcha* houses. The *katchi bastis* that were developed are known as Hazi colony, Panchmukhi Hanuman, Ashokpuri, Bais Godam, Chandrashekhar ki Bagichi, Purohitji ke Basti, Bassi Sitarampura and Dhannadas ki Bagichi.

The post-independence period with the declaration of Jaipur as a state capital experienced a major change, and it became a guiding factor in the location and distribution of *katchi bastis*, though social factors have also played a role in their formation.

The growth trends (Table 6) of *katchi bastis* indicate that in the decade 1941–51 there has been a very high growth rate of these *bastis* due to the exodus of displaced people. In the following decades the growth rates were 116.48 per cent (1951–61), 47.24 per cent (1961–71), and 164.68 per cent (1971–81). The population of *katchi bastis* had increased to about 2.56 lakhs in 1981.

Table 6 *Growth of Katchi Bastis in Jaipur*

Year	*No. of Bastis*	*Population*	*Growth Rate in Population*	*K.B. Population as % of Total City*
1901	15	2,000	—	1.2
1911	17	2,198	9.90	1.6
1921	19	2,250	2.30	1.9
1931	21	2,390	6.20	1.7
1941	21	2,500	4.00	1.4
1951	60	30,309	111.00	10.4
1961	60	65,605	116.00	16.3
1971	109	96,604	147.00	15.2
1981	178	2,55,690	162.00	25.2

The locational distribution of *katchi bastis* clearly indicates that the majority of the bastis have emerged near work centres, and the major concentration of clusters is in the northwest and west of the walled city. The other major chunk of *katchi bastis* is located along the bypass near Jawahar Nagar and along NH-8.

These *bastis* developed on the open public lands, which were proposed for public facilities, parks, playgrounds, plantation etc. They have also encroached upon major roads, hindering the smooth flow of the traffic.

Administrative and Managerial Failure

Implementation of the Master Plan is a process that needs special administrative and managerial skills and expertise. Though JDA was constituted with expertise, and had directors of town planning, engineering, finance and law, the effective action was not taken by them, partly due to the political setup and largely due to the lack of initiative and active participation by the administrative authority. Generally, in case of metropolitan towns, after preparing the Master Plan, a metropolitan authority is constituted in addition to the local authority, which decides the policies about the location of industries, regularisation of land, dealing with conversion cases, location of major economic activities etc. In the case of Jaipur, such authority was not established at the regional level. A senior IAS officer was appointed as the highest executive authority as commissioner in Jaipur and all other officers including four directors were subordinate to him. Thus he prevailed over the technical, legal and financial advices given by four directors.

The administrative failure can be noticed in the sense that no effective action was initiated against the developments taking place in violation of the Master Plan. The number of changes in land use cases permitted by JDA clearly reveals this fact.

Lack of Public Participation

The success of the plan largely depends upon its acceptance by the people. Many good plans fail simply because of the non-cooperation of the people. In the case of Jaipur, JDA or any office authority did not follow the procedure of the plan preparation in which large-scale public participation was asked for. Under the act every plan should be notified to the public for its objection. For this the plan should be advertised in the local newspapers to make it known to the people, so that they can voice their objections, if any. This was not done in Jaipur. Therefore there was no public response to the Master Plan and people considered it as an obstacle in the development. People were totally against the Master Plan, and it resulted into large-scale violations of the Master Plan proposals.

In the light of the above, it may be observed that the Master Plan could not be implemented due to various facts, like performance problems in planning, land acquisition, legal action, delay in plan preparation, *katchi bastis*, cooperative housing societies etc.

Conclusions

Jaipur is one of the fast growing metropolitan cities of India having a population of 2,23,4319 (2001). During the last decade 1991–2001 it has registered the highest growth rate of population, i.e., 59.37 per cent. The municipal area of Jaipur has increased from 6 km^2 in 1927 and 65 km^2 in 1941 to more than 200 km^2 in 1991. The urbanised area has increased from 4047 hectares in 1971 to more than 12,141 hectares in 2001.

The comparative study of the Master Plan of Jaipur prepared for 1971–1991 and 1991–2011 reveals the changing character of the urban fringe areas. The physical growth of Jaipur cutting into the rural landscape has changed the character of the fringe area and produced a landscape vastly different from either rural or urban. The rapid increase of the population has led to an ever-increasing demand of the town to capture the fringe area, and thus changing the internal structure of the city. The irregular developments on the fringe areas of Jaipur have become a liability, as they become a part of the urban complex in so far as provision of the infra-structural facilities and specific amenities are concerned. Nearly 10 million hectares of agricultural land has already been lost due to unplanned growth. In the urban fringe of Jaipur a maze of irregular residential colonies of co-operative housing societies has cropped up during 1980–2001 providing it a rurban character.

The study of the earlier Master Plan (1971–91) indicates that some of the industrial areas like Sudarshanpura, Jaipur South and Jhotwara area developed in the past have now become a part of Jaipur urban complex giving a distinct character to the city.

The new proposed Master Plan (1991–2011) of Jaipur Development Region has been prepared covering an area of 1464 km^2 comprising 385 villages. The Master Plan proposes 32 urban nodes out of which 20 nodes fall under urbanisable area of Jaipur city for 2011 and the remaining 12 nodes have been proposed all over the region as guiding growth potential of satellite towns.

The case study of Jaipur urban fringe area upholds the hypothesis that the fringe of Jaipur is an area of political conflict, so far as the land values and land grabbing are concerned. The study further reveals degradation of environmental and resource based fringe areas, its amorphous character, and the changing and expanding fringe during the independence period and, therefore, the fringe of Jaipur needs to be saved from a chaotic growth.

References

Master Plan 1971–91, Urban Improvement Trust, Jaipur, 1976.

Master Plan 1991–2001, Jaipur Development Authority, Jaipur 1998.

18

Integrated Approach for Characterisation of Urban Fringe Area

A Study for Bangalore City

DAKSHA C. BARAI, SUDHA RAVINDRANATH AND J. KRISHNAMURTHY

Many of the cities and towns of the developing world have demonstrated an unprecedented growth both in terms of spatial spread and population rise over the last few decades. This has been mainly due to industrialisation, shifting focus of the governmental policies, coupled with a steady rural–urban migration and also urban-urban migration. The consequence of the spatial growth of the cities has resulted in the changing facade of the fringe areas, i.e., the space segment lying in between urban complexes and the vast rural countryside. It has been observed that in general the fringe area is subjected to various kinds of unplanned growth, environmental degradation and destruction of natural resources. In its own right it becomes imperative to conduct a systematic study of the fringe areas and suggest better plans for its management and development.

Bangalore is best known as the "Fastest growing city in Asia" and the "City of the 21st Century" for the potential investors from abroad and as a "Silicon Valley of India" for the global electronic and computer giants. With its population of 5.96 million in 2001, the city ranks fifth amongst the nine million cities in the country. Much of the population increase can be attributed to the high population growth rate and rural–urban and urban–urban migration component, impacted by rapid industrialisation, relocation of some high-tech industries from Bombay to Bangalore and setting up of software and multinational companies in Bangalore. The city has grown in the past from a mere 28.85 sq. km. in 1901 to 364 sq. km. in 1996 about 13 times over 95 years engulfing many rural areas into it. By and large the engulfing has been taking place all around the built-up area of the Bangalore city. The changing character of the fringe area of Bangalore City has produced a landscape that is neither urban nor rural in its pure terms. The transition from rural to fringe, fringe to urban is the characteristic phenomena, that change the life style of the people, environment etc.

Aim

The present study has been taken up to understand the growth of Bangalore city in general, more specifically the developments taking place in the city's fringe area using remote sensing and GIS techniques substantiated by field work.

The specific objectives of the study are as follows:

- To map the change in spatial extent of the city over different time,
- To highlight the changes in the land use pattern in the fringe areas,
- To study the impact of urban growth on the life styles of the people in the fringe areas through case studies,
- To study the impact of globalisation on land use changes in Bangalore city and its fringe areas.

Study Area

Bangalore City has a colourful past and began life as the "village of the half baked gram" in early 1400s. The impact of the history of Bangalore is seen in its present day structure of the city with remnants of the Kempe Gowda's fort of 1500's, the cantonment of the British period and the palaces of Tippu and Hyder Ali of late 1800's. Physiographically, Bangalore City is located on a ridge top passing through the centre of Karnataka plateau from west to east, which is greatly dissected by the streams of Koramangala, Challaghatta and Naravanaholla, leading to the development of three projecting spurns. The land towards west of the watershed, though not very high, is very rugged and badly dissected by a large number of streams, all taking a southerly course. This defines the general slope of the land, either to the south or southwest (Singh, 1964). The ridge and valley topography of Bangalore has uniquely supported the creation of a large number of man-made lakes. These lakes form chains, being a series of impoundments across streams and sources of ground water recharge.

Bangalore has grown over the decades both in size and population, and as is evidenced from Table 1, population growth has been rapid during the last few decades. Originally, Bangalore was planned for a small population of 2 to 3 lakhs with small-scale commercial activities. The spatial growth of Bangalore has been in a phased manner. Chamarajpet, Basavanagudi etc., were some of the oldest residential areas to develop around the city core, with the core area comprising of city market, Chikpet, Balepet, etc. Residential and commercial activities were found in this core area. With the establishment of cantonment by the British, in early 1900's some more residential areas sprang up in the cantonment area to accommodate housing for defence personnel. The industrial development, with the setting up of Hindusthan Aeronautics Limited (HAL), Hindusthan Machine Tools (HMT), Indian Telephone Industries (ITI), Bharat Electronics Limited (BEL), Bharat Heavy Electricals Limited (BHEL) and other public and private sector industries during the period 1940 to 1960, further contributed to the development of more residential areas like Malleswaram, Vyalikaval, Palace Orchards, Vijayanagar, etc., and the overall city's spread (Barai, 1993). With the increase in the population and development of industries in the subsequent periods, the city started expanding, leading to development of land uses, which were totally unplanned and formed with an inadequate foresight.

With regard to transport, Bangalore is well developed and connected with the major cities of South India. Two National highways, NH-7 (Bombay-Salem connecting route) and NH-4 (Hyderabad-Madras connecting route) pass through the Bangalore City. The State Highway, SH-17, connects Bangalore with Mysore City. There are many major and minor district roads connecting the city to Doddaballapur, Chickballapur in the north, Kolar in the northeast, Kanakapura, Anekal on the south, Magadi in the west, and Tumkur in the north-west (Figure 1).

Figure 1 *Proposed Bangalore Metropolitan Area: Major Road Network*

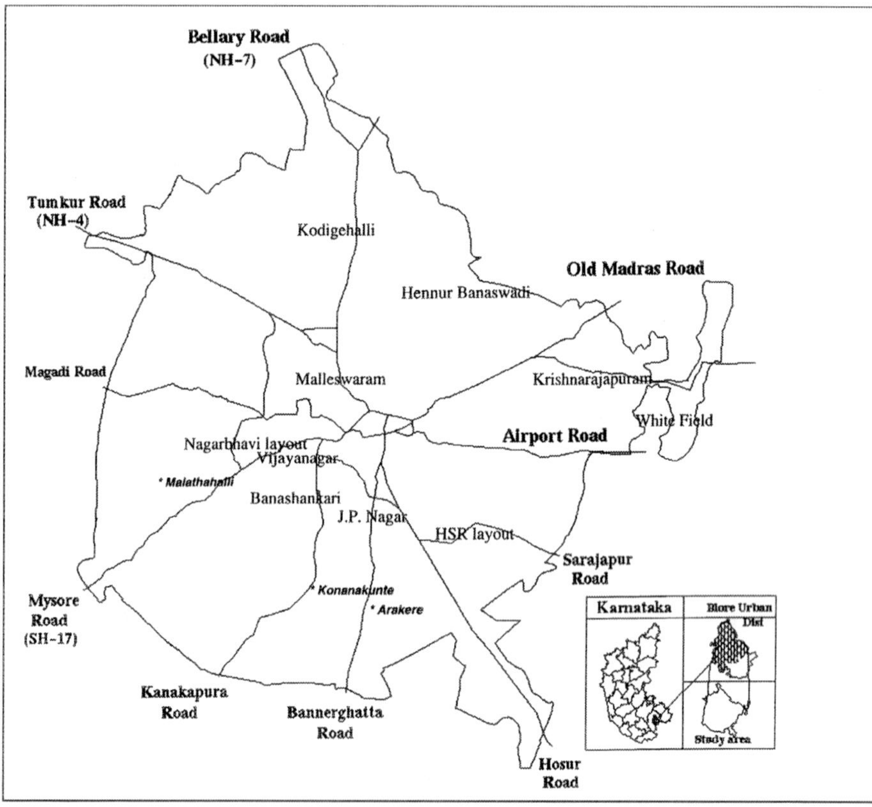

The fringe area has been delimited by Bangalore Metropolitan Region Development Authority (BMRDA) to envisage Doddaballapur, Kolar, Channapatna and Tumkur, an attenuated quadrilateral marking the probable and farthest limits of the metropolitan influence of the city (Prakasa Rao and Tewari, 1979). In his study on impact of metropolitan centres on rural transformation, Boregowda has delimited the fringe of Bangalore city as 30 km. radius (Boregowda and Mahadev, 1978)

However, in the present study, an area of 565 km^2 identified by the BMRDA as the potential urban development area for 2011 AD, has been considered (Figure 2) as the total study area. Beyond this boundary, an area of 682 km^2 has been identified as the green belt.

Figure 2 *Proposed Bangalore Metropolitan Area: Zone Boundary, 1991*

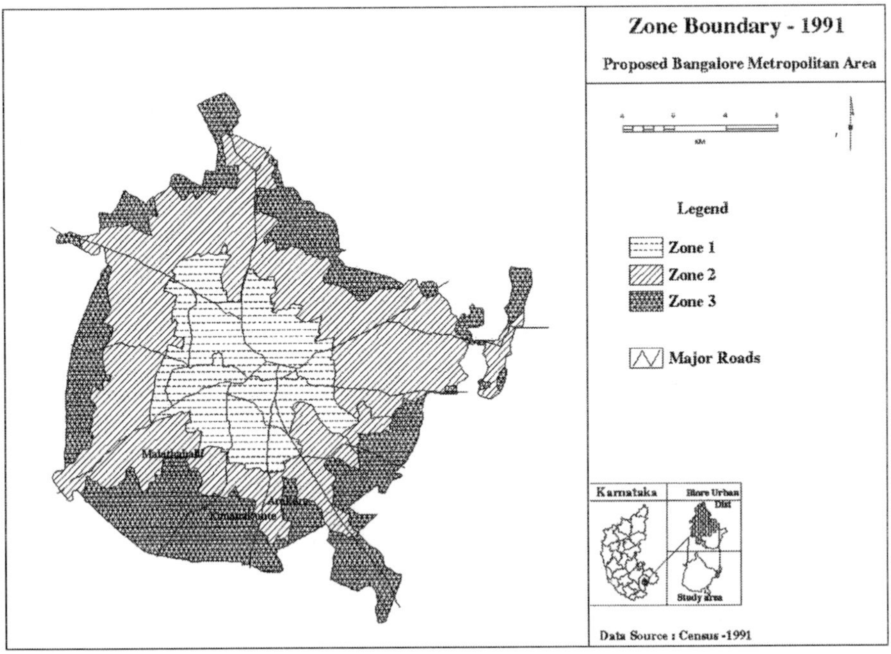

Table 1 *Decadal Population and Growth Rate of Bangalore*

Year	*Population*	*Decadal Increase*	*% Decadal Population Growth*
1961	12,06,961	4,27,984	54.94
1971	16,64,208	4,57,247	37.88
1981	29,21,751	12,57,543	75.56
1991	41,30,288	12,08,537	41.36
2001	59,60,000	18,29,712	44.29

Methodology

Remote sensing data, conventional maps and household primary survey data form the major source of data for the study. Satellite data of SPOT and IRS 1C have been used to generate products of Bangalore city and surroundings for two points of time viz., 1988 and 1996. Digital image processing techniques have been adopted to merge high-resolution panchromatic data with medium resolution multi-spectral data available from the satellites to generate images at 6 m spatial resolution. The photographic products produced at 1:25,000 scale have been interpreted using visual interpretation techniques, and land use maps have been preliminarily prepared. Ground verification of the land use classes has been carried out and final land use/land cover have been prepared. The road network, drainage network and extent of localities have been updated using the satellite data, and spatial database has been created in GIS environment. Overlay, dissolve, buffering and other techniques have been used to identify urban sprawl and urban land use changes over the years.

In order to identify representative fringe area for detailed study, the entire study area has been divided into three zones based on the classification of administrative units as per the Department of Census (Census of India, 1991). Zone-I comprises of the census wards which lie within the city corporation limits and is totally urbanised. Zone-II comprises of the areas identified as urban outgrowths and Zone-III is the area with rural component. In the present paper, the areas comprising Zone-II and Zone-III are considered as the inner urban fringe area. In order to understand the urban influence as well as the problems encountered by the residents of these inner fringe areas, three localities viz., Malathahalli, Konankunte and Arakere all located in Zone II in the west, south and south-east part coinciding with the direction of urban sprawl have been selected. Malathahalli is away from the main Bangalore-Mysore State high way but at the same time has the educational institutions within it. Konankunte and Arakere localities are located on the main roads which are experiencing rapid industrial development. To understand the characteristic in the life style of the people living in these localities, a detailed household survey has been carried out and information such as respondent's education level, occupation, income, movement pattern, housing, shopping and perceptions of their living environment etc. have been collected. By integrating information derived from remote sensing and GIS techniques along with field data (household survey), fringe area have been characterised.

Results and Discussions

Urban Land Use Changes

Remote sensing data record information essentially on land cover from which the land-use information is derived. Thus, a land use map interpreted from the satellite data depicts spatial distribution of different types of land use classes/categories present in it. In the present study, greater emphasis has been placed on the urban land use categories rather than general land use categories. To cite an example, the built-up category has been divided into many subclasses viz., residential, industrial, commercial, recreational etc.

Land use maps of 1988 and 1996 generated by interpreting the satellite data have been subjected to a change detection analysis. The results of the analysis are given in Table 2 and graphically represented in Figure 3. From the analysis, it has been observed that there has been an increase in residential area at the expense of agricultural areas in 1996 as compared to 1988.

Residential areas: The residential category on the whole has increased in 1996 in comparison to the residential areas as noticed in urban land use map of 1988. The increase has been mostly towards the eastern, western and the southern side of the study area. It can be seen from the table and figure that between 1988 and 1996, under the residential category, the four sub-categories viz., dense, medium, low built-up and new layouts have increased. However, the increase has been maximum in the dense built-up category and new layouts. There has been tremendous growth of dense built-up category in the northern and northeastern side especially in Hennur, Banaswadi, RT Nagar, Mahadevapura, Hoodi areas, mainly due to the industries located on the eastern side. Another reason for this increase in residential areas is due to the

Figure 3 *Land Use Changes between 1988 and 1996*

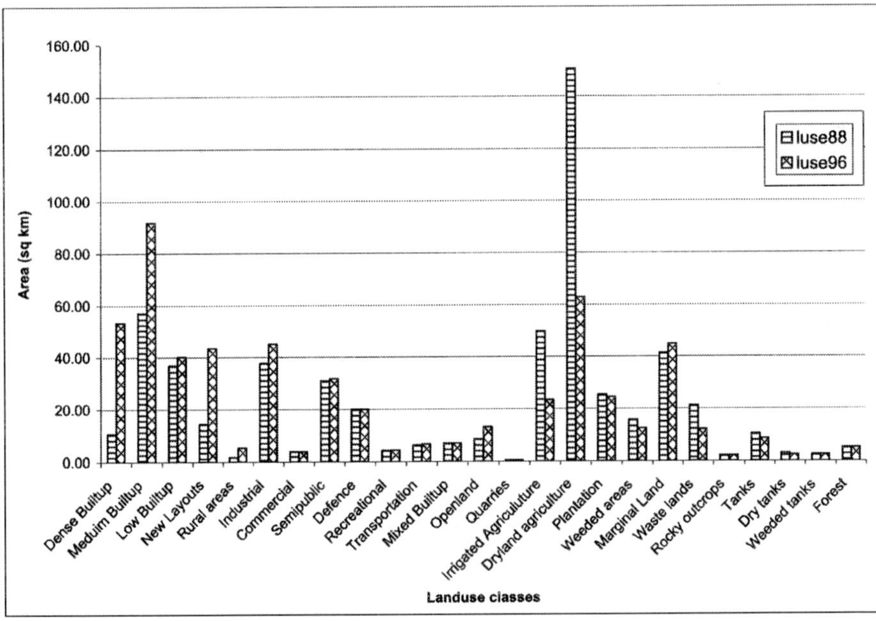

construction of the Technology Park on the Whitefield Ring Road in the east, and also the Outer peripheral ring road connecting the old Madras Road with the Bellary Road, which has accelerated the urban growth because of its accessibility to other parts of the city.

The areas, which were seen as new layouts in 1988, have become built-up category, either medium or low. A few examples in this respect are, the layouts at Hennur-Banaswadi, Kodigehalli (layout of the Telecom Department), Banashankari, J.P. Nagar in the south, Chandra layout, Prashanth Nagar, etc. in the west, which have become low to medium dense built-up areas in 1996. Some of the new layouts in 1996 are seen as large patches on the southern side, in between Hosur and Kanakapura Roads. These new layouts are the ones mostly developed by private builders, which are often opted by people working in the industries. Nagarabhavi layout, OMBR layout, east NGEF layout, AECS layout in the western side and layouts formed near Arakere, Begur, Royal Residency and Hulimavu on the Bannerghatta Road are a few examples of the new layout formations. Some of the major reasons that can be attributed to the new layout formations and residential built-up activity could be due to educational institutional growth on the western side and industrial growth in terms of software offices in the southern side of the city.

The industrial growth is mostly seen on Hosur, Bannerghatta and Kanakapura Roads on the southern side and on Whitefield and Krishnarajapuram on the east. The ground survey has revealed that software industries of Infosys, Honeywell, Microsoft and a range of upstart companies across the Ring Road through Koramangala to Whitefield Technology Park and Hosur Industrial estate, Public sector industries like ITI, HAL etc. are also located here. These areas have developed industrial areas in juxtaposition with residential areas in coexistence with commercial pockets and public utilities.

Agriculture areas: In the agricultural category, the dryland agricultural area has reduced in 1996 to about 1/3 of its area as compared to 1988, while the irrigated agriculture area has decreased in 1996 to about 1/2 of its area as compared to 1988. The agricultural areas, especially the irrigated, dryland agricultural and marginal areas have reduced more in the southern, western and north-western side and converted into built-up category or into new layouts. Close to Kengeri tank, dryland agricultural areas have been converted into marginal lands, which is likely to be used in future for residential purposes. The irrigated areas belonging to the Hebbal and Nagavara Kere areas have reduced and been transformed into built-up. Likewise, the irrigated areas close to the Hosur Road have also reduced in area. The dryland agricultural areas in between Hosur road and Bannerghatta road as well as between Bannerghatta road and Kanakapura roads have many new layout formations belonging to private builders, company layouts and Central Government layouts. There has been decrease in the plantations.

Table 2 *Changes in Land Use Statistics from 1988 to 1996*

Land use category	*Land use 1988 (km^2)*	*Land use 1996 (km^2)*	*Change (km^2)*	*% Change*
Residential:				
Dense Built-up	10.73	53.40	42.67	397.67
Medium Built-up	57.13	91.79	34.66	60.67
Low Built-up	36.80	40.08	3.28	8.91
New Layouts	14.50	43.45	28.95	199.66
Industrial	37.72	45.04	7.31	19.38
Commercial	3.84	3.84	0	0.00
Semi-public	30.80	31.70	0.90	2.92
Defence	19.98	19.98	0	0.00
Recreational	4.36	4.37	0.01	0.23
Transportation	6.28	6.71	0.43	6.85
Mixed Built-up	7.06	7.06	0	0.00
Open Land	8.63	13.15	4.52	52.38
Quarries	0.38	0.38	0	0.00
Agriculture:				
Irrigated agriculture	49.82	23.35	–26.46	–53.11
Dryland agriculture	150.55	62.90	–87.65	–58.22
Plantation	25.32	24.46	–0.87	–3.44
Grass/weeds	15.80	12.53	–3.27	–20.70
Marginal Land	41.34	44.78	3.44	8.32
Waste Lands	21.22	12.15	–9.07	–42.74
Rocky outcrops	2.14	2.16	0.02	0.93
Tanks: Tanks	10.46	8.67	–1.79	–17.11
Dry tanks	3.07	2.45	–0.62	–20.20
Weeded tanks	2.56	2.48	–0.08	–3.13
Forest	5.25	5.25	0	0.00

Wastelands have decreased to about 1/3 of its area in 1996 as compared to 1988. Wastelands found in the western side and the southern side have declined in areal extent and are converted into residential built-up category, especially those close to the Ring Road, connecting Mysore and Kanakapura Roads. Many of the tanks in the study area except a few of them maintained by the Department of Forest are polluted with weeds or are totally dry with grass grown in them. These dry tank beds are used as playgrounds or for dumping garbage by the public. Apart from this, there are tanks surrounded by built-up areas, which over a short span of time will be converted into dry tanks as their source of water is blocked due to construction activities. Tanks of Challaghatta, Jarganhalli, Puttenhalli etc. are the ones, which are totally dry and having grass cover. Nagarvarakere, Arekere, Hulimavu, Begur etc. are the ones surrounded by constructional activity, which are endangered.

The change in land use categories over different time frame is an important factor for understanding the overall urban land use patterns. The category wise change that has occurred over the land use existed in 1988 by 1996 has been worked out and results are presented in Table 2. It can be made out from the table that nearly sixty-six per cent of the dryland agriculture area in 1988 has undergone changes in 1996. Of this 66 per cent, the changes due to residential activities amount to 20 per cent and new layout formations amounts to 17 per cent. Similarly, 58 per cent of the irrigated agricultural area of 1988 has undergone a change, of which 23 per cent is under built-up category. The loss in plantation category of 1988 is to the tune of 30 per cent towards built-up category in 1996, but has been compensated by new plantations in other areas. Only 17 per cent of the new layout category of 1988 has remained as new layouts and the rest has been converted into residential category in 1996. Nearly, 37 per cent of the area under wastelands in 1988 has been converted into residential and new layout formations in 1996. It has been observed that the potential agricultural land is neglected and gradually converted to marginal lands, which finally get converted, to layouts by real estate developers. The above discussions clearly brings out the fact that due to mounting pressures of increasing population, people have taken up developmental activities, that too mainly residential, in lands earlier devoted to agriculture or lying as wastelands. This trend has also been observed earlier by other researchers (Prakasa Rao, 1979, Behera et al., 1986).

Similar such observations have been reported by various studies carried out for other cities by Hussain (1980), Hussain and Siddiqui (1982), Madalena Neiro Pereira (1996) and Shupeng Chen et al. (2000).

Influence of Urban Growth on the Life Styles of People in the Fringe Areas

The development in the inner urban fringe areas of Bangalore city has occurred haphazardly without adhering to any contiguous land use patterns giving rise to infrastructural problems. Besides this, problems in fringe areas are in a transitional stage which has led to resource degeneration in terms of converting agricultural land to non-agricultural uses such as housing, industry, marriage halls, resorts, commercial shops etc. In these areas, pollution is evidenced by the conversion of natural lakes and wastelands into built-up areas and disposal sites.

As discussed earlier, these problems have been studied for three localities, viz., Malathahalli, Konankunte and Arakere in the inner fringe of Bangalore city where rapid urban transformations are observed. In general it has been observed that the development in Arakere and Konankunte has been more rapid than in Malathahalli.

Malathahalli, is an example of a typical urban outgrowth, which is experiencing the urban influence and at the same time has retained the rural ambience. One can still observe the rural atmosphere in the core village with houses having tiles or zinc sheets used as roof tops, narrow, unmetalled and winding roads and lack of proper municipal civic facilities. Malathahalli is significantly influenced by the existence of important educational institutions in and around it viz., Bangalore University, Engineering College, Institute for Social and Economic Change, Atomic Energy Centre, National Law University, Homeopathy Centre etc. which has prompted urban growth. This urban influence, in turn, has brought about a change in the living styles of the people, which is evident from the survey. It has been observed from the survey that there has been an occupational change from primary towards secondary and tertiary where people are working in factories, in educational institutions, having their own shops etc. Most of the houses have modern gadgets like TV, telephones, refrigerators etc. Residents use two wheelers for their transport and have modern constructed houses. Though valuable agricultural land has been converted to new layout formations, housing, commercial activities associated with the needs of educational institutions. New layouts have been acquired for group housing schemes by public and private companies viz., ITI, BEL etc.

In the case of Konankunte and Arakere localities located on the two important major district roads, the development has been very rapid. There has been transformation of the land with the agricultural areas being converted into housing areas, software companies, farmlands, residential schools, factory outlets of branded Indian and multinational companies interspersed with government and private housing society layouts. The major semi-skilled and unskilled work force in many of the small-scale industries located on the main roads is from Konankunte and Arakere. However, there are subtle differences in the development activities occurring in these two localities. Konankunte has housing layouts of banks, teachers etc. in the interior and on the main roads, it has small-scale industries. Arakere village on the other hand has multi-storied apartments complexes, foreign banks with ATM, software companies are found in the main and arterial roads. Housing layouts in various stages of formations are found in Arakere. Apart from this, traditional brick kilns close to the water source still exist. Thus we see a strong multinational influence on the main arterial roads connecting these two localities in terms of exclusive resorts, commercial structures, multinational banks with ATMs, self-contained apartment complexes and industrial estates.

From a comparison of the three localities on various socio-economic factors it is observed that there is a strong urban influence felt on the socio-economic aspects of the residents. The influence is more perceptible in the patterns of education, occupation, income, type of houses, household amenities, vehicles owned, modes of transport used, etc. of the residents. In terms of the educational background, most of the respondents surveyed have SSLC as a basic educational qualification. All the three localities have more number of people in the income group Rs 5,000. People are employed more in business and services than in agricultural activities. Most of the houses are main houses with brick and cement construction. Most of the houses have water and electricity. Slightly more than 50 per cent of the houses have sewage connections and toilets within the house. One third of the houses have telephone facilities and have TV, tape recorders, mixers, sofa sets, dining tables, refrigerators etc., all indicating a strong urban influence. Most of the people use LPG connections in addition to kerosene for cooking. All the three localities have bus connectivity, and to a certain extent educational and medical facilities. Most of the residents have vehicles for their daily movement, with more people owning two wheelers. Unlike a typical village, all the three localities surveyed have shops like groceries, vegetables and fruits, milk booths, STDs, ice-cream and juice parlours, medical clinics, drug shops and pathology laboratories, Xerox copying centres, cyber cafes etc., which are more characteristic of an urban centre. On the whole, one can notice a substantial urban influence on socio-economic aspects of the residents in all the three localities, although it varies marginally. Some of the needs expressed by the residents for improving the condition of the localities are improvement of roads, proper waste collection and disposal, supply of corporation water, transport, proper sewage and drainage facilities, etc.

Impact of Globalisation on the Changing Land Uses in the Fringe Areas of Bangalore City

Globalisation is an extension of an internationalisation of economic activity that has a history, marked by a radically increased mobility of capital and international integration of production and control facilitated by advances in communication and transport technology (Marcuse and van Kemper, 2000). Globalising cities especially in India articulates itself as emerging metropolitan agglomerations where they play a vital role as centres of production, distribution and consumption as points of potential power and command. They are preferential locations of multinational companies and gateways of foreign brands, westernised life styles and consumption patterns. Since liberalisation Pune, Bangalore and Delhi have benefited from new economic opportunities (Dittrich, 2000).

Bangalore city as the state capital of Karnataka and in the heart of the Asia-Pacific region has emerged as the busiest software development centre and the fastest growing city in India. Bangalore's emergence as one of the busiest software centres with global giants to small local enterprises is engaged as end user application products and services ranging from accounting systems to specialised niche market products or customised services. The population doubled from 1981 to 1998 and is likely to touch seven millions by 2010 A.D. Most of the growth is by migration especially from Pune, Bombay, Delhi, Chennai etc. rather than natural increase.

The case of Bangalore points that globalised market areas of the periphery represents the "edge cities". The effects of globalisation is seen more on the south-eastern and eastern side where growth is due to software technology park at Whitefield and Hosur industrial estates on Hosur road, which is a private industrial estate housing software company, smaller industrial parks on the periphery of Bannerghatta road, Old Madras road, Airport road etc. Impacts of globalisation are seen along the peripheries which are marked by super markets (Food World type), pizza joints, multinational banks, ATM centres, resorts, clubs, pubs, self contained apartments etc. which mark 'edge cities', giving rise to a pastiche of disarticulated spaces. Thus, the growth of the city has brought about globalisation changes in land uses tending to bring out unplanned growth especially along the margins and also work culture of its residents. Konankunte and more so Arakere are typical examples of developing 'edge cities' where globalisation impact are felt. This impact of globalisation is not felt so much in the western, northern and north-eastern parts of the city. The western section is educational and industrial, while the northern and eastern section is influenced by colonisation. These are areas where old land uses exist and older areas are subject to urban renewal and space and colonial culture restricts a global impact.

From the study it is observed that there is marked urban influence in the inner urban fringe area where development has occurred haphazardly in unplanned layouts and apartments springing up in the midst of software and multinational companies. Hence the existing narrow winding roads are disproportionate to the development of the built-up areas and growing traffic on them. Roads during rainy season are a source of hazards creating bottlenecks on one hand and accidents on the other. Absence of storm water drains due to poor planning gives rise to flooding of the roads and low lying areas. Water is scarce on the peripheral areas due to over exploitation of ground water, and the Cauvery water in its IV stage has not yet reached all apartment complexes and is still inadequate. Lorry water tankers are a common sight in all apartment complexes.

Conclusions

In the present study an integrated approach of using remote sensing, GIS and house hold surveys has been demonstrated in characterising the developments taking place in the fringe area around Bangalore city. These developments are occurring at a rapid pace and in a haphazard manner bringing about changes in the land uses, services, life styles of people etc. Some of the problems and issues emerging due to the unplanned development taking place in the fringe areas have brought out the need for a continuous monitoring through remote sensing and GIS for a planned development. However, for planned development there is a need for a co-ordinated approach wherein the various service providers of the city, like the Bangalore Development Authority, Bangalore Metropolitan Transport Corporation, Bangalore Telephones, Bangalore Water Supply and Sewerage Board etc., have to work in close co-ordination with each other. Recently, the Bangalore Agenda Task Force (BATF) and the NGOs, which have its stakeholders both from public and private enterprises, have been making efforts in planning and monitoring the growth of Bangalore city.

References

Barai, D.C. (1993): Perspectives on Industrial Development in Karnataka, in N.P.K. Sinha and M.B. Singh (eds) *Perspectives on Industrial Development in India*:109–136

Behera, G., P.P. Nageswara Rao, C.B.S. Dutt, B. Manikiam, P. Kalakrishnan, J. Krishnamurthy, K.M. Jagadeesh, K. Ganesh Raj, P.G. Diwakar, A.S. Padmavathy, and R. Parvathy (1985): Growth of Bangalore City since 1900 based on Maps and Satellite Imageries. ISRO-EOS-TR-55–85, ISRO, Bangalore

Boregowda, P. and P.D. Mahadev (1978): Impact of Metropolitan Centers on Rural Transformation: A Case Study of Localities around Bangalore, *National Geographer*, XIII (2): 105–116

Census of India (1991): *District Census Handbook – Bangalore*, Part XII– A, Village and Town wise Primary Census Abstract, Dept. of Census Operations, Karnataka

Census of India (1991): *District Census Handbook – Bangalore*, Part XII-B, Village and Town wise Primary Census Abstract, Dept. of Census Operations, Karnataka.

Dittrich, C. (2000): Globalization and Vulnerable Livelihoods in Bangalore, South India., in Axel Drescher, Christopher Dittrich and Fred Kruger (eds), *APT-REPORTS on Urbanization Vulnerability and Resource Management in Developing Countries:* 44–54.

Hussain, M.I. (1980): Urban Expansion or Encroachment, *Geog. Review India*, 42 (2): 131–139.

Hussain, M.I and N.A. Siddiqui (1982): Urban Encroachment on Rural Lands: A Case Study of Shahranpur City (1950–73), *National Geog. J. India*. 28, Parts 1 and 2:186–196.

Pereira, Madalena Neiro (1996): Urban Management Using RS Techniques, *Proceedings of the Special Plenary Session of International Astronomical Federation on Population, Dynamics and Management of Urban Environment*, at Beijing, China: 17–22.

Marcuse, P. and R. van Kemper (2000): Conclusion: A Changed Spatial Order, in Peter Marcuse and Ronald van Kemper (eds), *Globalizing Cities: A New Spatial Order*, Blackwell Publishers, Oxford, Malden (Massachusetts)

Prakasa Rao, V.L.S., and V.K. Tewari (1979): *The Structure of an Indian Metropolis: A Study of Bangalore*, Allied Publishers Pvt. Ltd. New Delhi.

Shankar K., K.M. Shivashankara, B.P. Sureshappa and B.J. Shivaraju (2000): Impact of Urbanization on Malathahalli, Unpublished M. Sc Project Report, Dept. of Geography, Bangalore University, Bangalore.

Shupeng Chen, Shan Zheng and Chuangji Xie (2000): Remote Sensing and GIS for Urban Growth Analysis of China, *Photogrammetric Engineering and Remote Sensing*, 66 (5): 639–644.

Singh, R.L. (1964): *Bangalore an Urban Survey*, Tara Publications, Varanasi.

Sudha, R. (2001): *Urban Monitoring and Planning of Proposed Metropolitan Area of Bangalore using Remote Sensing and GIS Techniques*, Unpublished Ph.D. thesis, Dept. of Geography, Bangalore University, Bangalore, 337.

19

The Structure and Dynamics of the Urban Fringe of Delhi

BALESHWAR THAKUR

Nature of Problem

The urban fringe, also called the rural–urban fringe, is a segment of space lying between the urban complex, on the one hand, and the vast rural countryside, on the other. It is the peripheral zone of the cities and is occasionally labelled as periurban fringe. The urban fringe is the zone of land adjacent to built-up urban centres and this zone may extend outward for about 48–80 km. The most important aspect about the urban fringe is that its land space handles most of the conversion from rural to urban and associated urban land uses as the population of cities grows. The lifestyles and preferences of the city dwellers change and thus land in the urban fringe remains under strong demand. Many people today want to live in open space surroundings and can afford to do so. The physical growth of cities cutting into rural landscape changes the character of the fringe area and produces a landscape vastly different from either rural or urban. The growth is very fast in Delhi as compared to other cities in India. This is due to the non-availability of any physical barrier around the city. For example, Mumbai cannot expand in the western and southern direction as the Arabian Sea restricts to do so. Therefore, all growth is in the vertical direction in Mumbai, whereas Delhi has ample scope to spread out horizontally and it happens in the same way. This expansion is at the cost of good quality agricultural land which affects the food production. The spatial pattern emerging from multi-directional growth is sprawl. The physical expansion of settlements between 1951 and 2001, therefore, has led to the decrease in rural villages and brought about a structural change towards urban growth. There is a great loss of agricultural land in the fringe area after land acquisition by non-farmers. Therefore, numerous changes are discernible in the type of land use after the change in land ownership. The migration process also contributes to the change in land use. However, many competitive authorities have been involved in the fringe development including the Delhi Development Authority (DDA).

Moreover, the private land developers take advantage of this situation. Potentially, being a part of the future city, the fringe of Delhi experiences spill over effects of non-agricultural functions of the city and, consequently, land space in the urban fringe is in urgent need of better administration, comprehensive planning and public protection.

Purpose of Study

Delhi metropolitan city is expanding in a haphazard manner beyond their administrative boundaries into the surrounding rural areas due to the absence of a regional approach in city planning, lack of coordination in the plans of multiple planning agencies and lack of proper resources. Delhi's fringe is also characterised by an unplanned shift from agricultural to mixed urban land uses, scattered urban development, misuse of natural resources, environmental degradation, and inadequate provision of infrastructure services. In order to have a sustainable development of the fringe zone, the megacity needs to be managed by using innovative planning approaches and new strategies of land management. The purpose of the study is: (1) to analyse the spatial spread of the fringe of Delhi; (2) to demonstrate the impact of urbanisation on natural resources in the fringe areas; and (3) to evaluate the existing programmes and policies for the fringe development and recommend suggestion.

Hypothesis

The fringe expands uniformly in all directions in absence of any physical obstructions and socio-economic influences from the nearby towns.

The Study Area

The location and administrative set-up of Delhi and its surrounding areas give a clear understanding of its fringe. This fastest growing and leading megacity of India is located in the State of Delhi, surrounded by Uttar Pradesh in the eastern half and Haryana in the western half. The State is divided into two tahsils, viz., Delhi and Mehrauli. For the purpose of development, the State is divided into Urban Delhi at centre which is surrounded by five Community Development Blocks, viz., Alipur (north), Kanjhawala (northwest), Najafgarh (southwest), Mehrauli (south) and Shahdara (east) consisting of villages of varying sizes (Figure 1). The surrounding villages and towns of Uttar Pradesh and Haryana serve the city as suburbs and satellite towns, respectively. The main satellite towns are Faridabad, Gurgaon, Rewari, Rohtak, Sonipat of Haryana and Ghaziabad and Noida of Uttar Pradesh.

Delhi is the largest city in North India with a population of 12.79 million in 2001. It is the third largest in the country, after Mumbai (16.36 million) and Kolkata (13.21 million). It is perhaps one of the oldest cities of India with a chequered history. The city is located on the banks of the Yamuna river, a tributary of the Ganges river, at a height of 212 m above sea level. It possesses the most central geographical location, 1,536 km. from Mumbai, 1,520 km. from Kolkata and 2,163 km. from Chennai. Geographically, the city occupies a commanding situation in the form of a gateway between the Himalayas, Aravallis and the Thar. Before 1947, despite being the capital of British India,

Figure 1 *Delhi: Location*

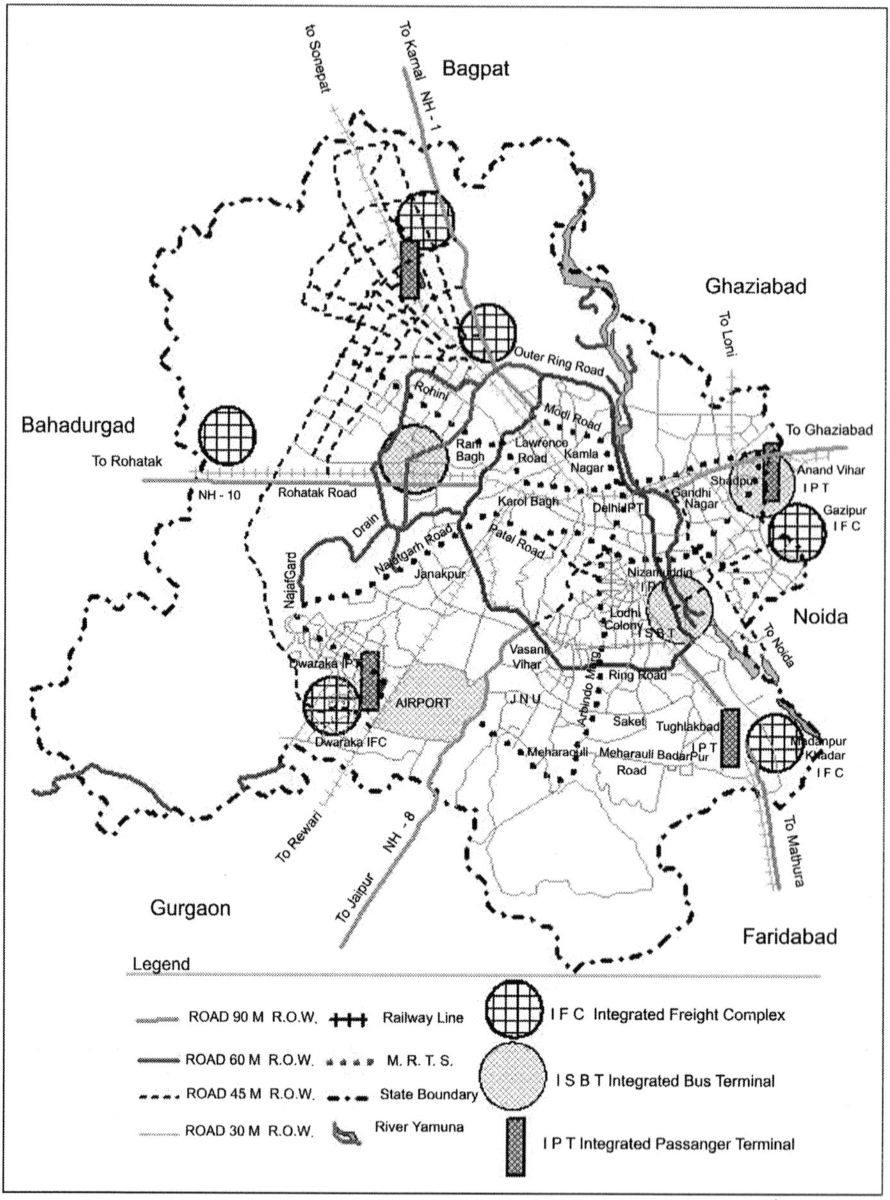

Delhi was a regional city. After Independence, the city has grown dramatically in population size and built-up area and since then, it has been receiving people from all parts of the country. It is estimated that the population has been increasing at a rate of 55 per cent or more per decade with a receipt of migrant population of about 2 lakhs each year. The city has been expanding its commercial, industrial and service bases. It is the national capital of the Indian Republic and the most important centre of political and economic power. It represents Indian culture and society as it has evolved through centuries. With the result, the city has witnessed an unparallel spatial expansion due to urban sprawl. Consequently, the urban area has increased from 46 km^2 in 1901 to 648 km^2 in 2001. Delhi is not only increasing in spatial terms in all directions due to urban sprawl but also experiences the adverse affects in its natural resources as well as its environment. The Delhi Development Authority has done a remarkable task of developing the city as a modern metropolis by giving shape to the inputs of urban planners. However, there appears to be a growing dissatisfaction over the way in which the implementation of the Plan has taken place.

Spatial Spread

Up till Independence, the boundary between the Delhi Urban Area and the surrounding rural areas was abrupt due to slow growth in urban population. Any small increase in the population of the city used to be absorbed within the existing residential areas. However, since Independence, due to the flow of new migrants into the city in search of work, education etc., the city has been expanding very fast encroaching upon the rural villages of the surrounding blocks one by one. Though, according to the Census, there is a sharp boundary line between *urban* and *rural* Delhi (which changes very frequently), the urban land use pattern and the socio-economic characteristics of the city change gradually outwards from the city. Even within a village (which the Census of India takes as smallest unit and converts the whole unit to urban area on the basis of changes in certain characteristics), the land use pattern and socio-economic characteristics are not homogenous. As a result, within the urban areas some rural characteristics and within the surrounding rural areas, some urban characteristics are observed. Therefore, gradually the concept of the "urban fringe of Delhi" emerged after Independence. The fringe can be defined as the transitional zone between the urban centre and the surrounding rural area in which the urban characteristics decreases and rural characteristics increases gradually outward (Ramachandran, 1989: 297). The urban characteristics are inversely proportional to the distance from the city centre, i.e., urban characteristics decrease with the distance from the city centre. Likewise, the rural characteristics are directly proportional to the distance from the city centre, i.e., rural characteristics increase with distance from the city centre. However, the rate of these changes, viz., changes in rural and urban characteristics are not uniform in all directions from the city centre. Towards the south and southeast, viz., towards NOIDA and Faridabad and Ghaziabad, the rate of decrease in urban characteristics is very slow.

It is very difficult to delimit the fringe around Delhi. In the Indian context, the inner boundary of the fringe starts where agricultural land uses appear near the city and extends up to the point where villages have distinct urban land uses or where some persons, at least, from the village community commute to the city daily for work or other purposes. On the basis of this, the inner boundary of Delhi can be delineated; but it is difficult to delimit the outer boundary, because urban land uses are found beyond hundreds of kilometres from the city centre, i.e within the rural belt in the form of educational institutions (residential schools/colleges), factories, godowns, industries etc. If the second criterion is considered for delimiting the outer boundary (i.e., daily commutation of some people to city for work or other purposes) then it is noticed that every day people commute from far-off places, e.g., from beyond Meerut to supply milk. This is possible due to the development of transportation facilities. Therefore, an intensive village level primary survey is required to delimit the fringe of Delhi.

In this study, to delimit the fringe of Delhi, understanding of spatial affiliation and close economic ties of the city with its surroundings are needed. Regarding the spatial affiliation, three regions are recognised at different hierarchical levels, viz., (1) the metropolitan city at micro level, (2) the metropolitan area or city planning area at meso level, and (3) the metropolitan region at macro level, respectively being designated as Delhi Urban Area (DUA) and National Capital Region (NCR) or Delhi Metropolitan Region (DMR). The Delhi Urban Area forms the core, i.e., the city, and DMA and NCR constitute two successive rings of contact around it (Figure 1). DUA extends as to the point where people can commute to the city core on a daily basis. Advanced means of long distance transportation and communication makes it possible to commute to the city for employment and education, and live outside it. It includes Delhi Urban Area, Narela (the town within Delhi State), and the towns of Ghaziabad, Faridabad, Bahadurgarh, Ballabgarh, Gurgaon and Loni, from the adjoining states of Haryana and Uttar Pradesh. The National Capital Region includes the Delhi State (1,483 km^2), Haryana sub-region (13,413 km^2) comprising the districts of Faridabad, Gurgaon, Rohtak and Sonipat; Rewari and Bawal tehsils of Rewari district; and Panipat tehsil of the Karnal district; Uttar Pradesh sub-region (10,853 km^2) including three districts, viz., Meerut, Ghaziabad and Bulandshahr; and Rajasthan sub-region (4,493 km^2) incorporating six tehsils of Alwar district. The National Capital Region beyond the Delhi Urban Area is primarily rural in character, dotted with lower order urban centres. They show tendencies of growth, related, one way or the other, to the growth of the main city. Thus, it can be concluded that the Delhi Urban Area forms the core, and DMA and NCR constitute two successive rings of contact around it, the former of intimate daily contact and the latter of moderate influence. Keeping the above economic interdependence between the region as well as the definition of the fringe in mind, it can be concluded that the inner boundary of the fringe should lie in between the DUA and DMA and the outer boundary should lie just beyond the DMA. Figure 2 (a and b) shows the inner and outer boundary of the fringe of Delhi, interpreted from the Landsat TM image acquired on 21st April, 1999. If this map is overlaid on the map showing, DUA, DMA and NCR, then it proves the tentative boundaries revealed from the study of spatial affiliation.

Changing Boundaries of the Fringe

Both the inner and outer boundaries of Delhi's fringe are not static. They expand rapidly with the expansion of the city. The metropolitan nature of Delhi is ever expanding since the beginning of this century because of the various spatio-temporal reasons. Before Independence, natural calamities were the centrifugal forces in rural India leading to a population influx into Delhi, but in the post-Independence period man-induced socio-economic centripetal forces fuelled a large-sized immigration into Delhi. With a continuously increasing number of immigrants, the physical size of urban Delhi has expanded. Figure 3 shows the spatial expansion of urban areas from 1951 to 1989. The Delhi Urban Area has expanded maximum during 1961–71 (32.68%) followed by the decades 1971–81 (32.62%) and 1981–91(15.78%), respectively. Though the Delhi Urban Area is increasing since 1961, the rate of increment varies distinctively. The rate of increment has decreased between 1961 and 1991 and after that it increased suddenly. From the spatial and temporal expansion of Urban Delhi, the expansion of the fringe and its frequently changing boundaries can be visualized. But, satellite images of two time periods are very helpful to get an exact picture of change in fringe boundaries. Figure 2 (a and b) shows fringe boundaries in 1974 and that of 1991 derived from the Landsat TM images. The fringe areas have expanded outward in 1999 but the boundaries have not expanded uniformly in all directions. Along the narrow Delhi-Ghaziabad corridor (1974), the urban area has expanded so much that Ghaziabad looks like a part of Delhi Urban Area in 1999. Within a span of 25 years, the corridors have developed between Delhi and Faridabad, as well as between Delhi and Gurgaon. The northern and western boundary of Delhi Urban Areas has expanded almost uniformly. The land use map derived from the image (1999) shows the outer boundary of fringe distinctively (Figure 2 a and b).

Figure 2 *Delhi in 1974 and 1999*

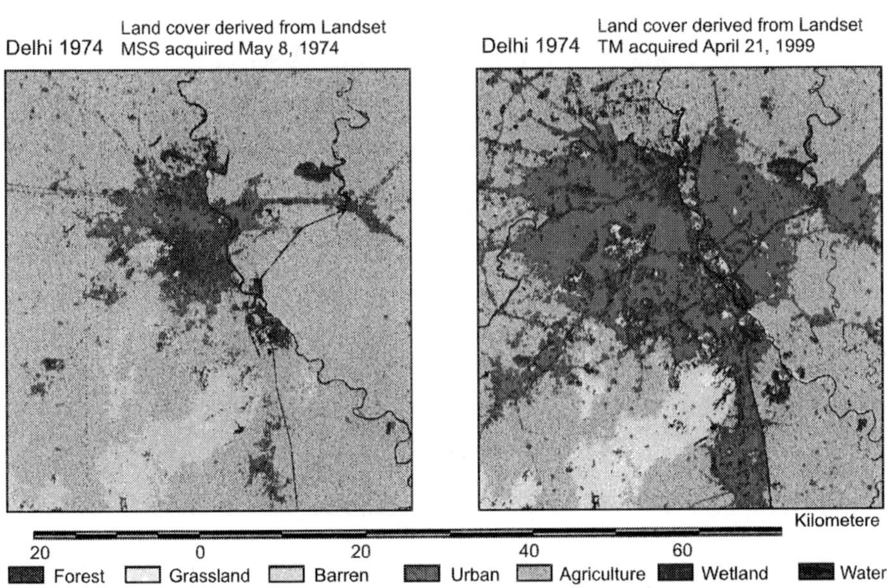

Patterns and Trends of Fringe Developments

The patterns and trends of development of the fringe areas of Delhi depend upon the physical features around the city and the existing trends of urbanisation. In contrast to the development plan of DDA, the fringe has expanded very fast towards the east, because migrants from all parts of highly populated Uttar Pradesh settle between Delhi and Ghaziabad in search of employment in Delhi. They settle there due to a number of reasons, viz., to benefit from the

Figure 3 *Delhi: Land Acquisition*

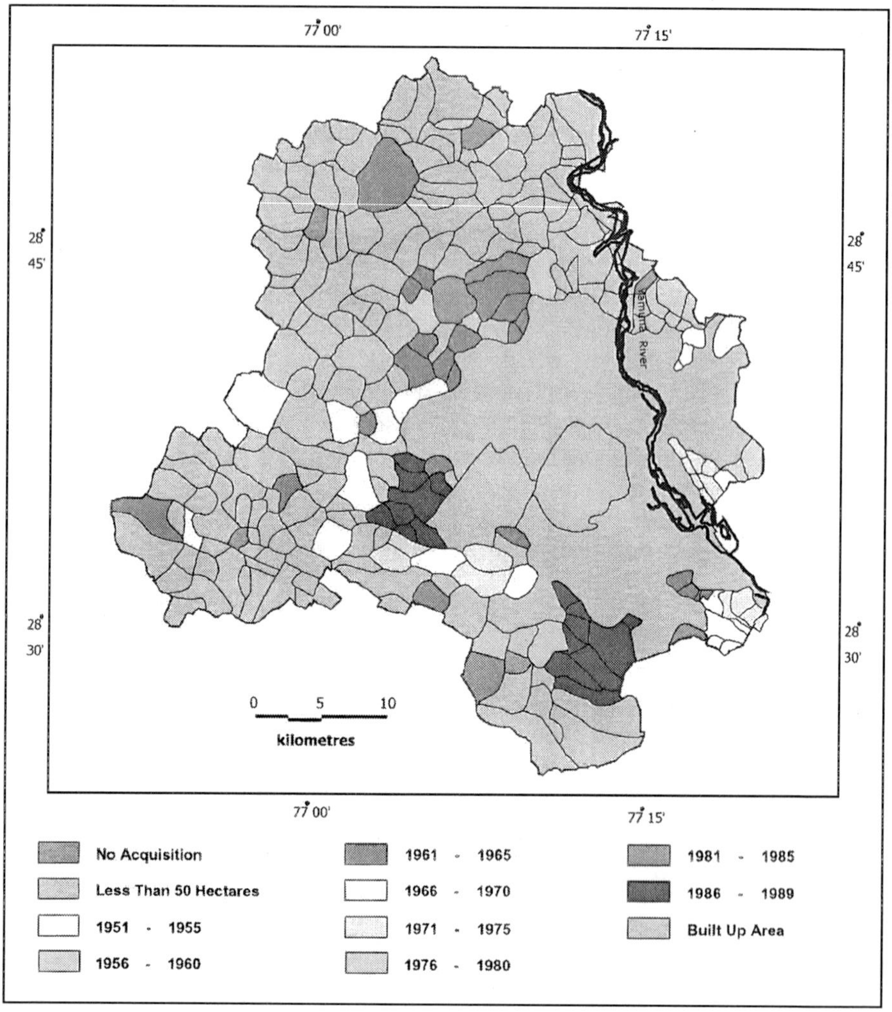

fertile lands between Yamuna and Hindon river; to find an employment opportunity in both the centres of Delhi and Ghaziabad and to get mental satisfaction by staying in their own state one/two km. away from their state boundary, though they have left their native places hundreds of kilometres away in Ghazipur, Banaras, Allahabad, Deoria, Sultanpur, Jaunpur, Pratapgarh etc. A distinct corridor (narrow urban zone) between Delhi and Faridabad has emerged due to the physical barriers on both sides of the corridor. These barriers are the barren and rocky lands of Delhi ridge towards the west and the marshy wetlands of the river Yamuna towards the east of the corridor. Likewise, due to the presence of barren/rocky lands towards east and low lying land towards west, Delhi has expanded towards Gurgaon in a narrow zone, making a corridor. Towards northern and western side, the fringe has expanded almost uniformly. This uniformity is again broken by the presence of recognisable physical or socio-cultural features. For example, towards Sonipat, the urban expansion has been slow due to the vast low lying areas of Yamuna. Again, very small and narrow corridors are developed breaking the uniformity of urban expansion towards north and west, where there are small surrounding towns. These towns are connected by roads (having shops/buildings on both sides) which may be called the outer boundary of the fringe.

Though the urban expansion has occurred much towards the east, i.e., in Shahdara and Loni, the standard of living of the people of the eastern fringe is very poor compared to the fringes of other sides. The density of population is very high in this area, resulting into congested slums and unauthorised colonies; most of the people work in government and private sectors, either in Delhi or Ghaziabad. Though it is the most fertile block with irrigation facilities obtained from Yamuna and Hindon river, less land is devoted to agriculture. Towards the southern side of Delhi, the fringe is well planned with huge multi-storied buildings of five star hotels, educational institutions, residential complexes etc. and low population density. The original fringe dwellers earn lots of money by giving their house on rent to the migrants who come from far-off places and settle in Delhi. Others become rich by either selling their lands for construction of huge buildings or leasing their barren/rocky useless land for mining coarse sand and building materials. The pattern and trend of the fringe development towards the northern and western side are totally different. Here, neither the congested slums like Shahdara nor the huge buildings like Mehrauli are found. Before fringe areas started to develop, people were engaged mainly in cultivation. Now, the fertile agricultural lands are mainly used for three purposes, viz., some lands have been acquired by DDA for development purposes (implementation in most of these places has not been started); some are used for sand mining, brick kilns or godown purposes (by which people get lots of profits); and the remaining lands are cultivated but give very low yields due to lack of interest by people.

Directional Characteristics of Fringe Development

The fringe developments around Delhi are different and quite contrasting when one compares their directional growth and characteristics. The pertinent question arises as to how the directional fringe development is related to micro relief features in the surrounding area (Figure 4). *Khadar* is a low lying area with recent river deposits. *Bangar* or the upper alluvial plain is composed of older deposits which covers the north-western section of the state. It is more elevated, fertile and drier than the *khadar*. *Bangar*, covering Alipur and Kanjhawala blocks, accommodates many brick kilns which supply bricks and tiles for the construction activities in the city. The southern part of the city is part of the Aravalli hills which is known as *Kohi* lands. It stretches far into Rajasthan and Haryana and forms the residential zone of the elite and upper classes. Thus, the micro-zonation of the land ecosystem in and around the city is related to diversified socio-economic activities. The following section therefore deals with features of five blocks consecutively.

Alipur Block

The Alipur block is located in the northern part of Delhi along the river Yamuna and is a part of Delhi's rural–urban fringe. It covers an area of 221 sq. km.

corresponding with dimensions of approximately 15×15 km. (Bentinck, 2000: 40). The eastern boundary of the block is formed by river Yamuna. The other water bodies found in the block are the Daryapur drain, the Western Yamuna Canal and the Nahri distributary. Alipur is mainly located in the *khadar* or riverine zone which has produced the most fertile land. The river alluvium is recent in age and is mainly confined to the narrow flood plains of Yamuna. The Yamuna enters the region from north of Delhi at an elevation of about 216 m and leaves it at 198 m above sea level. The general direction is almost due south. Along the banks of river, the water table remains stable at less than –6 m., as we move away from the riverine tract there is a drop in the water table reaching to –18 to –24 m. The soil of the area is in general silty sand. Therefore, all the parts of the block are under agricultural use and are classified as cropped land. This is because all the 53 villages have an easy access to hand pumps, tube wells, lift irrigation and canal irrigation. Consequently, Alipur is the main supplier of vegetables and flowers. The block contains three Census towns, i.e., Alipur, Narela and Prahlad Pur Bangar. The urban sprawl mainly occurs at the expense of productive agricultural land. Narela is becoming the commercial and industrial part of North Delhi which is famous for foodgrains mandi (Master Plan Delhi 2021, 2007). Other important centres are Sanjay Gandhi Transport Centre for Transport and Warehousing facilities. The National Highway No.1 (Grand Trunk Road) running towards Amritsar separates the block into an eastern and western part. The farmhouses developed on both sides along the G.T. Road are another attraction of this block. Some of the important villages like Jagatpur, Burari, Ibrahimpur, Mukhmelpur, Zindpur, Tigipur, Bakhtawarpur, Tajpur Kalan and Hamidpur are located in the eastern part, while Pansali, Siraspur, Khera Kanal, Barwala, Khera Khurd, Holambi Khurd, Holambi Kalan, Ghoga, Bhorgarh and Mamoorpur are found in the western part (Dahiya, 1998: 37). People living in these villages are active daily commuters to the city. Rohini is a twenty year old residential sub-city in northwest Delhi. It is the second largest sub-city after Dwarka which has more than 50 sectors, Sector-3 being the largest and Sector-2 the smallest. Its neighbouring areas are Pitampura, Mangolpuri, Badli, Mukarba Chowk, Shahbad, Daulatpur and Bawana.

Kanjhawala Block

The Kanjhawala Development Block is located in north-western part of the National Capital Territory, with its headquarters of the same name. Kanjhawala is centrally located in the block. It was earlier known as Nangloi and after delimitation in 1997 it became a separate block by itself (Singh and Mohan, 2008: 262). The block forms part of the northern fringe of Delhi bordered by Alipur block to its east, Najafgarh block to its south and urban Delhi to its southeast. The block comes under the *bangar* or the old alluvium in the north and *dabar* in the south. It consists of sandy loam and fine loam soil with high moisture. *Dabar* is also known as old *khadar*.

Najafgarh Block

The Najafgarh block is the largest block of the National Capital Territory of Delhi which occupies its south-western part. The block is bordered by the

Kanjhawala block on the north, by the city and Mehrauli blocks on the east, and by the state of Haryana on the west and south. The geographical extent of the block is 311 sq. km. which contains 72 villages and 5 urban centres (Tuli, 2000). The rural population amounts to 54 per cent of the total population and the urban population to 46 per cent. The block is densely populated 28 per cent population of the total rural population of NCT. The block is mainly composed of the alluvial plain which is *dabar* in character. The *dabar* covers a low drainage basin to the west of the Delhi Ridge and the drainage of the hills collects in the natural receptacle. It is also known as old *khadar* which is productive. The plain is flat with an average elevation of 215 m above mean sea level. The area is drained mainly by the Najafgarh drain which originates from a *jheel* located in south-western part of the block and flows northeast ward. 61 per cent of the area is cultivable and 81 per cent of this land is irrigated. Water requirements are largely met from the available groundwater resources, extensive development of which has resulted in the widespread depletion of the groundwater table. The surface water supply is very limited, therefore, people depend more on the replenishable but exhaustible groundwater resource. There are four Census towns, namely, Bindarpur, Nasirpur, Palam, and Roshanpura in this block. The Airport is also located in the *dabar* area which covers 24 sq. km. area. It is the busiest airport in India, handling 46 million passengers and it handles more than half of the air traffic in South Asia. It is the 8th largest passenger terminal of the world. In 2008, a 4.43 km. runway was inaugurated. Earlier, it was called as Palam Airport and was built during the Second World War. Now, it is called as Indira Gandhi International Airport. It contains seven Terminals: T1 is domestic, T2 is the International, and T3 is Integrated Terminal. T4 and T5 are made for later stages of growth followed by Haz Terminal and Cargo Terminal.

An important cluster of farmhouses or holiday homes has been found to be concentrated in southwest Delhi along Rajokri-Kapashera and Bijwasan-Najafgarh Road. Farmhouses are preferably located in clusters rather than in isolation because of physical insecurity and problems of theft in isolated locations. Such agglomeration forms a cohesive unit and reduces the chances of burglary, theft and murder. The distinctive feature of the growth of farmhouse culture in the block is that it has brought profound changes in the socio-economic character of the surrounding communities. The rural people are largely dependent on agriculture, but, after the sale of land to the people from outside their village, their dependency on agriculture has been considerably reduced (Kaushik, 2005). Another distinctive feature of this block is the location of Dwarka sub-city adjacent to the airport and the Najafgarh foodgrain market.

It is a part of the historic colony of Papankala which has been developed under the 'Urban Expansion Project' of DDA. Dwarka is bounded by the National Highway No. 8, Outer Ring Road, Najafgarh Road, Pankha Road, and Rewari railway line. It is well connected with metro rail with a total eight of metro stations. It is one of the largest residential areas in Asia which has been formulated under 'zero tolerance policy' (no misuse can be tolerated). It is the only sub-city which has been developed as residential township unlike Gurgaon or NOIDA. The sub-city has been planned with 29 sectors and there are 57 societies. The population of the sub-city is 11 lakh and the total area is 5,648 ha.

Figure 4 *Delhi: Physiographic Regions*

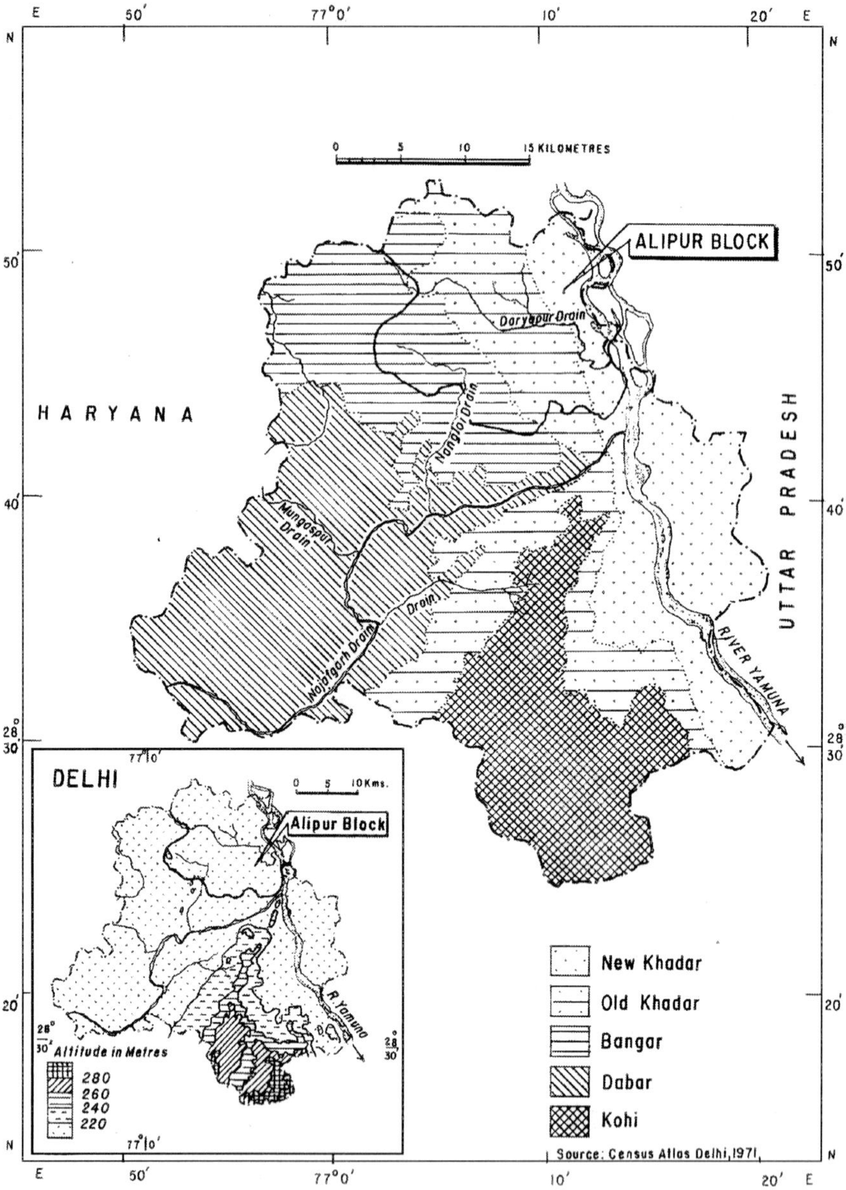

Mehrauli Block

The block is located in south Delhi with varying physical features. It is bounded by Najafgarh block and Gurgaon district on the west, City block on the north, Faridabad district on the east and Gurgaon district on the south. The block covers a rocky region surrounded by the hilly extension of the Aravalli range running through this area, reversal of slope and green reserve forests. Thus, the block presents a considerable variety of relief, interspersed by the inclusion of Aravalli outliers (Vasudev, 1989). The land is less fertile and agriculture is difficult. The rocky and hilly topography provides an attractive environment for higher class housing and recreational land use. Physiographically, this is called as *kohi* land, in local dialect, which forms the residential zone of the elites and upper classes. This area is dotted with many farmhouses owned by the elite class of Delhi. The Chattarpur region south of the Qutub Minar is the hub of farmhouse culture which developed during early 1960s. This was largely due to the proximity of the area to rich residential areas of South Delhi like Defense Colony, South Extension, Saket, Malviya Nagar, Vasant Kunj, Vasant Vihar, Gulmohar Park, Chankya Puri and Panchsheel Marg located in the southern triangle south of Connaught Place (Thakur and Sagu, 2007: 502). The scenic natural landscape provided by the longitudinal Aravalli ridge and high speculative land values associated with the spread of the city in this region were other attractive features for the location of farmhouses (Aggarwal and Kaushik, 2005: 63). Also, the development of a farmhouse in Chattarpur by one of the late Prime Ministers of India may have also encouraged such early growth (Aggarwal and Kaushik, 2005: 63). Further, it was joined by retired bureaucrats, businessmen, politicians and elites of the society like doctors, engineers, and advocates. By and large, the Vaishyas and Punjabi community own the farmhouses. In the early 1970, DLF (a private estate developer organisation) developed a cluster of farmhouses around Chattarpur village located south of Qutub Minar. Since then, there was a rapid increase in the number as well as absolute growth of farmhouses (Kaushik, 2005). The number rose from a mere 20 in the early 1970s to 300 in 1980, to 900 in 1990 and to a peak of 1,200 until 1996 (Aggarwal and Kaushik, 2005: 63). The pattern of growth thus resembles a logistic growth process, typical of innovation diffusion, and has reached a saturation (plateau) stage at present. The main clusters of farmhouses have developed south of Mehrauli along Chattarpur-Asola-Bhatti Road, Sultanpur-Mandi Road and along Mehrauli-Gurgaon National Highway. The average size of farmhouses is five acre only. These farmhouses are responsible for the excessive withdrawal of groundwater to irrigate their horticultural activities and to meet other necessary wants. The groundwater resources are in the most critical state of depletion due to its over-exploitation. Other economic activities like brick kiln industry and small industrial units also affect groundwater extraction resulting into low levels from –10 to –20 m. These changes exert a great pressure over agricultural land uses.

Shahdara Block

This block covers the whole of East Delhi across the river Yamuna. Physiographically, the block lies between the Yamuna and the river Hindon covered under newer alluvium. Therefore, it is called the new *khadar* belt. Urban expansion across the river was slow till the construction of new roads and bridges over the river (Tyagi, 1982: 173). Thus, a large majority of villages across the river were incorporated late into the urban limits during 1961–1971 period (Tyagi, 1982: 173). The Shahdara block is characterised by an absence of elite colonies and farmhouses observed elsewhere and by a very high density of population in resettlement colonies, slums and jhuggies and unauthorised colonies which have mushroomed in East Delhi. Two planned industrial areas developed in the 1980s are Jhilmil Industrial Area and Patparganj Industrial Area. The unplanned industrial areas are at Shahdara and the small-scale and household industries are predominantly found in high density areas. Shahdara Industrial Area accommodating 241 industrial units along with 88 establishments other than industrial units is small (Sharma, 2010: 225). The ownership pattern of the industrial units shows that most of the units are small in size as 79 per cent of the total firms are owned by single proprietors, followed by 13 per cent of enterprises with partnership and 7 per cent registered as private limited enterprises (Sharma, 2010: 227). The main industrial activities engaging the maximum number of firms are the manufacture of precious and non-ferrous metal, followed by insulated wires and cables, wholesale of non-agriculture intermediate products and maintenance and repair of motor vehicles (Sharma, 2010: 227). Shahdara covers two MCD (Municipal Corporation of Delhi) zones: North and South. It is also divided into Purana Shahdara and Navin Shahdara, the old part is not planned but the newer is. The colonies and villages of Shahdara fringe zone are Nand Nagri, Saboli, Ghonda, Loni, Bhagirathi Vihar, Johripur, Dilshad Garden, Vivek Vihar, Seemapuri, Anand Vihar, Hasanpur, Harsh Vihar, Karkarduma, Patparganj, Mayur Vihar, Kalyan Puri and Trilok Puri. An important colony of the East is Patparganj which was established as industrial location. Later on, the area was divided into two parts: (a) only residential apartments, and (b) an industrial area. DDA developed the Group Housing System which is well linked to Connaught Place, Nehru Place, ISBT (Inter-State Bus Terminus), and Railway Station by Metro Rail.

Natural Resource Depletion and Degradation

Being part of Indo-Gangetic plain, Delhi and its environs are rich in land resources with very fertile alluvial soil up to the depth of about 100 m. Delhi is also rich in both surface and groundwater resources. The river Yamuna flows within the state dividing it into two unequal parts. The Western and Eastern Yamuna Canals also supply water to the places away from Yamuna river (Figure 1). As the soil is permeable, groundwater is also obtained within few metres from the surface leaving very few pockets. Other renewable resources include vast forest stretches on ridge areas, along the river Yamuna and small patches in almost all villages; and sands for construction purpose in the Yamuna basin. The non-renewable resources include the reserves of coarse sands, stones and China clay towards the south, i.e., in Mehrauli block and towards Gurgaon. The mode of utilisation of these resources has changed with rapid urbanisation which leads towards resource depletion and degradation. This is explained in the following paragraphs.

Towards the northern, eastern and western fringe of Delhi, people used to grow two/three crops from the fertile alluvial soils using both surface and groundwater during the dry period. But, with the urban expansion, these fertile lands are used for residential and industrial purposes. Congested slums have developed on the fertile lands in Shahdara block. Likewise in Alipur block, the farmlands are used for godown purposes. Some farmers prefer to lease out their land for brick kilns and sand mining. Due to the heavy demand for bricks and sands in urban areas for construction purposes, people get immense profit within a very short period. As result, the soils get depleted and the lands become waste after few years. Renewable soil resources become non-renewable. The land used for brick kilns develop gullies which infect the nearby agricultural land. As a result, the neighbouring farmers are also forced to lease out their land for the same. In this way, acres of fertile agricultural land get converted into brick-kilns in the first phase, which further get converted into permanent waterlogged areas and wasteland in the second phase. In most of the places it is found that the brick kilns destroy the irrigational network, due to which the production of agricultural land located far away from the brick kilns gets affected too. The fertile agricultural land in the fringe areas also becomes polluted due to the disposal of solid wastes of urban areas. The agricultural lands of Rithala, Shahdara, Badli and Okhla are used for dumping wastes from the city areas. The height of these waste dumps increases gradually and then they look like huge land features. Most of the solid wastes from the urban areas are non-biodegradable. During the rainy season, gullies are developed on these dumps which also infect the nearby areas. When the infected rain water percolates into the ground and reaches the groundwater table, the groundwater also gets polluted.

Not only the fertile lands, but also the water resources of the fringe areas get depleted and polluted. The river Yamuna is getting polluted day-by-day as the sewers of the urban areas are disposed into the river. If this is not checked, the river water cannot be used for drinking purpose in the near future. On the other hand, due to the increase in population in Delhi, the demand for drinking water and other industrial purposes gradually increases, which leads to groundwater depletion in many pockets of Delhi and its fringe.

The urban fringe of Delhi has witnessed a sharp fall in groundwater level. While the condition of the north and northeast blocks is more or less stable, the south and southwest blocks are losing water on an average rate of 1.5 to over 2 m annually. The most severely affected areas are Badarpur, Sarita Vihar, Mohan Industrial Area, Tehkhand and adjoining area, Sainik Farms, Godaipur, Jaunapur, Kapashera, Mahipalpur, Chattarpur, Rajokri, Dwarka, Vasant Gaon, and JNU. Here the level has gone down by 1.5 to 2.5 m. The areas with the highest groundwater depletion are those which are not or had not been getting regulated Delhi Jal Board Supply. Greater declines have been recorded in the areas in central Najafgarh block, Kakraula and Chattarpur basin, Sidulzaib and Tigri village of Mehrauli block. Besides the geology and slope gradient, innumerable tube wells and farmhouses have resulted in the drastic fall of groundwater (Kamil, 2007: 77). Also, the unplanned urbanisation is causing havoc as a consequence of extensive concretisation in the capital, as the rainwater is not at all allowed to infiltrate, the water table is not getting replenished (Kamil, 2007: 79). Conversely, the water table has come up in the Bhatti mine area because steps taken up by the government to stop mining in the area has seen a huge improvement in the groundwater table. Levels have also gone up in isolated pockets in Pusp Vihar.

Dozens of villages of Alipur, Kanjhawala, Najafgarh, Mehrauli and Shahdara blocks are being supplied contaminated groundwater. They have depicted comparatively higher electrical conductivity and dissolved salts. The Central Groundwater Board in collaboration with the Central Pollution Control Board had conducted a survey in 1998 by collecting 303 groundwater samples from different location and depths in Delhi. It made clear that groundwater in most parts of Delhi is highly contaminated with fluoride, nitrate and heavy metals like lead, chromium and cadmium which should not be used for drinking purposes without treatment (Central Groundwater Board, 1997). It also indicated that there is no serious problem in Shahdara, but, by and large the entire Kanjhawala block and Najafgarh block have saline groundwater except along the Najafgarh drain and south-western part around Samalkha.

The disposal of garbage in a well managed land is termed sanitary landfill site. But the problem in most sites is uncontrolled space, where domestic, commercial, industrial and hospital wastes are dumped. Crude dumping is adopted for the disposable of waste in low-lying areas. Its unscientific management, therefore, leads to serious problems. The landfill sites situated at Okhla, Bhalsawa and Ghazipur on the fringes are increasingly polluting Delhi's groundwater and even surface water bodies. Leachate is characterised by a high content of organic pollutants, metals, acids, dissolved salts and micro-organisms. For instance, the leachate formed at the Okhla landfill site is gradually contaminating the groundwater used by residents. The leachate from the Bhalsawa site pollutes the Yamuna and the site at Ghazipur contaminates the Hindon Canal water. The Master Plan of Delhi 2021 (2007) has estimated that Delhi would require sites of 1,500 acres; however, the size of the present three sites being used by MCD at Ghazipur, Bhalsawa and Okhla is less than 150 acres. On the other hand, the Yamuna river has sustained Delhi over centuries, but today it is gasping for breath. The river has been defiled, desecrated and left for dead. It has been reduced to being a stinking drain and its sanctity and ecological significance will soon be the stuff of a legend.

Towards the southern part Delhi, i.e., in Mehrauli and Gurgaon areas, the story of resource utilisation, depletion and degradation is different. In Mehrauli block, the main occupation of the people was animal rearing as their land was not suitable for agricultural. By rearing buffaloes, they used to supply milk and its products to the city. But, now they lease out their land to mine coarse sands and stones etc. (used for construction purposes) and make profit. As a result, the pasture land gets, little-by-little, converted into a mining area. Mining operation is going on mostly in Badarpur and along the Delhi-Faridabad and the Delhi-Gurgaon corridor. The local people also quarry China clay available in some pockets and make good profit by selling the show-pieces made of it. These non-renewable resources would be depleted very soon due to the heavy demand in Delhi, Gurgaon and Faridabad. One positive thing in Delhi and its surrounding area is the increase in the green belt area. Though the village records show a constant decrease in forest land, the satellite images show an increase in forest land. However, logging is prohibited in this area as the green belt is needed to absorb air pollution in Delhi. Though vegetation does not give ready cash, it helps in protecting Delhi's environment.

Policies for Fringe Development

The concept of 'urban fringe' is more theoretical as it is called by different names, such as urban fringe, rural fringe, sub-urban areas, urban periphery, suburbs, extended urban areas etc. There is no statutory boundary or limit, which can precisely define it. As a result, it is very difficult to formulate policies towards the development and management of the fringe. Besides this, the fringe is a very delicate area which has a complex administrative structure with overlapping fringe, towns and rural areas from the adjoining three states.

The need for planned development of Delhi and its surrounding areas was felt in the early 1950s and the First Plan of Delhi was prepared in 1956 by the Town Planning Organisation. It was followed by the Master Plan of Delhi, i.e., MPD 1962–82, which was formulated on 1st September 1962 and envisaged as "Framework for guiding development". Major contribution of this Plan was diversification of activities in the neighbouring districts; delineation of "Delhi Metropolitan Area" etc. It also outlined efficient circulation network and extensive lung spaces. The Second Master Plan of Delhi, i.e., MPD 1982–2001 came into force on 1st August, 1990. It proposed a balanced regional development through formulation of NCR Planning Board and envisaged planning of Delhi in context of its region. The significance of this Plan vested in the healthy organic development in Delhi's urban extension by checking undesirable and conflicting land uses. To name a few, this includes planning development of Mayur Vihar, Sarita Vihar, Vasant Kunj, Rohini, Dwarka, Najafgarh and Narela etc. It also outlined a set up of a monitoring system to register the changing socio-economic profile of the community. Physical infrastructure was also included in this Plan. In the absence of such framework, during the Plan implementation process earlier, there has been a large area of unintended growth like unauthorised colonies, squatter settlement, informal sectors etc. With the experience of strategies of these two Plans and on the basis of planning studies by highly qualified professionals from various fields, the present plan has been modified. The modified document is entitled as "Master Plan for Delhi 2021". The plan ensures an appropriate balance between population distribution and housing, employment, infrastructure facilities, shopping centres and transportation etc.

The First Plan of NCRPB (formulated during Second Master Plan) was approved by the Board in 1988. This Plan visualized a goal of "a balanced and harmoniously developed region leading to dispersal of economic activity and immigrants to Delhi, thereby leading to a manageable Delhi". Though the exercise of preparation of this NCRPB Plan was quite elaborate and time-consuming, it failed to achieve its objectives due to weaknesses in implementation for lack of resources. A review of Plan conducted in 1999 pointed out the weaknesses in the Plan and based on these reviews, the NCRPB prepared another Plan with the perspective for the year 2021. The exercise of preparation of The Regional Plan, 2021 based on the recommendations of the study group is in progress and the draft report has been prepared for this discussion in the Board. The plan is aimed to promote growth and balanced development of NCR.

The plan framework for the development of NCR is envisaged through four policy zones: The NCT-Delhi, Delhi Metropolitan Area (excluding NCT-Delhi), remaining part of the NCR and Highway corridor zone. As per the Plan, no new major economic activities except those necessary to sustain the local population should be permitted in the NCT-Delhi. The opportunities in DMA excluding NCT-Delhi should be maximized to enable it to compete with the NCT-Delhi in terms of economic activities, transport systems, housing and other infrastructures and quality of environment. The rests of the NCR should have a policy of accelerated development of both urban and rural areas. Planned and regulated development has been proposed along the National Highway converging at NCT-Delhi.

Drawbacks

1. Though all these plans and policies sound very good, but they lack in implementation level mainly due to the lack of resources; lack of interest of bureaucrats who formulate the plan and politicians who rule the region; difference in opinion of the officials from different government departments involved in these plans; no involvement of private sectors; outdated municipal and town planning acts etc.
2. There is a tendency to convert agricultural land in the fringe for residential and commercial use without the presence of matching infrastructure such as roads, sewers, drains, water, power supply and other social amenities. It is commonly observed that the implementing agencies make piecemeal efforts to contain this type of fringe area development, which are often short-lived.
3. The unauthorised construction in fringe areas is a very common feature. The long time gap between land acquisition and development in those lands leads to unauthorised encroachment in most parts of the fringe areas.
4. According to the policy of land acquisition, the notification for acquisition of particular land is generally announced through the English newspapers, keeping in view that the farmers who have objection against the acquisition can write to DDA. As in the rural areas the circulation of English newspaper is low, farmers do not get information about it. They become the prey of it and get the price of compulsory acquisition. In this process, they lose the attachment to their land and do not hesitate to sell the remaining land for unauthorised colonisation through the intermediation of colonisers and land mafia. This leads to loss of agricultural land, on the one hand, and increase in urban sprawl, on the other hand.
5. The documentation of development areas is not properly maintained and there are ambiguities in respect to boundaries and extent of development areas, land status and land use. It is necessary to computerize the records of development areas overlapped with layers of revenue maps and zonal development plan/land use proposals.

Suggestions

The problems of fringe area are more of a management, which requires efficient coordination among the various implementation agencies. It is essential to comprehend those reasons, which can explain the problems faced by the agencies at the implementation level.

The modification of existing municipal, town planning, land acquisition and other related acts are required as they do not fit in the present situation. In this process the suggestions of local communities and private sectors should be taken along those of the government officials.

With the advent of modern digital technology, the availability of high-resolution images would be very much helpful in monitoring the growth of fringe areas along with the stages of development process during the implementation of the plans. The detection of unauthorised development and timely containment of some would definitely facilitate the implementation of Master Plans. Further, it would be desirable with the help of remote sensing technology and high resolution images to delineate existing fringe areas.

Conclusions

The following conclusions may be drawn from this study: (1) The expansion of the city has not been regular and uniform in all directions because of physical factors and the administrative policies of the government; (2) the *khadar* and *bangar* lands of East Delhi and West Delhi have prohibited the upper class and the elites of the society to construct farmhouses or holiday homes; on the other hand, Mehrauli block, Najafgarh and Alipur block have large number of farmhouses particularly along Chattarpur-Asola-Bhatti Road, Sultanpur-Mandi Road, Mehrauli-Gurgaon National Highway, Rajokri-Kapashera, Bijwasan-Najafgarh Road, G.T. Road close to Alipur and Alipur-Narela Road. Three clusters of farmhouses are distinct, because location of the farmhouses is preferred among clusters rather than in isolation; (3) As has been argued that the dynamics of directional fringe developments are operating in dissimilar directions, i.e., agriculture based in north, northwest, west and east, and scenic and luxury living based in the south and southwest. This question certainly requires further investigation, but based on the evidence presented here we advance the hypothesis that fundamental differences in the physiographic characteristics play a crucial role in the socio-economic and environmental differentiation of the fringe. This is quite acceptable because of Delhi's location on floodplains, old alluviums and the Aravalli ridge. (4) There is preponderance of corridor developments in the fringe, near the city; the corridor is a part of the fringe, while some distance away it becomes discontinuous. The corridors identified are: (a) Alipur-Sonepat, (b) Nazafgarh-Bahadurgarh, (c) Delhi-Gurgaon, (d) Delhi-Faridabad, (e) Delhi-Ghaziabad, (f) Mundka-Bahadurgarh, (f) Mayur Vihar-NOIDA, (g) Delhi-Ghaziabad-Meerut, and (h) Delhi-Loni-Baghpat; (5) The urban fringe of Delhi has witnessed a sharp fall in the level of groundwater and decline in water quality all around which have raised concerns; (6) The fringe development is a dynamic process and ever changing its boundary. Therefore, its identification and delimitation is a tedious task which can be based on a proper field survey of the villages within a radius of 10–20 km. from the city.

Acknowledgements

The author is thankful to Dr Punyatoya Patra, Associate Professor of Geography, Aditi Mahavidyalaya, Bawana (University of Delhi); Rajesh Kumar Abhay, Ph.D. Scholar and Rajiv Gandhi National Fellow, Department of Geography, Delhi School of Economics, University of Delhi; Dr Atul Kapoor, General Manager, ML Infomap Pvt. Ltd., Katwaria Sarai, New Delhi; and Miss Anika Kapoor, Urban Planner, INTACH, Lodi Estate, New Delhi for their help in preparation of this paper.

References

Aggarwal, S.K. and S.P. Kaushik (2005): Growth and Diffusion of Farmhouses in the National Capital Territory of Delhi, *Punjab Geographer*, 1(1): 61–69.

Bentinck, J. (2000): Unruly Urbanisation on Delhi's Fringe: Changing Patterns of Landuse and Livelihood, Groningen: *Netherland Geographical Studies*, 270.

Dahiya, A. (1998): Environmental Implications of Groundwater Resource Utilization: A Case Study of Alipur Block, Delhi, M.Phil. Thesis, Department of Geography, University of Delhi.

Kamil, A. (2007), Depletion and Degradation on Natural Resources in and around Delhi, M.Phil. Thesis, Dept. of Geography, University of Delhi.

Kapoor, A. and Thakur, B. (2008): A Geographical Analysis of Land Acquisition for Urban Development: A study of Delhi, in B. Thakur (ed.), *Perspectives in Resource Management in Developing Countries*, Vol. 3: *Ecological Degradation of Land*, New Delhi: Concept, 277–295.

Master Plan Delhi 2021 (2007), Delhi: Rupa and Company.

Prakash, S. (2005): Growth of Farm Houses in National Capital Territory and its Impact on the Socio-Economic and Spatial Urbanisation of Local Community, Ph.D. Dissertation, Department of Geography, University of Delhi.

Ramachandran, R. (1989): *Urbanization and Urban Systems in India*, Delhi: Oxford University Press, 293–321.

Sharma, P. (2010): *Structure and Growth of Mega City: An Inter-Industry Analysis*, New Delhi: Concept.

Singh, R.B. and J. Mohan (2008): Brick Kiln Industry and Related Land Degradation in Rural–Urban Fringe of Delhi, in B. Thakur (ed.), *Perspectives in Resource Management in Developing Countries, Vol. 3: Ecological Degradation of Land*, New Delhi: Concept, 261–276.

Thakur, B. and A.K. Sagu (2007): Locational Analysis of Elite Residential Colonies in Delhi, in B. Thakur, G. Pomeroy, C. Christopher, S.K. Thakur (eds), *City, Society and Planning*, New Delhi: Concept, 494–522.

Tuli, S. (2000): Assessment of Groundwater Resources in Rural Delhi: A Case Study of Nazafgarh Block, M.Phil. Thesis, Department of Geography, University of Delhi.

Tyagi, V.K. (1982): *Urban Growth and Urban Villages*, New Delhi: Kalyani Publishers.

Vasudev, P. (1989): Geomorphology of the Delhi Region, M.Phil. Thesis, Department of Geography, University of Delhi.

20

Urban Fringe of Vadodara

Development and Transformation

VIMALA RANGASWAMI

Vadodara ranked sixteenth out of thirty-five urban agglomerates and is one of fastest growing metropolitan cities of India. Human settlement here dates back to 1000 B.C. Despite several phases of ups and downs in its growth, owing to historical reasons and changes in its physical sites, Vadodara has witnessed its transformation from a settlement covered with dusty narrow streets and unclean houses to a town with magnificent infrastructure under Maharaja Sayajirao III. The physical change was accompanied by various economic and social reformations, which accelerated its growth and development.

The municipal limits of Vadodara city up to 1911 more or less continued to be 12.80 km^2 with the density fluctuating between 9,112 in 1872 and 7,761 per km^2 in 1911. In the next three decades between 1922 and 1941, the area increased to a little over 13 km^2 and a density to 11,605 per km^2. 1951 was the year when Vadodara recorded the highest density of 12,505 persons per km^2. Between 1951 and 1061, the city limit extended by almost three times to 47.70 km^2, and later, after attainment of the status of Municipal Corporation in 1966, the city agglomeration spread over 78.13 km^2 of which 57.50 km^2 was within the municipal limits. Rapid industrialisation and growth of services led to an explosion in population during the 1961–71 decade. Between 1981 and 1991, Vadodara grew horizontally to 108.22 km^2 with the density of population increasing from 6,784 to 9,715 (Figure 1).

With the population of 14,92,398 of the urban agglomeration in 2001 the density works up to 13,500 per km^2, if the present limit of the city remains unchanged (Table 1). The overall gross residential density of the developed parts of Vadodara is about 100 persons per hectare. The southern and western parts of the city are less inhabited and less developed compared to the eastern part of the city, where the density recorded is more than 1,500 persons per hectare.

Figure 1 *Vadodara City: Development Plan of Fringe Area, 2011*

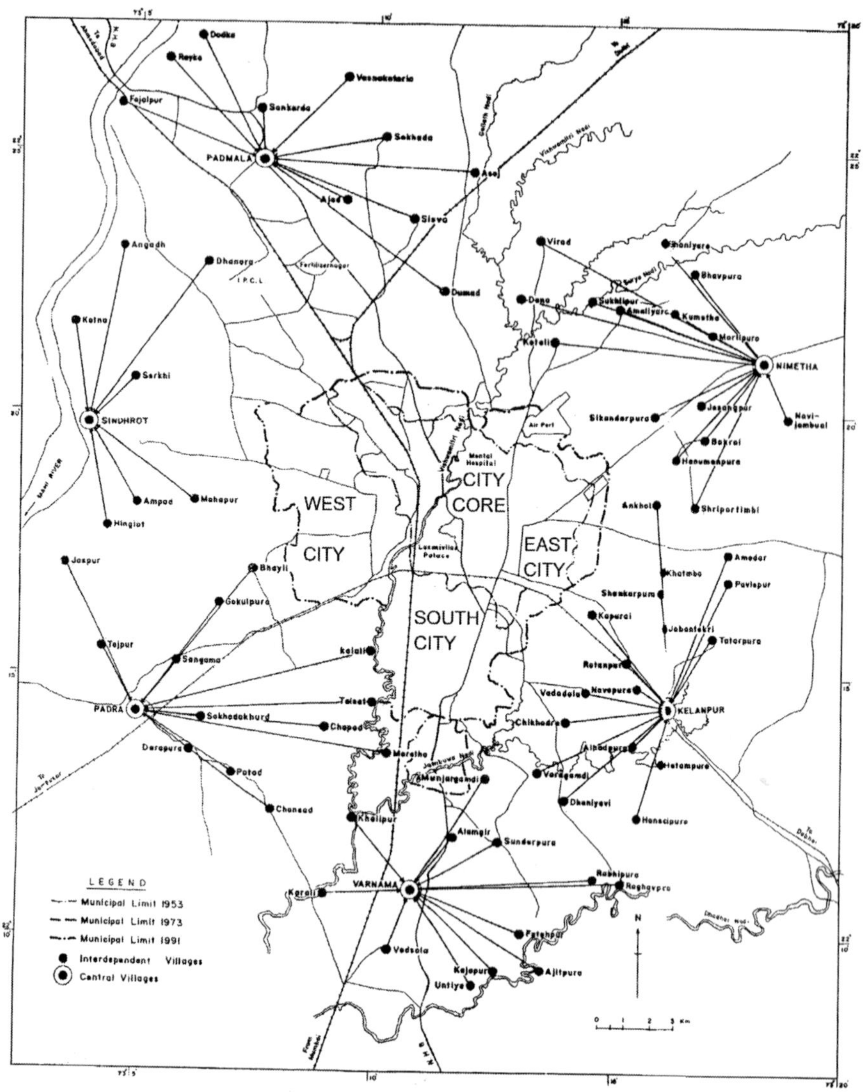

"Throughout the world, new urban development occurs mainly on vacant land around the fringes of built up areas. This happens because the rate of return on private and public investment in new buildings and other improvements is much higher there than elsewhere. Hence the "natural" forces of urban land markets generate the basic "inside-outward" pattern of urban growth found almost everywhere in the world", (Downs, 1973, p.1).

It is anticipated that the increase in all income groups in the presently developed areas will require more housing and other urban facilities resulting in overcrowding, vertical expansion, new growth areas around the urban periphery and the filling up of vacant lands. The localities on the west of the river Vishwamitri and the broad gauge railway line, which runs from north to south of Vadodara city constitute the newer development and represent the fastest growing area. This part of Vadodara stands out significantly in the urban fabric by its up-market, commercial land uses and several posh residential pockets, although some industrial area also falls within the boundary.

Table 1 *Population of Vadodara Municipal Corporation and its Outgrowths (Census of India 2001)*

Sr. No.	*Outgrowths*	*Urban Agglomeration*	*Population 2001*
1	Undera		12,389
2	Karodiya		11,527
3	Harni		4,819
4	Sama		20,515
5	Sayajipura		8,602
6	Bapod		12,902
7	Kapura		8,080
8	Kalali		2,208
9	Chhani		25,593
10	Total Outgrowths		1,06,635 (7.54%)
11		Vadodara Municipal Corporation	13,06,035
12		Vadodara MC + Outgrowths	14,12,670
13		Nandesari (CT)	7,259
14		Nandesari (INA)	2,815
15		Vadodara Urban Agglomeration	14,92,398

Source: Census of India, Baroda District 2001 (Provisional Census Abstract)

Thus with the growth of population, Vadodara will also be transformed structurally and arealy changing the present landscape and the density pattern.

Population Growth

From 1881 to 1991, Vadodara recorded a tenfold increase in its population. Between 1951 and 1971, there was a substantial growth due to rapid industrialisation following the formation of Gujarat State in 1961 and the mass exodus from rural hinterland. The city witnessed the laying of metalled roads and reconstruction of the bridge connecting new residential areas in the north on either side of river Vishwamitri. With the increase in the spread of city limits, the population crossed the million mark during the 1981–91 decade, ranking Vadodara as the 16th of 23 metropolitan cities of India.

The heavy inflow of immigrants to Vadodara is rather unique in the entire district. The rich cultural heritage, the impressive university, which is the only kind in Gujarat with English as the medium of instruction, the busy commercial centre with a large service area and the cosmopolitan population nurtured by Maharaja Sayajirao and impelled by various industries and organisations of defence, electronics, communication and others are responsible for the magnetic attraction of the city. Estimates of migrants to Vadodara city as in 1981, 1991 and 2001 are presented in Figure 2. Out of the total increase of 57.4 per cent during the 1971–81 decade, two thirds was accounted for by immigration. In fact, the natural increase of population has been on the decline due to better health services and health care facilities. Statistics derived for the year 1985–86 places the birth rate at 20.4 per 1,000 and the death rate 5.3 per 1,000.

Figure 2 *Growth of Population and Area of Vadodara City*

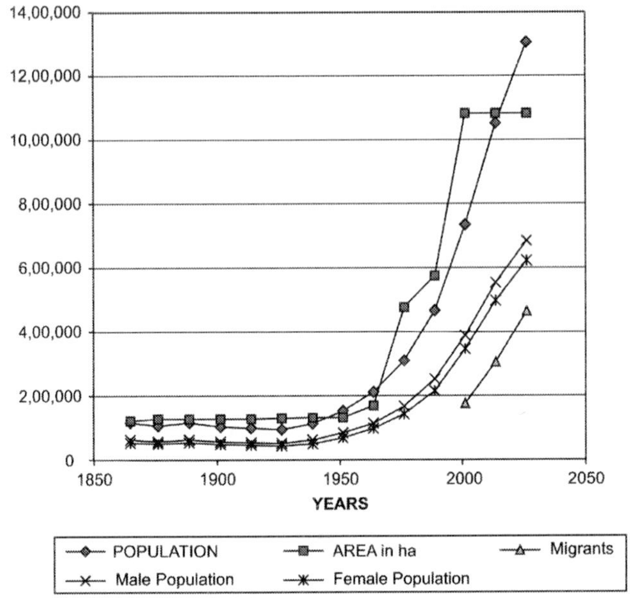

Source: Census of India Baroda District, 1951. 1961. 1971. 1991, Census of India 2001, Baroda District Provincial Paper 2.

Table 2 *Vadodara City: Classification of Main Workers 1981 to 2001*

	1981			*1991*			*2001*		
	Total	*Male*	*Female*	*Total*	*Male*	*Female*	*Total*	*Male*	*Female*
		in %			*in %*			*in %*	
Main Workers	2,14,037 (100)	91.22	8.78	3,11,212 (100)	88.58	11.42	4,19,459 (100)	85.84	14.16
Cultivators	1.14	95.57	4.43	0.99	95.57	4.43	0.39	96.48	3.52
Agricultural Labourers	1.54	73.23	26.77	1.30	77.52	22.48	0.48	65.68	34.32
Household Industries	1.53	82.32	17.68	1.56	79.63	20.37	1.18	61.20	38.80
Other Workers	95.89	91.59	8.41	96.15	88.79	11.21	97.95	86.20	13.80
Total Population	7,34,443			10,51,390			13,06,035		

Source: Census of India, Baroda District 1981, 1991, 2001 (Provisional Census Abstract).

According to the demographic projections, the increase in the total workforce between 1971 and 2001 was estimated to be 3,24,000 against the net increase of more than a million population during the same period (Table 2).

This net increase in the workforce is anticipated to take place in the sectors of manufacturing, allied activities and services, which will further increase the congestion, sprawl and density of the city.

Land Use Pattern

Of the total area of the city of 108.22 km^2 in 1991, 53 per cent was developed. Open spaces and vacant lands were estimated to be 10 to 20 per cent of the developed areas. Large areas of underdeveloped land were under agricultural use, and these were either on the outskirts of the city or in between the major arterial roads. The pattern of land use is more or less similar to other cities, which have grown from historic cores. The industries have sprung up on the outskirts of the city in all directions; however, the overall development of Vadodara is more in the western part, which is the most sought after and valued area of urban expansion.

To a certain extent, the admixture of developed lands and vacant lands in the developed and underdeveloped areas have kept the city open and green, but has posed serious problem for city planning. It has greatly increased the cost of providing infrastructural facilities to the disintegrated and scattered parts of the city. And, therefore, the facilities and amenities enjoyed by some segments of population in one area widely differ from those enjoyed by the population in other areas.

Table 3 gives the break-up of the proposed land use of Vadodara Urban Development Authority (VUDA) area up to 2011. It is evident from the table that, the urban limit would increase from 108.55 km^2 to 240.03 km^2 of which 54.67 per cent would be covered by residential uses, nearly 20 per cent by roads and railways and 10 per cent by industries.

Table 3 *Proposed Land Use 2011 A.D. of VUDA Area*

Sr. No.	*Description of uses*	*Existing land use in sq. km. 1993*	*Proposed land use in sq. km.*	*Per cent to total Urbanisable Area*
1	Residential	41.07	131.24	54.67
2	Commercial	1.51	7.79	3.24
3	Industrial	19.57	24.64	10.26
4	Open Space and Garden	2.80	15.66	6.23
5	Restricted Area	6.33	6.58	2.74
6	Roads and Railways	32.89	45.89	19.11
7	River, Tank	4.38	8.23	3.42
	Total	108.55	240.03	99.67

Source: VUDA – Draft Development Plan – Revised (1993–2011) Part A. Planning Proposal Vadodara.

The bifurcation of the Bombay State into Maharashtra and Gujarat in 1960 led to the movement of a large number of people and the shift of industrial and commercial ventures into Gujarat. Good agricultural land in the proximity of urban areas disappeared under unplanned, unrestrained uses. The town planning activities were limited to the municipal boundaries of the towns while much of the new developments took place in the periphery outside the city limits.

The Gujarat State Government, under the Gujarat Town Planning and Urban Development Act 1976, constituted Urban Development Authorities for urban areas including areas outside the urban limits. The Vadodara Urban Development Authority came into existence in February 1978 empowered to prepare and execute development plan for Vadodara Municipal Corporation and areas within the limits of 103 towns and villages around the city. Planning of the urban and industrial centres was to be considered with planning of agricultural development. The aim of the development plan was to ensure economic and physical development through a balanced, integrated programme of diversified and decentralised urban area. The main thrust in the Development Plan was the promotion of a more harmonious land use pattern. One of the significant characteristics of the land use pattern of the city was that nearly 32 per cent of the total area was vacant and underdeveloped, when the plan was envisaged.

In order to contain the urban sprawl and further pressure of population on Vadodara city, VUDA in its Development Plan had identified ten growth centres in its jurisdiction to act as a counter magnet between the taluka headquarters and the city. The plan envisaged was to diffuse, decentralise and diversify the process of development, through the creation of these "mini-counter magnets" against the pull generated by the city. Improper communication facilities and inadequate and inefficient mass transit failed to stimulate the growth centres, which were founded without strong incentives. "Forced" migration of people depending on public transport made it harder for the low-income workers to reach the place of work. Residential development in proximity to the place of work is a necessity to workers who may have to work in shifts in a factory and either have to walk or cycle to work. The main strategy to counter balance the concentration process in Vadodara by an equally strong dispersion process by promoting growth centres seemed far from achievement.

A revised Development Plan 1993–2011 has been prepared for VUDA jurisdiction totally covering an area of 714.56 km^2: 108.00 km^2 area within the Vadodara Municipal Corporation and 606.56 km^2 area of 104 villages. It plans to accommodate an additional population of 1,348,318 within the limits of VUDA.

The fringe area around the highly urbanised and developed parts of Vadodara comprises 186.6 km^2 that are proposed for residential use in the Revised Development Plan 1996. In addition, the developing areas of Harni, Vemali, Sama, Chhani, Karodia, Koyali, Undera and Ankodiya in the north, which are not specified for residential use, but have developed, nonetheless beyond the permitted area surrounding the village *gamtal* (core) are also included. The Refinery and IPCL Townships also fall within the area. To the east of Vadodara, portions of Sayajipura, Bapod, Danteshwar and Kapurai are included. To the south are included Tarsali, Makarpura, Gambura, Haneja, Talsat, Vadsar, Kalali, Akadra and Bil. To the west are included Samyala, Brayli, Tandalja, Vasna Saiyad, Sevasi, Khanpur, Golri and Gorwa (Mona Desai, 2002: 59).

Scattered tenements have mushroomed amidst agricultural fields. The areas are serviced by village roads and roads constructed under Town Planning Schemes. Major roads to Ahmedabad, Godhra, Ajwa, Nurieta, Vaghodia, Dabhoi, Mumbai, Padra and Ambusar, Borsad and Koyali connect the area with the main city. Some of the areas lie already within the municipal limits of Vadodara.

The fringe area, which forms a part of the VUDA area is spread over 9,787.08 hectares constituting 13.7 per cent of the VUDA area and 38.25 per cent of the developed area (non-agricultural development). Since 1971, the population in this area has risen from 1.37 lakhs to almost 3.52 lakhs in 2001. The gross residential density of the area increased from 14.06 persons per hectare to 36.72 per hectare keeping pace with the increase in the density of development

As permitted in the zoning regulations, the development is residential, commercial and industrial, spread out with horizontal zoning. Almost 30 per cent of the built-up area is residential and the remaining 70 per cent agricultural development. The sparse development has large areas that are underdeveloped and are left vacant (Desai, 2002: 122).

There has been a spate of tenement developments especially in the eastern, southern and northern fringe. To cope with the projected population of 26,20,648 by 2011, VUDA has made several changes in the zoning pattern to increase the stock of urbanisable area. (This is approximately 4,17,000 persons more than the projected population for the year 2001). The authority envisages changes in the residential areas at the Municipal level, fringe area level and rural area (Table 4).

In the previous plan, a sizable area around the existing industrially developed area was kept as industrial zone. As the industrial policy is not in favour of developing industries in VUDA area, majority of these lands have been found unutilised and vacant. Hence, it was decided to convert the industrial area into residential area, i.e., Danliswar, Gorura, TPS No. 13, Alcadra etc.

Many of the areas, reserved by the Municipal Corporation have been reduced and designated for either residential or local commercial zone.

Table 4 *The List of Reserved Plots (other Public Institutions)*[1]

Sr. No.	*Name of Institution*	*Area in hectares*	*Estimated cost in lakhs of Rs*
1.	Gujarat Housing Board	423.30	4,228.20
2.	Gujarat Slum Clearance Board	216.20	198.44
3.	Gujarat Rural Housing Board	42.50	6.38
4.	Gujarat Narmada Sarovar Nigam	35.00	210.00
5.	Gujarat State Road Transport Corporation	17.00	233.50
6.	Government of Gujarat	8.50	170.00
7.	M.S. University	34.30	686.00
8.	B.M.C.	118.29	1,683.98
	Total	895.09	7,416.50

Total Estimated cost of Land Acquisition for Reservation:

For VUDA	Rs 2.30 crores
For other Agencies	Rs 74.16 crores
Total	Rs 76.46 crores

On the periphery of the Municipal Corporation the rate of population increase has been significant, e.g., in the north, Gorwa, Chhani, Ranoli, Sama, Harai etc., in the east Sayajipura, Bapod, Tarrali etc., in the west, Ankodia, Sevasi, Bhayali, Alladrra etc. Looking to the development trend, required urbanisable area and demand and considering the physical barrier the following new areas have been added to the urbanisable area:

1. At Kapurai, Tarsali between the eastern bypass and Vadodara municipal limits.
2. At Gorwa, Undera.
3. At Ankodya, Sevasi, Khanpur, Bhayali between proposed 40 m. wide road and urbanisable area and Narmada canal in the north.

Transportnagar

VUDA plans to set up an area with modern facilities exclusively for stationing heavy commercial vehicles. This 'Transportnagar' will be outside the VMC. VUDA has acquired almost 90 per cent of the required 56 hectares at a cost of Rs five million. The site is on the junction between Vadodara-Godhra State Highway and the Vadodara-Mumbai bypass on National Highway 8. VUDA plans to construct special godowns for specific needs, petrol pumps, shops, auto ancillary outlets, a post office, octroi counter, banks, restaurants, hotels and *dhabas* (wayside inns). The main reason behind this project is to move a major chunk of the heavy traffic jamming the inner city roads towards the periphery of the city. (http//www.baroda-online.com/diary html#expressway)

Having failed in the attempt of activating growth centres around Vadodara, the VUDA has embarked on a new concept of exploring central villages. For this purpose Padamla, Nunetha, Kalanpur, Varama, Padra, Singhrot have been identified, with their own group of villages within their service area. It is planned to provide higher order facilities and good amenities at these six central villages, so that they could develop sound linkages and interdependency within their group. This would also reduce the burden on facilities available in the mother city.

Facilities like colleges, technical schools, hospitals, theatres, town hall, parks and play grounds, library, health centres, work centres, post and telegraph facilities, picnic spots, swimming pool, water supply, drainage etc. are proposed to be developed at these six central villages, so that they can serve their group of villages in a better way.

1. In the northeast, the intervention by VUDA has developed Darjipura as a '*transportnagar*'.
2. Saw mills and timber dealers are found in Sayajipura and Harni.
3. In the east, the residential development is more pronounced along Vaghodia-Dabhoi roads especially in the vicinity of Bopod and Kapurai.
4. In the south, Tarsali is developing as a residential area. There are also nondescript tenement developments at Maneja.
5. The southwest has seen a spurt in the development of private run schools.
6. The west has several group housing schemes, some of them with defined character.
7. The northwest has several planned residential societies with tenement topology.
8. The development in the north is mostly of tenement type.

The restricted area in the northwest and northeast serves as a buffer to the expansion of residential development in that direction.

The recreational facilities at Ajwa, industrial establishments, private educational institutions and ashrams (religious institutions) at Vaghadia and the Dabhoi road have led to the development of traffic on these routes. This served as an impetus to residential developments for those having connections in the east.

The location of industries in the south triggered the demand for housing in the proximity. The western fringe is dominated by high-rise commercial complexes along the major thoroughfare and by homes of high-income group levels. Increase in the population and shortage of good schools have initiated the establishment of branches of reputed schools, dental colleges, hospitals and clubs. The proximity to the public sector undertakings in the northeast has led to the development of housing along the entire north.

Conclusion

The land under urban use has been extending beyond the municipal limits year after year. Consequences of the morphological and demographic growth of Vadodara are manifested in the tremendous pressure on the basic amenities available to its present population. The infrastructural needs of the society and its population are likely to increase beyond the capacity of local authorities to cope with. Vadodara is inadequate in public transport systems and chaotic in its traffic situation. Private vehicles are increasing by leaps and bounds, despite the narrow and crowded streets, non-availability of parking places, traffic congestion and increased air and noise pollution. Potable water is becoming a rare commodity and quality of life in the crowded parts of the city is deteriorating.

There are several constraints to the growth and the development of the city, which stands in the way of integration and of interaction among various functional areas of the city. Industrialisation and urbanisation without long term city planning have affected the morphology of the city and the quality of life of the city dwellers. The fringe is often characterised by unhealthy and eye sore developments like mushrooming of multi-storied apartment complexes without proper and adequate parking facilities, sporadic growth of slums with immigrants from the 2001 earthquake affected areas and outward migration of people from the riot-torn settlements. Simultaneously a substantial increase in informal sector has also contributed to the deterioration of the pleasant environment for which the city was known in the past.

The agricultural lands, open vacant lands, are being devoured by various environment-unfriendly structures of concrete for residential, commercial or public entertainment purposes. Gated housing colonies with clubhouses, swimming pools, international schools, ashrams also occupy huge expanses of the fringe area. With free flow of money through financiers and banks, many from the crowded parts of the city move to the newer housing units that are larger, more stylish and offer more amenities. These new neighbourhoods contain clusters of housing units – duplex houses, single homes, and apartment blocks of basically similar quality, style and price. They are all either built by a single developer or group of developers, catering to the middle income or wealthy groups in society.

The Municipal Corporation, the Urban Development Authority and some voluntary organisations are striving hard to keep Vadodara economically vibrant, environmentally healthy and culturally rich, but the problem before them is one of coordination and financial constraint. If VUDA is steadfast in its commitment towards the planned development of urbanisable area and integrated rural development through detailed town planning schemes and infrastructure development in the fringe area, and gives priority to accessibility and connectivity by constructing new link roads and bridges and guaranties water supply, drainage, electricity, then the haphazard growth of ill-conceived housing units can be curtailed.

Based on the trend of city functions and inter-relations with functions of other urban centres in the region, VMC and VUDA should keep in mind the economic, social and geographical cohesion of the city. The problems generated by the urban development processes can be effectively tackled only through coordination of various governmental bodies and public participation. VUDA and VMC and the railways could make use of the existing railway lines, both broad and metre gauge, to build up an efficient local transport network and thus facilitate communication between the city and the fringe.

Note

1. VUDA – Draft Development Plan – Revised (1993–2011) Part A, Planning and Proposals, Vadodara.

References

Desai, Mona (2002): *The VUDA Development Plan: A Critical Appraisal*, Unpublished dissertation. (M.Tech. Degree)

Directorate of Census Operations: *Provisional Population Totals 2001*. Gujarat, Ahmedabad

Downs, Anthony (1973): *Opening up the Suburbs: An Urban Strategy for America*, New Haven and London, Yale University Press.

http://www.censusindia.net/results/million-plus.html

Rangaswamy, Vimla (1998): Vadodara: A City Overwhelmed by Growth, in R.P. Misra and Kamlesh Misra (Eds), *Million Cities of India* (Vol. II), Sustainable Development Foundation, New Delhi.

Sandhu, Ravindra Singh (Ed.) (2003): *Urbanization in India, Sociological Contributions*, Sage Publications, New Delhi.

Vadodara Urban Development Authority: Vadodara Shehari Vikas, Satta Mandal, 2000, Vadodara. VUDA

——, Draft Development Plan – Revised (1993–2001), Part A, Planning and Proposals, Vadodara, VUDA

——, Varied Revised General Development Control Regulations 2000, Vadodara, VUDA.

21

The Outgrowths beyond Municipal Limits in Gujarat

A Study on Some of the Demographic Characteristics and Related Changes

K.M. KULKARNI

Urban fringe is a dynamic spatial concept, which generally refers to an area between rural and urban settlements with their mixed characteristics of land use and population. Under the influence of an ever-expanding city, the urban peripheral areas undergo a sea change in terms of land use, population, employment, income and culture. This process of transformation in the urban fringe is induced by the rising pressure on land resource and associated phenomena of migration not only from the impoverished rural areas but also from the crowded core areas of the city. The outward expansion of the city engulfs several fringe villages (outgrowths) allowing them to remain intact and compact as village pockets in urban dynamics. This urban onslaught swallows villages, transforms agricultural land into either residential or industrial land. The rate of change and outward movement of the fringe directly, positively and proportionately depends on the size and functional complexity of the city. Among the several changes that occur in the urban fringe, those related to land use, institutional development and population are important. The residential development mainly includes farmhouses, spacious bungalows, tenements, duplex flats, row houses and spacious apartments in high-rise buildings with all modern facilities and designs, over and above a temple, a garden, open space, etc. The institutional development in the fringe area includes religious institutions (Gurudwaras, Derasars, replica of Balaji temple (Tirupati), Vaishnodevi, Ayyappa temple, ISKON temple etc. of various other sects of India), specialised educational and research institutions (engineering, medical, dental, consumer, education and research, chemical and pharmaceutical, etc.), social institutions (Civil Hospital, specialised hospitals, High Court, electricity grids, water filtration and purification plants, sewerage treatment plants, bus depots, etc.), commercial institutions (clubs and motels, star hotels, garden restaurants, roadside eateries (*dhabhas*), car show rooms, petrol pumps, company go-downs, company service stations and engineering works, poultry and dairy farms, business houses, coal depots, marble and stoneware works, saw mills, brick kilns, private bus depots, etc.), and the development of industrial units depending on the local prevailing conditions in relation to location, direction, quality of land, earlier industrial units and general wind conditions. Along with these changes in land use, transport network also changes especially to expressways, freeways, highways and ring roads in juxtaposition with other road networks to maintain and promote a free and efficient movement of traffic within the city including fringe areas as well as inter-city movement without creating any kind of bottlenecks. The third most significant change in the urban fringe is related to population composition. The population dynamics here is seen in terms of population size and density and includes the biological, social, cultural and economic characteristics and migration aspects. Except the residential occupancy in the fringe areas, the other population characteristics and their changes are not very visible. In this context, an attempt has been made to analyse and understand the changing population characteristics of fringe areas, i.e., outgrowths beyond the municipal limits of 39 Urban Agglomerations of Gujarat by size class. The present study offers us a necessary base for locational planning for providing social infra-structural facilities such as housing, health, education and social security, etc.

Objectives

The present study aims at (a) understanding some of the demographic characteristics of the outgrowths vis-à-vis the municipal towns of all the Urban Agglomerations of Gujarat. (b) It also intends to monitor the kind of demographic changes that have been taking place within the city limit and beyond the city limit during the last twenty years. (c) It tries to understand the nature of relationship between the demographic characteristics of outgrowths and the size class of their urban agglomerations.

Study Area and Data Base

The present study on demographic characteristics and change covers 125 outgrowths of all the 39 Urban Agglomerations (2001) of Gujarat by their size class. The necessary data of some selected demographic characteristics are obtained from the Provisional Population Totals – Paper-2 of 2001 on Rural–urban distribution, and Paper-3 of 2001 on workers and their characteristics (Census of India, 2001). The Census data on demographic characteristics are cross tabulated by municipal towns and their outgrowths in order to understand the nature and intensity of relationship between city and fringe (core-peripheral relations). Among them growth rate, sex-ratio literacy, and work participation in agriculture, household industry and other services are important.

The Outgrowths beyond Municipal Limits

Just outside the limit of Municipal towns sometimes certain specialised functions develop but these areas may not themselves qualify to be treated as towns but they are treated as outgrowths (OGs) by the Census Department. These outgrowths may be either totally new developments or overgrown and transformed rural settlements under the impact of municipal body. However, the impetus for the growth of outgrowths depends on the size, function, location and direction of inter-urban interaction. The million plus cities Ahmedabad, Surat and Vadodara of Gujarat have a larger number of outgrowths (about 29 per cent of the total number of outgrowths of Gujarat), and they are growing faster in terms of population, functions and land-use changes. Another 16 large cities (Class-I cities), which have a Municipal Corporation, share 50 outgrowths representing 40 per cent of all the outgrowths of the 39 urban agglomerations of Gujarat. This shows that the phenomenon of urban fringe development is of greater reality in case of million plus cities and also of large cities rather than medium sized cities. Gujarat has in all 125 outgrowths belonging to 39 urban agglomerations of million cities and Class I, II and III towns. All the outgrowths account for 19 per cent of the population of urban agglomerations. However, this percentage shows wide variation in their distribution by size class. 57 per cent of the total OGs population of Gujarat is concentrated beyond the municipal limits of only three million cities. Another 35 per cent of OGs population is spread out beyond the city limits of Class I cities (19 in number).

Population Dynamics of Outgrowths

The population size is constantly changing in the fringe area as it is developing rapidly. The number of outgrowths have increased from 48 in 1981 to 125 in 2001 and the increase is more in case of million (13 to 36) and Class I cities (12 to 50). The absolute population of outgrowths increased from 1,75,992 to 27,44,226, and percentage wise from 2.67 per cent to 18.92 per cent during the period 1981–2001. The annual percentage growth rate of the outgrowths of million cities was 74.24 and of Class I cities 190.86 during the same period (Table 1). This shows vibrant urban fringes of larger cities in terms their demographic condition. The annual population growth rate in OGs is significantly higher compared to their municipal towns. However, in terms of absolute increase in population, there is no comparison between them. The three million cities and 19 Class I cities and their outgrowths record a substantial increase in population as compared to the urban agglomerations and outgrowths of Class II and III categories. The average size of outgrowth shows positive association with the size class of urban agglomeration. The average size of outgrowths ranges from 3,652 in case of Class III Urban Agglomerations to 43,546 in case of million cities (Table 1).

Literacy Patterns of Outgrowths by their Urban Agglomeration Class

The percentage of the total literacy and the female literacy (2001) of the outgrowths do not show a significant positive association with their urban agglomerations. This difference may be explained by the lower literacy rate of the rural as well as migrant population living within the outgrowths. The outgrowths of the million cities have a relatively low level of literacy including female literacy compared to the literacy patterns of outgrowths of other size classes. The percentage of female literacy in urban agglomerations and outgrowths shows greater differences compared to the percentage of total literacy. The maximum difference of 13.90 per cent in female literacy is observed between the outgrowths and their million cities (Table 2). 66 per cent of the total outgrowths of Gujarat have not only recorded high literacy rate of more than 75 per cent (2001) but also their urban agglomerations show more than 75 per cent of literate population. 18 per cent of the outgrowths show 65 to 75 per cent and the remaining 9 per cent of the outgrowths show less than 65 per cent literacy when their urban agglomerations showed more than 75 per cent literacy (Table 3). Two per cent each of the OGs showed less than 65 per cent and more than 75 per cent of their respective UAs literacy rate (i.e., 65 to 75%). Although the majority of the outgrowths (66%) show higher literacy of more than 75 per cent, which is the same as the category of their urban agglomerations, there is a clear lag in the literacy level of outgrowths from their urban agglomerations to the extent of 4 to 12 per cent (Table 2).

Table 1 *Number of Urban Agglomerations and Outgrowths and their Population by Size Classes in Gujarat during 1981–2001*

Urban Size Classes and Population (2001)*	*Number and Population of Urban Agglomerations*		*Number and Population of Outgrowths*		*Average Size of Outgrowths*	
	1981	*2001*	*1981*	*2001*	*1981*	*2001*
Million Cities	01 24,15,195	03 88,23,140 (12.54)	13 98,914	36 15,67,659 (74.24)	7,609	43,546
Class I (51,20,172)	10 30,12,609	19 47,19,911 (2.83)	12 24,591	50 9,63,260 (190.86)	2,049	29,429
Class II (17,63,253)	13 8,90,226	10 7,27,702 (–81.26)	17 37,712	30 1,81,792 (19.10)	2,218	6,060
Class III (17,25,504)	04 1,44,952	07 2,30,202 (2.94)	04 12,816	09 31,515 (7.30)	3,204	3,652
Class IV (6,47,684)	02 38,694	— —	02 1,959	— —	980	—
Total	30 66,01,676	39 1,45,00,955	48 1,75,992	125 27,44,226		

(Figures in bracket indicate average annual percentage of population growth rate during 1981–2001) (* Includes the population of independent towns)

Table 2 *Percentage of Total Literacy and Female Literacy of Urban Agglomerations and their Outgrowths of Gujarat (2001)*

Size Class	*Percentage of Total Literacy*	*Percentage of Female Literacy*
Million Cities	84.74	78.56
OGs	72.02	64.60
Class I UAs	83.69	79.65
OGs	79.08	69.03
Class II UAs	83.01	75.81
OGs	79.06	70.64
Class III UAs	80.31	72.13
OGs	75.33	63.23

Table 3 *Percentage Literacy in Outgrowths of Class I, II and III Urban Agglomerations of Gujarat, 2001*

UAs of Class I, II and III Categories	*Outgrowths*			
	Less than 65% Literacy	*65–75% Literacy*	*More than 75% Literacy*	*Total*
Less than 65%	—	—	—	
65–75%	01 (I) 01 (II) 03 01 (III) (2.5)(2.4)	—	02 (I) 02 — (1.67)(1.6) —	03 (I) 01 (II) 05 01 (III) (04)
More than 75%	07 (I) 03 (II) 11 01 (III) (09)(8.8)	16 (I) 06 (II) 26 04 (III) (22)(18)	56 (I) 23 (II) 83 04 (III) (69)(66)	79 (I) 32 (II) 120 09 (III) (96)
Total	08 (I) 04 (II) 14 02 (III) (11)	16 (I) 06 (II) 26 04 (III) (21)	58 (I) 23 (II) 85 04 (III) (68)	82 (I) 33 (II) 125 10 (III)

Note: Average per cent of Rural Literacy in Gujarat – 62.06
Average per cent of Total Literacy in Gujarat – 69.97
Average per cent of Urban Literacy in Gujarat – 82.59

Female Proportion in Outgrowths and their Urban Agglomerations

By and large, the female proportion of outgrowths shows a positive relation with their size class of urban agglomerations. The million cities of Gujarat show 851 females per 1,000 males (2001) whereas their outgrowths recorded only 780 females per 1,000 males. However, there is no difference in the female proportion of UAs of class III and their OGs (915) in both the areas (Table 4). The predominance of male population in million cities is due to male selective migration (who are adult, single, also illiterate), who get into an unorganised sector of the city economy as domestic help, cook, plumber, carpenter, sweeper, masons, hair-dresser, hawker, etc. The proportion of the female population in the outgrowths of Gujarat varies greatly depending on the economic activities of the urban area. The lowest sex-ratio is recorded in the outgrowth of Jamnagar, i.e., port area, with 112 females per 1,000 males. Vadod (236) and Bamroli (493), two outgrowths of Surat city, also record a low female population. Similarly, Shaijpur-Gopalpura (625) of Ahmedabad city and Hamsapur (634) of Patan record a low female proportion. During the period 1981–2001, the female proportion has shown an overall decline in urban agglomerations of all classes whereas such a decline is observed only in the outgrowths of million cities (Table 4). However, there is an improvement in the sex ratio of the outgrowths in all other categories during 1981–2001, which is due to the phenomena of female migration by marriage. Out of a total of 125 outgrowths of Gujarat 82 outgrowths (65.6%) belong to Class-I UAs, of these 32 (39%) have recorded less than 879 females per 1,000 males. Only one-third of these OGs belong to those class-I UAs which also have less than 879 females per 1,000 males (Table 5), and remaining two-third OGs show low female proportion compared to their respective UAs. Eleven OGs of Class-I UAs have more than 945 females per 1,000 males whose respective urban areas have low female proportion of

901–922. This may be due to family migration or young couples settling down in outer areas. There are four outgrowths in Gujarat recording more than 1,000 females per 1,000 males. Among them the highest sex ratio is in Nani-Kadi of Kadi Town with 2,183 females per 1,000 males. This may be due to the heavy out-migration of males for work purpose. Other outgrowths are Jitodiya (1173) of Anand town, Mangrol (1,064) of Mangrol town and Valsad (1,033) of Valsad town. Thus the sex ratio among 125 outgrowths of Gujarat shows wide variation in the sex ratio with a minimum of 112 in the port area of Jamnagar to a maximum of 2,183 in Nani-Kadi of Kadi town. However, the average female proportion of all outgrowths is 877, which is lower than the average of urban agglomerations (898).

Table 4 *Female Population per 1,000 Males by Size Classes: 1981–2001*

Urban Size Class	*Urban Agglomerations*		*Outgrowths*	
	1981	*2001*	*1981*	*2001*
Million Cities	871	851	845	780
Class I	922	910	832	906
Class II	946	917	854	905
Class III	929	915	891	915
Total	917	898	856	877

(Average sex-ratio of Urban Gujarat – 879, average sex-ratio of total Gujarat – 921 and average sex-ratio of Rural Gujarat – 945)

Table 5 *Sex-Ratio of UAs and their Outgrowths by Size Class, 2001*

Size Class of UAs		*Number of Outgrowths*					
		Less than 879	*879–900*	*901–922*	*923–945*	*More than 945*	*Total*
Less than 879	I	11	—	01	—	01	13
	II	03	—	02	—	01	06
	III	—	—	—	—	—	—
879–900	I	10	02	04	01	02	19
	II	06	01	—	—	—	07
	III	02	—	—	—	01	03
901–922	I	10	08	08	01	07	34
	II	—	—	—	—	01	01
	III	—	—	02	02	02	05
923–945	I	—	03	04	03	—	10
	II	04	—	01	04	02	11
	III	—	01	—	—	—	01
More than 945	I	01	—	02	02	01	06
	II	01	01	—	01	05	08
	III	—	—	—	—	01	01
Total	I	32	13	19	07	11	82 (65,6%)
	II	14	02	03	05	09	33 (26.4%)
	III	02	01	02	02	03	10 (8.0%)
Grand Total		44	16	24	14	23	125 (100.0%)

Work Participation Rate in Outgrowths and their Urban Agglomerations

The average percentage of main workers (excluding marginal workers) in urban Gujarat amounts to 31.26 per cent and in rural Gujarat to 35.11 per cent, and in Gujarat as a whole to 33.66 per cent. About 52 per cent of the outgrowths of Gujarat show more than 33 per cent of the main workers, which indicate characteristics closer to rural workforce (Table 6). Of these, 35 per cent of the outgrowths are of Class-I urban agglomerations. The percentage of non-agricultural workforce is quite significant in both the urban agglomerations and the outgrowths. Except the million cities and their outgrowths, all other size classes show the difference of 10 to 15 per cent in the non-agricultural workforce between cities and their outgrowths. This also implies that the outgrowths have 10 to 15 per cent more of agricultural workforce than their cities/urban agglomerations reflecting their partly rural character (Table 7). The percentage of agricultural workforce in urban agglomerations and outgrowths shows negative correlation with their size classes whereas the percentage of non-agricultural workforce shows positive relation. Loss of workforce in the agricultural sector represents a gain of workers in the non-agricultural sector, this is observed during 1981–2001 period except in the million-city category. In this category there is a marginal increase in the agricultural workforce and a marginal decrease in the non-agricultural workforce (Table 7). This phenomenon may be due to the annexure of fringe villages as outgrowth of million cities and also due to the development of farmhouses, nature clubs, party-plots, nurseries and parks, etc.

Table 6 *Percentage of Main Workers in Outgrowths of Urban Agglomerations of all Classes, 2001*

Participation of UAs	*Out-growths*									*Total OGs*		
	Less than 31%			*Between 31 to 33%*			*More than 33%*					
	I	II	III	I	II	III	I	II	III	I	II	III
Less than 31 %	09	07	01	06	03	01	08	04	01	23	14	03
31 to 33 %	08	04	–	13	03	–	17	04	05	38	11	05
More than 33 %	02	01	01	–	01	–	19	06	01	21	08	02
Total	19	12	02	19	07	01	44	14	07	82	33	10

Note: Figures indicate number of OGs.

By and large the percentage of workforce in the category of cultivators, agricultural labourers, and household industry (HHI) is low in both the cities and their outgrowths of all size classes (Table 8). However, outgrowths and medium sized towns show relatively higher percentages of workforce in these categories except the category of household industry where outgrowths have a low percentage and cities have a relatively higher percentage. In the category of 'other workers' the difference between cities and outgrowths is to the extent of 5 to 12 per cent (i.e., OGs have lower percentage). The million cities (03) and Class-I Cities (14) of Gujarat show more than 95 per cent of their workforce in the category of 'other workers' whereas Class-II (15) and Class III (07) cities have 89 and 83 per cent of workforce in this category respectively. The outgrowths of Class III towns record 70 per cent and outgrowths of million cities show 90 per cent of workforce in other workers category.

Table 7 *Change in Percentage of Agricultural and Non-Agricultural Workforce of Cities and their Outgrowths (1981–2001) (by Size Class)*

Size Class	*Percentage of Agricultural Workforce*				*Percentage of Non-Agricultural Workforce*			
	1981		*2001*		*1981*		*2001*	
	Cities	OGs	Cities	OGs	Cities	OGs	Cities	OGs
Million +	0.33	2.57	0.55	8.24	98.54	95.78	91.45	91.77
Class I	2.19	25.19	1.73	13.23	96.40	74.57	98.02	87.98
Class II	7.39	44.36	6.49	18.00	90.22	53.24	93.51	81.97
Class III	14.19	46.82	14.17	29.39	82.65	48.80	85.80	70.59

Table 8 *Percentage of Workforce in Sub-Categories, 2001*

Size Class	*Cultivators*		*Agricultural Labourers*		*Household Industry*		*Other Workers*	
	Cities	OGs	Cities	OGs	Cities	OGs	Cities	OGs
Million +	0.24	2.41	0.31	5.83	2.41	1.64	97.04	90.13
Class I	0.94	5.49	0.79	7.74	2.05	3.63	95.97	84.35
Class II	3.25	6.95	3.24	11.05	4.02	2.15	89.49	79.82
Class III	5.66	8.40	8.51	20.99	2.89	0.50	82.95	70.09

Thus, the preceding discussion brings out the significant differences in some of the selected demographic characteristics by Municipal area and beyond (OGs). The outgrowths are dynamic in terms of land use development and demographic structure. The outgrowths of the past have become part of the present urban land and society, and the present outgrowths will become the entity of future metropolis or urban landscape. The outgrowths are a typical phenomenon of large cities (Class-I and Million Cities have 69 per cent of total outgrowths of Gujarat) recording a high percentage of annual growth rate (97.5%), relatively low percentage of literacy (72 to 79%), low female proportion (780 to 915 per 1,000 males) and high per cent of main workers including agricultural workforce (cultivators and agricultural labourers). Based on the understanding of these demographic characteristics, the outgrowths of Gujarat should be developed in terms of land use, various socio-economic and cultural institutions and transport and communication networks.

Acknowledgements

My thanks are due to Mr Rajeev, a Senior Geographer of Census of India (Gujarat) who provided me the necessary data.

References

Hyma, B. and G. Dattari (1976): The Growth of Metropolitan Sub-Centres of Madras and their Development, *Indian Geographical Society*, Golden Jubilee Volume. Madras, pp. 52–64.

Kulkarni, K.M. and Ila S. Joshi (1981): The Walled City of Ahmedabad. Two Outer Areas: A Study in Urban Contrasts, *Ekistics*, Vol.48, no.287, (March-April): 129–133.

Kulkarni, K.M. and C. Thangavel (1983): Demographic Characteristics and Functional Base of Urban Agglomeration and their Outgrowths in Gujarat, India, *Trans. Inst. of Indian Geographers*, Vol.5, No.2 (July): 127–136.

Lal, H. (1987): *City and Urban Fringe: A Case Study of Bareilly*, Concept Publishing Company, New Delhi, pp.43–73

Sita, K. and C.D. Deshpande (1976): Ratnagiri and Goa: A Contrast in Regional Inputs, *Indian Geographical Society*, Golden Jubilee Volume, Madras, pp.188–197.

Sita, K. (1999): Urbanisation – Policy and Reality: A Study of Maharashtra, *Indian Social Science Review*, Vol.1, No.1:117–135.

22

Nashik City

A Study of its Urban Sprawl

S.R. Latkar

The world witnessed an unprecedented growth of the urban population, towards the end of the 19th century. The latest estimate shows that by the end of the twentieth century, the world will have 2.95 billion people living in urban areas, out of which 1.96 billion people will be in developing countries and it may rise to 3.94 billion, i.e., 50 per cent of the total population with some 80 million cities. Today Nashik is already one of them. The big metropolitan cities in India will have 20 to 30 million people and the total urban population will probably expand to 660 million from the present. Thus, the developing countries will face the problem of hyper-urbanisation. Such urbanisation is due to rural depopulation, so the urban centres will show very high growth rates.

Urban Sprawl, Fringe

The large urban centres progressively extend their social and economic influence to the surrounding urban field. This creates mental or perceived urbanisation and gradual urbanisation of nearby rural settlements, i.e., social transformation of traditional rural societies into urban societies.

The outward spread of urban centres into the nearby rural areas is called an *urban sprawl.* It is a continuous process, which absorbs the peripheral villages into the urban economic system. This process can be explained as the urbanising villages, urbanised villages and the suburban development and the rural–urban fringe. It is mainly due to increasing population, over-congestion and high land values in cities.

The industrial economic development is responsible for rapid growth of medium cities and the process of suburbanisation has already begun, influencing the environment or the ecology. Suburbanisation of Indian cities is like a graft, which is imposed on the indigenous growth of cities, in the form of scattered development. This latest urban phenomenon deserves urgent attention, as the future urban growth of large cities will be located here and proper urban planning is required before the present conditions start deteriorating further. The urban fringe can be defined as "The actual physical extension of the urban areas outside their corporate limits in the nearby rural areas."

The city does not grow outward in well-defined advancing rings, with a rapid complete development as is theoretically assumed. The sprawl is clearly haphazard moving rapidly in one direction, skipping and exploding in another, while in some areas it may be very negligible in extension. The rural–urban fringe consists of rural territory pierced by finger-like projections of urbanised land use. So, the fringe is actually a real extension of the city itself. Here the land uses are in a state of flux. It is a situation, which needs proper urban planning, direction and control.

So the fringe growth is irregular with tentacles of urbanity and embayment of rurality like "an octopus". Patrick Geddes named the fringe development as a polypus, i.e., the city grows by the addition of new cells or tissues of surrounding villages. It is like the cancer cells, which affect other healthy cells and grow in their size.

The present study is an attempt to find out the development of fringe area and the urban sprawl of Nashik city. The interest in this topic came about due to the inclusion of some twenty nearby villages into the corporation area of Nashik. Recently Pune and Kalyan-Dombivali Corporation limits were extended by inclusion of nearby villages. The reason for including a large number of villages into Nashik city may have been political, economical, commercial, etc. Many people living in such villages opposed this inclusion and the decision to omit some villages from the corporation area was forced upon the administration. Today the city of Nashik has an area 376.23 sq. km., which is second largest area after the city of Mumbai. Hence Nashik city, which is showing signs of urban sprawling, presents an interesting case study to analyse the various aspects of rural–urban fringe.

Development of the City

The existence of the city of Nashik can be traced back to the early stone age, on the right bank of an "S" shaped Godavari river. The Juni Gadhi (old fort) is an alluvial mound, 80 feet high, 410 feet long and 320 feet wide where the original city development started. The traditional settlement of *Panchavati* developed in the Aryan period on the left bank. The name of Nashik refers to nine hills or *Nav-Shikha* on which the present Nashik city is growing. It is a well-protected site from the seasonal floods of Godavari. In the Muslim period the city was known as *Gulshanabad* when the city started growing in the southern direction and different gates and Puras were added. During the Maratha period the development was along the banks of the river and a new town or Pura with different Peths was added.

Under British rule the city further expanded in the western direction. The earlier development was mainly between the two rivers, the Godavari in the North and Nasardi in the south. Nearby towns like Nashik Road (railway station in 1861), Deolali cantonment and Bhagur grew independently within a distance of 17 km.

Nashik, a district headquarters, is a typical, old, medium sized Indian urban centre whose development was shaped by historical and religious factors. Various periods from prehistoric to modern, through epical, historical Muslim,

Maratha and British period left their imprints on its growth. It became an administrative headquarters during the British rule with a western type of development, which was responsible for its special growth away from the core area (Figure 1).

Figure 1 *Nashik City: Historical Development*

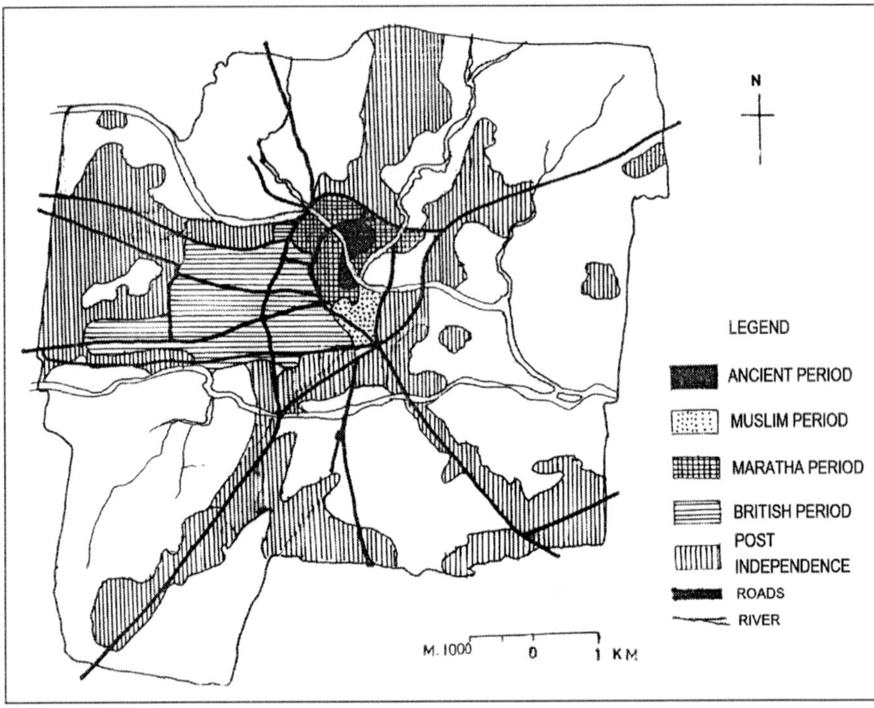

Nashik is situated in the western parts of the Deccan plateau on 20° north latitude, and 73° 51'east longitude, on the bank of the sacred Godavari river, 597 m above A.S.L. Nashik, a temple town with some two hundred temples, is known as a Banaras or Kashi of western India, where Sinhasta Mela is held after every twelve years, which explains the historical and religious importance of the city of Nashik.

Nashik was a very small city in the 19th century and at the beginning of 20th century, it started growing slowly. Up to 1941, centripetal forces were more dominant. But from 1951 onwards, Nashik showed rapid population growth due to centrifugal forces acting upon its core development (Figure 2).

The city limits were expanded from time to time from 12.8 sq. km. in the year 1881 to 58.28 sq. km. in the year 1981 before the corporation came into existence.

The city shows all morphological components, such as indigenous city (core), the new expansion beyond the walled city, the western type British period development such as civil lines, district court, collectorate, special areas, railway station, and cantonment and later development of bastis, slums, village enclaves (Vadaala, Kaamatwade, Deolaligaon, Vihitgaon) and new suburban growth (Anandvalli, Gangapur, Satpur, Ambad, Upnagar).

Figure 2 *Population Growth of Nashik City and Nashik Urban Agglomeration*

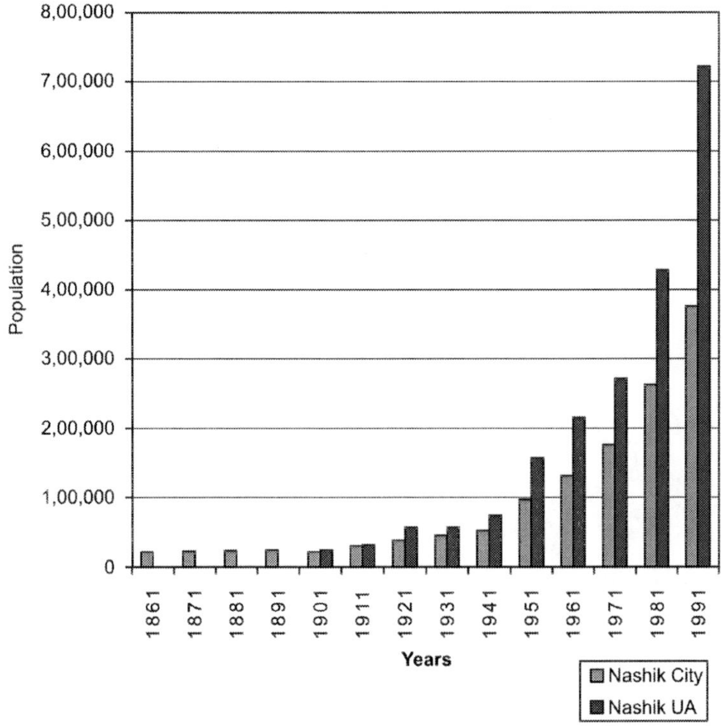

Nashik shows multinuclear model of a city because the present corporation includes three former municipalities and twenty nearby villages. The nearby urban areas in its vicinity were excluded though they are a part of Nasik's Standard Urban Area and urban agglomeration (Figure 3 and 4).

Figure 3 *Nashik Municipal Corporation Limit*

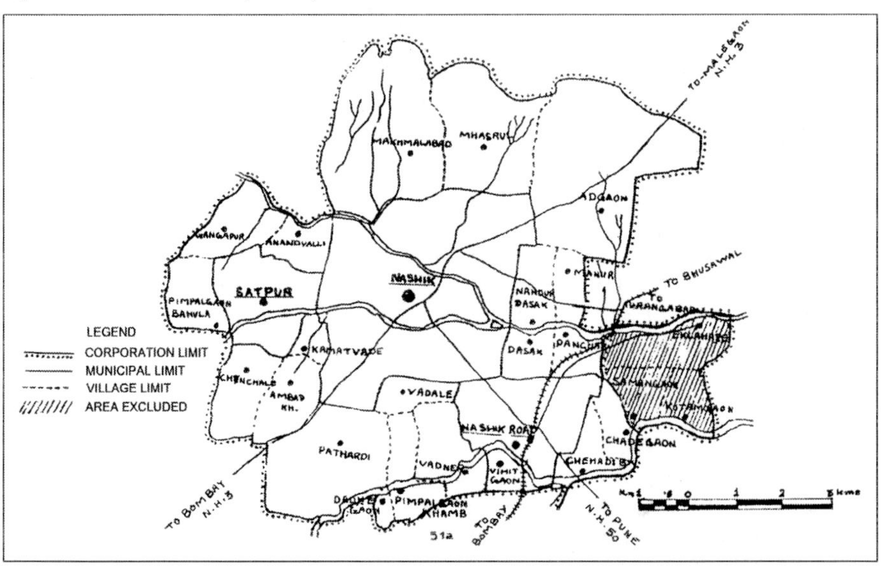

Figure 4 *Nashik City: Standard Urban Area*

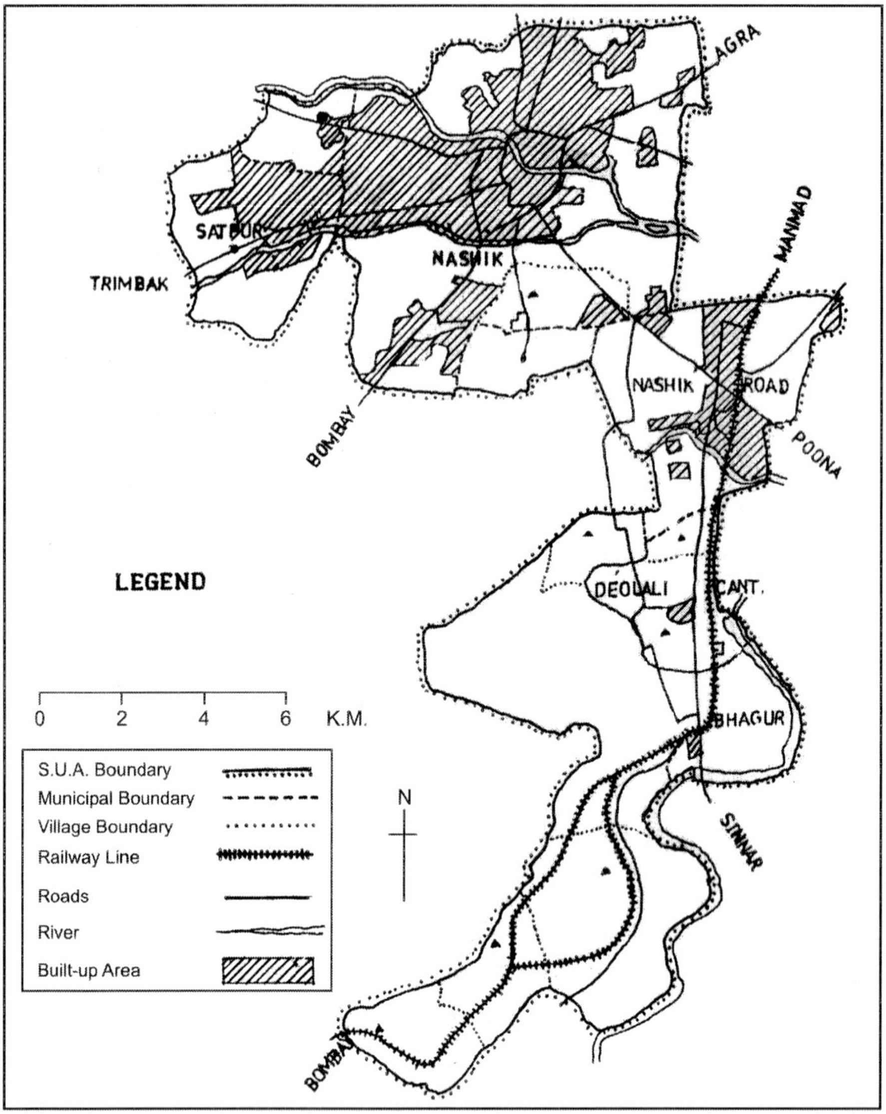

Delineation of Urban Fringe

From the works of eminent Western and Indian geographers, a great deal of information has emerged on the methods of the fringe demarcation for the present study. Several criteria suggested and used by them, were combined in this study to assess the zone of urbanisation and to distinguish it from the surrounding rural areas.

Various criteria such as the topographical attributes, land use characteristics, land values, building and construction activity, ratio of non-agricultural workers, demographic characteristics such as growth of population, density, sex ratio, literacy and female literacy rates, means of transport, such as frequency of city buses, travel time and distances have all been considered in this study.

Figure 5 *Population Growth of Nashik City and Component Settlements of Nashik Urban Agglomeration*

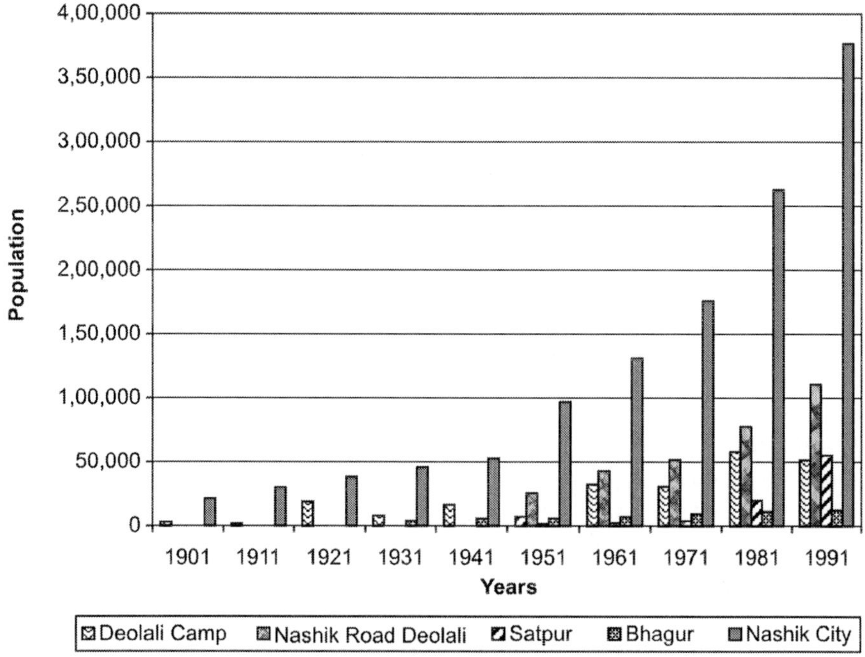

The study showed that the demographic criteria, ratio of non-agricultural workers and transport were highly significant in the Indian context.

Figure 6 *Rural–Urban Fringe of Nashik City: Non-Agricultural Workers as the Percentage of Total Workers, 1981*

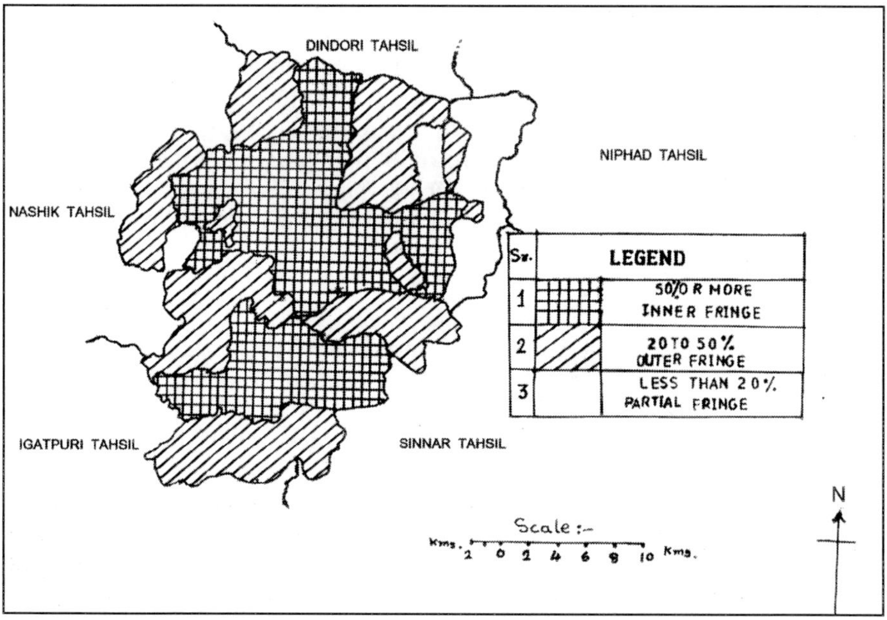

Rural–Urban Fringe of Nashik

Two fringes were identified, one inner and the other outer. The delineation of inner and outer fringe boundaries varied depending on the criteria used and as such it was found that they do not coincide with each other.

Nashik is an over bounded city. Still the inner and outer fringe areas continue to extend beyond the corporate limits, due to the exclusion of nearby urban centres, i.e., Eklahara, Deolali Camp and Bhagur. The compactly built-up area shows the radial pattern along the major arterial routes. The city has expanded rapidly in the western, southern and south-eastern directions due to the physical barrier of Godavari in the north and main central railway line in the east.

Findings

The Nashik municipal corporation area consists of 91.52 km^2 of urban and 284.71 km^2 rural area (three former municipalities and twenty nearby villages). The administrative boundary demarcation was a political decision and was influenced by the Ceiling Act applicable to former municipalities (the Urban Ceiling Act extends to five km. beyond municipal boundaries and one km. beyond the corporation boundaries). Thus, all neighbouring 20 villages were included, even though some of them do not show urban characteristics. The exclusion of urban areas like Eklahara, Deolali cantonment and Bhagur cannot be justified, while the inclusion of 20 nearby villages appears anomalous as this appears to be only to fulfil the prerequisite population required for obtaining a status of corporation for Nashik.

The suburban development started with added industrial functions in the early 70's. Prior to that, the centripetal forces encouraged rather the core development than the centrifugal forces, resulting in the outward migration of functions and the people. So, the neighbouring rural areas gradually became a part of the fringe when Nashik's population increased beyond hundred thousand.

The average extension of inner fringe area is shown as 249.80 km^2 (including nearby urban centres). But actually it is only 176.55 km^2. The outer fringe area is about 282.77 km^2, which even extends into nearby tehsils. This shows that the present corporation area of 376.23 km^2 is not justifiable as the city is over bounded. There are some villages, which show rural characteristics and it seems that urbanity was imposed upon them artificially. These villages face the problem of identity and are the least priority areas for development of urban civic services and infrastructure.

The so-called developed areas in the city also face some problems due to its scattered and patchy development. The land reservations, vacant ceiling lands, green belts and no development zones allow residential developments in just 20.1 per cent area and only 51.9 per cent area is available for all types of urban developments. The land values have therefore sky rocketed due to these extraordinary restrictive factors. There are some 85 slums with 20 per cent of city population (1991). This is very high percentage for a medium city like Nashik.

The lack of adequate supply of civic services is due to large unmanageable area, lack of adequate financial resources and scattered development. The findings of primary data reveal some interesting points, 69 per cent of respondents interviewed were migrants and settled in Nashik in the 80's and plan to stay permanently here due to good climatic conditions and better living conditions of Nashik. The migration tables available for Nashik show that people are coming from within the state and from other states of India and many rural people are seasonal migrants. They come to the city in search of jobs.

Due to above factors, Nashik showed decadal variation of population of 55.03 per cent in the year 1981–91, which is fourth rapid growth rate among the ten major cities of Maharashtra.

Conclusions

The demarcation of the fringe area of Nashik has brought out certain glaring inconsistencies and defects in drawing out administrative and urban limits and to verify the assumptions.

The cities greatly influence the surrounding rural areas, which gradually merge into the urban economic system of the cities. The impact of cities decreases as the distance from the city increases.

Similarly the land values, population densities, percentage of non-agricultural workers, literacy rates also decrease but the sex ratio increases.

The road network extends the inner fringe areas to about 10 km. or 30 minutes travel time from the city centre by bus.

The growth of city proper increases as its power of impact over its surrounding area. The physical barriers restrict the city growth in all directions. The radial or linear development waits for the infilling of the in between areas, which lags behind the arterial routes.

The different classical models and the theories about urban patterns were not strictly seen in the case of Nashik.

Nashik, therefore, appears close to a multiple nuclei model with functional diversity, but an economic segregation is not very clear in the form of distinct zones, but the social and the communal segregation is more clearly visible in the form of natural areas within Nashik city.

Suggestions

Though the present corporate area is not justifiable, it can be used for the purpose of planning the future urbanisable area, which lies in the rural–urban fringe today. Presently the decentralisation of functions, neighbourhood development projects and the *basti* improvement schemes are urgently needed for the systematic and orderly growth of the city. Similarly, the internal traffic needs urgent improvement and planning of commercial, industrial, residential areas with improved civic services and parking facilities, because Nashik has already started growing rapidly beyond its corporate limits. The work of underground drainage system and the widening of the main arterial roads have just begun. The state transport department operates the city bus service and the corporation does not have its own bus system. For the effective internal movement an effective modern system of mass transportation is required, as many areas do not have proper connections with the city centre due to the physical barriers of Godavari river between the northern and the southern part. So there is urgent need of proper urban planning and political will to implement the master plan for the city. Nashik has in the future to play the role of third node of industrial development in the western part of Maharashtra after Mumbai and Pune since it is equidistant from both the cities.

References

Camphell, James M. (Aug. 1883): Gazetter of Nashik Presidency, Vol. No. 16.

Census of India (1981): Administrative Report (Census Handbook) Maharashtra, Series 12, Part I-A.

Census of India (1981): General Population Tables, Maharashtra, Series 12, Part II-A.

Census Handbooks – Nashik District 1951–1961, 1971–1981.

D.D.T.P. – Town Planning Report Nashik, Region and Nashik Corporation Area.

Gazetteer of India (1975): Nashik District (Revised Edition).

Mahana, P.P. (1986): Census Handbook 1981, series 12, Maharashtra Part XIII, District Census Handbook, Nashik District.

Nashik Municipality (1965): Jeevan Ganga (1864–1964), Nashik Municipal Centenary Report.

23

Stagnant Town in a Metropolitan Fringe

The Case of Sandor in the Shadow of Mumbai

V.S. Phadke and V.S. Rao

The Problem

Evolution of rural–urban fringe is concomitant to urban expansion and consequent spill-over of urban population and function into the surrounding area (Andrews, 1942; Whitehand, 1967; Johnson, 1974). Greenfield locations lying beyond city limits attract population because of both "push" and "pull" factors. The main among the former are the high land values and complications in dealing with the land available in the city area (Burns and Ness, 1981); the latter, on the other hand, operate because of attractiveness of green-field areas, which are land-rich, cheap and generally pose little difficulty in processing of land deals (Dillman, 1979). It is not surprising then that fringe locations have a competitive advantage over those in the city (Farris, 2001). The fringe thus becomes a premier region of growth as it also possesses several non-ponderable values such as more open space, cleaner air and water, less congestion and noise and better environment in general to raise a family when compared to city and suburbs (Daniel, 1998).

The demographic spill-over generally moves along the traffic corridors as access to city remains a prime consideration, but the settlers also seek urban infrastructure to ensure a comfortable living even after the shift. The existing towns in the fringe thus grow rapidly as a result compared to rural areas in the vicinity (Barkley and Henry, 1996), simultaneously with the settlements located along major traffic arteries. One, therefore, finds a great diversity within the fringe zone with areas of disadvantage lying in close proximity of affluent areas (Taylor and Jope, 2001). Diversity also exists with respect to cause of fringe growth. Barkley et al. (1994) have identified mixed patterns of population change in metropolitan areas of South Carolina.

Some towns in the fringe, however, defy the simple norm stated above and it is probably the result of some unique local factors constraining their growth. In all probability, the factors could be internal such as lack of adequate living space, inhospitable environment or scarcity of free goods like water. One cannot, however, rule out the role of external factors such as relative inaccessibility or competition from other growing urban centres in the vicinity, which outright divert metropolitan spill-over to such advantageously located towns. It is desirable to understand the relative role of such factors with a view to appreciating the process prevailing under such a situation.

The Context

The present exercise is an offshoot of a larger study of marginal towns of Maharashtra, 1961 (Dept. of Geography, University of Mumbai 2003). The towns belonging to census classes V and VI in the year 1961 were analysed in order to understand the nature of change in their status during the subsequent census periods up to 2001. It was revealed that not all such towns with a favourable location have grown rapidly, others have demonstrated either sluggish growth or even stagnation; some have declined and finally got declassified. Generally, the marginal towns in the shadow of Mumbai have shown a phenomenal growth due to metropolitan spill-over.

Sandor, a marginal town in the vicinity of Mumbai (Figure 1), has not only failed to grow beyond snail's pace, but has also shown a decline in the growth rate in the initial stages and even absolute demographic decline during the decade 1991–2001 (Table 1). From the population of 5.640 in 1961, it has barely attained a size of 8,841 in 1991; then onwards it has declined to 8,336 in 2002. This is despite the fact that other towns in the vicinity have shown a considerable growth during the past four decades, especially since the eighties.

Virar lying at a greater distance from Mumbai, for example, has grown from a size of 9,413 in 1961 to that of 1,18,945 in 2001. The corresponding figures for Bhayandar, a town at the edge of Brihanmumbai, are 6,974 and 5,20,301 respectively; its demographic expansion during the last decade is primarily related to incorporation of vast rural area in its fold. Vasai also shares this common experience although its growth is not phenomenal. Some new towns such as Nala Sopara, Manikpur, Navghar have also emerged and swelled; Manikpur, for example, was merely a dormitory suburb in mid-seventies (De'Mello, 1975). Why has Sandor failed to grow while all other urban centres in the vicinity have shown a considerable growth? The present paper attempts to explore into the demographic stagnation of Sandor when there is urban growth all around.

Table 1 *Towns to the North of Mumbai: Growth of Population*

Town/Year	*1961*	*1971*	*1981*	*1991*	*2001*
Bhayandar	**6,974**	**10,598**	**25,646**	**1,75,605**	**5,20,301**
Manikpur		7,610	9,531	10,032	
Navghar				25,080	
Navghar-Manikpur					**1,16,700**
Sandor	5,640	6,705	7,927	8,841	8,336
Vasai	22,598	30,594	34,940	39,781	49,346
Waliv					15,312
Gokhivare				6,696	19,772
Nala Sopara				**67,732**	**1,84,664**
Virar	**9,413**	**12,713**	**23,303**	**57,600**	**1,18,945**
Kophrad					5,267

Source: Census of Maharashtra, 1961–2001.

Virar lying at a greater distance from Mumbai, for example, has grown from a size of 9,413 in 1961 to that of 1,18,945 in 2001. The corresponding figures for Bhayandar, a town at the edge of Brihanmumbai, are 6,974 and 5,20,301 respectively; its demographic expansion during the last decade is primarily related to incorporation of vast rural area in its fold. Vasai also shares this common experience although its growth is not phenomenal. Some new towns such as Nala Sopara, Manikpur, Navghar have also emerged and swelled; Manikpur, for example, was merely a dormitory suburb in mid-seventies (De'Mello, 1975). Why has Sandor failed to grow while all other urban centres in the vicinity have shown a considerable growth? The present paper attempts to explore into the demographic stagnation of Sandor when there is urban growth all around.

Figure 1 *Sandor: Space Relations*

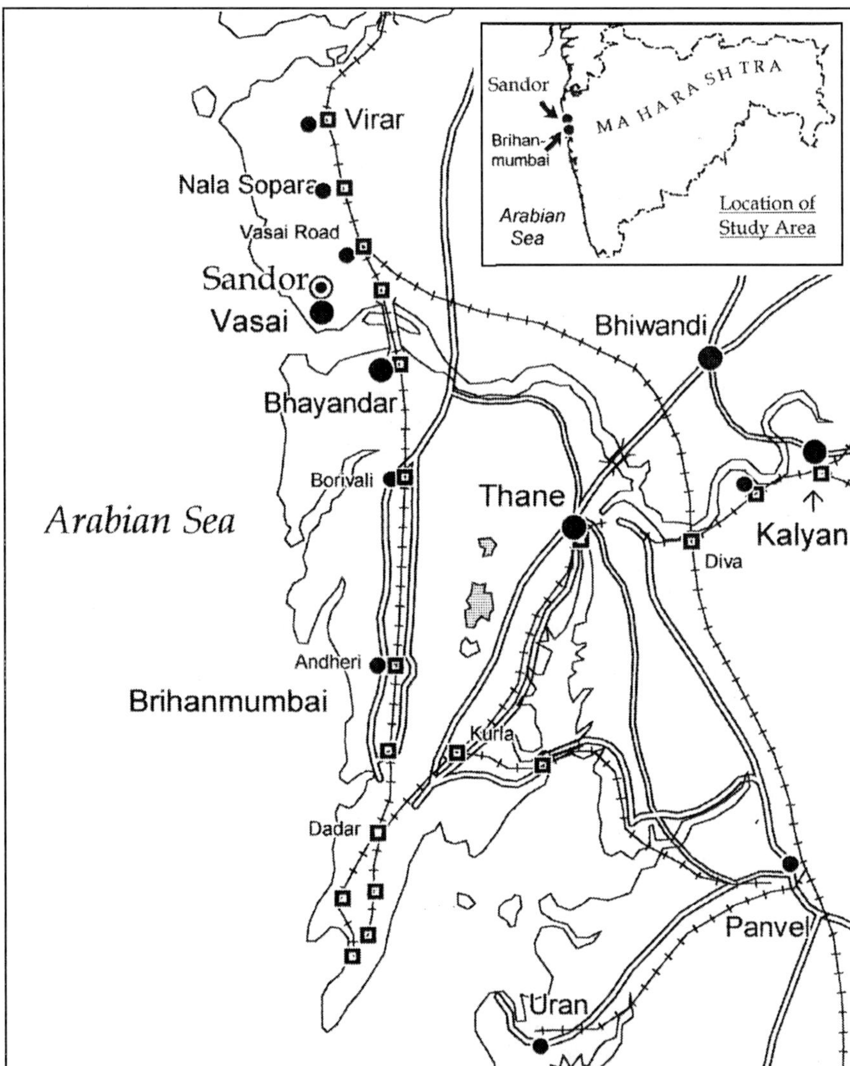

Data Sources and Methodology

Causal factors responsible for the demographic stagnation – external as well as internal – could be many as indicated earlier. Influence of each of these factors were sought be studied with the available secondary sources of data to start with. Topographical maps of the area, settlement map of the township and S.T. Bus timetable at Vasai Railway Station proved useful in this respect, apart from the Census data. Absence of secondary data with respect to some aspects was overcome through generation of primary data by extensive field observations. In general, the ethnographic research design was used in data collection, as people were rather reluctant to give information in writing (Atkinson, 1979; Goetz and LeCompte, 1984). Tabulation and mapping helped in getting answers to some of the questions raised.

Accessibility to Vasai Road

An analysis of bus flows originating from Vasai Road Railway Station to the different settlements in the vicinity indicated that Sandor has adequate number of buses to take daily commuters to the station (Figure 2). There are very few buses however, originating from the place as such and commuters have to depend on those passing through the township. Such a problem does not exist in the case of Vasai, which is the bus terminus. For nodes around the railway stations, such as Bhayandar, Navghar-Manikpur, Nalasopara and Virar, the problem does not exist except in the case of those who stay too far from the station. Today, however, share-autos are also available and inaccessibility cannot be taken as the adequate ground for demographic stagnation.

Competition from the other neighbouring centres exists because of accessibility factor mentioned above; but even here, it is noteworthy that the township of Vasai has grown, though not phenomenally, despite its inaccessibility relative to other centres.

Pattern of Settlement

The settlement of Sandor is organised into hamlets that derive names from some feature of local significance, e.g., Taadlai, Madodi, Dev Talav etc. (Figure 3). Hamlets are not widely separated and one finds a smooth transition from one hamlet to the other. The houses inside the hamlet, however, are not clustered; they are of farmstead type with every house associated with a farm. Generally, the houses face the lanes and farms lie in the rear. The open space in between two houses is devoted to tree crops such as coconut. A trail through the settlement does not give an impression that it is a town, as there is no usual hustle and bustle, although census authorities had designated it as a town in 1961 itself; there is neither noise nor congestion which is a characteristic of even a small town. The nature of housing, however, is quite impressive in many sections and this, along with the amenities locally available, is an adequate indicator of urbanisation. From the spacious nature of settlement, it is clear that the argument that the settlement could not grow because of lack of adequate physical space does not stand. In fact, there is considerable scope for expansion, if desired.

Figure 2 *Sandor Vicinity: Bus Frequency*

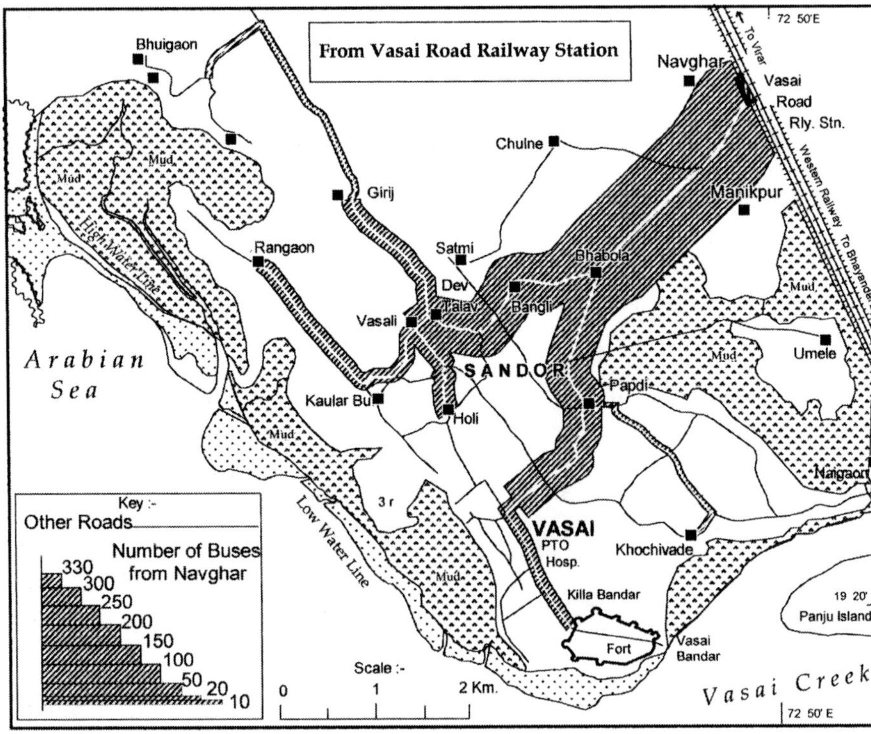

Figure 3 *Sandor: Pattern of Settlement*

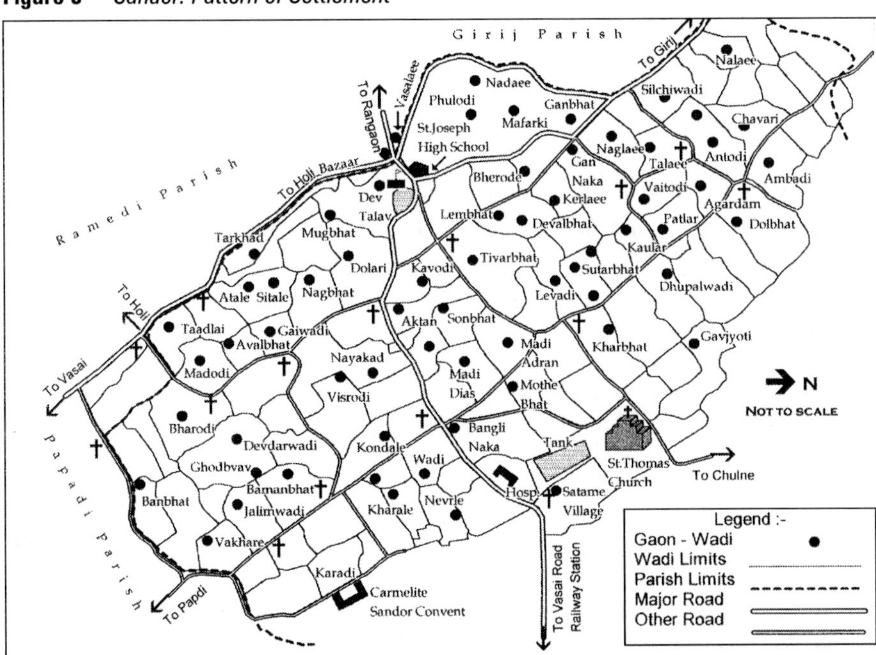

Physical Environment

An examination of the terrain condition of the Sandor environs indicated that the town is located on the old stabilised sand dunes with a reclaimed marshy area to the east (Figure 4). There are virtually no physical constraints for construction and urban expansion. In fact, a lot of urbanisation has already taken place on the terrain to the east that was more discouraging. Visiting metropolitan dwellers would envy the area and give top locational preference, if allowed to move into it.

Even water is available in plenty and less than 5 per cent of the residents depend on external sources of water (Table 2). Water supply is generally considered adequate and sweet (non-brackish). The people have, however, complained that it is hard and this poses some problems to health, apart from those such as thick coating of calcium salts on inner surface of vessels, discolouring of utensils faced in day to day life or difficulties experienced while washing clothes. It is noteworthy, however, that the problem is even more severe in the fast growing urban centres such as Navghar-Manikpur, Nala Sopara, Virar, where the residents have to depend on tanker water drawn from villages in the vicinity of Sandor. This adequately refutes the argument related to the inhospitable environment as an explanation for stagnation.

Table 2 *Nature of Water Supply in Sandor: Adequacy and Quality*

Attribute	*Percentage of Respondents*			
Source	*Users*	*Adequacy*	*Hard Nature*	*Sweet in Taste*
Well	85.37	80.49	75.61	78.05
Bore-well	9.76	9.76	9.76	7.32
Tap (External Source)	4.87	2.44	2.44	4.87
Total	100.00	92.69	87.81	87.24

Source: Field enquiries

Socio-Economic Set-up

The social set-up of the township is rooted in its history. Being located in an area colonised by the Portuguese way back in the sixteenth century, one finds an imprint of the same even today. The heterogeneity exists on religious grounds and this is a factor of considerable importance in shaping the attitude of the residents towards development. Catholics, forming about 80 per cent of the population, dominate the social scenario. Hindus form a poor second in quantitative terms. Muslims and other religious groups are so small in terms of numbers that they hardly play any significant role in decision-making.

The life of the Christians is focused on the Church and this has helped them to constitute a community interest. Traditionally, they were farmers involved in the supply of perishables such as milk and vegetables to the city of Mumbai; banana too was an important crop (Kshirsagar and Chavan, 2002). Betel vines formed a notable feature of the farm landscape at a later stage, and the existence of Vasai Pan Marketing Sahakari Society Ltd. is reminder of the past glory in this respect. The Church had, however, helped to create awareness by diffusion of information through regularly held masses. This has aroused the need to take education, including technical and professional. Today, one finds hardly anybody who does not aspire to take higher or technical education. The Church has not only provided the infrastructure like schools but also the other forms of logistic support such as scholarships. The Catholic Co-operative Bank supplemented these facilities by providing soft loans for various purposes. It is not surprising, therefore, that at least one or two members from almost every household have migrated to countries such as Dubai, US or Singapore either to take higher education or seek an employment. This effort has been facilitated by the small family norm adopted by the people engaged in non-agricultural jobs. Other adult members, except very old people, are employed outside the town, primarily in Brihanmumbai.

Currently, the primary source of income is thus earnings from non-agricultural employment although the farm activities continue to provide supplementary income by way of raising cash crops for Mumbai market. Those who are outside India continue to maintain contact and provide financial support. The number of STD/ISD booths and foreign courier service available in the town are important evidences in this respect. That the community is financially well off, is adequately reflected in real estate development. Almost all the households belonging to this community own a spacious bungalow type house that uses costly building materials such as marble or granite and has a unique architectural design. Sofas, TV, VCR/VCP are common items of use and a two-wheeler is considered a necessity. Occasionally, one also finds a four wheeler stationed in front of the house.

The community is interested in a calm and peaceful life, and this factor has helped resisting the entry of the outside element. There is a vehement opposition to sale of land to outsiders, especially builders from the city. There are instances of the community stalling the construction projects for the fear of contamination of ground water without proper drainage system. This is considered particularly necessary in an area where the capacity of the existing natural drainage channels is limited. People are also afraid of the social pollution. The community is extremely possessive, however, and has not hesitated even a bit to disown the tribal families who provided cheap farm labour in the past. This is the result of a recent legislation that made it compulsory for the owner cultivators to part with a piece of land for such people; tribal families have now been rehabilitated elsewhere.

The **Non-Christians**, by contrast, are traditionally farmers, oilseed crushers, toddy extractors or rural artisans. They are educationally poor and still depend on the local job market. Apart from cultivation, some of them work as farm labourers, transport operators or traders. The Vasai Shetkari Vividh Karyakari Sahakari Society Ltd. formed by the people of Sandor, has helped in creation of jobs such as spice making, where these people, particularly females, find some seasonal employment. Being financially poor and having limited landed property, these people are too eager to sell agricultural land as farming is becoming costly day by day. There have been such attempts to sell land this way but the majority community that controls the Village Panchayat has succeeded in stalling them. These people maintain cordial relations with the Catholics for obvious reasons.

Figure 4 *Sandor Vicinity: Terrain Characteristics*

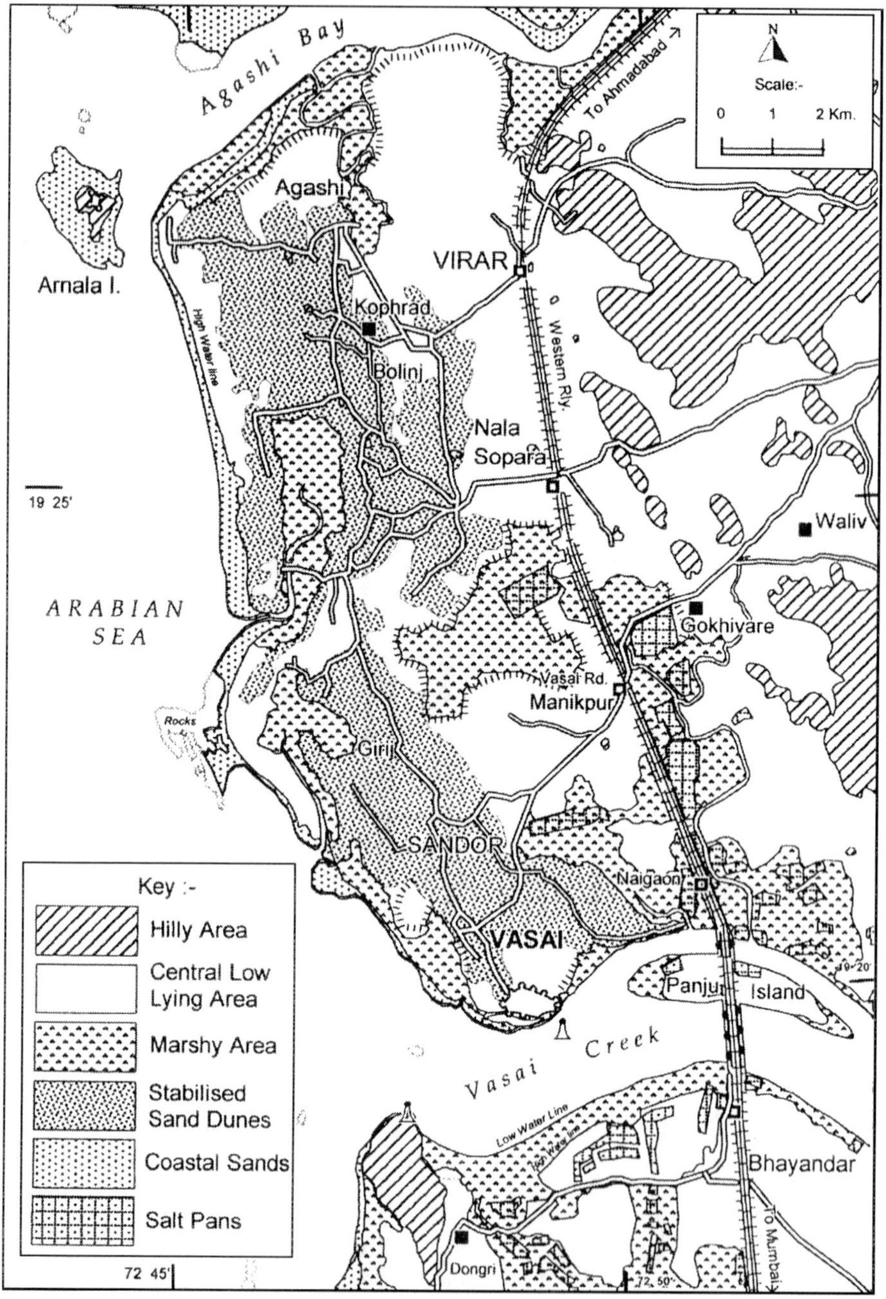

The Harit Vasai Movement has helped motivate the residents to resist urbanisation efforts. With opening up of the Vasai-Virar Region for development and launching of the new plan for the Mumbai Metropolitan Region, there was an official sanction for taking urbanisation to this area (BMRDA, 1995). Sandor falls in "green zone" but still builders lobby is making an effort to encroach upon the available space. Fortunately, people were in a position to resist such development.

Lessons for Urban Fringe Managers

The case of Sandor is atypical and suggests that the educated segment of the fringe community is increasingly becoming aware of the ills of unplanned urbanisation; this is in keeping with the experience elsewhere (Margulis and Sagan, 1999). NIMBY (Not In My Back Yard) factor is becoming prominent to successfully resist haphazard growth of the urban fringe (Fulton, 2001). It also means that local community alone could manage the fringe well given opportunity and encouragement. However, such an initiative needs sacrifice and the moot question is how long this would continue effectively. The community of Sandor is nearly homogeneous and the Church factor has held it together. Would this provide adequate force to prevent development of fissures in the community, especially when there is a nexus between politicians, administrators and the builders? Any disruption of the social fabric would reverse the past trends and pent up forces would find easy passageways through newly opened floodgates. Moreover, this environment could hardly be replicated elsewhere and hence it is doubtful whether the model would have ecological validity. It all depends on the attitude and internal cohesion in the society.

We started the discussion by considering Sandor as a "stagnant town". At the end, it appears that the adjective is a misnomer and we should realistically call it a "green town" that has effectively stemmed harsher impacts of metropolitan expansion from reaching its precincts by managing to preserve its green areas. Halting metropolitan sprawl on a perpetual basis seems a rather unfeasible proposition; however, the process could be delayed if the community with a quest for a livable city fringe draws, side-by-side, appropriate lessons from the earlier experiences.

References

Andrews, R.B. (1942): Elements in the Urban Fringe Pattern, *Journal of Land and Public Utility Economics*, 18:169–83.

Atkinson, P. (1979): Research Design in Ethnography, in the Open University (ed.) Research Methods in Education and Social Sciences, Research Design, 3B, Milton Keynes, 43–81.

Barkley, D.L. and M.S. Henry (1996): Big City Lights and Small Towns: Conflicts or Confluence, Center for Community Economic Development, CEN, Newsletter No. 237.

Barkley, D.L., M.S. Henry and S. Bao (1994): Metropolitan Growth: Boon or Bane to Nearby Rural Areas? *Choices*, Fourth Quarter:14–18.

BMRDA (1995): Draft Regional Plan for Bombay Metropolitan Region, 1996–2011, Bombay Metropolitan Regional Development Authority, Mumbai.

Burns, L.S. and K.V. Ness (1981): Decline of the Metropolitan Economy, *Urban Studies*, 18:169–80.

Daniel, T. (1998): The Struggle to Manage Growth in the Metropolitan Fringe, Proceedings of the 1998 National Planning Conference, AICP Press, New York.

De'Mello, A.A. (1975): Manikpur as a Dormitory Suburb, Unpublished M.A. Dissertation, University of Mumbai.

Department of Geography (2003): Marginal Towns of Maharashtra – 1961, Unpublished project work, M.A./M.Sc. Part II, University of Mumbai.

Dillman, D.A. (1979): Residential Preferences, Quality of Life and Population Turnaround, *American Journal of Agricultural Economics*, 61: 960–66.

Farris, J.T. (2001): The Barriers to Using Urban Infill Development to Achieve Smart Growth, quoted in W. Fulton (2001), Loc cit.

Fulton, W. (2001): Comments on J. Terrence Farris's "The Barriers to Using Urban Infill Development to Achieve Smart Growth, *Housing Policy Debate*, 12 (1): 41–45.

Goetz, J.P. and M.D. LeCompte (1984): *Ethnography and Qualitative Design in Educational Research*, Academic Press, London.

Johnson, J.H. (1974): *Suburban Growth*, John Wiley & Sons, London.

Kshirsagar, P.J. and A.P. Chavan (2002): Marketing of Banana in Thane District of Maharashtra, *http://www.indiangronet.com*

Margulis, L. and D. Sagan, (1999): Second Nature: The Human Primate at the Borders of Organism and Mechanism, *Umass Magazine*, 4 (1): 24–9.

Taylor, J. and S. Jope (2001): Poverty on the Metropolitan Fringe, *Social Action and Research*, Brotherhood of St. Laurence, Fitzroy (Australia).

Whitehand, J.R.W. (1967): Fringe Belts: A Neglected Aspect of Urban Geography, *Transactions, IBG*, 41: 223–33.

24

Managing the Peri-urban Interface of Mumbai

A Case Study of the Vasai-Virar Region

GITA KEWALRAMANI

Urbanisation in developing countries is characterised by the concentration of population in metropolitan cities. With a population of 11,914,398 in 2001, Mumbai, the financial and commercial nerve centre of India, is one of the largest urban agglomerations in the world. The severe limits of space imposed by the physical configuration of the city, which is insular in character and comprises of a narrow north-south strip of land confined to a 30 degree wedge, exacerbates the problems associated with excessive concentration of population and activities (Figure 1). The constraints imposed by physiography dictated the spatial spread of the city onto the mainland in the north. The front zone of urban expansion took place along the suburban railway, resulting in linear fringe areas, which are characteristic of the metropolis. Thus, though in the contemporary period it is the automobile that has had a major impact on urban form, in the present context it is the railway, which has dictated the spread of the city.

Continuous influx of population into Mumbai, acute paucity of land, inordinately high cost of real estate and crumbling infrastructure combined with a highly efficient suburban railway network and policy initiatives aimed at containing the congestion in the metropolis have contributed to the spread of population and activities into the peripheral zone. In the sixties settlements located along the Central Railway experienced rapid growth of population. The ban on locating medium and large industrial units within the city by the Municipal Corporation of Mumbai in 1961 led to establishment of industrial estates in Thana, Kalyan, Ulhasnagar. Other urban centres, e.g., Dombivili, developed as dormitory suburbs, providing cheap housing for workers in the city. The cities along this axis absorbed most of the spill-over of urbanisation and industrialisation from Greater Mumbai resulting in an urban continuum, which together with Mira-Bhayandar and the portion of Navi Mumbai in Thane District was incorporated into the Mumbai Urban Agglomeration. While the growth rate of Greater Mumbai has slowed down in recent decades, the Urban Agglomeration has continued to grow apace. In 1991–2001 growth rate of the city was 20 per cent while that of the Urban Agglomeration was 55.5 per cent, indicating thereby the trend of diffusing urbanisation. The railway stations are

Figure 1 *Vasai-Virar Region: The Study Area*

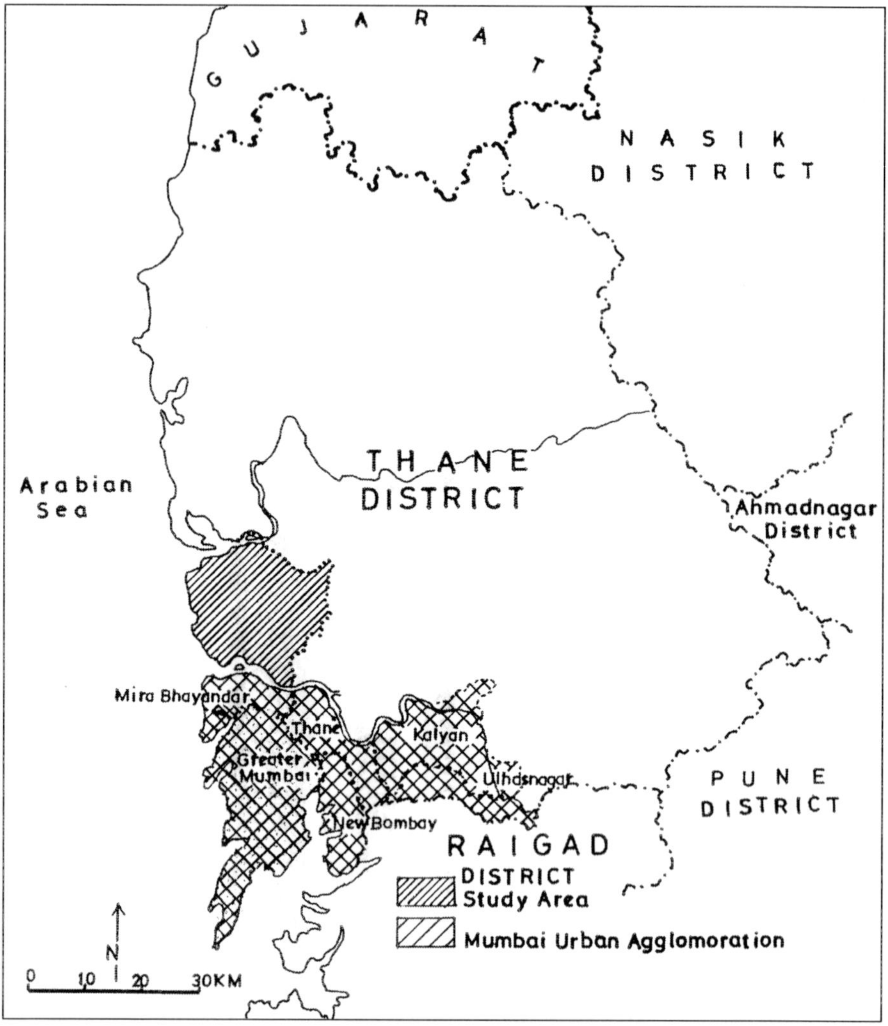

the focal points of growth while traditional subsistence agriculture continues to hold sway in the rural areas. In 1970 with the basic objective of curbing further growth of the mega-city, the State Government initiated the development of Navi Mumbai (New Bombay) as a counter magnet of Mumbai. 18,824 hectares of land, including the urban areas of Uran and Panvel towns and 95 villages in Thane and Raigarh districts were acquired by the City Industrial and Development Corporation (CIDCO) – the Special Planning Authority (SPA) for the region. Self-sufficiency in terms of job locations and shelter were to be the key to the emergence of the new city. It was expected to have twenty 'development nodes' with a total population of 2 million and about half a million jobs. The largest planned city development project in the country, however, did not take off as envisaged. Lacking infrastructure, an economic base and a rail link with the metropolis the population of Navi Mumbai in 1991 was 3.5 lakhs against a target population of 21 lakhs (BMRDA, 1995). The establishment of the suburban railway network in 1991 connecting the twin city with the metropolis triggered its growth of, and by 2001 it had reached a population of 7,85,833. Nonetheless, currently only 7 of the originally planned 20 nodes have been developed. Though the industries in the area provide 50–60,000 jobs, majority of the workers, are employed in the tertiary sector in offices located in Mumbai. Thus this 'pole of relief', which was planned as an economically vibrant city, has evolved as a dormitory for Greater Bombay. The twin city lacks a rural base and thus does not satisfy the criterion of an urban fringe which has been defined as a frontier in space where the returns to land from traditional and customary urban land uses are roughly equal to the returns from traditional and customary rural land uses. The third axis along which the city has spread is to the northwest along the western railway. The periurban interface in this zone has experienced some of the fastest urban growth rates in the country during the last three decades. This tract, the Vasai – Virar region, is not contiguous to Mumbai. It is not only separated from the metropolis by the Ulhas creek but by another urban area: Mira-Bhayander. Though the latter has been given the status of an independent urban centre, it is a continuum of the megalopolis and a part of the Mumbai Urban Agglomeration. The Vasai-Virar region, unlike the urban development along the Central Railway and Navi Mumbai, enjoys a symbiotic relationship with the metropolis. It provides perishables, manpower, recreational facilities, low cost shelter and space for some unwanted land uses such as dairying in return for a market for agricultural produce and job opportunities offered by the metropolis. It was therefore selected as the study area for an in depth analysis of the urban fringe of Mumbai.

The Study Area

The Vasai-Virar Region, a cohesive administrative unit – a tehsil, occupies an area of 380 sq. km. and is separated from Mumbai by the Ulhas creek. The distance from the southern tip of Mumbai to Virar, which is located to the north of the region, is 60 km. The region is well connected to Mumbai, both by the suburban railway, which provides Mass Rapid Transit to the city, and by a four-lane national highway. There are 202 daily train services between Mumbai City and the study area between 4.00 a.m. and 1 a.m. In addition, 10 long distance trains, which are also used by commuters, halt at stations in the area. The region is also connected by shuttle train services to the industrial nodes of Tarapur and Bhiwandi, which are located in the vicinity. In 2001, 794,739 people, of whom 70 per cent are urban, were located within its confines, in 7 towns (3 with a population over one million) and 67 villages. The flight of population into the region, which took place along the railway corridor taking advantage of cheap and efficient access to the city, was mainly confined to the low income and lower middle income groups, which could not be accommodated in the city due to the high costs of real estate (residential property in South Mumbai currently ranges between Rs 13,500–18,000/sq. ft.). The highway, on the other hand, mainly caters to goods traffic to and from Mumbai to Western India. Due to rapid growth of population since 1971 the Vasai-Virar

Table 1 *Population of Settlements in the Vasai-Virar Area*

Settlement	*Population*	*Population*	*Growth rate %*	*Population*	*Growth rate %*	*Population*	*Growth rate %*	*Population*	*Growth rate %*
	1961	*1971*	*1961–1971*	*1981*	*1971–1981*	*1991*	*1981–1991*	*2001*	*1991–2000*
G Zone	78,262	97,766	24.92	1,24,353	27.19	1,44,891	16.52	1,71,823	18.59
Vasai	22,598	30,594	35.38	34,940	14.21	39,781	13.86	50,252	26.32
Nala Sopara	10,573	15,163	43.41	20,177	33.07	67,732	235.69	2,25,000	232.19
Navghar	9,987	16,110	61.31	23,126	43.55	59,324	156.53	1,15,000	93.85
Virar	5,930	16,364	175.95	29,063	77.6	57,600	98.19	1,05,000	82.29
Waliv Region	3,711	5,167	39.23	9,162	77.32	16,067	75.37	37,824	135.41
Balance U Zone	10,839	13,099	20.85	15,500	18.33	20,324	31.13	24,452	20.31
Total U Zone	63,638	96,497	51.63	1,31,968	36.76	2,60,828	97.64	5,57,528	113.75
Region	1,41,900	1,94,263	36.9	2,56,321	31.95	4,05,719	58.29	7,94,739	79.77

G Zone – Green Zone; U Zone – Urban Zone

region was notified by the Urban Development Department of Government of Maharashtra as a Special Planning Zone in August 1988. Thus, the study area is unique in that it is one of the few fringe areas in the country where a special purpose authority bridging urban and rural areas has been created. Conventionally institutions of local government tend to be either urban or rural in focus; and district and regional governments do not adequately link urban and rural concerns. The periurban interface promotes and maintains livelihoods in both urban and rural areas. Activities in both areas rely upon it for flows of labour, finance, market produce, communication and access to the natural resources. Thus the provision of institutional cover is critical to the management of the periurban interface. However, despite the existence of institutional support the rapid demographic growth of the area has brought in its wake congestion, overcrowding and inadequacy of infrastructure which is a relative measure of mismatch between the need and availability of housing, water supply, drainage facilities, open spaces, intra- and inter-urban transport etc. Woefully inadequate though the amenities are, it must also be noted that their very presence is significant in a developing economy.

Growth of Population

The failure to stabilise Mumbai's population coupled with the failure of Navi Mumbai to evolve as a dynamic node, the success of the Back Bay reclamation scheme which resulted in the rapid growth of commercial jobs in the Central Business District of the metropolis to which the study area was connected by suburban railway, the paucity of affordable housing for the middle and lower income groups in Mumbai and the presence of open lands situated outside the purview of the Urban Land Ceiling Act contributed to the dynamic growth of the Vasai-Virar region. An average decadal growth rate of 115.02 per cent was registered during the last forty years. This however varies from 29.89 per cent in the rural areas to 115.02 per cent in the urban areas. There are also sharp contrasts in the growth rates of the urban centres. While those straddling the railway have experienced explosive growth (Nala Sopara has an average decadal growth of 507.02%) the towns lying away from the railway, e.g., Vasai have growth rates, which are similar to that of the rural areas. This highlights the significance of time cost for workers employed in the metropolis. Due to the rapid growth of the towns the proportion of urban population to total population has increased from 44.85 per cent in 1961 to 70.15 per cent in 2001.

Land Use

Land use in the region is closely associated with the physiography. Four distinct areas are observed, and the impact of urbanisation varies significantly in each of them (Figure 2 and 3).

Coastal belt: Adjoining the coast is a narrow belt barely a km. wide, comprising the eroding beach zone, backed by living dunes, rising to a height of about 5 m. Behind this are a series of north-south running, linear stabilised fossil dunes, of average height 2–3 m above sea level, separated by long, narrow depressions. It is an extremely fertile and productive sandy loam tract, intensely irrigated with a large number of shallow percolation wells. Since the

Figure 2 *Vasai-Virar Region: Landuse*

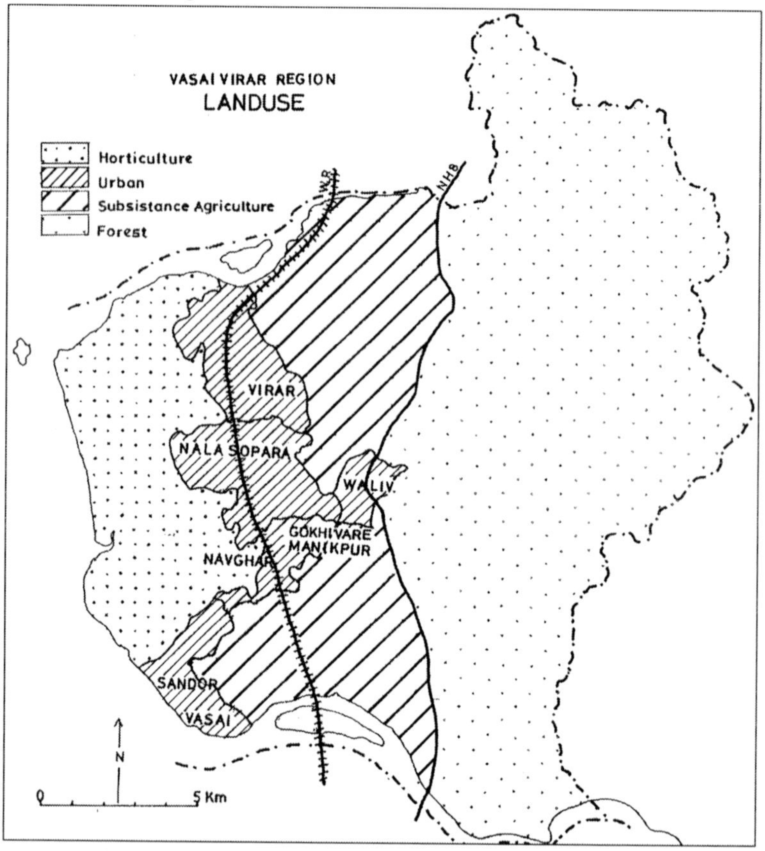

construction of the railway in 1858 this belt evolved as a classic example of the "Free Cash Cropping Zone" in von Thünen's model of agricultural land use. As the linkages with the city have intensified during the last few decades, the farmers have made agriculture more intensive, substituting less remunerative cash crops by more remunerative ones. Floriculture has taken over from bananas and vegetables, which dominated earlier. The flowers are transported by train to markets in Mumbai. A few large farmers have developed forward linkages and have their own retail outlets in the city. Flowers are also exported to Dubai. Vegetables are often inter-cropped with the flowers. Being bulky and a relatively cheaper commodity they are sold in the local urban market. This highly labour intensive activity is highly suited to the area, which is characterised by a dispersed settlement pattern, small farm holdings with an average size of 1,000–2,000 m^2 and cheap labour. This activity is likely to get a boost in the future as a flower auction house, the first of its kind in the country, is slated to come up on a 15–acre site at Goregaon, a Mumbai suburb along the western railway, under the aegis of the Maharashtra Agro-Industries Development Corporation. The project has already been cleared by the State Government and will cater to both the export market and the Indian one. Fishing, a traditional occupation in the coastal area is confined to artisanal fishermen. Catch has been dwindling in recent years due to trawling, development of the offshore Bombay

Figure 3 *Vasai-Virar Region: Past Configuration*

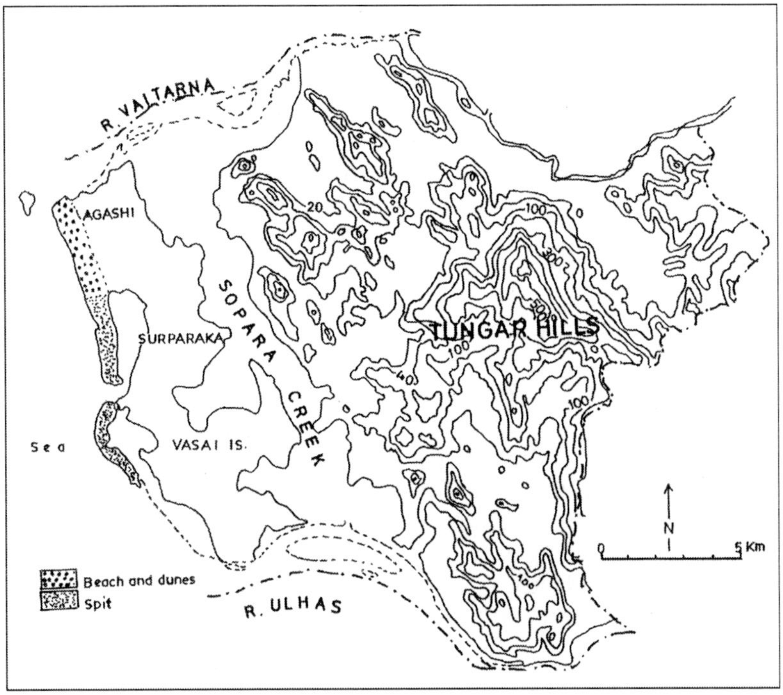

High oilrig and pollution. Despite organising themselves into co-operatives and developing forward linkages with Five star hotels in Mumbai the profits of the fisher folk continue to decline. They claim that while three years ago they earned Rs 500 a day, today they barely manage to recover the cost of diesel and ice. Inland fisheries have been developed during the last two decades in two large fresh water ponds, which have been given on contract to local farmers by the village authority. Exotic species of fish are bred here, the fingerlings are obtained from Calcutta and the fish marketed in Mumbai. The scenic beaches in the area are a recreational site for the lower middle-income groups in Mumbai who visit the area by train. There are about 15 small resorts, none of which have a sea front, and provide cheap accommodation. The beaches are dirty and in addition to fishing activities are also used as cremation grounds. Dredging for sand is also common in the coastal areas.

The Central Lowlands: This belt, which is a vast mud flat, flooded during the monsoons by rainwater and reached by tidal waters during high tides, marks the area of the erstwhile Sopara-Agashi creek. Roughly in the centre runs a railway on an embankment, 2–3 m high. This is the zone where the rural character of the fringe has been abruptly replaced by a more urban profile in terms of land use, employment, income and culture. It is a high-density residential area. All the million towns, which are contiguous to each other, are located here. These dormitory towns extend to a maximum of 2 km. on either side of the railway and are inhabited by the middle and lower income groups, taking advantage of cheap and efficient access to the city. 64 per cent of the housing stock is occupied by the lower income groups, 15 per cent by middle income groups, 20 per cent by the economically weaker sections (in both organised as well as unorganised sectors) and just 1 per cent by the upper income groups[1]. Housing thus comprises mainly of high-rise blocks with apartments ranging in size from 275–450 sq. ft. Initially, the residential complexes were small in size, plinth levels were low, quality of construction was poor and there was often no proper access to the buildings. In most cases no fill was undertaken, so the buildings were susceptible to sinking and flooding of the ground floor. In recent years the trend has shifted towards large complexes with higher plinths, proper approach roads, schools, parks, playgrounds, and shopping centres have been constructed. A shuttle bus service to and from the railway station is also being provided by some builders.

Eastern Lowlands: This belt, with an average height 4–5 m. above sea level, has been formed by coastal alluvial deposits. The eastern margin of this tract is marked by the Mumbai-Ahmedabad National highway. It is dominated by small, nucleated settlements and subsistence agriculture based on paddy cultivation. The high value cereals are used for human consumption, while the low value rice straws have a ready market in the dairy units, which are located in the area. Irrigation is non-existent as the water table is at a depth of 100–120 ft. Brick making and sand dredging have proliferated in recent years to cater to the vibrant construction industry.

The highway has promoted the growth of secondary and tertiary activities. A number of non-hazardous, non-polluting, and not water intensive small-scale industries, such as those manufacturing engineering goods, garments, packaging material, plastics and electronics have come up in the industrial zone demarcated by CIDCO. The industrial units employ mainly unskilled, temporary labour and backward and forward linkages with the study area are extremely limited. A few dairy farms have shifted into the area from Mumbai. The labour, which shifted from the city along with the units, is from North India. Milk is supplied to Mumbai by road. This is an example of an undesirable land use being shifted out of the city. There is a need to ensure effluent treatment and disposal to prevent solid waste pollution. This is vital as there is a proposal to shift another 60,000 cattle into the area by The Animal Husbandry and Dairy Development Department, Government of Maharashtra. A provision of 350.25 hectares has been made for this purpose in the development plan. A few recreational complexes have also come up along the highway to cater to the needs of upper middle class population from the city.

Eastern Hilly Area: It is an area of rugged terrain, with maximum height 662 m, about 10–15 km. broad running parallel to the coast at a distance of 15–20 km. from the shore. The main hill complex runs NNW-SSE with offshoot spurs especially to the south. The dominant vegetation comprises tropical moist deciduous forests. Small settlements, many with declining population, dot the landscape.

Impact of Changes in Land Use in the Periurban Interface

The intermingling of urban, rural and natural systems in the peri-urban interface has created both problems and opportunities, which have significant impact on people's livelihoods.

Problems

Rapid growth of population has given rise to numerous problems in the urban areas associated with lack of infrastructure and the peculiar physiography of this belt.

Lack of Infrastructure

(i) *Water:* The urban areas suffer from acute water scarcity. Till 2000 only 10 million litres of water was supplied daily (mld) to the towns, catering to less than 1/4 of the demand. In Virar, which received the least water, the supply was for one hour a day, rotation wise in different areas. Moreover, the quality of water is questionable, as part of it is not treated. Since 2000, the supply has been enhanced to 30 mld, i.e., 60.58 litres per capita per day (lpcd). As per the National Commission of Urbanisation the quantity of water to sustain human life at a minimum standard of hygiene under acute drought conditions is 70 lpcd and under normal conditions the requirement is 140 lpcd. The current supply is therefore less than 50 per cent the prescribed quantity. It is also relevant to note that there is no supply of piped water to unauthorised colonies and to non-municipal areas. The shortfall of water is met by tankers, which supply water from ground water sources. This water is hard and of doubtful quality – random measurements show pH values up to 9. It was estimated by the Government of Maharashtra that 5 million litres of water was being extracted from the region daily in 1993.

(ii) *Sewage:* There in no central sewage system in the region. Individual houses/colonies construct septic tanks with soak pits, a method geologically unsuitable to the region. Marine clay soil is impervious and as the ground water table is high, detention period is inadequate resulting in overflow into the low-lying areas and open drains along the road. This leads to ground water contamination. In some pockets the sewage flows into natural ponds, which are regularly used for bathing and washing purposes. During the dry season, the quality of water deteriorates rapidly and BOD levels are dangerously high. Samples of surface water taken by the Maharashtra Pollution Control Board in January 2000 reveal dissolved oxygen levels at 5.0, BOD levels 3 days later at 38.0 and COD at 236.0. This water therefore is not fit for any use. There is only one public sector sewage treatment plant in the study area, which is inadequate and the lone private plant functions only as an aerator, disposing the 'treated' sewage into natural drains.

(iii) *Drainage:* The drainage network covers only 10 per cent of study area. High tide water penetrates up to 8 km. inland from Vaitarna and Vasai creeks into the Central Lowlands due to the low-lying nature of the terrain. During the monsoons, run-off from the eastern hills aggravates the problem. The railway embankment to the west forms an artificial ridge, preventing the free flow of water. In 2001 this resulted in the flooding of many industrial units, which are located in the foothills. In addition, piecemeal development of the area has resulted in isolated pockets being artificially raised thereby creating obstructions to the natural drainage system, leading to water logging. Extensive filling-in of the land for construction in tracts to the west of the railway line has reversed the natural direction of flow of water resulting in flooding of the coastal belt during the monsoons.

(iv) *Transport:* The roads in the region are inadequate and excluding the National Highway are poorly maintained. There are few East-West linkages from the national highway to the developed regions in the west. Significantly, though the urban areas are contiguous they are not connected by road; the railway provides the only direct linkage between them. The 26 km. stretch between Virar and Borivali in North Mumbai is the second heaviest passenger section on the Mumbai suburban network. The average number of southbound morning peak-hour passengers is about 25,000 and average train occupancy ranges from 2,100–2,500 per train, which is super dense crush load. Bus services are inadequate which has given rise to rampant use of three-wheelers, which though convenient are highly polluting. Price-wise it is highly competitive as up to four people share the services, which operate along fixed routes with flexible stops.

(v) *Electric supply:* Lack of sufficient number of substations and the existence of overhead transmission lines results in constant power failures.

Ground Water Quality

Heavy demand by urban households for water has threatened supplies in the rural areas, which need water for agriculture and domestic consumption. Overexploitation of water from wells in the rural areas has led to salinity ingress in the coastal tract. Samples of water collected from this belt in 1993 reveal that 85 per cent samples have Total Dissolved Solids over the optimum limit of 500 ppm. 15 per cent samples show chloride concentration above the optimum limit of 200 ppm for drinking purposes while in one sample the value was as high as 2,700 ppm. All samples showed total hardness values exceeding 300 ppm, the highest desirable level concentration for drinking water; in one sample the value was as high as 1,341 ppm. The pH values of all the samples were close to or above 8. Some samples with values exceeding 8 were located inland indicating that high salinity in these areas is not related to sea water intrusion, since pure sea water rarely exceeds pH 8.0. There appears to be an independent pH increasing source such as high carbonate content in the soil (Report of water sample analysis by AFPRO, Ahmednagar). Degradation of groundwater will have a major effect on the livelihood of the rural population as the irrigation dependent, highly intensive agriculture characteristic of the area would not be possible if salinity ingress continues unabated.

Coastal Erosion

Constant dredging of sand for construction has contributed to erosion along the western coast. During the last 30 years the sea has intruded about 100 metres inland in the south – eastern part of the study area. Five years ago, the government dumped stones to construct a protection wall of sorts but the barrier remains incomplete due to financial constraints. It has been estimated by the Maharashtra Maritime board that Rs 76,00,000 are required to complete the wall. Due to the ingress of the sea, the compounds of the fisher folk are being washed away during the current monsoon season. They have resorted to stacking gunny bags of sand around their houses and dumping stones but these measures have been of little help. If dredging is not discontinued and measures are not taken to contain coastal erosion, the problem is likely to get aggravated in future as waves during the monsoon move shoreward through water several meters deeper than normal and break against land that is poorly shaped to absorb wave energy.

Excessive Use of Fertilisers and Pesticides in the Horticultural Belt

Intensive agriculture has given rise to increasing use of chemical fertilisers and pesticides, which will lead to environmental damage. In recent years there is an increasing demand in Mumbai for organically produced agricultural products. Organic vegetable farming should be undertaken by the farmers in order to tap this lucrative niche market. This will also ensure sustainability of this highly productive area.

Inadequate Economic Base

Though some industrial development has taken place most of the manufacturing units are small in scale, employing few workers, most of whom are on daily wages. The rapid growth of population in the area has resulted in a higher demand for locally supplied, household oriented services like schools, shopping facilities, medical services etc. Nonetheless, comparison of data based on the Economic Census (workers are enumerated at the place of work) with Census data (workers are enumerated at the place of residence) reveals that if all the workers are employed from the region (which is incorrect) only about 35 per cent of the workers are employed locally. This points to an employment-population imbalance in the region. Chronic shortages of water and electricity are the major hurdles in achieving industrial growth.

Growth of Slums

Explosive population growth in the area has been accompanied by the rise of informal settlements. Though there are a few pockets in the towns, growth of slums has mainly taken place during the last 2–3 years on a large tract in the green zone along the road connecting Nala Sopara to the National Highway. They occupy government and private as well as tribal land and comprise squatters who have been removed from the National Park, the vicinity of the airport and railway tracks in Mumbai. Thus though the periurban interface has not been tapped for the development of special physical infrastructure for the city, such as airports, sewage plants and landfills which often lead to large-scale environmental impacts, a considerable amount of land in the green zone has been encroached by slum dwellers which originally lived in the city. The growth of slums reflects the inadequacy of housing in the region for the economically weaker sections of the society. In view of this in 1998 CIDCO started providing incentives to projects where developers constructed at least 60 per cent of the tenements of less than 25 sq. m built up area. This has worked well and 26 schemes comprising 1600 tenements of built up area between 18–25 sq. m have been approved. To date 140 tenements in 6 schemes have been completed. Though CIDCO monitors the quality of construction it does not have any say in controlling the prices. Today these tenements cost between Rs 1,75,000–2,25,000 inclusive of stamp duty and other charges for registering the sale deed. In addition to the above the SPA needs to take additional steps to enhance provision of housing to the poor. The 'site and service scheme' that provides households with small plots with basic services and helps them to build their own houses should be promoted on government land.

Opportunities

Agricultural Employment

Agricultural intensification has led to a greater need for farm workers as well as higher wages. Currently daily wages range from Rs 60 for women to Rs 80 for men. This is equivalent to that of casual workers employed in the small-scale industries in the area. This not only benefits poor agricultural workers but also enables poor farmers to compensate for small farm size by working on the farms of others.

Non-Agricultural Employment

Urbanisation characteristically results in diversification of the economy. As observed above, brick kilns and sand dredging provide additional income in areas of subsistence agriculture. The growth of towns has promoted the growth of the trade and service sectors to cater to the needs of the local population. Cheap and efficient transport links also provide opportunities in the metropolitan job market. A large proportion of the youth in the western horticultural tract have taken up tertiary sector jobs in Mumbai, while the older generation looks after the farms adding considerably to the family income. This has contributed to economic prosperity in the region, which is evident in the widespread renovation of houses in the area.

Better Access to Health and Education Services

In earlier years educational facilities in the rural areas was mainly confined to primary level schools. Today, in addition to secondary level schools, three Arts/Science/Commerce colleges have come up in Virar, Vasai and Nala Sopara. In addition, there is a homeopathic Medical College and Technical School in Virar and a Government Polytechnic at Navghar for industrial training. In addition, there is a Rehabilitation Centre for the Handicapped. Though there are no large government hospitals, a number of private hospitals have mushroomed. Advanced medical care is still lacking and there is no blood bank in the area.

Markets for Selling Rural Products

Mumbai provides a lucrative market for flowers and milk produced in the area. The local urban market is tapped for vegetables, which are a bulkier commodity to transport than flowers.

Role of Grassroot Movements in the Area

Grassroot movements have played a crucial role in conserving the fertile agricultural land in the region. Community structure has been of vital importance. 65 per cent of the population in the horticultural tract are Christians. Christian missionaries have played a significant role in promoting education; consequently most of the population is literate. A priest, Father D'Britto, who was able to draw all members of the community together, has been at the forefront of these movements. Under his leadership the 'Harit Vasai Samiti' (Green Vasai Movement) was formed which fought to prevent urban uses infiltrating prime agricultural space. Under the aegis of the organisation 1255.59 hectares of this tract, which were included in the Urban Zone in the Development Plan of the area were re-converted to the Green Zone. The other local movement 'Pani Bachao Mahila Andolan' was also initiated at his behest. The 'Pani Bachao Mahila Andolan' (Women's Save Water Movement) was launched to prevent exploitation of groundwater resources in the area. Women were put in the forefront to counter the aggressive tactics employed by the owners of water tankers who were purchasing water from the villages in the area. Water quality monitoring was undertaken by the organisation in 1990 to provide a technical base for presenting the problem of seawater intrusion to the people and the government. Based on their findings the government restricted the selling of fresh water from open wells. Water samples taken in 1998 show that in most cases there has been a reverse trend in the values for chloride and hardness, which indicates that seawater intrusion into the aquifer zone has decreased.

Role of Planning in the Area

Due to the rapid growth of urban population in the study area since 1961 the Bombay Metropolitan Regional Development Authority (BMRDA) identified Virar, Navghar-Manikpur, Nalasopara and Sandor as dormitory towns in the Development Plan (1971). The rest of the region was included in the Green Zone. Development plans for the towns were prepared by the Assistant Director of Town Planning, Thane District, which had no statutory basis and showed complete disregard to the availability of physical infrastructure (e.g., the proposed source of water supply for the development taking place was groundwater sources (wells)). Only Vasai town had a statutory development plan. Initially developers bought cheap agricultural land outside urban control. Apart from construction of tenements, no value addition in terms of physical or social infrastructure was made by the builder. The Town Planning Department of the State Government on its part encouraged this trend by excluding these areas from the Urban Land Ceiling and Regulation Act and granting post facto sanctions to the unauthorised constructions. Thus the area designated for urban use increased from 773 hectares in 1973 to 2353 hectares 1983/84 to 8578 hectares in 1988. As the planning initiatives were confined to merely increasing the extent of urban area, the region suffered from lack of co-ordinated development and serious deficiencies in the provisions of essential municipal services and amenities in the towns. The uncontrolled and haphazard development prompted the government to appoint BMRDA as the SPA in December 1988 to prepare an integrated development plan for the region. In May 1990 the

Government abruptly replaced BMRDA with CIDCO as the SPA for the region. One of the main duties assigned to the latter was to carry out a land use survey for the study area and prepare a Development Plan. Without carrying out the former CIDCO published a draft Interim Development Plan in the same year, adding another 2000 hectares in nine different pockets to the Urban Zone. Six of these pockets, with an area of 1,255.59 hectares, were from the horticultural tract. It was only due to the public protests organised by the Harit Vasai Samiti that these pockets were returned to the Green Zone in November 1992. This example is a reflection of the arbitrariness with which Development Plans are prepared in the country. Other functions delegated to CIDCO included formulation of development control rules, granting permissions or development and taking action against unauthorised construction in the Urban Zone. The provision of infrastructure is under the jurisdiction of different statutory bodies/authorities such as Public Works Department, Maharashtra Water Supply and Sewerage Board, Western Railway, Maharashtra Industrial and Development Corporation, Forest Department, Department of Telecommunication etc. CIDCO has to collaborate with these agencies for the provision of physical and social infrastructure required in the region. The main source of revenue for the Special Planning Agency is development linked levies which include 'Development Charges', Water Source Development Charges, Fire cess, scrutiny fees and miscellaneous receipts. The only other source of finance is the Rs 4,000 million interest-free loan granted to it by the government. The income generated is inadequate to meet the needs of the development activities scheduled. The agency already has a deficit of Rs 5,960 million and an additional Rs 1,05,900 million are needed for infrastructure projects proposed in the area. The Special Planning Agency therefore is severely handicapped by the restricted nature of its mandate coupled with the lack of funds. The existence of a regional plan has given direction to the location of various land uses in the study area. Most of the economic activities have come up in the areas designated for them. It has however, failed to meet its objectives in terms of provision of physical, utility and service infrastructure. There was no master plan of infrastructure development in the region declared urban till the Draft Development Plan for the area was published in September 1995. In addition, the large number of agencies involved is a major constraint. Each of these finds its own agenda, and none has an overall view of the region. Thus though it is possible to tap water from Rajivali and Sativali, this has not been possible because the necessary permission has not been granted by the Forest Department. As a result water is now been obtained from Surya Dam (Figure 4). Inadequate resources have further aggravated the complexities of management of the region. The planning agency is dependent on government grants for the implementation of many of its infrastructure projects including water supply. Financial grants are often sanctioned in an arbitrary and ad-hoc manner and are sometimes dictated by political compulsions rather than the needs of the society. This has resulted in poor quality infrastructure, which has taken place on a piecemeal small-scale basis, area by area, rather than in a planned manner with a regional perspective. Water supply is a case in point as is the haphazard development of drainage facilities. This is in sharp contrast to the situation in Navi Mumbai where

Figure 4 *Vasai-Virar Region: Water Supply Schemes*

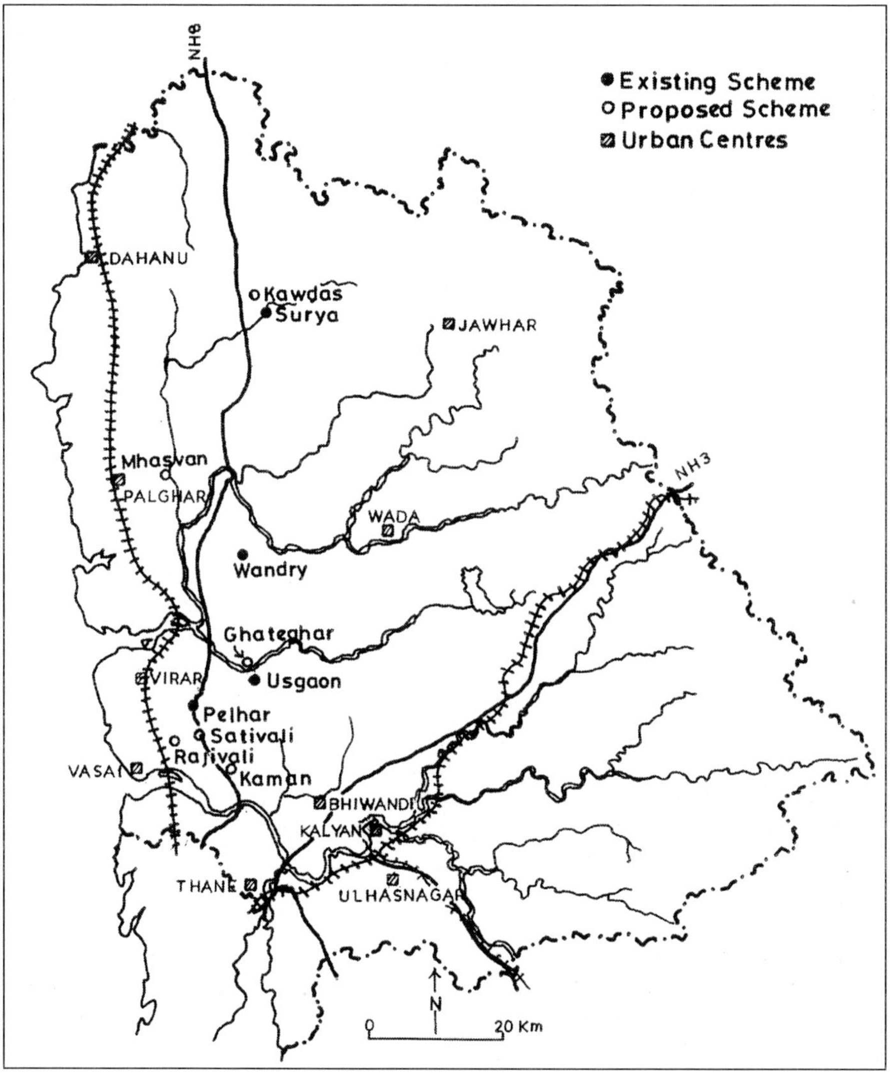

CIDCO is not only the planning agency but also the implementation agency. Here all privately owned land was acquired by the Government and handed over to CIDCO and the land itself was the major resource for financing development. Though acquisition of privately owned land is not the ideal solution, government owned land could be transferred to the CIDCO in the Vasai-Virar Region to enable it to garner some resources. Considering the scale of the project (The Vasai-Virar Region is larger in extent than Greater Mumbai and Navi Mumbai) and the cost involved for its development it would also be prudent if the government allows CIDCO to enhance the Development Charges from Rs 70/m^2 which is very nominal. It is of vital importance that the Special Planning Agency is financially sound for systematic development of the region.

Conclusion

The rapid growth of population in the periurban fringe has been driven by congestion and high cost of living in the metropolis and a resulting trade-off between high-cost of living in the city proper with all the amenities, and an affordable way of life in the fringe. Urban colonization has taken place along the railway. Unfortunately, there is no recognition of local geography and this region, which was a creek, suffers from poor drainage. The prime agricultural tracts of the region have essentially remained intact, thereby avoiding a parasitic dependency of the city. Generally it is assumed that in the age of globalisation clinging to the farm economy is anachronistic as well as irrational. Social factors have played a significant role in ensuring the survival and prosperity of agriculture on land impacted by urban price pressures. It is also important to note that while agriculture may not be friendly to all environmental values, it does serve to protect open space and provide other amenity values of importance to the community. In addition, agricultural land uses make little demand on local public services.

The suburban residents, the most numerous set of actors on the urban fringe suffer from an acute paucity of infrastructure. This is despite institutional measures in place. The dynamic nature of the periurban interface has made it difficult for institutions to adapt to the demands of change. It is in this context that the future policy options have to be viewed. CIDCO has submitted the Draft Development Plan of the region to the Government and has applied for termination of its appointment as the Special Planning Agency for the region once it is sanctioned. This raises the question of putting in place an appropriate institutional framework in the near future. The debate would centre around two options:

- Enhance the role of CIDCO from just a planning agency to an implementation agency as well as in the case of Navi Mumbai.
- Decentralise the planning process and delegate the responsibility to the individual local bodies as recommended by the 74th Amendment of the Constitution.

The chairpersons of the four municipal councils in the area and the Sabhapati Panchayat Samiti have already filed a writ petition in High Court challenging the validity and competence of CIDCO as SPA. While decentralisation is desirable certain modifications are suggested in the current administrative set-up. It is recommended that the four municipal councils in the area, which are contiguous to each other, are merged to form a Municipal Corporation. This will have a positive impact not only from the point of view of co-ordination but also financially. The revenue generated by the combined Municipal Corporation through taxes and octroi coupled with development linked levies, if effectively and efficiently managed can propel it into a vibrant, self sustaining urban area. It is also open to question whether the Village Panchayats have the will or the money power to assert their autonomy. It is of vital importance that the development of the entire region should be in the hands of a technically competent and financially sound body. Otherwise planning will continue to be plagued by ambitious goals but limited resources. In addition, the processes of social and environmental change taking place in the periurban interface need to be considered in the light of complex rural–urban interactions. Since these take place across space between 'urban' and 'rural areas', an integrated approach for the entire region is desirable. As the growth of the metropolitan regions (which are the engines of growth in developing countries) continues there will be a tendency for space needs to be met from the urban fringe. The rural–urban conflicts in the region are thus apt to intensify in the future, not dissipate.

Note

1. As per a survey conducted by CIDCO in 2002.

References

Kewalramani, G. and S. Srivastava (1999): Development Strategies and Environment Issues: A Case Study, in Abha Lakshmi Singh (ed.) *Resource Management*, B.R. Publishing Corporation, pp. 271–291.

CIDCO (1992): Interim Development Plan of Vasai-Virar Sub-Region, Brief Report.

CIDCO (1995): Draft Development Plan of Vasai-Virar Sub-Region, Development Control Regulations.

CIDCO (1998): Modified Draft Development Plan of Vasai-Virar Sub-Region, Report – 1998.

IV

Bombay Suburbs in Retrospect

25

The Suburbs of Bombay

*Fifty Years Ago**

K.R. Dikshit

The rise of suburbs is almost an inevitable phase in the history of a city's growth. It occupies the rural–urban fringe, which *"may be defined as the area of transition between well recognised urban land and the area devoted to agriculture"* (Wehrwein). The suburbs denote a period of transition when the rural landscape gradually changes to obtain the characteristics of the urban complex. The process of evolution is linked with the areal growth of the city. The expanding city projects outward in stages which one may term dotting, lineation, compaction or filling up and finally the physical accession to the city. The process may continue with a pace depending upon the stage in the life of a city. A fast growing suburb throws light on the vigour of the city, and its expansion, no doubt, results from rapidly multiplying functions.

The suburban growth is also a manifestation of the changing city structure (Colean, 1953), which shows a shift of population, trade and industry to locations in the out-lying parts of the city.

The suburbs quite apparent in the thinning out of the structures on the outskirts of the city and easily distinguishable because of inadequate development of urban characteristics defy any objective demarcation. To put them in a zone defined by sharp boundary lines will mean ignoring the realities of the process of urban growth. The compact urban fabric loosening outward is similar to the sedimentary rocks formed by series of beds. The degree of compactness near the core and looseness on the outskirts can be compared with the process of lithification, which chronologically decreases from the oldest bed at the bottom to the youngest at the top. In case of the city the arrangement is horizontal from the core outward while in the case of rocks it is a vertical formation. In fact it is a continuum and faces the same problem of zoning and demarcation as any other phenomenon of spatial distribution.

As for the functions, suburbs are believed to be *"highly differentiated segments showing greater specialisation in functions than characterises the urban unit as a whole"* (Harris, 1943: 84). This, however, is not always true, though the spatial pattern

* Reproduced from K.R. Dikshit (1961) The City of Bombay: A Study in Urban Geography, Chapter VII, unpublished Ph.D. thesis, Pune, pp. 569–648.

of functional specialisation in the suburbs is more advanced than in the city. Unlike many other suburbs, Bombay suburbs present a unique case in so far as the location of the city on an island has imposed serious limitations on its expansion in all directions, except to the north, where the island is linked with the mainland by railways and roads. The routes of transport, however, have not been able to establish a contiguity of built-up area from the city outwards because of the interposition of the Mahim creek between the city and the mainland.

It is quite a problem to demarcate the suburbs on the map. The difficulty of demarcation arises from the imperceptible urban rural gradient along the railways and roads, the urban characteristics on the other hand are of little value in fixing the outer limit of the suburbs as in any case the communities away from the core of the city show only a few traits of urban community organisation. The occupational structure of the settlements hardly provides a suitable criterion, as the non-agricultural population predominates even in very distant villages. And if all the villages with predominantly non-agricultural population are included in the suburbs, much of it will present a predominantly rural landscape without any compactness though within the orbit of city's immediate influences. In the present case the municipal limits is taken as the approximate outer margin of the suburbs. It must, however, be admitted that it is not a very plausible proposition, and the author prefers a discussion of the growth and expansion of the suburbs to their subjective demarcation.

In contrast to what is suggested here, in the usage of most writers the term "suburbs" appears to denote an urban place outside the corporate limits of the large city, but either adjacent thereto or near enough to be closely integrated into the economic life of the central city (Duncan and Reiss,1950). This was the case with Bombay even a decade ago but the extension of the corporation area has covered all the suburbs and the latter have no technical existence for the corporation though one can certainly make them out on the ground.

Greater Bombay commands at present an area of 169 sq. miles (437 km^2) of which the city proper (the city on the island) covers only 26 sq. miles (67 km^2). The remaining area of 143 sq. miles (370 km^2) though popularly known as suburbs, no longer figures in the municipal records under this name. The suburbs – the parts of Greater Bombay not included in the city – are the result of the last hundred years of evolution and a very rapid growth of industries after the Second World War.

The Growth of the Suburbs

In the middle of the nineteenth century, the northern part of the city (on the island) was occupied by the then suburbs, which later with the commissioning of the cotton textile mills in the city developed into an industrial area. The city, then, was not showing signs of a sprawl and the inadequacy of space was not felt. Besides, the absence of suitable transport limited the choice of the places of residence. A population of six to seven lakhs was suitably accommodated on the island. The laying of railways after 1853 and the availability of suburban trains opened the way to cheap and convenient life in a rural setting without having to forego the advantages of gainful employment in the city. Living in the suburbs was cheap and did not involve long distance commuting.

The city was, however, growing functionally and commuting, which at one stage was introduced by economic considerations, became in due course, as the suburbs grew, uneconomic apart from being wearisome. In the beginning of the twentieth century the sprawl of the city and the consequent growth of the suburbs were readily perceptible in the expansion of the already existing nuclei of some settlements. This trend of urban growth was soon recognised and the area in the immediate north of Mahim creek was named "Bombay Suburban Division and District". The administration of this area lay under the jurisdiction of Thane district – the administrative district just north of Bombay.

Table 1 *Size and Number of Settlements and Population of Bombay Suburban District in 1921*

Size of Settlements	*No. of Settlements*	*Population*
Under 500	40	9,387
500 to 1,000	10	7,097
1,000 to 2,000	13	17,352
2,000 to 5,000	10	32,688
5,000 to 10,000	4	30,986
10,000 to 20,000	—	—
20,000 to 50,000	2	55,330
Over 50,000	—	—
Total	79	1,52,840

Source: Census of India 1921, Vol. VI Bombay Presidency Pt. II, p. 6

The above table when summarised gives some very concrete facts.

Table 2 *Towns and Villages, Occupied Houses and Population in 1921*

Bombay Suburban District	*Settlements*		*Occupied houses*		*Population*	
	Towns	Villages	In Towns	In Villages	Urban	Rural
	4	75	6,315	16,990	70,377	82,463

Source: Census of India 1921, Vol. VII Bombay Presidency Pt. II, p. 2. It is noted that though the number of settlements with a population above 5,000 was six, only four settlements were classed urban.

The four towns appearing in the above statement are Bandra, Kurla, Ghatkopar and Santacruz. Of these the first two, larger and comparatively older, formed the nucleus for rapid suburban spread in the beginning of the 20th century (Figure 1).

The origin of these two towns is not a subsequent event to the development of Bombay, though their later growth has derived much support from the city. The first one, Bandra, if not older, is at least as old as Bombay. Located on higher ground and overlooking the sea it had a very strategic site and commanded Mahim Bay, which was fortified by Muslim rulers. Later the village attracted the attention of the Portuguese especially the Jesuit fathers, who claimed the land for themselves as well as for their college and mission paying a quit-rent according to the prevalent feudal law (Da Cunha, 1990). The cathedral together with the church became the nucleus, and the religious significance of the place became an important factor in its growth; later the place became a strong hold of catholic Christians. Even today the population of Bandra consists of a majority of Christians.

The other town, Kurla, was a village with a fairly large population. This gained in importance after the laying down of the railways between Bombay and Thana in 1853. In 1921 it was mainly a centre of rural supplies for urban needs and stood exclusively on its economic importance in contrast to Bandra, which had a religious base for its development.

Figure 1 *Decadal Growth of Three Towns of Bombay Suburbs*

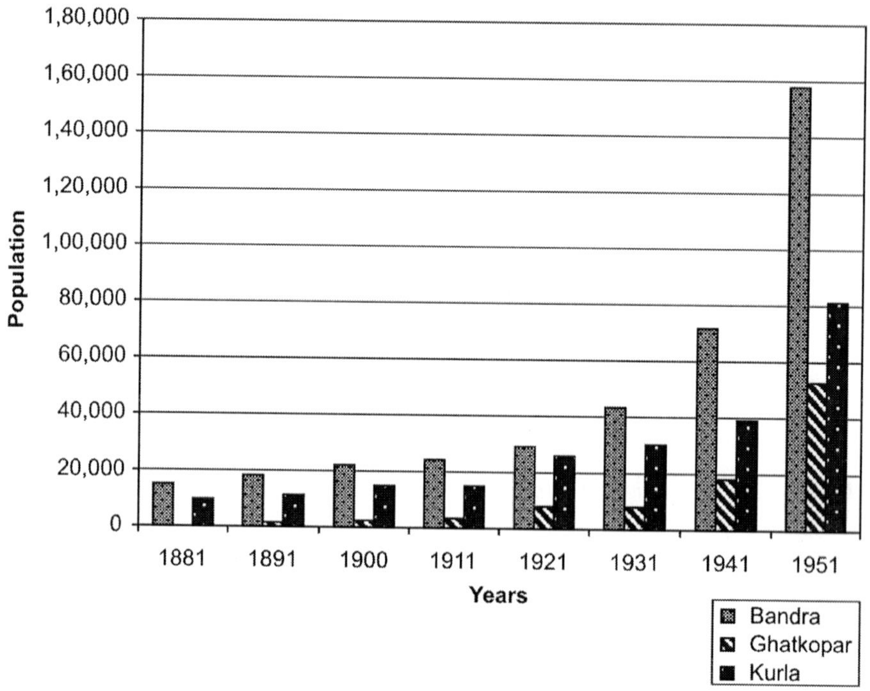

This explosion of the population in the suburban centres resulting from inadequate residential accommodation in the city and the consequent spill-over led to rapid urbanisation and a progressive increase of settlements in the larger population groups and a diminution in the number of villages. Though the changes in the outline of the Bombay Suburban District have affected the results of comparison, the fact remains, that a number of settlements with more than 5000 population have cropped up in the twentieth century.

By 1930 the process was quite advanced and a few centres like Bandra and Kurla[1] had become all-important suburban centres and had set the train of development that continues even today. Apart from these two important towns the number of settlements claiming the status of a town continued to increase from 1921 onwards. This is obvious from the following table.[2]

Table 3 *Changes in the Number of Town and Villages and in the Rural and Urban Population in Bombay Suburban Area*

Year	No. of Towns	No. of Villages	Urban Population	Rural Population	% of Urban Population	% of Rural Population
1901	2	77	36,906	56,317	40	60
1911	2	77	39,367	61,963	39	61
1921	4	63	70,377	82,463	46	54
1931	4	75	84,230	89,763	48	52
1941	8	69	1,96,444	54,703	78	22
1951	10	33	4,67,354	32,901	93	7
1961	The suburban area is merged with Greater Bombay					

There has been a progressive increase in the number of towns as also in the urban component of the total population of the suburbs right since the beginning of the present century. The enlargement of municipal limits in 1957 saw as many as 16 towns in the suburbs letting the rural population dwindle to mere seven per cent showing that not only did the villages grow into towns, but even the towns with the urban facilities have attracted more population from smaller settlements thereby increasing the urban population. In fact, urbanisation is accompanied by 'de-ruralisation'.

The unexpected decrease in the number of settlements in 1951 resulted from the boundary adjustments of Bombay Suburban district, which was subsequently replaced by a few suburban wards of Greater Bombay. Therefore, whereas the area of the 'Suburban district' was 142 sq. miles in 1921 and 153 sq. miles (396 km^2) in 1941, it dwindled to 90 sq. miles (233 km^2) in 1951 and thereafter only remained a part of Greater Bombay, which included both the city proper and the suburbs. The limits of Greater Bombay were further extended in 1957 to cover an area of 167 sq. miles (433 km^2) which almost corresponded with the old 'Bombay Suburban district' of 1921, thus bringing under the Municipal Corporation 78 villages and 16 towns, all with a population of 1.3 millions, besides the main city. Associated with the increase in the number of towns is the rise in population density in the suburbs, a fact, which speaks for the urbanisation trend.

In 1961, all the settlements – small towns and villages – were merged in what is known as Greater Bombay and no longer remained separate entities. The population count in this area has been adapted following the Census pattern in Bombay city and the entire suburban zone is divided into wards, sections and circles with areal adjustments that have obliterated the old village boundaries.

While the population increase in the suburbs has been gearing itself to gradual acceleration, the density though always on the rise, has shown a very erratic rate of increase. Density variations in this case, apart from being a function of population growth, have been also affected by the accession of sparsely populated countryside. This explains why a three fold increase in suburban population between 1951 and 1961 swings back on the density scale showing an increase of less than thirty per cent. Apart from the general increase in population and density, individual towns in the suburbs have grown considerably (Table 4).

Figure 2 *Progressive Urbanisation and Decline in Rural Population in Bombay Suburbs*

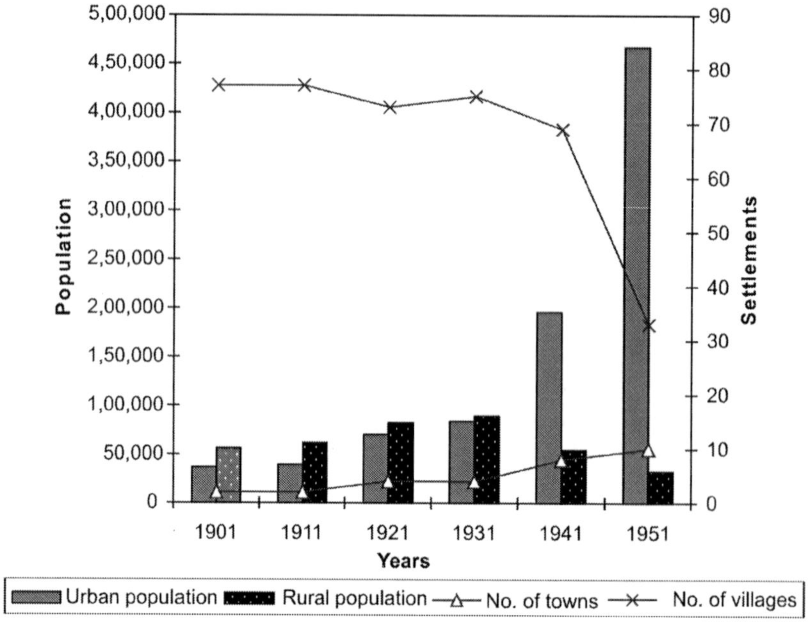

In all these cases a rapid rise in population is observed during the recent years after 1941 (Figure 1). The mounting figures of 1951 are the result of growing industrialisation of the country and the consequent rise in the population of Bombay and its suburbs since the city has tended to form the nerve centre of the western industrial zone of the country.

Table 4 *Variation in Population Density of Bombay Suburbs over the Last Sixty Years*

Year	*Area in sq. miles*	*Population*	*Variation*	*Variation in %*	*Density per sq. mile*	*Density variation in %*
1901		93,223				
1911		1,01,330	+ 8,107	+ 9		
1921	142	1,52,840	+ 51,510	+ 51	1,076	
1931	142	1,74,013	+ 21,173	+ 13	1,166	+ 8
1941	153	2,51,147	+ 77,134	+ 44	1,641	+ 41
1951	65.5	5,00,255	+ 2,49,108	+ 99	7,637	+ 365
1961	141.23	13,80,123	+ 8,79,868	+ 175	9,772	+ 28

Density figures and variations worked out with the help of Census Books of Bombay 1921, 1941, 1951, 1961.

Changes during the Ten Years 1941–1951: There has been a tremendous rise both in population and density of Bombay suburbs during the decade 1941–51. The population has gone up by 175 per cent. This is the maximum decadal increase recorded since the turn of the century. This enormous increase in suburban population suggests indirectly congestion on the island – a phenomenon, which has forced the new entrants to the urban community to find shelter in the suburbs.

The factors responsible for the growth of suburbs and the increasing degree of their urbanisation can be summarised as follows:

(i) Overpopulation in Bombay city and lack of available space for residential and other purposes.
(ii) Quick and efficient transport facilities available between the city and the suburbs.
(iii) Preference for the suburbs as suitable industrial sites and the consequent development of a large number of industries and shift of people from the city to the suburbs.
(iv) Lower cost of living, low house rent and taxes in the suburbs.
(v) Shifting of many institutions, public utility services and other social amenities to the suburbs making the city proper a less sought after place.

The railways and the automobiles have further helped the process by encouraging commuting and throwing open a large area of suburbs to city dwellers or the new arrivals, who not addicted to the life of the city found the undeveloped suburbs more akin to the villages they migrated from. Though the city's population is still increasing, a stage of stagnation has almost arrived and the increase in population of Greater Bombay, henceforth, will mean an increase in the population of the fast expanding suburbs.

The expansion of the city by way of what is termed by McKay[3] the *'metropolitan invasion'* has proceeded unimpeded with the increasing tempo and has engulfed the land in the suburbs transforming the face of the country. The following words of Mc Kay depict vividly the way rural areas are transformed.

"The metropolitan invasion would take its start from the central community. Its movement, we make liken to a glacier. It is spreading unthinking ruthless. Its substance consists of tenements, bungalows, stores, factories, bill boards, filling stations, easing stands and other structures whose individual hideousness and collective haphazardness present that unmistakable environment which we call the 'slum', not the slum of poverty but the slum of commerce. This substance conceived as a projecting, crawling glacial flow, makes its journey along each of the radiating highways. The villages of the locality are welded together into a common suburban mass without form or articulation, the integrity of each former village is ironed away; its local government is merged in general administration; the personality evaporates. Beyond the villages, the lines of flow growing thin and puddy and continue their inroad towards the hinterlands."

Land Use in Suburbs

No statistical data are available to show quantitatively the distributional pattern of land use in the suburbs. A tentative land use map has been prepared by the author based on fieldwork and personal observations (Figure 3). The nature of land use in Bombay suburbs does not fit into the theoretical framework of uniform rings of urban land use. On the other hand, it agrees to some extent with McKay's idea of finger like projections. Functional specialisation is virtually nonexistent in the suburban and one does not find an exclusively Singh type of suburbs based on the functional structure of the locality. An exception to this may be formed in the groups of residential colonies clustered together, which one may compare with the dormitory suburbs of the West. Bandra, Juhu and Parle-Andheri are the cases in point. In fact, the suburbs are very complex and the land use seems to have been largely influenced by geographical factors.

Figure 3 *Land Use in Bombay Suburbs*

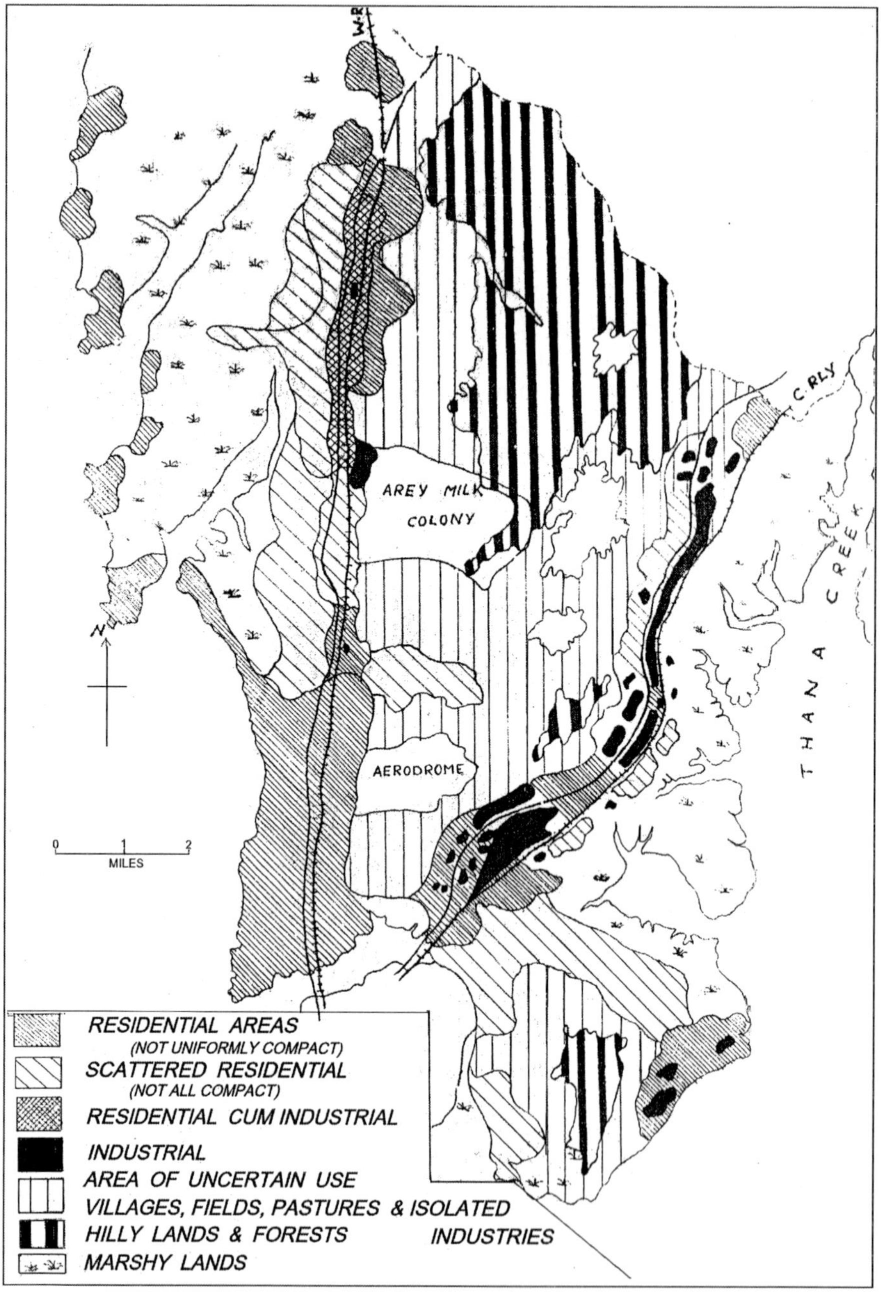

The development of cultural landscape has more commonly adhered to the zone below 50 ft. above sea level. The area below 50 feet is most developed, competed for by all different types of land use. In its outlines it resembles a fork, the two tongue of which project out from the main island. Only a small portion of this area along Thane creek has remained undeveloped largely because of its marshy nature. Transport routes, industrial plants, residential structures, and a very small area of agriculture represent the prominent modes of civilisation in this belt. Practically all the settlements with more than 5,000 population with the sole exception of Kanheri lie in this altitudinal zone.

The land between 50' and 250' contours is irregular, sloping both east and westwards from the central hilly terrain. The development is minimal. Only scattered villages practising subsidence farming in the piedmont zone form a link between the forest economy of the hills and fishing on the coast. The two water reservoirs – Vehar and Pawai – are located in this area.

The area above 250' contour is too steep and unsuitable for habitation and the steep rocky and unproductive slopes remained untouched except in rare cases along valleys. The higher parts in the suburbs are, however, likely to be developed into national parks. Residential and sloping areas near the railway stations have been followed both to the north and south by the land either left unused or claimed in parcels for agriculture, industries and in certain cases even for brick kilns.

The landmass in the suburbs is oriented to the larger interest of the urban community than to the immediate requirements of the existing villages. An extensive sea-beach at Juhu, Aerodrome at Santa Cruz and many developed holiday camps and pleasure resorts have sprung up, not so much for the local population as for the urban community as a whole. Agriculture in the suburbs is no longer an important occupation of the people. Small patches of land at the foot of the hills covered by medium textured soils form the ground for cultivation. Rice is grown in small fragmented fields. Land and particularly the soil are not very suitable for gardening or horticulture due to absence of level land and non-availability of perennial supply of water. The eastern shoreline is studded with saltpans covering a narrow but extensive belt along Thana creek.

More than anything else accessibility has been a dominant influence on the nature of land use. A particular mode of development has been promoted or retarded because of accessibility considerations. Most of the activities where transport is a factor give preference to accessibility and topography of terrain. This accessibility is defined in terms of proximity to some means of transport. The suburban land use starts with displacing agriculture far inland from the main thoroughfares. The vicinity of which is much in demand. In fact, soil capability in the suburban region has no relevance to land use. Even the fertile patches of soil available for cultivation do not receive the attention due to them. Farming often turns uneconomic because of high urban taxation and the high price of land soon tempts the farmer to make some fortune by selling out the land and settling down to occupation other than agriculture. In growing suburbs agriculture is really very much out of tune, and is soon dislodged by other uses of land.

To start with the suburbs were mostly residential and the residential land use has gravitated either along the western seacoast from Bandra to Manori or in the two narrow fork-like projections mentioned earlier. The western sea face has only a few residential colonies like Versova and Madh.

It may be noted that the development along the western sea face of the suburbs – the most suitable site for residential buildings – is rather slow. In fact, there does not appear to be any competition, and the whole of the sea face from Bandra northwards is not at all compactly built up. In this sector the suburban development of the city presents a contrast with the development of the western countries, where sea face enjoys a priority and the coastal line of buildings stands almost like a wall often obstructing the view of the sea. In Bombay suburbs the case is just the contrary, the neglect of rather than the indifference to the attractive sea face is more a reflection of distance as a barrier, lack of accessibility and inadequate transport for movement in the city or for commuting than the dearth of appreciation of splendid building sites or the charm of a sea villa.

A very large section of population of Bombay depends on public transport and likes to be conveniently located in respect to the main transport thoroughfares. The number of people owning automobiles is insignificant and this further reduces the chance of quick sea face residential development in the suburbs. The few residences that have come up are confined only to the western sea face of the suburbs. A few villas of rich people, a few moderate residential quarters in nucleated patches but above all the fishermen's hut is all we find. In fact it is marshy and unsuitable for residences. The developed narrow zone along the transport routes attracts most people and over 75 per cent of the East-suburban population lives in this zone. But even here the density of structure is not uniform and the development more or less patchy.

The location of residences (Figure 3) close to the railway lines follow from the fact of accessibility measured in terms of distance from the railway station or a bus stop. Bus services, however, were extended to the suburbs rather recently, when the residential colonies had already established themselves in the ribbon along the railway.

The suburban dwellers rely on commuting for their jobs and such proximity to railroad is a key factor in their choice of residence. The opening of a large number of bus routes during the last fifteen years has helped commuters to penetrate the central part hitherto inaccessible by trains. The noticeable result is a diffusion of residential colonies, often quite far from the railway stations. The improvement of the transport has not only promoted the pace of suburban development but is also changing its character from a ribbon to a more uniformly built suburb. To be sure while the railways initiated the suburban spread by dotting – the stations being the nuclei – the automobiles are responsible for starting a process of filling up that may lead to a more compact suburb.

Unlike the human beings the industries still retain their preference for proximity to railway lines. The fact is that the railways are still the most effective media of bulk transport, which the industries need.

The land above the 250 feet contour is hilly and rugged, partly forest covered. It is zone of scenic beauty and a haven of wild life. Much of it is demarcated as National Park. This natural green belt while providing the urban dwellers with all diversions from daily life has created a bottleneck of communications, which are confined to the lowland between this hilly terrain and the two shores. It has also restricted the choice of industries and other economic activities.

There is very little specialisation of function in the suburb and one does not find an exclusively single type of suburb, based on its functional structure in one locality.[4] The functional structure of a greater part of suburb cannot be precisely defined: patches of land occupied by single function appear, but they cannot make a definite type of suburb. It is only in the south-western part that a big residential patch appears represented by Bandra, Juhu and Parle-Andheri. The suburbs in Bombay are comparatively of a complex type, where residential and industrial suburbs are interwoven. Side by side there exist residential colonies, industrial plants, brick kilns, small gardens and even vacant land. Parts of suburbs may be classified as primarily industrial or residential, stressing the importance of one or the other function. The land offers sites for some of the necessary services, which do not find place in the city. The aerodrome at Santa Cruz, slaughterhouse at Bandra, a flying club close to the Airport and many picnic spots are all located in the suburbs. Inside the suburbs maximum development is always near the railway stations, which form the core of a particular suburban area.

Nature and Distribution of Settlements in the Suburbs

The incorporated area of Bombay suburbs had 78 settlements in 1951. These settlements no longer appear on record and their physical existence no longer presents the aspect of a decade ago. The distribution of the small villages has been guided mostly by topography. Transport seems to be a secondary factor, since most of the villages in suburbs antedate the present transport thoroughfares, which were to serve a larger economic function of Bombay and its hinterland and not the small villages. The development of Bombay, while attracting a number of transport routes, has on the contrary initiated a trend of depopulation in smaller villages and a size growth of bigger ones. The superimposition of the contour map on the distribution map of the settlements shows that the villages, which have established themselves on comparatively level land, have avoided the steep slopes.

Table 5 *Settlements at Different Elevations (1951)*

Vertical range from A.S.L.	*No. of Villages*	*No. of Towns*	*Population of the Villages*	*Population of the Towns*	*Total number of Settlements*	*Total Population*
Below 50 feet	44	16	64,127	574,109	60	638,236
Between 50 and 250 feet	13	1	11,377	13,575	14	24,952
Above 250 feet	4	—	2,720	—	4	2,720
Total	61	17	78,224	5,87,684	78	6,65,908

Besides, about 75 per cent of settlements have kept to the area below 50 feet contour, and practically all the towns have occupied level land. The growth of villages into towns in the suburbs has followed the transport thoroughfares, which in turn have preferred flat land to ensure maximum economy in their laying, maintenance and run closely to 50' contour.

The land between 50' and 250' contour is traversed frequently by small rivulets coming from the higher altitude and thus causing a recession of 100' contour. The narrow piedmont zone sloping gently westward has provided sites for fourteen villages, which still exist and are linked by roads. These villages though still alive are unmistakably declining. A few of these Vehar and Gundgaon were classed deserted in 1951. Even the other villages remote from the transport routes are either fast dwindling in their population or have reached a stage of stagnation.

Figure 4 *Settlements in Bombay Suburbs*

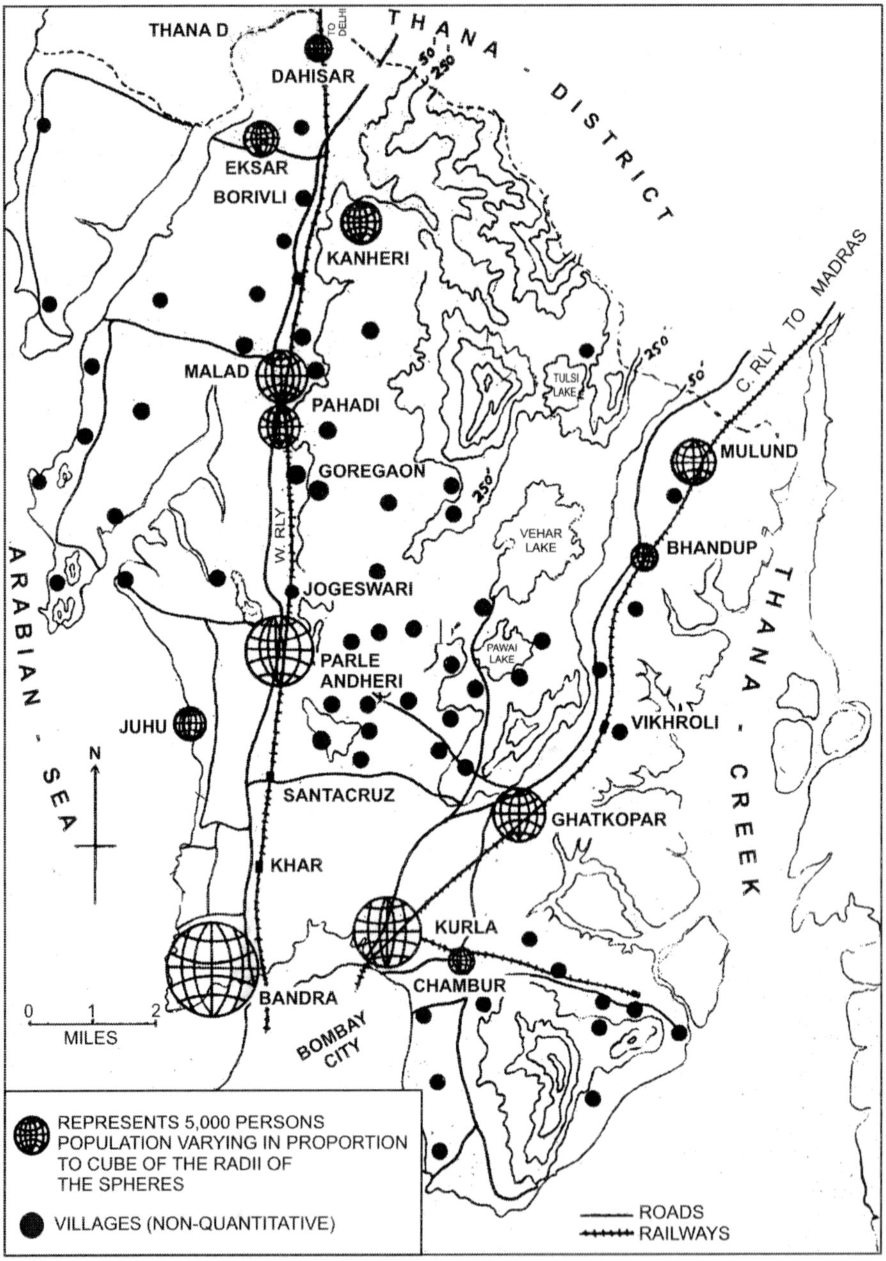

There are only four villages at an elevation of more than 250' ASL, where the land is rugged and covered with forests. More correctly these are hamlets inhabited by some backward tribes who are often daily wage earners.

A major part of the development area lies in the following belts:

1. Western seashore,
2. Along Western Railway, Ghorbundar road and between the two,
3. Along Central Railway, Bombay Agra road and in between.

The western seashore is conspicuous by the presence of beach and facing the open stretch of the Arabian Sea has attracted navigators since long. The presence of forts like Bandra and Madh bears testimony to this fact. The coastal shipping has promoted a number of small fishing ports like Manori and Varsova. But more important than either the historical significance or the economic advantages of the close association with the coastal navigation are the aesthetic considerations weighing heavily in favour of the western shore. It is well drained and sandy covered with coconut groves in contrast to the eastern creeky shore that is virtually marshy. The residential area development has, therefore, remained insignificant on the eastern shore, and even on the western sea face the pace is moderately slow. The other two belts are the areas of maximum development – confined between the railways and the roads – these linear zones have the advantage of flat terrain and convenient transport.

Along with the settlements the distribution of population in the suburb also reveals some significant facts. The density decreases with the distance from the city (Figure 4) but this decrease does not follow a uniform gradient. The maximum density of more than 10,000 persons per sq. mile is just north of Bombay city, and it decreases to less than 1,000 along the transport arteries in some sectors of the suburb. Away from the transport routes and in the hilly tract, a population density as low as ten to the sq. mile is recorded.

Undeveloped, under-developed and well-developed areas depending upon the early or late initiation of development and other site conditions often interrupt the gradient intermittently. The initial nucleation shows itself in the density pattern for a considerable length of time till an extensive area around the nucleus is uniformly well developed. But apart from this, the gaps in the density gradient often reflect a change in the land use. The Aarey milk colony in the western suburb or a number of heavy industries in the eastern suburb, do not show a variable degree of development result from the spatial structure of certain functions.

The occupational structure when classified under agricultural and non-agricultural classes of livelihood gives another result (Appendix, Table 6). In majority of the villages more than 90 per cent of the population is engaged in non-agricultural means of livelihood. The villages having a lower percentage of non-agricultural population are close to the seashore. This does not, however, show inadequacy of urban influences but is a reflection of the flat land, which occupies many people with salt collection and growing of vegetables. Occupation seems to have responded more readily to the urban influences than the density of population. The improved mobility has led to a quick adjustment to employment opportunities in the city and a change in the occupation. The change in population density needs not only a permanent migration but also building of more residences and hence is slow.

Orientation of Industries in Bombay Suburb

The typical ribbon pattern of Bombay suburbs is at least in part the result of the orientation of industries developed during the last twenty-five years (1935–1960). The industries are located in both the eastern and the western sector of the suburbs (Figure 5). From Kurla northwards, as far as Mulund, the

Figure 5 *Important Industries in Bombay Suburbs*

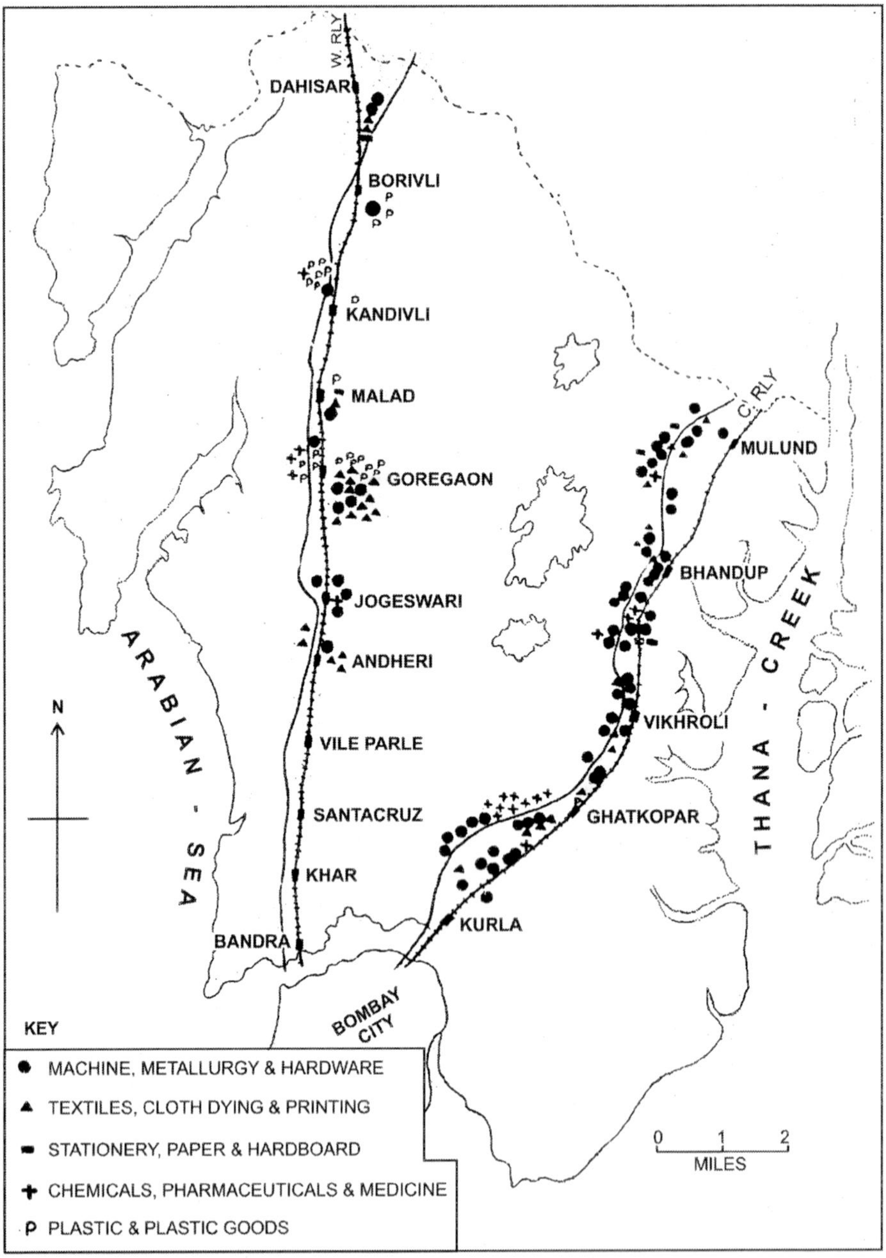

narrow strip between the Central Railway and the Bombay-Agra road is dotted with many industries, mostly of manufacturing type. The western suburb, on the other hand, is characterised by small-scale manufacturing or processing plants located predominantly along the western railway but quite often also along Ghorbundar road. Such small plants do not look for an exclusive industrial enclave, but have located themselves near the railway stations usually in a complex of residential buildings.

The location of these industries in 'Metropolitan Bombay' and more specifically at their present sites in the peripheral zone of the city is governed by certain economic laws, in which geographical factors are a major determinant. The growth of the industries in Greater Bombay is a part of the general economic strategy to develop industries in large urban agglomerations. Their orientation to transport and to the big cities, which were the hubs of transport, was the outcome of inadequate transport facilities in the country in the 19th and the early part of the 20th century. In the initial stage of industrial development, it was the lack of railways and good metalled roads in the country that brought about the establishment of pioneer mills in the port-towns; and later on the policy of the Indian railways favouring unduly the port towns in the matter of freight rates and transport facilities led eventually to a congestion of industries in these port towns at the expense of regions in the interior (Sharma, p. 207). Secondly, the importance of being close to the transportation ganglia was critical for industry and commerce and for their labour force. Accordingly, "*large cities developed close to the ganglia and particularly at the nodes of transportation system – at the juncture of the rivers and the railroads – and the industry competed for space closeby these nodes*" (Vernon, 1957, p. 18). The relative importance of these considerations have since greatly changed and the truck and the automobiles have loosened considerably the bonds of manufacturing plants toward large urban areas and allowed them to consider location more distant from urban centres. While transport may be a prime factor in urban industrial location, the industries in Bombay have aimed at advantages, which mean much more than mere facility of transport.

The suitability of Bombay to industrial location has increased manifold because of the port, the effective transport link that the city has with other parts of the country. Great ports where ocean transport lines converge and are linked up with a transport network of converging lines provide sites immune to heavy terminal charges because of the change from one form of transport to another. Inherent in the preference for port towns as industrial centres is the tendency to evade such costs by locating factories, especially those using imported materials, in the port themselves. There are many industries in Bombay suburbs which use imported raw materials.

Besides various aspects of production economy, the distributional aspect of the industrial enterprise has also influenced their location. For many of the goods processed or manufactured at Bombay, the city with its complex of industries and sizable population offers a market. What factors are decisive will vary from industry to industry and shall be reviewed while examining closely the type and the location of industries.

These industries can be grouped in the following categories:

1. Industries where loss of weight is negligible after processing. Godrej, Premier Automobiles, Crompton Parkinson and many others come in this group.
2. Industries where weight is not an important factor and the transport does not affect them seriously like plastics, pharmaceuticals and light chemicals.
3. Industries where imported raw materials are used, and because of their weight losing property need be processed in the port town.

4. Lastly there are industries which do not have the necessary raw materials nearby, nor do they import them but do occupy the present location because of the market being a very important factor in their location.

In the first group are placed the industries, which mostly process goods out of steel and some other raw materials which do not lose much weight even after processing. The Godrej – a firm manufacturing office equipment, cupboards, furniture, typewriters – is hardly guided by the cost of raw material, or else it should have been never located in the Bombay suburbs about a thousand miles away from its steel suppliers in Eastern India. Since the "freight rates generally progress with the stages of fabrication"[5], it is more economic to manufacture the heavy equipment, which do not undergo much loss in weight, in the market area and sell locally without undergoing heavy transport charges than to manufacture them at a distance and spend heavily on the transportation of the manufactured commodity. In the above case the question of location has been a matter of judicious selection by the owners because "*where a single raw material is used in the manufacture of an article without loss of weight in the process, location can be at the source of the material, at the market or at any point in between*"[6], but preferably at the market as the transport of processed material is costlier than the raw material. Godrej is primarily market oriented. Similar case is presented by Premier Automobiles, which assemble cars, though transport in this case is a more important factor since some parts are always imported. More important reason for its location near Bombay is its dependence on a variety of products from other manufacturing concerns and a vast local market.

The second group of industries mentioned above include CIBA, CIPLA, Johnson, Asian Paints, May and Baker and many other industries. Located in the suburbs they have preferred proximity to Bombay because of special distributional advantages. Secondly high cost goods like medicine and paints with low bulk are not very much affected by transport, though freight rates for them are higher. The sources and the kind of raw materials are so varied and so many in number that they no longer play a significant part in locational decision of the industry. These industries – viz., pharmaceuticals, paints and chemicals – with their raw materials not very bulky obtained from various sources have tended to follow large industrial complexes to avail of some processed articles needed in their manufacture and to find ready clientele for their own goods.

There are other industries, which cannot but locate themselves on the coast. The two oil refineries Burma Shell and Stanvace are suitable examples. They belong to the category of those processing plants where the raw material loses considerable bulk after processing. In the western suburb, 'Bharat Plastics' provide another case.

The considerations above show the role of market as a factor in the location of certain industries in the neighbourhood of Bombay. As a matter of fact to an industrialist it is not just choosing between the economic of production and that of distribution, but what matters most to him is the maximum profitability that is a function of all economics effected in both production and distribution apart from the trend of prices. The factors, therefore, decisive of location are many and vary with the individual enterprise.

Interdependence of units of production is also partly responsible for a concentration of industries in the metropolitan area as this procures for the unit the advantages obtained by the proximity of related processes and production. An apt example of this type is the neighbouring location of WIMCO, manufacturing matchboxes, and Morarjee Dharamsee Chemicals producing chemicals at Ambarnath. The latter concern takes special interest in the requirements of the former.

Bombay also offers for its large-scale industries in the city and neighbourhood, certain large-scale economics. Available in the city or in the neighbourhood are the advantages of better transfer services and broader and more flexible labour market. In addition there are many kinds of auxiliary services catering to business in general – banks, utility services, fire and police protection and others – which can do more effective job in larger communities. Interest, property insurance and utility rates are generally lower in larger cities.

Besides all these reasons, the effective regional demand of the buying capacity of the people are important points in favour of industrial location and the prosperity of Bombay and the Western Indian region have exercised considerable influence on the promotion of industries. The above observations relate to the location of industries in Bombay city region and neighbourhood, where they continue to cluster despite the time honoured idea of their areal decentralisation and dispersion. Many Indian economists are critical of this agglomeration of industries in a limited area. It is argued that while there are enough economic and technological reasons for the development of industries in Bombay city region it does not show much of social justification.

To be sure, the huge concentration of industries in and around Bombay has become as much of a problem in urban planning, as it is a constraint in urban development. In modern days the cause of decentralisation and dispersion is advocated and the intervention of the government is sought to control any further worsening of the situation. At present the municipal corporation has taken very effective steps to stop any further location of large manufacturing or processing unit inside the city, but even otherwise industries have shown a general preference for the suburb especially during the recent years.

With the growth of the city was felt the inadequacy of space, and modern standard of hygienic living considered the existence of factories in the heart of the city antisocial. The new industrial plants, therefore had to locate themselves at the suburbs where they chose a place of their convenience. This, however, did not present any conflict between the civic life and the industrial interests as the latter had practically all the advantages of city location extended to them, besides their being able to procure cheap land and easy transport facilities. In Bombay the suburbs extend only in one direction and provide the transport available at Bombay.

The early history of industrial development is however repeating itself with the tremendous growth of the city. The suburbs do not represent a neglected zone of urban periphery to be taken at will by the industries. Once again the residential quarters find themselves face to face with industries. So what happened on the island is also happening in the suburbs and once again we have the residential areas right under the smoking monsters. The pull of market proximity to the port and other facilities never allowed the industries to go far beyond the city's orbit, which goes on increasing with the time and so does the permissible distance for industrial location.

The shift of the industries to the suburbs is not necessarily a result of demand for land for residential purposes or a move of releasing urban congestion or to conform to the principal of planning. Often they find suburbs more convenient to them. A factor in the shift of industrial location from the centre of the city to the suburbs is the expansion of productivity of certain firms. This is the case with all industries that have moved to the periphery, not only in Bombay but even elsewhere. Besides there are also associated problems like high labour costs, taxes, traffic congestion, onerous city fire and health ordinances etc. which are responsible for movement of industries to the suburbs, but none of these factors has primacy over the space problem.

The question of external economics is significant to the industries. The industries in the suburbs are in a disadvantageous position with regards to the external economics which were easily available to the centre, but the modern gigantic size of the concerns have helped them to provide their own external economics. The fractional transport, service facilities added space, materials and labour so indispensable in some industries are available in the suburbs.

The modern technical developments have also had a hand in fostering the growth of many industries in the suburbs. This is particularly so, where the batch production has been replaces by continuous production. Such shift characteristically involves a basic change in the flow of materials inside the factory and implies a regular flow to a fixed station. This can be seen in operation in 'Anil Hard Board', which is occupying an extensive area and is located on the sea face near Vikroli[7].

The forces, which are responsible for the location of the industries in the suburbs, are summarised by Hoyt as follows:

> While factories are still predominantly located in great metropolis area, they are now at the fringe of these area rather than at the centre, because the advantage of cheap land permitted one storey factories and continuing of industrial operations, railroad freight car service to the factory and low taxes, can best be served on the periphery of the city, where the outer railroad belt lines, the auto truck and automobiles furnish transportation for goods and for labour.[8]

The distribution of industries in the suburbs shows some interesting features (Figure 5). Most of the large and heavy industries are located in the eastern suburb while the western suburbs developed predominantly light industries and small enterprises. In the eastern suburb, engineering, hardware, asbestos, motor, hard board, and even machine manufacturing industries are located while on the western side the industries produce mostly plastic, stationery goods, chemicals and textile processing. Among the factors affecting the nature of industries in the two suburbs, transport and terminal costs are very important. A large area of the hinterland of Bombay is served by Central Railway, and a location along this ensures a smooth distribution without the delay involved in transit. Goods can be rolled on the same wheels to different parts of U.P., Bihar, Madhya Pradesh, Mysore, Andhra and Madras, since these places are connected by Central Railway. The Western Railway on the other hand covers a considerably small portion of the hinterland on the western side of the country, and the distribution of goods from the western suburb to other parts of India will not only entail more of terminal cost but also delay because of transhipment necessary at many places in course of transit.

The western suburb, on the other hand, is connected to a very narrow zone of hinterland served by Western Railway. Only those industries, therefore, have established themselves where the transit costs are negligible or which cater to the local market. These are the light goods manufacturing concerns which, granted the essential component of an enterprise – the land, labour, capital, water and power – do not have much of consideration for very effective transport means.

The eastern suburb is directly linked with the port and the inflow of necessary imported raw materials for the industries is smooth. It has the same convenience in obtaining supplies from or distributing finished goods inland. Disposal of effluents presents no problem and can directly be discharged in the Thane Creek. Enough competition or the lack of it, with other types of land use quite often becomes a decisive factor in the location of industries. This competition does not affect the industries economically, as with their vast financial structures, they can always outbid the promoters of residential colonies, but public demand for residences and the land for them works through legislation introduced by Municipal Corporation under the pressure of the public opinion. The eastern suburbs – much of it marshy – did not attract the residential colonies and the industries had no difficulties either in open competition or because of legislation. In fact, the eastern suburbs remained neglected for a very long time as sites for residences. One, however, finds now residential colonies, coming up in the low-lying marshy land least suitable for them. In contrast the western suburb has developed elaborate residential areas, on level land and not far from the hills, and the industries had no free hand to set their foot anywhere.

Transport as a Factor in the Development of Suburbs

The one-sided urban sprawl in Bombay to the north has adhered to the major transport thoroughfares. The suburbs to the north have been traversed both by Western and Central Railways, charging from the island, making between them an angle of 40 degrees, and two roads which later give out multiple ramifications covering a very large part of the country. In the western suburb, radiating from the city is the Western Railway with Ghorbunder road running parallel on its west. The latter connects the city with Bulsar, Surat, Broach and many coastal cities. The eastern suburbs are traversed by the Central Railway and the Bombay Agra road, running very close to the railway track. The bulging suburb east of Kurla is served with a loop branching off from the main track at Kurla. The railway tracks occupy a belt of 100–200 yards, covered with multiple tracks of Central Railway main and suburban railways which run as far as Karjat. The eastern and western suburbs are joined at many points by transverse roads, thereby increasing the accessibility to the interior. The development and building activity in the suburbs have been guided by the economy of transport and have sought places close to the main stream of urban influences that follow the most important transport routes. In the extended Bombay suburban zone, transport has influenced both the dwelling places and industrial location.

Both the automobiles and the railways have widened a worker's choice of residences. He can find a residence not only in the vicinity of his place of work but anywhere within a reasonable distance from where commuting may be possible without being uneconomic and strenuous. The concentration of population along the transport routes is an evidence of its significance in the suburban life of the city. The railway stations of the suburban railway have been the most powerful nuclei for later clustering of structures. They are not just stopping points for the trains but a virtual gateway between a particular arrondissement and the rest of the city, an effective rendezvous for the people, a point of convergence before the population is diffused for work during the day and above all a point that collects and radiates urban influences. The likeness of a particular place in the suburb bears to the city varies with its distance from the city. The outer fringe of a particular suburban is most unlike the city, while near the station, the urban functions tend to enlarge and accentuate themselves. The commuters always tend to be as close to the station as possible. Railway stations have helped urbanisation of the small rural settlements. Most of the stations between Kurla and Thana on the Central Railway and Bandra and Dahisar on the Western Railway are small shopping centres and often small towns having sizable population. Transport lines, no doubt, have introduced a lack of symmetry in the morphology of the suburbs.

Commuting

The area between the city and the outer limit from which the ebb and flow of the human movement is effected is called the commuting area of the city in America. The persons making the to and fro journey are usually termed commuters (Dickinson, 1957).

Commuting has become a spectacular phenomenon in the life of the city of Bombay. The most regularly running trains of Bombay suburbs make it possible to move as many as 40 miles (65 km.) from their residence to the place of work. On the Western Railway the suburban trains reach as far as Virar while on the Central Railway as far inland as Karjat. Though commuting apparently seems to have solved many difficulties created by lack of accommodation in the city, it has started a train of undesirable developments. To quote F.G. Osborn *"the transport industry which began by making it possible for city people to 'live out and work in' seems to end by making it possible to work anywhere and live nowhere"*[9].

The trend for commuting has gradually moved up in Bombay with the increase in its population and expansion of its suburbs. This is obvious from the increase in the number of suburban trains operating on suburban section of Western and Central Railways during the last five years (1955–59). In 1955 the number of trains run during a 22 hours working day was 301; this was raised to 333 in June 1957 and again to 347 in October 1957. By now the figure is almost doubled. In April 1959, over 650 trains were run during 22 hours of a working day. During 'rush hours', between 8 and 11 in the morning and 5 and 8 in the evening trains were run every 3½ to 5 minutes. At other times the usual interval is 15 minutes. This phenomenon of quick transport contributed significantly to the mobility of labour. Socially it has been able to preserve the family as a single unit making it possible for its members to work at different places, without having to stay away.

The spatial pattern of commuting area is a function of various consideration involved in commuting. These may be summarised as under:

1. The time taken in commuting to reach the place of work and back,
2. The cost of travel,
3. Inconvenience of the journey.

In the majority of cases the cost and time are directly proportionate to each other, since a place closer to the city will cost the commuter less by way of railway or bus fare and will entail only a moderate waste of time in travelling. This simple travel-time cost relationship is more than complicated in cases where distance is no indication of the time taken in commuting. This happens because the introduction of a second factor – distance from the main thoroughfares – that permits or retards accessibility. Many places though not very distant from the city in terms of linear measurement are away from the main transport thoroughfares, and commuting from them takes more time than places quite far away on the main transport route. Such places lie in the hilly areas, between the two railways or further at a longer ordinate distance from the railway beyond Thana or Borivili.

In such cases the difficulty of transport is obvious. Uncertain and inadequate means of transport force one to cover the distance to the nearest railway station either on bicycle or on foot. The effectiveness of transport for commuting decreases not only with the increase in the distance from the city, but also on the transverse distance of a settlement from the nearest bus or railway station. This simple principle governs the order of preference for a place as a residence of a commuter. Commutability, therefore, varies directly with the convenience of travel and inversely with the time spent in travel. Distance and cost appear rather secondary however, difficult to fit these relationships in the frame of a mathematical function, and magnitude of commuting may show a marked departure from the expected trend, or the choice of place may be purely arbitrary.

Every day about two lakh people move to the city. This includes the people both to Churchgate and Victoria Terminus. This number more than four times that of the pre-war period is an important force in the functional organisation of the city and is responsible for the large day time population of Bombay's CBD and many other busy locations. Commuting though very important is not indispensable and with proper planning much of this wearisome travel could be minimised if not completely eliminated.

Notes

1. "Bandra and Kurla are becoming large towns. This is due to organised development, to house building schemes and to the efficiency of the electric railway system which is turning the greater Bombay area into a definite unit with features approximately to those prevailing in London and other countries where an enormous population lives within a narrow radius ... The Bombay suburban area, despite setbacks for the time being due to financial slump which restricts the amount of money available for building upon new sites shows every sign of development into a large scale city of the modern type and is in this respect probably unique in India", Census of India, 1931, Vol. VIII, Pt. I, Bombay, p. 46.
2. Usually a settlement of more than 5,000 population according to Indian Census is called a Town. In this case all such settlements have not been included, because compactness has been taken into account. Figures worked out from the reports.
3. Quoted from George S. Wehrwein 1942, p. 218.

4. C.D. Harris (1943, p. 8) has classified six types of suburbs viz. (1) Industrial fringe, (2) Industrial, (3) Complex with industrial more important, (4) Complex with residential more important, (5) Dormitory, (6) Mining and Industrial.
5. Fulton, Maurice and L. Clinton Hoch, 1959, p. 51.
6. Ibid, p. 51.
7. Continuous process reduces the movement of labour and the use of moveable machines in the plant. Since it is ordinarily easier to engineer a continuous flow of material in a single level plant than in multi storey structures, this development has encouraged a preference for horizontal layouts in large plants. As a result large establishments tend to avoid cramped sites more than they did in the past; the overwhelming preference for open sites, where horizontal expansion in any direction is needed, is relatively unimpeded.
8. Homer Hoyt, 1940/41, p. 847.
9. Quoted from K. Liepman.

References

Colean, Miles L. (1953): *Renewing our Cities*, Twentieth Century Fund, New York.

Da Cunha, J. Gerson (1900): Origin of Bombay, *Journal of Bombay Branch of Asiatic Society*, extra number.

Dickinson, R.E. (1957): The Geography of Commuting, *G. Review*, Vol. XLVII, Oct.: 521–38.

Duncan, O.D. and A.J. Reiss (1950): *Social Characteristics of Urban Rural Communities*, John Wiley, New York, p. 117.

Fulton, Maurice and L. Clinton Hoch (1959): Transport Factors affecting Local Decision, *Economic Geography*, Vol. 35, Jan., p. 51.

Harris, C.D. (1943): A Functional Classification of the Cities in USA, *Geog. Review*, Vol. 33: 84.

Hoover, E.M. (1948): *Location of Economic Activity*, McGraw Hill.

Hoyt, Homer (1940–1941): Forces of Urban Centralisation and Decentralisation, *American Journal of Sociology*, Vol. XLVII, p. 843.

Liepman, Kate (1944): *The Journey to Work*, Kegan Paul, London, p. 9.

Sharma, T.R. (1959): *Location of Industries in India*, Hind Kitabs Ltd, Bombay, 3rd ed.

Vernon, Raymond (1957): Production and Distribution in Large Metropolis, *Annals of the American Academy of Political and Social Sciences*, Vol. 314, p. 18.

Wehrwein, G.S. (1942): Rural Urban Fringe, *Econ. Geog.* Vol. XVIII: 217–218.

Appendix
Population Distribution and its Occupational Nature in Bombay Suburbs

Town or Village	*Area in sq. miles*	*Population*	*Density of population per sq. mile*	*Agri-cultural population*	*Non-agri-cultural population*	*% of agri-cultural population*	*% of non-agri-cultural population*
1. Bandra	8.65	1,57,856	18,240	860	1,56,996	0.54	99.46
2. Parle Andheri	6.63	1,15,438	17,410	1,454	1,13,948	1.26	98.74
3. Juhu	1.31	7,327	5,593	22	305	0.30	99.70
4. Ghatkopar	3.95	52,633	13,320	298	52,335	0.56	99.44
5. Kurla	2.88	81,240	28,210	488	80,752	6.00	94.00
6. Bhandup	0.85	11,813	13,900	565	11,248	4.78	95.22
7. Chambur	2.80	18,841	6,759	277	18,564	1.47	98.53
8. Marol	3.06	5,792	1,893	266	5,526	4.50	95.50
9. Vadhavali	0.69	5,964	8,644	53	5,911	0.88	99.12
10. Varsova	1.79	10,450	5,939	341	10,109	3.33	96.67
11. Mulund	5.60	27,148	4,846	637	26,511	2.34	97.66
12. Malad	7.00	45,134	6,448	459	44,695	1.01	96.11
13. Pathadi	3.20	16,360	5,113	249	16,111	1.52	98.48
14. Kanheri	0.50	13,575	7,688	70	13,505	0.21	99.79
15. Dahisar	4.30	5,749	1,337	842	4,907	14.64	86.36
16. Eksar	2.50	8,253	3,302	748	7,505	9.00	91.00
17. Anik	1.85	675	365	205	470	30.30	69.70
18. Asalpe	0.23	79	344	—	79	—	100.00
19. Bapnala	0.07			No Population			
20. Borla	0.86	2,656	3,008	76	2,580	2.86	97.14
21. Pwada	0.08	489	6,112	66	423	13.50	86.50
22. Chakla	0.42	1,950	4,643	52	1,898	2.66	97.34
23. Chandvali	0.28	648	2,314	127	521	19.60	80.40
24. Devanar	2.73	1,988	734	395	1,593	19.80	80.20
25. Harijali	1.32	2,367	1,793	21	2,346	0.88	99.12
26. Kajur	0.99	1,707	1,724	176	1,531	10.31	89.69
27. Kandivali	0.51	1,542	3,024	81	1,461	5.25	94.75
28. Kopari	0.60	27	40	—	27	—	100.00
29. Madh	0.61	4,387	7,193	316	4,071	7.20	92.80
30. Mahul	3.84	2,970	774	518	2,452	17.40	82.60
31. Majar	1.45	2,404	1,657	16	2,388	0.67	99.33
32. Manbudruk	0.72	117	163	36	81	30.70	69.30
33. Mandla	1.63	666	409	11	655	1.65	98.35
34. Mankhurd	0.93	2,622	2,819	115	2,507	4.38	95.62
35. Marwali	0.75	596	795	244	352	40.95	59.05
36. Mohili	0.80	1,604	2,005	5	1,599	0.31	99.69
37. Mulgaon	0.54	356	659	109	247	30.62	69.38
38. Nanala	1.30	92	71	—	92	—	100.00

Cont'd...

Cont'd...

39. Oshivara	1.84	1,374	747	73	1,301	5.31	94.69
40. Parjapur	0.41	407	993	25	382	6.14	93.86
41. Paspoli	1.46	457	313	13	444	2.84	97.16
42. Powai	1.32	629	477	22	607	3.49	96.51
43. Sahar	1.05	3,735	3,557	353	3,382	9.45	90.55
44. Saki	0.31	311	1,416	5	305	1.60	98.40
45. Tirandaj	0.51	588	1,003	38	550	6.46	93.54
46. Trombay	1.66	2,540	1,530	180	2,360	7.08	92.92
47. Tungwe	0.55	1,268	2,306	18	1,250	1.31	98.69
48. Vikroli	0.87	1,470	1,690	328	1,142	22.31	77.69
49. Vyaravli	0.35	79	226	46	33	58.23	41.77
50. Nahur	1.80	1,313	730	33	1,280	2.51	97.49
51. Vehar				Deserted			
52. Gundgaon				Deserted			
53. Tulsi	3.40	28	8,235	—	28	—	100.00
54. Klerabad	0.80	5	6.25	—	5	—	100.00
55. Maroshi	N.A.	378	—	224	154	59.26	40.74
56. Magathna	7.40	2,599	352	242	2,357	9.31	90.69
57. Poisar	2.90	3,906	1,347	214	3,692	5.47	94.53
58. Akurli	1.70	2,392	1,407	63	2,329	2.63	97.37
59. Vadhwan	0.20	7.91	3,956	—	791	—	100.00
60. Kurad	0.30	1,588	5,294	105	1,483	6.61	93.39
61. Ara	0.20	2,452	12,270	22	2,430	0.89	99.11
62. Goregaon	1.60	1,592	796	36	1,556	2.26	97.74
63. Dindoshi	0.50	508	1,016	338	170	66.53	33.47
64. Chincholi	0.30	1,440	4,800	7	1,433	0.48	99.52
65. Sai	2.90	88	30	23	65	25.00	75.00
66. Mandpeshwar	0.20	233	1,165	21	212	9.01	90.99
67. Borivili	0.90	153	170	110	43	7.19	92.81
68. Gorai	5.00	1,333	267	459	874	34.43	65.57
69. Manori	4.50	2,485	552	902	1,583	36.20	63.80
70. Charkap	1.10	650	590	283	367	43.54	56.46
71. Kandivali	2.10	3,396	1,617	296	3,100	8.73	91.27
72. Sampouli	0.20	205	1,025	64	141	31.22	68.78
73. Marve	0.30	692	2,307	36	656	5.20	94.80
74. Akse	0.20	155	775	85	70	54.84	45.16
75. Malvni	5.30	3,953	576	529	2,524	1.73	98.27
76. Valni	0.70	2,666	3,809	64	2,602	2.40	97.60
77. Erangal	1.80	743	413	272	471	36.61	63.39

Contributors

Gerhard Bahrenberg, Professor, Institute of Geography, University of Bremen, Bremen, Germany. (gbah@uni-bremden.de)

Bhawana Bali, Research Scholar, Department of Geography, Panjab University, Chandigarh.

Daksha C. Barai, Professor of Geography (Retd.), Bangalore University, Bangalore. Smt. J-204, Mantri Woodlands, Bangalore.

Christopher C. Benninger, Architect and Planner, India House, Balewadi, Pune. (christopher@ccba.in)

V.G. Bhide (Late), Former Vice-Chancellor, University of Pune, Pune.

Pippa Deodhar, Department of Geography, Punjab University, Chandigarh.

D.N. Dhanagare, Professor of Sociology (Retd.), University of Pune; Former Vice-Chancellor, Shivaji University, Kolhapur. (dhanagare.dn@gmail.com)

K.R. Dikshit, Professor of Geography (Retd.), University of Pune, Pune. (rvdikshit@vsnl.com)

G.R. Diwan, Architect Planner. B1, Kumar Aashujana, Sinhagad Road, Panmale, Pune.

Anjali Kalamdani and **Kiran Kalamdani,** Architects and Urban Designers. Flat No. 4a, First Floor; Navkar Towers, Near Kamat Hospital, Chinchwad, Pune.

Rajeev Kathpalia, Professor, School of Planning at CEPT University, Ahmedabad.

Gita Kewalramani, Department of Geography, University of Mumbai, Mumbai. (gitakewalramani@gmail.com)

J. Krishnamurthy, Scientist, Regional Remote Sensing Centre, Bangalore.

Pankaja Kulabkar, Political Scientist, B-5, Bank of India Housing Society, Taware Colony, Pune. (pkulabkar@yahoo.com)

K.M. Kulkarni, Professor of Geography, Gujarat University, Ahmedabad. (drkmkad1@sancharnet.in)

S.R. Latkar, Head, Department of Geography, H.P.T./R.Y.K. College, Nasik. (shrilatkar@yahoo.co.in)

Chinmoyee Mallik, PhD. Scholar, Centre for the Study of Regional Development, School of Social Sciences, Jawaharlal Nehru University, New Delhi.

R.N. Mishra, Professor, Department of Geography, University of Rajasthan, Jaipur.

Sandeep Parkhi, Architect Urban Planner, C-10, Swanand Society 2, Sakhar Nagar 2, Pune. (sandpark77@yahoo.com)

Chittaranjan Pathak, Former Professor of Regional Planning, I.I.T., Kharagpur. (cr_pathak@hotmail.com)

V.S. Phadke, Professor of Geography (Retd.), University of Mumbai, Mumbai. (vinayakphadke@hotmail.com)

Vimala Rangaswami, Professor of Geography (Retd.), M.S. University, Baroda. (rangavimala@hotmail.com)

V.S. Rao, Department of Geography, University of Mumbai, Mumbai.

Sudha Ravindranath, Scientist, Regional Remote Sensing Centre, Bangalore.

Sucharita Sen, Associate Professor, Centre for the Study of Regional Development, School of Social Sciences, Jawaharlal Nehru University, New Delhi.

H.S. Sharma, Professor of Geography, University of Rajasthan, Jaipur.

K.D. Sharma, Professor of Geography, Panjab University, Chandigarh. (sharmakd@pu.ac.in)

Jean Steinberg, Professor, Institute of Urbanism, Université de Paris 12, Val-de-Marne, Paris. (jeansteinberg@yahoo.fr)

Vinod Tewari, Director, National Institute of Urban Affairs, New Delhi.

Baleshwar Thakur, Professor and Head (Retd.), Department of Geography, University of Delhi, Delhi. (bthakur21@gmail.com)

Hanuman Singh Yadav, Professor, Department of Regional and Economic Growth, Barkatullah University, Bhopal. (hanumansinghyadav@gmail.com)

Index